Police Defensive Handgun Use and Encounter Tactics

Police Defensive Handgun Use and Encounter Tactics

Brian A. Felter

Defensive Weaponcraft Training and Consulting, Inc.

A BRADY BOOK
PRENTICE HALL BUILDING
Englewood Cliffs, New Jersey 07632

LIBRARY OF CONGRESS
Library of Congress Cataloging-in-Publication Data

Felter, Brian.
    Police defensive handgun use and encounter tactics / Brian A.
  Felter.
         p.   cm.
    Bibliography: p.
    Includes index.
    ISBN 0-89303-798-2
    1. Police shootings. 2. Pistol shooting. 3. Police training.
  I. Title.
  HV8031.F47 1988
  332.2'32--dc19   87-32783
                                                       CIP

Editorial/production supervision: Nancy Menges
Cover design: Diane Saxe
Manufacturing buyer: Robert Anderson

©1988 by Brian A. Felter
Published by Prentice-Hall, Inc.
A Division of Simon & Schuster
Englewood Cliffs, New Jersey 07632

The information contained in this book follows years of extensive researching, gathering, testing, and developing to present safe and effective methods for using a service handgun. Safe and judicious firearms use and practices are stressed extensively throughout this book. If approached, used, and adopted with good common sense, these methods will serve you well. The author accepts no liability for any injuries to persons or damage to property resulting from the application, use, combination, or adoption of any of the techniques, methods, procedures, tactics, or information contained or implied in this book. Further, the techniques, methods, procedures, tactics, and information presented here are in no way a substitute for departmental firearms training programs.

Printed in the United States of America

10 9 8 7 6 5 4 3 2 1

ISBN 0-89303-798-2

Prentice-Hall International (UK) Limited, *London*
Prentice-Hall of Australia Pty. Limited, *Sydney*
Prentice-Hall Canada Inc., *Toronto*
Prentice-Hall Hispanoamericana, S.A., *Mexico*
Prentice-Hall of India Private Limited, *New Delhi*
Prentice-Hall of Japan, Inc., *Tokyo*
Simon & Schuster Asia Pte. Ltd., *Singapore*
Editora Prentice-Hall do Brasil, Ltda., *Rio de Janeiro*

*This book is dedicated to
my father, **Walter T. Felter,**
without whose guidance, years
of teaching, and firearms skills,
this book would not have been possible.*

Contents

Foreword

There is very little in this world that is genuinely new. Particularly in the area of contemporary self-defense training, most concepts that serve as the basis for all modern instruction were first thought of and contemplated by our spiritual antecedents long ago. We present-day instructors travel, investigate, experience, observe, research, take what is most useful, and (hopefully) incorporate all of it into a scintillating and comprehensive training program. The best instructors think of themselves as neither progenitors nor guardians of knowledge. We are merely the current trustees. It is our solemn responsibility to incorporate what enhancements we can and pass it on. It follows that the most accomplished of us are the master communicators. The author of this volume, my colleague Brian Felter, is one of the very best communicators around today.

I met Brian for the first time back in 1981 when I was instructing a defensive firearms course in the Washington, D.C., area. At the time, I had been a contract instructor for several years, and like most people involved in defensive firearms instruction, I was living hand to mouth. Brian was both a student and an associate instructor, and we had the opportunity to work together on that and many subsequent occasions.

I continued to write and instruct, and Brian did the same. In this defensive firearms training business we are all so impoverished that independent instructors are not really "competitors," since we all need each other. We try to work together, sharing information and opportunities. Brian was never one to insist that he was always right, nor would he withhold knowledge from other professionals. He shared it freely. That is one reason we got along so well.

This, therefore, is a book on the subject of defensive shooting, written by one of the instructors in this field most qualified to do so. Unlike many of the shallow and frivolous contemporary texts on this subject, this volume is authored by someone who has a depth of understanding of this topic rivaled by few. He knows of what he speaks.

In addition, Brian is an excellent and innovative writer. The reader will both enjoy and profit from this manual. Some know. Some can communicate. Brian is one of the few who can do both.

John S. Farnam

Preface

In society, police officers serve as the highly visible symbol of civil authority—engaged in maintaining law and order and functioning as the flux between opposing factions. In their varied role, officers must be prepared to respond and handle calls that extend from the mundane to the lethal. What will each day bring, what awaits on the street: only shift's end will tell.

Day to day, officers nationwide are engaging in a profession that can instantly place them at the center of a lethal encounter, fighting for their lives. In preparation for this possible eventuality, they are issued service handguns and trained at the academy in an effort to provide them with the necessary means for coping with an armed threat as the ultimate enforcement of their authority. All too often, this training falls very short of the desired skill level necessary to deal effectively with an armed threat and regain control of the situation. This is not stated to discredit departmental training; departments are faced with the, at times monumental, task of training and qualifying large numbers of officers with limited resources. This is stated to point out a sizable void that exists between departmental firearms training programs and the *modern,* defensive weapon use techniques, tactics, and training, involving the full spectrum of encounter management. Officers must be provided with the means to fill this void: furthering and expanding the vital *officer survival* knowledge essential when dealing with lethal encounters.

Within the last several years, the fore-thinking segments of the law enforcement community have recognized the need to substantially increase *officer survival* awareness and training. The importance of this need cannot be understated, as the use of firearms in assaults on police officers has increased at an alarming rate. Police officers are dealing with a *newer,* more highly trained criminal element—more and more frequently arriving on the scene ready for an encounter: wearing bulletproof vests, armed with shotguns and semiautomatic high-capacity handguns, increasingly outnumbering the police officers, and often having the advantage in *both* weaponry and numbers. It is thus becoming more and more difficult to stop the threat effectively and control the situation.

Today, every officer must be provided with *the most modern training in the use of his or her service handgun and its associated tactics and completely versed in all areas of encounter management.* Few things, if any, in an officer's career will be as life threatening as an armed encounter, and he or she must be able to control the immediate environment with the means at hand: *the service handgun and his or her ability to use it effectively.*

This book is the "college course" in the police use of the service handgun. The *survival skills* contained herein are founded in the four factors employed to stop a lethal encounter: *mental set, encounter tactics, weapon use skills, and preparation.* It provides you, the working police officer, with a step-by-step understanding of how these factors work in concert to produce *a skilled weapon user who possesses the tactical knowledge and mental set to control his or her environment should a threat present itself.* The "college course" cuts right to the meat of the subject. You are a police officer, you have been through an academy firearms training program. Now, refine your skills with a course that fully covers the service handgun and all the *survival techniques* necessary to win an armed encounter.

This may be the most important book you will ever purchase for yourself or your family. Read it, learn it, and every time you go 10-8, you will have the skills necessary to be a survivor.

Brian A. Felter

Acknowledgments

In any work such as this, many people are ultimately involved: family, friends, fellow instructors, and others. All of these people have influenced or assisted in the realization of this project in one form or another. I take this time to acknowledge some of them.

My beginnings in firearms use and defensive weaponcraft originated under the tutelage of my father, *Walter T. Felter.* Without his instruction and guidance this book would truly not have been possible. Many of the lessons I learned from my father were to become quite a few of the modern defensive truths of today. I owe a large, loving debt to my father, whose skill and training were the crucible that formed my early and later firearms abilities.

Continuing with my family, my wife, *Bonnie Felter,* contributed extensively to this work by producing all the line drawings contained in this book. As a talented artist, she worked for months on the exacting drawings that provide greater understanding of the techniques covered. Her contributions, for these drawings and in many other respects, are greatly appreciated.

A very special thanks goes to *Jim Horan* for his great assistance throughout this and other projects. A good friend, Jim is also a knowledgeable defensive practitioner and instructor. If a knowledgeable hand was needed, he was always there, at the right time, with many excellent ideas.

Another good friend and associate, *John Pepper,* helped form my understanding of many practical considerations and realities. A master defensive user, he is most noted as the inventor of the excellent "Pepper Popper" reactive steel target, used in practical competition around the world. Throughout years of working together—while experimenting, designing, and running IPSC matches and practical research tools—a large amount of defensive information was generated. John is a true practical innovator, master shot, and excellent defensive firearms instructor.

The teachings of **Colonel Jeff Cooper** directly influenced much of my defensive thought. Both his written word and in-person instruction clarified many defensive truths. Most of my in-person association with Colonel Cooper was spent with pen and pad in hand, saving the defensive information that this master instructor transmitted. I am truly grateful for the learning experiences he has provided me, which have greatly expanded my knowledge in this field.

John Farnam, another friend and associate and a very talented, well-known defensive instructor, deserves mention here. John has been around for years, developing the fine-tuning defensive techniques that have expanded the art form. During our time spent together and in communicating, many defensive ideas have surfaced and been refined.

Also, the help provided by **Massad Ayoob, Ray Chapman,** and **Michael Harries** is greatly appreciated. All three are very well known defensive firearms tacticians and instructors, and through their excellent work in the development of defensive and survival techniques the law enforcement community has greatly profited.

Special thanks goes out to **James Hollmann** for his help with this project. A good friend and associate, Jim is a very knowledgeable defensive weapons and officer survival instructor.

Special thanks also go out to **Dave Tracy** and **Dave Smith,** both of whom are well-noted officer survival instructors, for their friendship over the years.

A man never forgets good partners and friends: **Ken Knox** and **Jim Stewart** are both of these and more. Here's to remembering those early years of gun handling and trips into the unknown.

Special appreciation goes to Beretta's **Warren Barron** and **Birger Boggild.** Both good friends for years, Warren has been a great help on many projects, and Birger's superlative firearms knowledge has expanded my understanding of handgun design and mechanical function. This special appreciation is also extended to Sigarms's **Bob Valantine, Rich Turner,** and **Harald Ocetnik.** Both Bob and Rich were very supportive of this project, and Harald supplied information from his extensive firearms knowledge. Special appreciation is also extended to Ruger's **Linda DeProfio,** DeSantis Holster's **Gene DeSantis** and **Denny Gaylor,** Bianchi International's **Richard D. E. Nichols,** and Horseshoe Leather's **Andy Arratoonian** for their assistance in this project.

The unsung hero of this book is **Scott Sorrell,** who was responsible for most of the excellent pictures that were rendered into line drawings. My hat is off to this gifted photographer for the excellent service and quality he provided: a truly professional craftsman.

Finally, special thanks go to several other people for a variety of reasons: **Bob Crovatto, Richard Azzaro, Jack Janetatos, Roger Burgess,** and **Linda Figurowski.**

1

Overview of Police Defensive Handgun Use and Encounter Tactics

This book may well provide the most complete coverage of defensive shooting techniques and encounter tactics ever presented under one cover. The techniques, tactics, concepts, and descriptions extend from technical details to tactical methodologies. The information presented can provide you with the survival skills necessary to conclude lethal encounters successfully. These skills are founded on four factors—mental set, encounter tactics, weapon use skills, and preparation—that must function together during the encounter. The reduction of any one of these factors will reduce your ability to survive. This book does not cover just weapon use skills, but provides you with all the vital factors that can increase your survival advantage.

This chapter is an overview of the entire book and provides an initial foundation of history, concepts, and central information that will be referred to throughout the book. As such, it provides you with a working knowledge of how defensive handgun use developed, defines basic terminology and concepts, and provides an understanding of how everything works together.

BRIEF HISTORICAL PERSPECTIVE ON THE MODERN DEVELOPMENT OF DEFENSIVE HANDGUN TECHNIQUES

Throughout the history of handgun use, from the time the first handgun appeared to the beginning of the twentieth century, techniques to improve the defensive use of the handgun have come and gone. History provides many insights into precursor techniques and methods of employment, but the true development of combat handgun techniques is a modern occurrence. The actual fathering of modern defensive pistolcraft began in the early 1900s and has developed to the art form it is today. Within the last 30 years, the growth and interest in defensive handgun use has produced most of the major technical advances. Many of the limits of defensive handgun use have been reached, although there is still much more to be learned and accomplished in perfecting the art form. Today, the main emphasis is on imparting these defensive handgun skills to those who need them. We now have the knowledge to provide the training.

This brief history of the development of modern defensive handgun techniques will take a look at some of the main influences during the past 75 years. Space does not permit a complete telling, but rather, we highlight some of the people, situations, and techniques that have helped develop defensive handgun use.

Captain W. E. Fairbairn and the Shanghai School

The foundation in the modern development of defensive handgun techniques started with Captain Fairbairn and his Shanghai school. His was the first major systematic approach to improve the effective combat use of the handgun.

Fairbairn was assigned as the officer-in-charge of firearms training for the Shanghai municipal police in 1910. Over the next 10 years, he worked to improve the firearms training of the police officers under him. During those years he made a complete study of police-involved shootings and from this study developed a method of firing and training to match the realities his officers faced—what eventually became known to many as the Shanghai school.

When enforcing the laws in the alleys and bars of Shanghai, the types of gunfights encountered were identical to those occurring today: close, fast, in poor light, with the criminal almost always taking the first shot. From his study, Fairbairn developed a method of instinctive shooting called ''shooting to live,'' in which one-handed instinctive shooting was used, by pointing the handgun out and firing below the line of sight. He felt that this was the best technique for the types of encounters that his officers faced. This technique and more were covered in *Shooting to Live,* by Fairbairn and Sykes. Much of what he experienced and discovered is still valid today: firing with two-shot bursts, shooting at moving targets, training during low-light conditions, the use of a fun house (at that time known as the mystery house), and surprise courses of fire. These developments, which were ahead of their time, did not initially catch on or survive, surfacing only when rediscovered and redirected years later.

Ed McGivern, Fast and Fancy

In the 1930s, Ed McGivern dramatically advanced double-action revolver shooting, demonstrating the full potential of the double-action firing mode. At that time the double-action revolver was almost always used in the single-action firing mode, with double-action considered only for the closest of situations. McGivern proved that double-action firing was quick and accurate at 25 yards and beyond, and that firing could be done exceedingly fast.

As an exhibition shooter, his skills and abilities were extraordinary and his feats at times unbelievable—some of his marksman skills being recorded in the Guinness *Book of World Records*. In 1938 his book *Fast And Fancy Revolver Shooting* was published, completely outlining all his experiments and developments in fast and fancy double-action revolver shooting.

During his career he trained thousands of police officers in defensive handgun techniques, much of which he developed. More than anything else, he showed us what the combination of the human body and handgun could produce in terms of speed and abilities.

FBI Training

In the mid-1930s, the FBI was one of the first police agencies to develop a *practical firearms training program* for both handguns and long guns. The practical police course (PPC) was developed at that time for revolver training and was a large step forward in defensive handgun use—step forward and away from the target-style shooting of the day. In an updated form the PPC course is still the premier law enforcement match for the double-action revolver, although now unrealistic in equipment and format used.

The most notable FBI firing technique ever to emerge was the FBI crouch. The crouch positioned the revolver at waist level, with the other arm across the chest, ostensibly to protect the heart, and the knees bent deeply to form the crouch. The aligning method was a body aiming technique, with the revolver locked into the body. Its use ended a long time ago, but it was one of the first "modern" techniques that departed from the basic one-handed target-shooting methods that were ineffective for defensive handgun firing.

Today, the FBI is still at the forefront of firearms training, instituting changes to keep its program current with the new developments in defensive handgun use, using such modern techniques as the Weaver stance and rollover prone position, to name a few.

Bill Jordan of the Border Patrol

A true defensive handgun master, Bill Jordan's knowledge and abilities on these subjects came from 30 years of law enforcement experience with the Border Patrol. During those years of work on the border, he developed exceedingly fast and accurate methods for employing the double-action revolver. He is most noted for his developments in the area of fast drawing and firing techniques for close range. His book *No Second Place Winner* covers precise techniques for drawing the revolver and firing it, the holsters used, modifications for defensive revolvers, combat-style shooting, gunfighting, and much more.

As the "father of the fast draw," his lightning fast drawing and point-shooting abilities have astounded thousands during demonstrations. But to the law enforcement community he has provided his greatest service, by presenting information to improve officers' performance with the service handgun, thus increasing officers' survivability. His techniques are still part and parcel of defensive handgun work.

The Law Enforcement Community

Prior to the 1940s there was little truly defensive law enforcement firearms training. What did exist was usually slow fire using the revolver in the single-action mode and firing at bull's-eyes (the double-action mode considered a poor second and used only when very close to the target). This type of firearms training had been used for the last 60 years to train soldiers and police officers in the use of the revolver. Although change was urgently needed, it would not occur to any large degree until 20 years later.

Until around the 1960s, the majority of law enforcement defensive handgun shooting was still being done in the *one-handed target shooter's stance,* often with the other hand placed in the pocket. At the same time, though, *two-handed stances* were being developed (or rediscovered). Innovators discovered that the two-handed firing grip increased the handgun's control and ability to "hit." Thus two two-handed stances came into being (in actuality being rediscovered): the point shoulder and isosceles stances.

The point shoulder two-handed firing stance held the handgun at chest level with the arms locked out, firing being done while looking over the handgun, below the line of sight. The isosceles two-handed firing stance, sometimes referred to as the turret stance, held the handgun *directly in* the line of sight with the arms locked out. Both of these two-handed firing stances dramatically changed law enforcement's defensive handgun techniques. Locked-out two-handed sighted firing stances now became the rule, and police officers' abilities to produce "hits" increased.

Today, the law enforcement community as a whole continues to upgrade and improve defensive handgun techniques and the associated tactics involved. The main problem still occurring is the large gulf that exists between individual departments. Some departments are constantly upgrading their firearms training programs, while other departments are still relying on training programs that are very archaic, being as much as 30 years old. Change must occur to upgrade the firearms training that police officers receive. This is the goal that must be worked toward continually, as police officers must be provided with the best survival-oriented training available.

Civilian Defensive Handgun Competition

Across the nation civilian clubs were also involved in defensive handgun techniques and engaging in competition to test the skills developed. Virtually none of these localized efforts were ever recorded and the knowledge gained was lost. A notable exception were the defensive handgun developments occurring at Big Bear Lake in California in the mid-1950s. At that location, Jeff Cooper, Ray Chapman, Jack

Weaver, Elden Carl, Thel Reid, and others began a form of handgun competition that would ultimately lead to the modern technique of defensive handgun use. First billed as leatherslaps, competitors fired one-handed, drawing from their holsters (leather).

From the experiments and developments that this group produced came much of the foundation of defensive handgun use and many of the techniques we use today. Probably the first was the speed rock, with the handgun being "rocked" forward and firing the instant it clears leather. Today, it is used as an instantaneous answer to a very close attacker. But the most notable technique developed was the Weaver stance, developed by Jack Weaver in 1958. This two-handed stance completely redirected defensive handgun use. Like a light in the darkness, this was the major step forward in defensive handgun use. The Weaver stance in exceedingly fast, exerting the best defensive control on the handgun, and is the most flexible defensive stance for the realities of lethal encounters.

The Birth of IPSC.   From the beginnings at Big Bear Lake, this style of competition initially spread over southern California with an organization of clubs called the Southwest Combat Pistol League. Within a few years, clubs sprang up across the United States and in other countries. In the early 1970s, the International Practical Shooting Confederation (IPSC) was formed, which would organize and promote worldwide practical pistol competition.

The principles of practical handgun use are founded in three equal factors: accuracy, power, and speed. Commonly referred to by the three letters DVC, for the Latin words *diligentia, vis, and celeritas,* it is triad of practical shooting. All practical competition is freestyle in form and allows the shooters to solve the problems presented in any way they choose. Realistic situations are presented and the shooters' skills—speed drawing, very fast and controlled firing, quick reloading, hitting moving targets, firing while on the move, assuming a variety of firing positions, and so on—are tested when solving these problems.

Practical competition's primary function has been as a research tool to develop, experiment, and test which handguns and associated systems for employing them are the most appropriate for defensive use. By being freestyle it provides the freedom to use that which works. Many of the defensive handgun techniques we use today were derived through this system of freestyle competition.

Jeff Cooper, the Father of Modern Defensive Handgun Use

If any one person can be referred to as the father of modern defensive handgun use, it is Jeff Cooper. His untiring efforts in the development of the modern technique have spanned 40 years, during which time he has been directly responsible for many advances, ranging from weapon use technique, to mental conditioning, to defensive philosophy, and beyond. Colonel Cooper is the president and founder of the American Pistol Institute (Gunsite) in Arizona, which provides start-of-the-art small arms defensive training (not just handgun, but also shotgun and rifle).

Colonel Cooper was also the founding director and now lifetime chairman of the International Practical Shooting Confederation, with much of its initial and later developments a direct result of his efforts. It is through his extensive and continuing work in the field of defensive firearms use, and the work of Gunsite's cadre of highly trained instructors, that defensive techniques and information are continually being researched, developed, and refined.

Today the Training Resources Exist for the Law Enforcement Community to Use

In defensive firearms training today, the information and defensive instructors exist—five of the most talented being Massad Ayoob, Ray Chapman, John Farnam, Emanuel Kapelsohn, and Chuck Taylor—and form a resource pool of defensive information that the law enforcement community must make use of. The defensive handgun information is well established and readily available for departments to take advantage of. Although differences exist in styles and techniques, we all are working toward the centralized goal of improving every officer's survivability.

Today, more than ever, law enforcement and individual instructors are working in concert to develop and/or implement the best firearms training programs available. The goal of improving every officers' survival advantage must be kept at the forefront and made part of every police department's commitment. Police firearms training must be continually refined and broadened to fulfill this vital need.

THREE SCHOOLS OF THOUGHT ON DEFENSIVE HANDGUN USE

Today there are three major schools of thought on defensive handgun use. As can readily be assumed within any body of knowledge, differences in techniques, tactics, and methods exist between these three schools of thought. We like to refer to them as left, middle, and right (borrowed from political usage to designate two extremes and a middle ground). The left believes that almost all defensive handgun use should be done with unaimed fire. The right, at the opposite end of the spectrum, believes that almost all defensive handgun use should be done with a locked-in two-handed sighted firing stance. The middle, a combination of the two, applies the best techniques of each to the total situations that can be encountered by using both aimed and unaimed firing techniques to their most appropriate use and best advantage.

Obviously, the left and right schools are widely varied on which style of techniques will work during real lethal encounters. The right firmly states that aimed fire from a two-handed stance is the best defensive firing technique and teaches that almost exclusively. For the most part they are absolutely right, but the realities of lethal encounters can demand one-handed and/or unaimed firing skills and officers must be prepared for these eventualities. The left firmly states that unaimed fire, either one- or two-handed, is the best defensive firing technique, considering that lethal encounters seldom occur over 15 feet away and happen so quickly that attempting to use aimed fire will place officers at a disadvantage. Both schools acknowledge that the other firing techniques have a place, but emphasize their aforementioned aimed or unaimed firing techniques.

If you had to pick only one of these schools, the right school of thought would be your choice, as this school provides the most effective methods for dealing with the total variety of lethal situations that could occur. In the final analysis aimed fire and a locked-in two-handed firing stance are most effective and used whenever possible. But that is the rub, as there are times when one or both cannot be used. Many more truths exist with reference to these schools and all the techniques involved, and these will be covered.

This book is based on the middle school of thought, where the best techniques are taken from the other schools and combined into a grouping of techniques capable of most effectively responding to all the varying types of situations that can occur.

THIS BOOK DEALS ONLY WITH LETHAL ENCOUNTERS

This book has been written to cover completely the gun fighting techniques and encounter tactics necessary to conclude lethal encounters successfully. As such, we are dealing only with the deadly force option. Deadly force must only be used in response to a lethal assault which is occurring at that moment which, if continued, would cause death or grave bodily harm and there is no other way to avoid or control it. Deadly force is the ultimate use of the authority given a police officer and the most critical decision that he or she will ever make. The decision to use deadly force, although the ultimate police decision, may have to be made in a split second for you to survive. The purpose of this book is to show you how to implement that decision into the actions necessary to survive.

We are dealing with gunfight situations where the bullets are flying or soon will be, with the threat(s) trying to kill you. Other police control methods that may be used are not the subject of this book; surviving lethal encounters is. The information presented here will provide you with the weapon use skills and tactical capabilities to survive a lethal encounter when a threat is trying to kill you. Tactical safety will be heavily stressed to keep you from making a deadly force mistake and firing on an innocent. Also, you will fully understand how to stop a deadly force decision if the situation instantly changes and deadly force is no longer required. Within the text, some discussion will involve other control options just short of using deadly force.

In the police function, many degrees of control exist, rising up the use-of-force ladder from verbal, to gestures, to physical blocks and holds, to nonlethal equipment, and finally to the deadly force option of your handgun. This book deals with the final control mechanism, deadly force. During a situation, you may have tried all the other control mechanisms and finally had to resort to deadly force, or you may have had to resort instantly to deadly force to stop an instant attack. Your deadly force option will be dictated by the situation and you must be instantly ready to use this option to survive.

Police firearms training must include training in the progression of force up and down the use-of-force ladder. Due to the large amount of information presented here and the space limitations involved, no other force options can be addressed in this book. Remember, the use of deadly force is always the final option—although depending on the situation, it may have to be the first option used.

WHAT YOU CAN EXPECT FROM THIS BOOK

When you purchased this book you took a positive step toward increasing your survival advantage. The journey toward any goal begins with the first step, but once that step is taken, you must continue moving in the direction of your goal. Hopefully, your goal is to become a professional weapon user, well skilled in defensive handgun use and encounter tactics. Do not be put off by the amount of material presented, but flow with the information, building your weapon use skills in a step-by-step progression. Before you know it, you will have trained-in and developed the skills of a professional weapon user. The decision is yours. You are a defensive weapon user by virtue of your job, but you can only be a professional weapon user by virtue of your trained-in skills.

Defensive and Professional Weapon Users: the Difference. These terms denote two different skill levels, or the dividing point between someone who just carries a handgun and someone who knows how to use it professionally. All police officers are defensive weapon users by virtue of their job. Day after day they carry their service handguns, but how proficient and professional are they in their use? It is a sad commentary that very few police officers are professional weapon users. It is also an interesting fact that most police officers have little interest in furthering their weapon use skills and knowledge. Their lives may depend on their abilities to use the service handgun successfully during a lethal encounter, but they rationalize that the odds are against it ever occurring. On the one hand, they are right: It may never occur. On the other hand, it may occur tomorrow or next week or when they least expect it, with the end result being tragic. This faulty reasoning will dramatically reduce their survival advantage. If confronted with a lethal encounter and fighting for their lives, they must now rely too heavily on luck to survive—and luck can be exceedingly cruel.

Any defensive weapon user can become a professional weapon user if he or she practices and trains in the reflexive sets and skills in the four areas of defensive handgun use: mental set, weapon use skills, encounter tactics, and preparation. A surprisingly small number of police officers on most departments would qualify as professional weapon users. It takes work to become one, but not as much as you may think. Your interest and commitment to improving your skills are the major factors.

Changing Habits. One of the main stumbling blocks to advancing your weapon use skills is resistance to change. If you find a better way of doing something and it works, you would be foolish not to change. But many officers resist changing handgun techniques, saying: "I've always done it this way and I don't think I can change." In reality, this is not the case: You can change if you want to. Approach this information with an open mind and if change is appropriate, institute the change.

You have demonstrated your desire to further your defensive handgun skills by reading and studying this book, thus greatly enhancing your survival advantage during a lethal encounter. The survival advantage can be yours if you prepare beforehand to make sure that it is.

THE BOOK'S TERMS

Chapter 1 is used to get everyone on line and headed in the same direction. This section is very important to that goal by defining the terminology used and how you are to view it. Throughout this book the various terms, descriptions, and nomenclature form a lexicon of defensive handgun use terminology that must be understood. But further, certain terms and concepts must be clarified right from the beginning, to explain certain mechanisms of this book. In this section we define certain terms, concepts, and uses that will be seen throughout this book. We present this section to get everybody oriented from the beginning. There are only a few items to be explained, but they will help your understanding of the information presented.

Handgun or Service Handgun. These terms are used interchangeably for a police officer's service handgun and can be any of the three service handgun design types: double-action revolver, double-action automatic, and single-action automatic. Precise nomenclature for both the revolver and automatic will be referred to in the book and is shown in the following drawings.

Strong Hand and Support Hand. In teaching defensive handgun use, the ability to teach both left- and right-handed officers successfully is based in individual terms for each hand—other than left and right. This is done to stop the problems caused by descriptions meant only for right-handed officers, with left-handed officers forced to figure it out. To end this problem, we switch the terms to strong hand and support hand.

No matter whether you are left- or right-handed, you have a strong hand and a support hand. The strong hand is your favored hand: If you are right-handed, your right hand is your strong hand and your left hand is your support hand. If

REVOLVER NOMENCLATURE:

1.1.

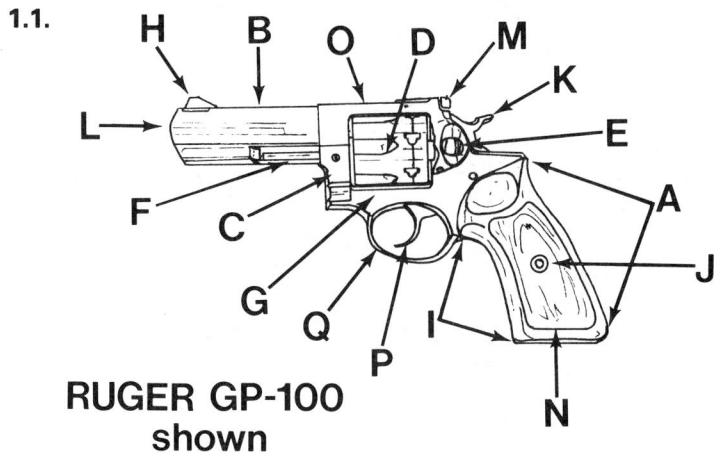

RUGER GP-100
shown

Figure 1.1 Nomenclature for the revolver: A, back strap area; B, barrel; C, crane (rotates cylinder out for loading); D, cylinder; E, cylinder release; F, ejector rod; G, frame; H, front sight; I, front strap area; J, grip/grip area; K, hammer; L, muzzle; M, rear sight; N, stocks (actual grip panels); O, top strap area; P, trigger; Q, trigger guard.

you are left-handed, your left hand is your strong hand and your right hand is your support hand. Your strong hand is used almost exclusively to grip the service handgun, with the support hand supporting it when a two-handed grip is used. By using the terms "strong hand" and "support hand," we have removed the identification problem. Just follow the strong-hand and support-hand use as written in the text and it will work no matter what "handed" you are.

The strong and support terms also reflect *all bodily parts* on each side of your body. If you are right-handed, your strong hand is your right hand, your strong leg is your right leg, your strong eye is your right eye, and so on. Divide your body down the middle; anything on the strong side is termed strong and anything on the support side is termed support.

For various techniques, though, a particular hand will be required, so *left* and *right* will be used to designate the precise hand used. If you see "strong hand" or "support hand," it is for whichever "handed" you are. If you see "left hand" or "right hand" it is for that precise hand.

Threat(s).   This book deals only with deadly situations where an assailant is attacking you. The term "threat(s)" will therefore be used for all references to suspects or assailants. Threat(s) are, at that moment, presenting a grave or deadly

1.2. **SEMI-AUTOMATIC NOMENCLATURE:**

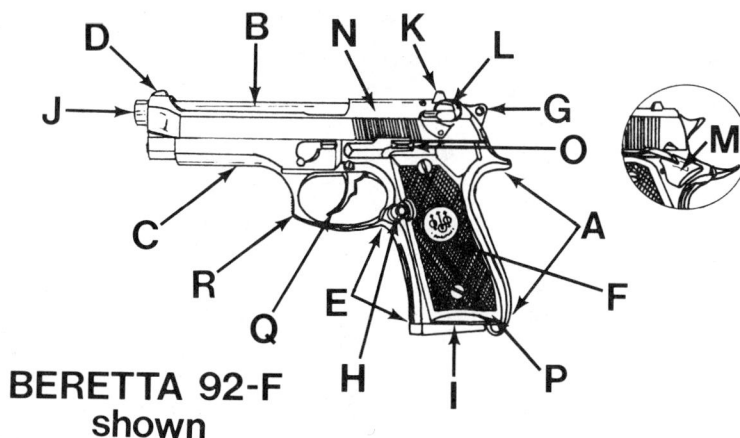

**BERETTA 92-F
shown**

Figure 1.2 Nomenclature for the semiautomatic pistol: A, back strap area; B, barrel; C, frame; D, front sight; E, front strap area; F, grip/grip area; G, hammer; H, magazine release; I, magazine well opening (magazine floorplate showing magazine in place); J, muzzle; K, rear sight; L, safety/decocking lever (slide mounted on double-action autos); M, safety (frame mounted on single-action autos; see small circular insert); N, slide; O, slide stop/slide release; P, stocks (actual grip panels); Q, trigger; R, trigger guard.

threat, which is your only justification for shooting in the first place. "Threat(s)" is almost always written in the singular(plural) form, to emphasize that you should always be looking for the next threat. All too often officers relax after the first threat has been stopped, many times completely neglecting the possibility of a secondary threat(s). The threat(s) is referred to in the neuter gender to reflect the fact that it could be either male or female. Whenever you see the term "threat(s)" always be thinking: a lethal threat, who can be anyone, and there is always one more threat than you have found.

"Hits". The terms "hits" is always placed in quotation marks, to emphasize the ultimate goal of weapon use skills—placing "hits." You must only fire as fast as you can and "hit" with every bullet. Make sure that every bullet is directed at the threat(s) and "hit" with the first bullet and every bullet after it. You must become "hit" oriented. Obviously, you will not "hit" every time, but you must be constantly thinking "hits."

These are the main terms that need to be defined initially to start everyone in the right direction. Many other terms will occur throughout this book. The main ones are defined in the glossary.

THE ASSETS SYSTEM

The ASSETS system is a very important part of your understanding of the total spectrum of defensive shooting and encounter tactics and will be referred to throughout this book. It reinforces the process you will be engaged in throughout a lethal encounter—finding out what is occurring and responding appropriately. The system's use began long before the encounter started, will be used throughout the encounter, and will continue long after the encounter ends. In other words, the ASSETS system is continually in use, especially for police officers, both on and off duty. This sytem is used to increase your ability to detect, respond to, and survive lethal encounters.

Mainly, the system increases your awareness of what is occurring around you, which will be used initially to detect that a possible threat(s) is about to present itself. If caught early, you are better prepared when the threat(s) does present itself. The ASSETS system is not difficult to understand; it merely reinforces what you should be doing at all times but especially during a lethal encounter.

The System

The ASSETS acronym stands for "assessing the situation and structure for the most effective tactics selection." When functioning, the acronym is broken down into its two parts: ASS and ETS. ASS is the continual process of always "assessing the situation and structure." This is done on a daily basis, every day; it did not just begin with the threat. You were using it long before the encounter started, will use it during the encounter, and its use will continue after the encounter ends. Once you have assessed the situation and structure, the ETS part comes into play. ETS is "the most effective tactics selection" and covers all the tactics and weapon use employed during the encounter. As the ASS part continually assesses what is going on and where it is taking place, the ETS part puts thought into action by applying the most effective tactics or weapon use to the encounter.

During the total encounter, ASS and ETS continually work together by mentally recognizing what is occurring around you, deciding on a course of action, and directing your tactics and weapon use. Stated generally, throughout the total encounter you continually assess the situation (what is occurring at the moment) and structure (the area you are in and structures around you) for the most effective tactics selection [the tactics and weapon use employed, in response to the situation and structure, to control or stop the threat(s)]. Think of this process as a chess player making moves and countermoves. As the encounter unfolds, it becomes a continual process of modifying your tactics and weapon use to fit the ever-changing situation and structure occurring throughout the encounter. As they change, you must modify your tactics and weapon use to fit them.

Both parts function together continuously throughout the total encounter. Assess what you have and where you are, and select the appropriate/timely tactics and/or weapon use to respond to it. This process is continually functioning to meet the changes that will instantly occur, and countering with the most effective tactics and/or weapon use.

ASS (Assessing the Situation and Structure)

The first part of the ASSETS System is always with you as part of your day-to-day activities. It extends throughout your life and creates an aware and prepared state of being that is constantly working. We use the illustration of a continuum line flowing through your life (stretching continuously from your past, through the present, and into the future) and the possible occurrence of lethal encounters as points along that continuum. The question is: How do you prepare to meet and survive lethal encounters whose rarity and unpredictability defy you to determine where along the continuum they will fall and in what form they will manifest themselves? The answer is the first part of the ASSETS system: continually assessing the situation and structure.

The first part of the ASSETS system, assessing the situation and structure, flows along the continuum that is your daily life (both on and off duty). Assessing the situation (what is going on around you) and structure (where you are) becomes part of your life, increasing your perception and awareness of people, places, and events around you. Throughout your life, you are expanding your senses into the immediate environment around you—heightening your awareness of everything going on around you. Not only have you increased your awareness to detect a pending lethal encounter (a definite adjunct to a police officer's continued life), but you have also heightened your individual perception, sampling and savoring of your environment and life itself.

You are cultivating a natural talent hidden within each of us. The use of this talent does not manifest itself in some obvious, overt change in your physical action—no paranoid adjustment to give you a *"nut"-like appearance*. It is hidden, covert, and yet nonetheless there, working to tell you many things that go completely unnoticed by virtually all around you. You are now in a position, at all times to know THAT something is about to happen, WHAT to do when (or before) it does, and WHEN to do it. As such, you are several steps ahead when the opening ceremony begins and are definitely a surprise to a threat(s).

Assessing the situation and structure did not just suddenly begin with the encounter, but was always quietly there, flowing along the *continuum line* that is your life. Understand, this not only functions to catch the *danger signs* and forewarn of approaching danger, but its use enhances your sampling and savoring of life itself.

The perception of a lethal encounter and the corresponding function of the ETS part (the total encounter from beginning to stabilization) appears as only one small moment on the continuum line, but one very critical and possibly lethal moment if you are not aware.

ETS (Effective Tactic Selection)

The second part of the ASSETS system, the most effective tactic selection, reinforces the use of tactics and/or weapon use. Police officers must understand that tactics are always used but that weapon use may not be needed.

Tactics.   The tactical part of ETS involves the tactics to be used during any situation and are dictated by the occurring situation and structure. In defensive small arms use, virtually all of the tactics are the same for whatever weapon you use. Tactics are fairly universal; simply apply the appropriate techniques for the weapon you are then using. The main point is that your response must always be tactical in nature, but will not always require a weapon use response. If it does, though, you must be ready to respond instantly.

Weapon Use.   The weapon use part of the ETS follows the three weapon use areas: handling, firing, and manipulating. Your individual weapon use skills must be trained-in reflexive sets that function automatically when needed. When the decision is made for a weapon use response, the handgun should already be up in your line of sight, as the sights are verified and the shot(s) fired. These skills function subconsciously; when needed, the skills are there.

The ASSETS system is not hard to understand and is used to reinforce what you should be doing at all times, especially during a lethal encounter. Both parts are continually functioning together throughout the total encounter to direct your response. The system was described here to provide an initial understanding of its function. Its use will become more apparent in other areas of this book.

SUMMARY

This chapter was provided to get everyone oriented and headed in the same direction. With the historical foundation, initial concepts, and central information covered, we begin building the weapon use skills and encounter tactics to increase your survival advantage.

2

Safe Gun Handling and Its Tactical Application

The first area covered in any weapon use is safety. Safety is a day-to-day function when carrying and handling a service handgun—necessity 100 percent of the time. In all likelihood you will rarely, if ever, have to use your service handgun to stop an armed attack, but you will always have to be safe with it. Safe gun handling begins with the four basic safety rules and a complete understanding of your service handgun. From these safety procedures, you move into an understanding of tactical safety that can keep a deadly mistake from ever occurring.

The service handgun will be in your hand on unknown or possibly dangerous situations on a daily basis. During those times, you will be searching with other officers and will no doubt come in contact with innocents (citizens who are not part of the situation) who stumble onto the scene. The double-bind is that you must always be "safe," yet ready to respond instantly to a deadly threat that may suddenly appear. If you are not safe and prepared, you may unintentionally kill or wound another officer or an innocent. You must handle your service handgun intelligently every day of your career.

In this chapter we discuss the four basic safety rules necessary for you to conduct a search safely, all the safety procedures for the service handgun, and the tenets of tactical safety—providing a complete understanding of what safety really involves.

Safety and the Defensive Weapon User

Most people think of safety and safe gun handling as beginners' lessons in the use of firearms. This is only partially correct, as a beginner must obviously be well versed in safety procedures. But further, the defensive weapon user—you, the police officer—must possess a total package of tactical skills to handle safely and effectively all the unknown or dangerous situations you may have to face. Tactical safety is very important and one of the skills that marks an expert defensive weapon user. One fact must be stated now so that everyone understands: Safety rules are not just for the inexperienced; they are for the experts, as part of their tactical use techniques. Remember, when using a weapon on dangerous or unknown situations, you are going in "hot" from two standpoints: high stress levels and a loaded weapon. During such tense undertakings, you can easily make a mistake. Tactical safety must be used to keep mistakes from happening in the first place and to lessen the impact of those you may make. Safety must be taken seriously as part of your tactical handgun use.

THE FOUR BASIC SAFETY RULES

Guns are mechanical devices and will not fire by themselves, but human intervention adds in the factors of common sense, reason, judgment, restraint, and good habits. The lack of any one of these can cause an unintentional discharge. It sounds like a lot, but really is not. There are just four basic safety rules that must be followed in your everyday use. If these rules are not followed, you are just an accident waiting to happen, and it may happen while you are right in the middle of a dangerous situation which can jeopardize your life or the lives of fellow officers. Prevent your first unintentional discharge from ever happening. As we all too painfully know, once a bullet is launched, it cannot be called back.

These safety rules are nothing more than common sense that makes good safety sense. If you take these rules seriously, memorizing and using them, your first mistake will never occur. Using these rules must become a safety reflex to maintain proper safety practices.

1. Consider All Guns To Be Loaded at All Times

There are no exceptions to this rule; be extremely serious about it. Treat all firearms as being loaded at all times. This does not mean that you disregard checking to make sure that a firearm is unloaded when handling it. When handing it to someone, when it is handed to you, and any time you think it is necessary, the handgun is checked to make sure that it is unloaded.

You must always assume that a firearm is loaded. Make sure that you always treat any firearm as loaded when handling it. People who do not can easily make a costly or fatal mistake, which will undoubtedly be followed by these words: "I didn't know the gun was loaded!" Do not let this happen to you.

2. Keep the Muzzle Pointed Away from Any Person or Thing You Do Not Intend to Shoot

This rule is the most violated of the four. Do not let the muzzle point at anything you do not want to shoot, especially do not let the muzzle cross your body or any-body else's. Officers too often forget this when searching together, creating very unsafe situations. Letting this occur is one of the most obvious signs of an unexperi-enced gun handler.

When handling or using a handgun, it is extremely easy for this to occur, as the firearm is short in length, being turned or pointed quickly and easily in any direction. People who let the muzzle of a handgun point at or cross someone seem inclined to say: "Oh, don't worry, the handgun isn't loaded." This is not to be excused, especially since it completely violates rule 1 and can get someone killed.

3. Keep Your Trigger Finger out of the Trigger Guard Except When Coming on Target Just before Firing

Many officers wrongly think that the trigger finger should be on the trigger or in the trigger guard at all times when the handgun is out, so that they can fire faster. This is definitely not true. You have more than enough time to "index" the trigger finger on the trigger as you are aligning on the target. When keeping your trig-ger finger outside the trigger guard, you are very safe, yet can instantly index the trigger finger (place it into the trigger guard on the trigger) and fire the handgun. In fact, you cannot physically line up the handgun on the target before you can place your trigger finger on the trigger. As such, you are very safe and just as quick to fire.

Disregarding this rule causes 95 percent of all unintentional discharges that occur. When handling or searching, it is amazing to see the number of officers with their fingers on the trigger. This is highly unsafe and tactically incorrect. Do not let yourself fall into this extremely bad habit. Keep your trigger finger out of the trigger guard until you are coming on target. The only exception to this rule is dry firing, only after checking the firearm to make sure that it is unloaded.

4. Be Sure of Your Target and Background

First, you must be sure of your target by positively identifying it before you shoot. In police work this translates into positively identifying the threat, which at that moment is engaged in a lethal attack which, if completed, will in all probability cause your death or grievous bodily harm, with no other options to control or avoid it. Make sure what you have. An officer must not shoot at a suddenly occurring sound or form in the dark. You must identify your target the first time every time. Second, you must be sure that the area around and behind the threat(s) is clear of innocents. In reality, most lethal encounters occur so quickly that there is little time to do anything but the reflexive actions to save your life, much less check what is behind the threat(s). But you should always be taking this into consideration when you think that a threat(s) may be present and hopefully engineer the situation to make sure that you are not endangering innocents. Also, a lowered firing position, especially kneeling, can change your angle of fire if innocents are present (see Chapter 13).

These four safety rules must form a safety reflex that is in place and working all the time. They should be ingrained to the point that you almost cannot make yourself violate any of these rules. These are all the safety rules that you will even need. Use them to make sure that you do not make your first mistake with a firearm. Memorize these safety rules and use them constantly. Remember, you may not have the luxury of a first mistake with a firearm, as your first mistake may be your last.

This point was tragically brought home by the death of a young officer on a building entry. Poised next to a door, ready to enter instantly upon its being opened, the officer held his service handgun in the up position, the muzzle unknowingly pointed at the back of his head. As the action proceeded, he reflexively flinched and the trigger finger, on the trigger, fired the handgun. The officer died instantly from a head wound brought about by not following the two most important safety rules: Keep your trigger finger out of the trigger guard except when coming on target, and keep the muzzle pointed away from yourself or any other person you do not intend to shoot.

TACTICAL SAFETY

Tactical safety is an understanding of the safety rules as they apply to tactical encounters or searches. The use of a firearm during a search begins with safety and the need is triple-fold during these times of high stress, as safety is coupled with an instant readiness to fire. Where speed is a main consideration in firing, the risks involved increase, as you are on a short trigger (instantly ready to fire). While searching an area you are at peak stress, all the while holding the weapon ready to fire instantly if needed. As such, the chance of an unintentional discharge or firing too quickly, before you really know what you have, is great. These can be eliminated or reduced only by training in correct tactical safety habits and consciously using them on all your searches or encounters.

Understand that tactical safety is one of the signs of a professional weapon user. Safety is not some basic skill left behind as one advances in weapon use, but its methods are continually practiced, used, and refined as part of your subconscious reflexive sets, although still part of your conscious thoughts. Tactical safety is expressed as a combination of search safety and weapon etiquette. These are virtually the same but will be explained separately to cover all their points.

Search safety are those practices that keep you and those searching with you safe from each other in highly charged search situations. As stated before: "You, and anybody with you, are going in 'hot' from two standpoints: weapons loaded and high stress." During these situations two things must always be done by you and any others involved: (1) Keep your trigger finger out of the trigger guard until coming on target just before firing, and (2) keep the muzzle pointed away from yourself or any other person you do not intend to shoot. These are commonsense rules, but you would be surprised how many officers do not follow them. The search situation is a fluid one, with officers moving around each other while searching. If search safety is not used, many dangerous situations can easily develop. The fact is that officers on searches (or other calls) are placing themselves in danger without even realizing it. They do not know it until one officer unintentionally shoots or almost shoots another officer searching with him. Make a constant effort to keep your head up, use common sense, and always follow these two vital rules.

Weapon etiquette is nothing more than the safe, professional way of manipulating the handgun. You can tell how much an officer knows about weapon handling just by watching him or her manipulate the service handgun on a search or other use. Is the officer safe, comfortable with its use, and professional? As you observe the officer, you will either feel comfortable (not having to worry about the officer's safety) or uncomfortable (have to keep an eye on the officer). Officers handling weapons in an unsafe manner are just as much of a lethal danger to themselves and others on the search as are the actual threat(s) they are searching for. Often an inept officer is a much greater danger, as he or she is armed and the threat(s) hiding is not or it is just an empty building. It is aggravating and you can bet it will not be tolerated for long.

As you practice and use tactical safety it become a subconscious routine or safety reflex that goes with the search, encounter, or any weapon use.

OTHER SAFETY FACTORS

Unintentional Discharges

Accidents with weapons are divided into two basic types of unintentional discharges: those occurring through poor technique and those occurring under the stress of the situation. Poor safety and weapon use techniques are responsible for the majority of unintentional discharges. These usually result in bullet holes in inanimate objects. Statements such as "I didn't know it was loaded," "I don't know how it went off," "I never touched the trigger, the gun malfunctioned" are heard all too often. In reality, the problem lies with poor safety habits and a lack of familiarity in using the weapon. Knowing your service handgun's safety procedures and following the four basic safety rules would stop all of these.

Stress-related unintentional discharges occur during the tense moments of an unknown or possibly dangerous situation. An innocent inadvertently appears on the scene, is taken for a threat, and the officer fires too quickly, before knowing what he or she has. This occurrence is usually triggered by the officer's feelings that there may not be enough time to save his or her life if firing is not done immediately. Under the stress of the moment, the innocent suddenly appears and the officer fires—*quick and tragic*. This problem can be corrected only by increasing officers' confidence in their ability to use the service handgun effectively and control the situation. With increased confidence, officers will know that they possess the skills necessary to stop the threat(s) quickly; thus providing the advantage they need when making quick shoot/no-shoot decisions.

You, the police officer, are ultimately responsible for your actions. All too often, unintentional discharges instantly turn into unintentional hits. If you are careless, do not follow the basic safety rules, and if your skills are inadequate, you are a liability on a police search. Your mistake could dearly cost you, another officer, or someone else. Remember, whatever your bullet unintentionally hits, you will be held accountable for.

One example dramatically illustrates just how quickly and easily a deadly mistake can occur. Two officers respond to the scene of a possible breaking and entering (B&E) in progress, where a resident returned home to find his front door opened. On the scene the two officers entered the house and began the search. At some juncture during the search, they split up to search the same floor (their first mistake). The first officer, after looking through the living room, pushed open the door to the bedroom. There standing in the dark shadows stood a figure with a revolver. Instantly, the first officer fired his revolver at the dark figure, missing her head by about an inch. You have probably jumped ahead of this narration and guessed that the figure in the bedroom was the second officer.

The point is: If you fall into the trap of not being serious about your search, not being prepared, and not using tactical safety, sometime along the way you will get caught.

Safety on the Draw and When Searching

When drawing and manipulating the handgun on the search, safety involves not only the safety rules and procedures but the use of any mechanical safety mechanism on the service handgun.

Safe trigger finger action is the same for all service handguns.   The safe action of the trigger finger is the same for the three service handgun designs: double-action revolver, double-action auto, and single-action auto. In conjunction with the trigger finger action, many of the autos have external safety levers which are also manipulated at various points.

When drawing and firing, the trigger finger is placed into the trigger guard and makes contact with the trigger *only* once the handgun is pointed at any part of the threat's body (or in its general direction) and the muzzle is well in front of your body. When searching, the trigger finger is out of the trigger guard (laying straight along the side of the frame), when either *searching* in the *holding* positions or *approaching* a possible threat location in the *firing* positions (these positions are discussed in Chapter 6). With the finger out of the trigger guard, if you are startled, accidentally fall or stumble, or come in contact with an object, you will not reflexively pull the trigger finger (gripping with the rest of the hand) and fire an unintentional round. *Only when the threat(s) appears [or you know the threat(s) is directly close] do you place the trigger finger on the trigger in preparation for firing.* Once the firing is completed and the handgun lowered [after making sure that the threat(s) has been stopped], the trigger finger comes out of the trigger guard and is placed along the side of the frame. Remember, the trigger finger is in the trigger guard on the trigger only as the handgun is coming on target just before firing.

Double-Action (D-A) Revolver.   The D-A revolver is the easiest service handgun to describe, as there are no external safety levers to push on or off. Just follow the safe trigger finger action when drawing and searching with the D-A revolver.

Double-Action Automatic.   The D-A automatic (auto) will be carried with the hammer down and the safety either "on or off." On the draw, either push the safety "off" and pull the trigger to fire, or (if the safety is already "off") merely pull the trigger to fire, just like a D-A revolver. When searching with a D-A auto, always follow the trigger-finger actions by keeping it out of the trigger guard until coming on target just before firing. If the safety was "on" in the holster, push it "off" as you begin your search. Once the D-A auto has been fired, the hammer will remain cocked. Once the encounter is over, push the safety "on" to decock (lower) the hammer safely and then push the safety "off" to make it instantly ready to fire again. Throughout the encounter use the *safe trigger-finger action* (keeping it out of the trigger guard as required) to keep the auto from firing. Most new D-A autos have *internal safety mechanisms,* so the D-A auto will not fire if the trigger is not pulled to the rear.

Single-Action Automatic.   The S-A auto will be carried cocked and locked (the hammer cocked back and the safety locked "on"). When drawing and immediately firing, the safety is pushed "off" just after the hands come together in a two-handed grip as the handgun is moving forward to be locked out into a two-handed firing stance. Keep the thumb on top of the safety whenever it is pushed "off." This is done to keep it from accidentally reengaging and stopping the auto from firing. When searching with an S-A auto, follow the safe trigger-finger actions already described and keep your thumb on top of the safety to be instantly ready to push it "off" if the threat(s) suddenly appears. Keep the safety "on" until you are ready to fire. Once the S-A auto has been fired, the hammer will remain cocked. Whenever the S-A auto is not firing, push the safety "on" (the hammer will not decock when the safety is pushed "on"). Once the encounter is over, keep the safety "on," reload as required and holster the auto.

Clearing and Checking the Service Handgun

When checking a service handgun, make sure that you keep the muzzle pointed in a safe direction and keep your trigger finger out of the trigger guard, then open the action and look into the chamber(s) to make sure that it is unloaded. When clearing and checking a service handgun, follow the steps listed below. (*Note:* These steps are presented under the functions of the service handgun in Chapter 3. They are included here to outline safe clearing and checking methods.)

The Revolver.   When clearing and checking a double-action revolver, follow these steps:

1. Keep the muzzle pointed in a safe direction and keep your trigger finger out of the trigger guard.
2. Press the cylinder release and swing the cylinder out.
3. Tilt the muzzle up to cause the cartridges to fall out (if two or three rounds have been fired, eject them manually by pressing the ejector rod).
4. Check the cartridges (or empty cases) and *look into each chamber of the cylinder* to make sure that the revolver is unloaded. Count the cartridges or cases just to be sure.

The Semiautomatic.   When clearing and checking a semiautomatic pistol, follow these steps:

1. Keep the muzzle pointed in a safe direction and keep your trigger finger out of the trigger guard.
2. Remove the magazine first. You are removing a number of possible unintentional discharges. Secure the magazine by placing it under your belt or in your pocket.
3. Grasp the slide with the support hand, the palm over the ejection port, as the auto is tilted away from the body. The slide is thus turned down at an angle and the magazine well opening is angled up. Make sure that the muzzle is still pointed in a safe direction.
4. Push the slide to the rear (if a single-action auto, the safety is pushed "off" first), ejecting the chambered cartridge into the palm of the support hand. As this is done, press up on the slide stop to lock the slide open.
5. Look into the chamber of the barrel to make sure that it is unloaded.

Always check the chamber! Never fail in this, whether checking an unloaded handgun or clearing a loaded one. When unloading an auto or revolver, make sure that you look into the chamber(s). When unloading an auto, after the magazine is removed and the slide is pulled to the rear, ejecting the chambered round, look into the chamber to make sure that it is unloaded. When unloading a revolver, after you open the cylinder and remove the cartridges, do not just count the cartridges; look into each chamber of the cylinder to make sure that it is unloaded. Make sure each and every time.

A Note on Automatic Loaded Chamber Indicators. A number of automatics come equipped with loaded chamber indicators, a small piece of metal that protrudes when a cartridge is in the chamber, indicating that the auto is loaded. Do not trust these. Generally, they work just fine, but they do not always function correctly and may indicate that an automatic is loaded when it is not. The automatic must be checked to determine whether it is loaded or unloaded.

Drawing and Dry-Firing Practice

When practicing drawing or dry firing, always check to make sure that the handgun is unloaded! Make sure that you check it twice. You must practice your drawing technique to train in the "holster-to-stance" reflexive set and use dry firing to improve your trigger manipulation. These must be done on a continual basis to improve your skill and confidence in your ability with the service handgun. Before you begin the practice, make sure that the service handgun is unloaded. Check it several times before starting. Similarly, when you reload the service handgun, check to make sure it is reloaded before you holster it. Remember, an unloaded handgun is never reholstered (hopefully, your firearms instructor does not have you reholster an unloaded handgun on the range). (*Note:* Drawing and dry firing are described later in the book; do not attempt these forms of practice until you understand them completely.)

Range Safety

A professional weapon user has a deep respect for his or her firearm and the lethal abilities associated with the carrying and use of it. The professional always conducts himself or herself in a safe manner.

At the range keep your handgun holstered (a holstered handgun is a safe handgun) unless otherwise instructed by a range officer or rule of the range. Keep your hand away from the holstered handgun except on the firing line. Also, never forget: The trigger finger is out of the trigger guard except when coming on target just before firing. Whenever you stop firing, even for a brief moment, take your trigger finger out of the trigger guard and lay it straight along the side of the frame. If involved in some type of assault course and moving between firing points, again, the trigger finger is outside the trigger guard.

Whenever engaged in any type of firing, never turn around with the handgun out of the holster. Keep facing downrange during firing and turn around only when the handgun has been holstered. The muzzle is always pointed downrange until the handgun is safely holstered.

When holding the handgun in your hand at any time, except when firing, the action will be opened. This is also the way any handgun will be handed to another person. If an auto, the magazine will also be removed. (*Note:* Whenever closing or opening a handgun's action, use two hands; never slam a revolver's cylinder into the frame or allow an auto's slide to slam into battery when it is empty. Treat the weapon with the respect it deserves, in a professional manner.)

When practicing on an unsupervised range, if any other shooters are present, give a loud warning that you are going to begin firing. If nobody has been shooting for a time, some of the other shooters may have taken their hearing protectors off and would like to be given enough warning so that they can put them back on. This is just general professional shooting manners.

Handgun Storage Safety

When an officer is off duty, the service handgun is usually kept at home. It is every officer's duty to make sure that the service handgun is safe and stored properly. Remember, the handgun is either holstered or stored safely. When you arrive home, it is never taken from the holster and laid down somewhere. If it is taken from the holster, it is stored safely—every single time. Children shoot, injure, or kill them-selves each year by service handguns that were laid down carelessly. Do not let this happen to your family. You must be completely responsible with your service hand-gun. Dog tired or not, your first responsibility is to secure your handgun safely when you come home.

As a rule, most officers also keep their service handgun as the self-defense gun of the house. If you keep your service handgun ready as a self-defense gun, a bal-ance between safety and availability must be arrived at. The balance will depend on each officer's decisions about his or her family and the living arrangements. Every-one living with the officer or visiting, from the children to Uncle Henry, must be taken into consideration. There will be times when there is no direct control over the handgun and certain procedures must be used to keep it as safe as possible.

Ultimately, each officer must make the decisions of where and how the service handgun will be stored. First, it must be kept out of sight. Untrained people often cannot resist picking up a handgun and handling it. Many accidental shootings in-volve someone who picks up a handgun left in plain sight. Do not let this happen; keep it safely hidden away. Your family (every member who is old enough) must be educated to have the same respect for the handgun that you do. Children are taught not to fear it but to respect the danger that can come from it and not to touch it if they should ever find it. When they are old enough they should be taught safe gun handling.

Several methods of storing a handgun can be used. Possibly the best method is to store the handgun and ammunition in separate places. If ever needed, both can be gotten and the handgun quickly loaded. Also, if the service handgun is an auto, it can be stored with chamber empty, hammer down, and a full magazine locked in place (if a D-A auto, the safety is also pushed "on"). If needed quickly (push the safety "off" if a D-A auto), pull the slide to the rear and release it to chamber the first round from the magazine. While the auto is quickly available, pulling the slide to the rear is virtually impossible for small children (especially with the hammer down). Again, carefully consider your particular living situation and safely store the handgun accordingly.

Several mechanical devices can be purchased that either completely contain the handgun in a locked box, or cover and lock the trigger, or lock the action open.

Although these are certainly safe, it will take longer to bring the handgun into defensive use. You must ultimately decide how to store your handgun safely. Once a method is decided on, use it routinely.

SUMMARY

In your day-to-day carrying and use of the service handgun, safety must become a conscious and subconscious routine that is used at all times. Remember, you must handle your service handgun intelligently every day of your career. Being safe and tactically correct is being intelligent.

3

The Three Service Handgun Designs and How They Function

The term service handgun elicits a variety of images, extending from old single-action revolvers to double-action revolvers and semiautomatic pistols; every size, type, and caliber is probably represented. Names such as Colt and Smith & Wesson (two long-standing, venerated U.S. manufacturers), Ruger, or several of the excellent European imports, such as Beretta, Glock, Heckler & Koch, and Sig-Sauer, all are synonymous with the service handguns used by police officers and military personnel. Throughout the history of law enforcement, the power these pieces of loaded mechanical steel possess is quite respectable—enough power held in one's hand to control the immediate surroundings readily when threatened or attacked by an armed criminal. Officers, by the authority given them under the law and their skill with the service handgun, have the duty and ability to stop a lethal threat—either by the use of the handgun or its threatened use. All this can be accomplished only if they use this power intelligently.

Whether it be the first or final analysis of any situation, the officer (user) is far more important than the service handgun (weapon). The service handgun is nothing more than a piece of emergency equipment, providing the officer with the means of responding to and solving a lethal encounter. As stated, the officer possesses the means of dealing with a lethal threat(s), but will he or she use it in a safe, effective, and intelligent manner? The service handgun's power must be used properly to save lives.

Contrary to what most believe, the service handgun is a defensive weapon and its primary purpose is actually to save lives. It fulfills this primary purpose by stopping lethal threats which endanger the lives of innocent citizens and officers alike. Defensive in intent and provided primarily to save lives during emergency situations, the service handgun provides officers with the ability to save themselves and others.

An explanation of all the various service handguns carried nationwide would fill one complete text alone. The purpose of this chapter is to familiarize you with the three types of handguns that will cover virtually 98 percent of all service handguns in use today. We are cutting to the heart of the matter—the three service handgun designs and how you optimally handle and use them.

A service handgun must be one of the three designs this chapter is covering: the modern double-action revolver, the double-action semiautomatic pistol, and the single-action semiautomatic pistol. Only these three designs should be considered as defensive sidearms/service handguns. Chapter 15, on back-up, concealable and off-duty handguns, will address the smaller, more readily concealable types of handguns.

The information presented here will give you a decided advantage in two respects: (1) it will improve your "handgun handling habits" by showing you the proper techniques for your own service handgun, and (2) it will increase your knowledge of virtually all handguns, improving your ability to place any handgun found or taken from threats in a safe condition. This chapter may seem like a lot of basics, but you must have a working knowledge of all the information presented here. We begin with an examination of the requirements of a defensive sidearm.

THE REQUIREMENTS OF A DEFENSIVE SIDEARM

A defensive sidearm, the service handgun, must provide you with the means of stopping a lethal threat(s) and regaining control of your immediate surroundings. We view the service handgun as a piece of easily portable emergency equipment that must possess certain capabilities to perform its task effectively. These capabilities (or requirements) can instantly become vital during a lethal encounter.

Most frequently, the lethal threat(s) that the service handgun is meant to stop occurs from arm's length to room-size distances (0 to 20 feet). They are usually quick to occur and quick to end. For this purpose the handgun is beautifully adapted: it is small, compact, light, easily carried, and can be brought into action quickly. (*Note:* The handgun's use is defensive in nature and fairly limited when compared with other firearms—shotguns, rifles, and so on—as its range is limited, its power is considerably less, and it cannot be used as efficiently. But when considering the police function, it is perfectly suited, the advantages far outweighing the disadvantages.)

Once we note that the handgun is well adapted for the task at hand, what requirements can increase its effective use when performing the task, thereby increasing your survival advantage during a lethal encounter? The first three requirements that follow are the most important requirements of a defensive sidearm.

The Three Main Requirements of a Defensive Sidearm

The three main requirements of a defensive sidearm are those most needed during a lethal encounter. When the engagement begins and the bullets are flying, these three will improve your chances of successfully stopping the lethal threat(s). They are shown in the order of their importance.

1. *Reliability*. First and foremost, the service handgun must be reliable. This is the most important requirement, as one fact stands out: If it will not function dependably, it is not worth having! This cannot be stressed enough. The service handgun must function reliably the first time you use it every time you use it. Reliability is the only requirement that is not traded-off for anything; first and foremost the service handgun must be reliable.

2. *Controllable fight stopping power.* The handgun must possess an acceptable degree of fight stopping power, yet must be relatively easy to control and "hit" with by all sworn members. As such, a balance must be made between fight stopping power and controllability.

The ultimate fight stopping power in a defensive handgun round is one that would stop a full-grown man within 2 seconds with one solid torso hit. In a handgun that could be considered for use as a service handgun, it does not exist (although it is closely approached by the .44 Magnum). Most cartridges generally used in service handguns run around the 40 to 75 percent fight stopping percentage level: .45 ACP and .357 Magnum, 60 to 75 percent; .38 special and 9 mm, 40 to 60 percent. These percentages are merely indicators to show the level of fight stopping ability each cartridge possesses. Variations will definitely occur due to load considerations, bullet configurations, and bullet weights, although the variations will tend to reduce the fight stopping percentage levels to the lower percentages shown (obviously overpowered or wildcat loadings are not considered here; these would have no bearing on police service handgun loads).

When dealing with controllability, you must be able to "hit" with the first shot and instantly get back on target for the next and subsequent shots. This effectively removes overpowered rounds such as the .44 Magnum, which is hard to control defensively, increasing dramatically the time it takes to reacquire the target between shots. (*Note:* The .44 Magnum loaded to controllable levels is an excellent defensive round.) Also, there are trade-offs that must be considered when dealing with *controllable fight stopping power:* overpenetration, political/social stigma (hollow points in some locations, any cartridge that is unfortunate enough to be labeled a killer round, fragmentation rounds, etc.), the actual service handgun chosen, and so on.

3. *Capacity*. The number of in-the-gun rounds is important for the increased ability to maintain a fight when faced with multiple threats. More and more, we are finding the team concept being used by criminals. The increased ability to engage

multiple armed threats continuously, coupled with improved reloading ability, is a must.

The foregoing main requirements outline the most important considerations of a defensive sidearm. Many other areas—safety in design, accuracy, other defensive features, and so on—are addressed in this chapter and throughout the remainder of this book.

THE THREE SERVICE HANDGUN DESIGNS

As stated in the beginning of this chapter, there are three service handgun designs that account for more than 98 percent of all police service handguns used nation-wide. A knowledge of these will give you a basic understanding of virtually all modern handguns. Obviously, within these three service handgun designs, there are many variations between the different manufacturers (Colt, Smith & Wesson, Ruger, Beretta, Sig-Sauer, Glock, H&K, etc.): safeties and safety systems, decocking mechanisms, magazine releases, exposed or unexposed hammers, and so on. It is less important to understand the many variations (except for several notable variations that will be examined at the end of this chapter) than it is to understand the working of the "three" service handgun design types.

The three service handgun designs that must be understood are the double-action revolver, the double-action semi-automatic pistol, and the single-action semi-automatic pistol. First, we must understand the difference between the double-action and single-action modes, then take a brief look at each design type. Second, we must proceed with the functioning of each design type, examining combat efficiency as we go.

Single-Action and Double-Action Firing Modes: What They Mean

The single-action and double-action firing modes. The double-action firing mode refers to the hammer being uncocked and having to be mechanically cocked by the trigger as it is pulled back, which brings the hammer back and drops it to fire the handgun. The single-action firing mode refers to the hammer already being cocked back and the trigger being pulled merely to drop the already cocked hammer and fire the handgun (the trigger not having to cock the hammer mechanically as it is pulled). The felt difference is in the weight of the trigger pull. In the single-action firing mode (with the hammer cocked back), the trigger travels a much shorter distance with a much lighter trigger pull then in the double-action mode. In the double-action firing mode (the hammer is uncocked), the trigger has a much longer travel distance (to be able to cock the hammer) and a heavier trigger pull weight.

cocked

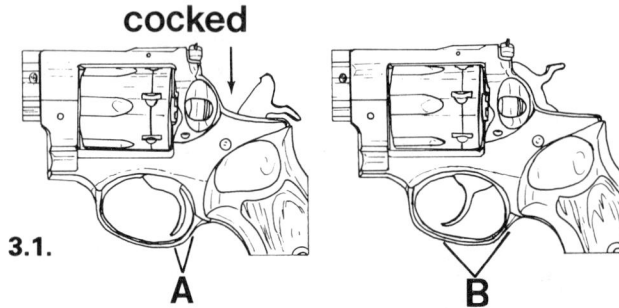

3.1.

A   B

Figure 3.1 With the hammer cocked, note the shorter trigger travel (A). With the hammer not cocked, note the longer trigger travel (B).

All handguns are designated as either single-action or double-action. For all service handgun designs, the double- and single-action firing modes function exactly the same way and every revolver or auto is designated as either a double-action or single-action handgun.

If a revolver or auto is referred to as double-action, either the single-action firing mode (the hammer being cocked first, then the trigger pulled) or the double-action firing mode (the hammer being uncocked and the trigger being pulled) can be used for the first round. All subsequent shots for the D-A revolver can be either double- or single-action, depending on the shooter's choice. All subsequent shots for the D-A auto will be fired in the single-action firing mode as the hammer is cocked by the action of the slide each time the auto fires.

If a revolver or auto is referred to as single-action, only the single-action firing mode can be used. All shots, whether fired first or subsequent, must be fired in the single-action firing mode. To fire the S-A revolver, the thumb must cock the hammer every time before the trigger is pressed. To fire the S-A auto [the hammer is already cocked to the rear as it is carried cocked and locked (hammer cocked and safety locked "on")], push the safety "off" and fire the first and subsequent rounds in the single-action firing mode. Just as with the double-action auto, the action of the slide cocks the hammer each time the auto is fired. (*Note:* The single-action revolver is only made mention of here and is not to be considered as a service handgun, as reloading time is exceedingly long and firing requires manually cocking the hammer for each shot.)

In use. When using the double-action mode, you take up the slack, then pull the trigger back in one smooth continuous motion to fire the handgun. As this is done, the hammer is mechanically cocked back and then dropped to fire the handgun. When using the single-action mode, you press the trigger back by smoothly increasing the pressure until the sear breaks and the hammer falls, firing the handgun. The hammer was already cocked and the only mechanical process is pressing the trigger until the sear (holding the hammer cocked) is disengaged, causing the hammer to drop instantly, firing the handgun.

As stated before, the felt difference is in the trigger. In double-action, the distance the trigger travels is longer and the amount of pressure applied by the trigger finger is greater. In single-action, the trigger travels only a very small distance and the pressure applied is a third to a half that of the double-action trigger pull. The double-action trigger pull ranges from 7 to 14 pounds and the single-action trigger pull ranges from 4 to 8 pounds. Anything less than a 4 pound trigger pull should not be considered for a service handgun.

The Double-Action Revolver

The majority of service handguns in use today nationwide fall into this category. The names Colt, Smith & Wesson, and Ruger are synonymous with the double-action service handguns officers carry. This country's love affair with the revolver has its foundation in the Old West, where the single-action peacemaker and those who were good with it still stir images that continue into the present. Only now is the semiautomatic pistol beginning to make inroads into territory long held (perhaps too long) by the revolver.

The revolver is recognized and named for its cylinder, which holds six cartridges (in a circular pattern) that "revolve" around the center pin, running through the middle of the cylinder into the front and back of the frame. Each time the trigger is pulled in double-action, or when the hammer is cocked and then the trigger is pulled in single-action, the "cylinder" rotates, bringing each cartridge (one after the other) up in line with the barrel and firing pin, and fires it.

The defensive firing modes of the D-A revolver.   When using the D-A revolver defensively, which of the two firing modes is used and for what situation? Double-action is the defensive firing mode, as it is the quickest method of firing the D-A revolver. Single-action is used only for speciality purposes, usually involving increased distance and time frames. You must have the time necessary to use the single-action firing mode and assume a steady firing position for the increased distance and/or difficult target.

When using the double-action firing mode: As the trigger is pulled to the rear, it manually cocks the hammer and rotates the cylinder to bring a new cartridge in line with the barrel and firing pin, and at the end of the trigger pull the hammer falls, firing the revolver. Firing the revolver is accomplished by one smooth, continuous pull of the trigger. For another instant shot, release the trigger and pull it again. The double-action mode has a heavier trigger pull weight than that of the single-action mode, but is a very fast method of firing. Even though the double-action firing mode is heavier, with practice it can be almost as smooth as the single-action firing mode.

In contrast, when using the single-action firing mode: You must thumb cock the hammer each time, then *press* the trigger to fire the revolver. As the thumb cocks the hammer back (to lock it in the cocked position), the cylinder rotates to bring a new cartridge in line with the barrel and firing pin. The hammer is now cocked to the rear and the revolver is ready to fire with a small press of the trigger, the action now being locked until the trigger is pressed. The trigger is then **pressed** a short distance, which releases the hammer to fire the revolver. The single-action firing mode has a lighter trigger pull weight but is a slower method of firing, because the hammer must first be cocked manually for each shot.

The double-action firing mode is used exclusively (98 percent of the time) in defensive revolver use—almost always involving very close gun fight distances with very short time frames. When functioning in a close, quick gun fight, you cannot afford the lost motions or time to cock the hammer before each shot. Too many things will be happening at once. Your major weapon use thought must either be "front sight/squeeze" (for aimed fire) or "lock-in/squeeze" (for stance-directed fire) every time you fire the handgun.

At longer ranges, with their usually increased time frames, the single-action firing mode can be used. In those situations you can benefit from the greater precision of the single-action trigger pull. As stated before, by using a single-action mode instead of a double-action mode, you will reduce the pressure needed to fire the revolver by a half to two-thirds. This will increase your ability to place a more accurate shot at longer distances. The reality of having to fire defensively at longer distances is very small, but if necessary, this can help. Remember, at no other time is the single-action firing mode used.

It should be noted that many departments do not allow the use of the single-action firing mode, going so far as to cut off (dehorn) the hammer spur and grind off the single-action notch on the hammer (so that hammer cannot be locked back in a cocked position). This is usually done to eliminate the problem of officers running around with cocked revolvers, which can present a definite safety problem.

Single-Action and Double-Action Semiautomatic Pistols

Used by this country's armed forces and European military and police forces for well over 70 years, the automatic has been less favored by our law enforcement community, which has clung steadfastly to the revolver.

The semiautomatic pistol (designated *automatic* in this work) is recognized for its angular appearance. With a slide atop the frame, the automatic is most noted for its ability to eject a fired case and reload the chamber with cartridges held in a magazine locked in place within the auto's grip area. Each time the auto is fired, the slide cycles (moving to the rear and then forward to again lock in place), ejecting the empty case (as the slide goes to the rear), and then chambering another cartridge from the magazine (as the slide goes forward). The magazine holds the cartridges under spring tension, pushing them up to feed into the chamber each time the automatic fires and the slide cycles. Each press of the trigger fires the auto and then instantly ejects the empty case and chambers another round from the magazine: the auto is instantly ready to fire again in the single-action firing mode.

D-A and S-A automatics, their defensive firing modes.   Automatics come in two basic design types, double-action and single-action. This refers to the automatic's ability to fire the first shot either double-action, by smoothly pulling the trigger, which will mechanically cock the hammer and release it, or single-action, by pushing the safety lever "off" and then pressing the trigger to drop the already cocked hammer. Once the first round is fired (either single- or double-action), all subsequent rounds will be fired "single-action," as the rearward movement of the slide will automatically re-cock the hammer in the process of ejecting the empty case and chambering the fresh round from the magazine. There are advantages and disadvantages to both which will be discussed completely.

The single-action auto is carried with the hammer cocked and the safety locked "on," referred to as cocked and locked. When loading, the slide is pulled to the rear and fully released, chambering the first round from the magazine. The hammer will remain cocked and the safety is pushed "on." The hammer must be cocked to fire the first shot, as the trigger mechanism cannot mechanically cock the hammer. To fire, push the safety "off" and press the trigger—firing the first shot in the single-action firing mode. Once the auto fires, the discharge recoils the slide to the rear (ejecting the empty case and cocking the hammer) and then the slide goes forward (chambering the next round from the magazine). The second and all subsequent rounds will also be fired in the single-action firing mode.

The double-action auto is carried with the hammer down and the safety either "on" or "off." When loading, the slide is pulled to the rear and fully released, chambering the first round from the magazine. The hammer will remain cocked until the safety lever is pushed "on," which will safely decock the hammer (it will safely fall and strike the rear end of the slide). The safety is pushed "on," the hammer safely falls, and then either leave the safety "on" or push it "off" (depending on the method used). The hammer does not have to be cocked to fire the first shot, as the trigger mechanism can mechanically cock the hammer. To fire, either push the safety "off" and pull the trigger, or if the safety is already "off," just pull the trigger (the same as firing a revolver), which will fire the first shot in the double-action firing mode. Once the auto fires, the same sequence of events occurs as with the single-action auto. The second and all subsequent rounds will now be fired in the single-action firing mode.

Carrying Modes.   The auto's design type will designate the carrying mode—how the automatic will be carried safely in the holster. The single-action auto will be carried cocked and locked, with the hammer cocked and the safety locked "on." To fire, the safety is pushed "off" and the trigger pressed. The double-action auto will be carried with the hammer down and either the safety "on" or "off." To fire, either push the safety "off" and pull the trigger, or if the safety is already "off," just pull the trigger, the same as a revolver. Once the first shot is fired from either auto, all subsequent shots will be fired single-action, as the slide re-cocks the hammer each time the auto fires.

The DA/SA Switch.   The real difference between D-A and S-A autos is the trade-off between safety and the ability to fire the first and all subsequent rounds in the single-action firing mode. Safety is a consideration that bears heavily on the service handgun selection process. Obviously training is the main factor to promote and maintain safety, but improving the safety features of an auto goes a long way toward improving safety during routine handling of the auto and during real situations.

The DA/SA switch occurs when firing a D-A auto and will happen between the first shot in the double-action mode and the second shot in the single-action mode (hence the DA/SA switch). This is the largest detraction for the double-action auto. When the first round is fired in the double-action mode, the trigger finger has to exert more pressure and travel farther for the longer and stronger trigger *pull.* Once the first round fires, the second shot will be fired in the single-action mode, with the shorter trigger *press,* that will apply less pressure. (*Note:* In function, no adjustment of the trigger finger on the trigger is needed, but an adjustment in how the finger pulls the trigger will be needed—the amount of pressure needed and trigger travel.)

On the first shot in double-action, the first joint of the trigger finger is used for the longer and heavier trigger pull. When the first shot is fired, many officers now readjust the trigger finger for the shorter and lighter trigger press, by placing the pad on the trigger. The trigger finger should not be initially readjusted (physically moved on the trigger), but adjust the trigger finger pressure on the trigger. This pressure adjustment becomes the DA/SA switch.

It is really a very minor "glitch" that is taken care of in training. The DA/SA switch is not a large problem if the trigger finger is not instantly adjusted on the trigger between the first and second shots. The first joint of the trigger finger should be used exclusively for the initial string of rounds fired—the first through the second and however many rounds are initially fired. Once the initial string is fired and the firing stops, the trigger finger can be instantly adjusted to the pad if desired. Wait until a lull in the action to readjust the trigger finger.

Safety and the DA/SA Switch.   The conflict arises from the perception that there is a trade-off between safety and carrying an auto cocked and locked for a continuous firing mode (single-action for the first and all shots). Adherents, supporting the single-action auto (invariably the Colt .45 auto or one of its look-alikes), contend that cocked and locked is safe. They are absolutely correct. It is very safe when used professionally. We will state right up front that the Colt .45 auto is a very safe automatic when handled properly, but that is the problem. For those officers who will take the time and practice with the single-action automatic, the Colt .45 auto is a superlative weapon, a joy to use, and very safe. For those officers, though, who will not take the time and practice: handling and procedural problems can occur at the user end. Carrying a single-action auto cocked and locked is the only proper and safe way to carrying it in a holster, the only defensive way to carry it. The main problem with cocked and locked is its unsafe appearance, looking as if the hammer is about to fall and cause an unintentional discharge. In reality it is a lack of knowledge that causes people to think it is unsafe. It is very safe when handled properly.

The D-A autos produced today use several different, very safe systems to safely decock the hammer once a round has been chambered (usually, a decocking lever that safely lowers the hammer). As such, the D-A auto is designed to be carried with the hammer down. On certain double-action autos (definitely not all), safety is improved by the addition of "internal automatic safety devices," usually connected to the trigger. These will render the double-action auto incapable of firing if the trigger is not pulled to the rear; in other words, if everything else goes wrong but the officer does not pull the trigger, the auto will not fire unintentionally. Also, the newer single-action Colt autos come with a trigger-activated firing pin block that locks the firing pin if the trigger is not pulled to the rear.

The first two shots are the real difference between the single-action and double-action autos: the smooth continuous firing mode of the single-action auto as opposed to the DA/SA switch from one mode to the other with a double-action auto. In reality, the switch is a minor problem. The first shot will be slightly quicker and more controlled from a single-action auto due to the single-action trigger press, being shorter and lighter. Once both autos fire the first two rounds, they function the same for the remaining rounds. The main advantage of either semiautomatic pistol is the single-action firing mode that greatly improves officers' abilities to place "hits."

With an understanding of single-action and double-action functioning, we continue with an in-depth study of the handling procedures for each of the designs: safety, loading, unloading, and holstering.

HANDLING PROCEDURES FOR EACH OF THE THREE SERVICE HANDGUN DESIGNS

Each of the three service handgun designs has its own set of handling procedures that must become safe handgun handling habits. During your day-to-day function as a police officer, the service handgun must be handled, loaded, unloaded, and holstered in a safe and knowledgeable manner. The following handling procedures are used to accomplish these tasks safely and easily. When practiced and used they form the safe handgun handling habits necessary to perform your day-to-day functions with the service handgun safely and efficiently. Do not skip this area, labeling it as "beginner knowledge," as these procedures, and how they tie in with your complete understanding of your defensive sidearm, will become very important.

The handling procedures for the three service handgun designs will be covered for both right-handed and left-handed officers. Find the area that covers your type of service handgun and your strong hand, then study and practice the procedures thoroughly to build your set of safe handgun handling habits.

Professional Handling. Start from the beginning to handle your service handgun professionally. Whenever you address and pick up your service handgun, do it correctly each time. Pick it up in the strong hand and assume a secure/safe master grip, with the trigger finger outside the trigger guard. Never pick up or handle the handgun in a funny or strange way; always handle it professionally, the way it was meant to be handled.

Even though you know the handgun is unloaded (do not ever assume that it is unloaded), check to make sure that it is unloaded. Always use the correct grip and proper safety procedures whenever a handgun is handled. Training-in the correct procedures will go a long way to improving your professional gun-handling abilities.

A Note on the Loading and Unloading Procedures and Securing the Loaded Handgun. The procedures shown here will follow the reloading procedures covered in Chapter 12 (consult the drawings there). The hand placement is the same, but the procedures shown here are naturally shorter, as you only have to accomplish one task (either to load or unload, as opposed to reloading, where the handgun will be unloaded and then reloaded). When engaging in everyday loading and unloading, the hand placement must be the same to train-in those movements that will be needed when reloading during a lethal encounter. Everything we train-in works towards improving our survival advantage during a lethal encounter.

When the handgun is loaded, immediately secure it in the holster. The loaded handgun is not laid down or placed somewhere else; it is secured in your holster. Too many problems can occur, not only with children but adults. Safety is a consideration 100 percent of the time. To accomplish this, no safety opening can exist. One slip is all that is needed for a tragedy to occur. If you are not ready to holster the handgun, do not load it.

Safe Handling Basics

Whenever you handle a weapon the basic safety rules must be followed. Of the four basic safety rules (see Chapter 2), two must be reemphasized with your handling skills:

1. Keep your trigger finger out of the trigger guard except when coming on target just before firing.
2. Keep the muzzle pointed away from any person or thing you do not intend to shoot. (Stated simply: For general handling, never allow the muzzle to point in an unsafe direction.)

Remember these two safety rules and always follow them as part of your primary safe handgun handling habits. If you are not safe in practice, you will not be safe in a real situation, which can lead to disastrous results.

Keep checking the handgun to make sure that it is unloaded. Whenever dry practicing or at other times when the handgun should be unloaded, check it as many times as needed—whenever handing it to someone, whenever someone hands it to you, and at any other time you think you should. Always treat every handgun as loaded, but check to make sure that it is unloaded when it is supposed to be. Be safe in your handling!

A Safety Note on the Trigger and Hammer. The trigger and hammer are not used during loading and unloading (except to lower the hammer on a single-action auto after it has been unloaded or to ease a double-action auto's hammer down when the safety is pushed "on"). They perform no function (except as stated before) when loading or unloading the three service handgun designs; yet the trigger and hammer are responsible for 95% of all unintentional discharges. Keep away from the trigger and hammer during loading and unloading. The trigger finger is placed into the trigger guard, on the trigger, only as you are coming on target preparing to fire. At any other time keep the trigger finger out of the trigger guard. Get into this habit and use it at all times. There are only three exceptions to this rule: (1) when engaging in dry-fire practice, only after making sure the handgun is completely unloaded; (2) when lowering the hammer on a single-action auto after it has been unloaded; and (3) when easing a double-action auto's hammer down when the safety is pushed "on" to lower the hammer after it has been loaded (an additional safety practice that is really unnecessary).

These safe handling basics cover all three service handgun designs and are always used, no matter which design type you are issued. They are covered first to make you completely aware of these important safe handling basics. Follow them and you may never have your first unintentional discharge. Remember, if you are not safe in practice, you will not be safe in a real situation.

Double-Action Revolver Handling Procedures

The D-A revolver requires the least amount of explanation, as there are no external safety features. The cylinder release (the only release or lever on a revolver) opens the cylinder for loading and unloading, and to fire the revolver you just pull the trigger. Although it takes the least amount of explanation, the defensive management of the D-A revolver will require more work and dexterity than will the semiautomatic pistol.

Loading or unloading the D-A revolver is extremely simple: Press the cylinder release, swing the cylinder out, insert the cartridges to load (or remove the cartridges to unload), and close the cylinder—very simple and easy, without touching the hammer or trigger. Holster a loaded revolver or safely store an unloaded revolver. (*Note:* There is no manual safety, but an "internal automatic hammer block" built in, which keeps the firing pin from touching and striking the cartridge primer until the trigger is pulled to the rear, dropping the block down.)

Check Your Rounds Before Loading. Before loading the revolver, check every round for any irregularities that can cause problems when firing or attempting to fire. Irregularities can be seen and felt and will appear as a damaged case, or a backward and/or not properly seated primer (a high primer), or improper bullet seating. A general visual check of each round and running your finger tip across the primer (to feel if it is high) will take care of these.

As a final test, open the cylinder and drop each round into one of the chamber holes in the cylinder and then tilt the revolver muzzle up to drop the rounds back out. Each round should easily enter and fall free from the cylinder's chambers. This will eliminate any oversized cases that can cause a tight fit. Eliminate any problems before they occur: Check your rounds.

Also make sure that the revolver is completely clean, especially under the cylinder star and any fouling between the end of the barrel and the front of the cylinder.

To check the cylinder's free rotation: with the revolver unloaded and your trigger finger out of the trigger guard, pull the hammer back slightly and with the other hand spin the cylinder. It should rotate (spin) freely. If it does not, find out what the problem is. If not readily diagnosed, take it to the armorer. (*Note:* If a Smith & Wesson or Ruger, hold the revolver in the right hand, with the left side of the revolver facing you, and spin the cylinder by running the fingers of the left hand down along the cylinder and off of it; the cylinder will spin for about a second. Repeat several times. If a Colt, reverse the process, as the cylinder rotates the opposite way. If unsure when a revolver is picked up, gently try each side; one will turn easily and one will not turn at all. Or you can use the arrowheads on the rear end of the cylinder as a guide; spin on the side where the arrowheads are pointing down.)

Right-handed procedures

Right-Handed LOADING of the D-A Revolver

1. Begin by holding the revolver in the master grip with the right hand. The trigger finger is out of the trigger guard and straight along the side of the frame. The revolver is held at waist level just in front of the body. The muzzle is pointed in a safe direction.
2. The right-hand thumb is placed on the cylinder release (if necessary, the master grip is eased and slightly shifted for better thumb contact on the cylinder release) and the left hand slides up to grasp the cylinder lightly (thumb on the left side and index and second fingers on the right side).
3. The right-hand thumb pushes the cylinder release and the index and second fingers push the cylinder out to the left, both fingers following it through the frame. The two fingers and thumb of the left hand now securely hold the opened cylinder, as the right hand leaves the revolver.
4. The right hand now picks up and loads the cartridges into the cylinder. The left hand holds the revolver so that the muzzle is pointing down, to keep the cartridges from falling out of the cylinder (or remaining slightly up, which will prevent the cylinder from closing).
5. Once loading is completed, the right hand regrips the revolver (the trigger finger is held straight along the frame, sliding between the frame and fingers of the left hand) as the left hand closes the cylinder.

The revolver is now loaded and holstered. Once loaded the revolver is holstered; it is never laid down.

Right-Handed UNLOADING of the D-A Revolver

1-3. are the same as those for loading the revolver.
   4. The right hand is now held directly to the rear of the cylinder. The left hand tilts the revolver up (so that the muzzle is pointing straight up) and all the

cartridges fall free into the right hand, which was tilted with the cylinder and formed a cup to catch the cartridges. If any cartridges should stick (all should fall free), the right-hand fingers can pull them free. Check the cylinder.

5. The cartridges are put down temporarily. Then the right hand regrips the revolver (with the trigger finger straight) as the left hand closes the cylinder.

The revolver is now unloaded and safely stored. An unloaded revolver is never placed back in the holster.

Left-handed procedures

Left-Handed LOADING of the D-A Revolver

1. Begin by holding the revolver in the master grip with the left hand. The trigger finger is outside the trigger guard and straight along the side of the frame. The revolver is held at waist level just in front of the body. The muzzle is pointed in a safe direction.

2. The left hand shifts back on the grip (the three fingers still holding onto the front of the grip) with the trigger finger coming to rest on the cylinder release, and the right hand slides up to grasp the cylinder lightly (the thumb touching the right side of the cylinder to push it open and the index and second fingers touching the left side of the cylinder).

3. The trigger finger pushes the cylinder release and the right-hand thumb pushes the cylinder out to the left, the thumb following it through the frame. The thumb and two fingers of the right hand now securely hold the opened cylinder as the left hand leaves the revolver.

4. The left hand now picks up and loads the cartridges into the cylinder. The right hand holds the revolver so that the muzzle is pointing down, to keep the cartridges from falling out of the cylinder (or remaining slightly up, which will prevent the cylinder from closing).

5. Once loading is completed, the left hand regrips the revolver (the trigger finger is held straight along the frame, sliding between the frame and the fingers of the right hand) as the right hand closes the cylinder.

The revolver is now loaded and holstered. Once the revolver is loaded it is holstered; it is never laid down.

Left-Handed UNLOADING of the D-A Revolver

1–3. are the same as those for loading the revolver.

4. The left hand is now held directly to the rear of the cylinder. The right hand tilts the revolver up (so that the muzzle is pointing straight up) and all the cartridges fall free into the left hand, which was tilted with the cylinder and formed a cup to catch the cartridges. If any cartridges should stick (all should fall free), the left-hand fingers can pull them free. Check the cylinder.

5. The cartridges are temporarily put down. Then the left hand regrips the revolver (with the trigger finger straight) as the right hand closes the cylinder.

The revolver is now unloaded and safely stored. An unloaded revolver is never placed back in the holster.

Double-Action Automatic and Single-Action Automatic Handling Procedures

The D-A auto and S-A auto are loaded and unloaded in virtually the same way. Make sure that you check the instruction manual provided with the service handgun and/or the instructions given by your firearms instructor for loading and unloading the handgun.

The auto is a two-unit system: the automatic itself and its readily detachable magazine. When loading, care must be taken to make sure that the magazine is fully seated and locked in place. If not completely locked in place, the first round from the magazine may not chamber when the slide is pulled to the rear and released, and/or the magazine may slide farther out so that the second round will not chamber, and/or the magazine may fall out completely and become lost. *You must make sure that the magazine is completely seated in the auto—locked in place—*before continuing with the reloading process.

Loading and Unloading the Magazine.   Since the auto is comprised of a two-unit system (the auto and its magazine), you must know how to load the magazine properly as a prerequisite to placing it into the auto. Also, procedures for unloading the magazine will be outlined.

Check Your Rounds before Loading.   Before loading the magazine, check every round for any irregularities that can cause malfunctions when the auto's slide cycles to eject the empty case and chamber the next round from the magazine. Irregularities can be seen and felt and will appear as a damaged case, or a backward and/or not properly seated primer (a high primer), or improper bullet seating. A general visual check of each round and running your fingertip across the primer (to feel if it is high) will take care of these. As a final test, disassemble the auto and take the barrel out. Now drop each round into the chamber and then tilt the barrel up to drop the round back out. Each round should enter easily and fall free from the barrel's chamber. This will eliminate any oversized cases that can cause a tight fit. Make sure that you check your rounds before inserting them into the magazine; this can be critical to the auto's functioning. Ammunition manufacturers, although following excellent procedures and inspections throughout the manufacturing process, cannot stop a few irregular rounds from slipping through when millions of rounds are produced. Check your rounds to be sure.

Load (charge) the magazine by following these steps: (1) grasp the magazine

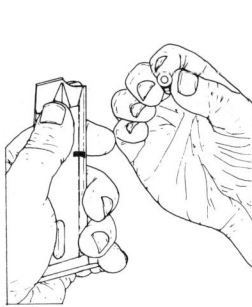

3.2.

Figure 3.2 Step 1

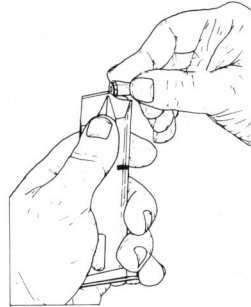

3.3.

Figure 3.3 Step 2

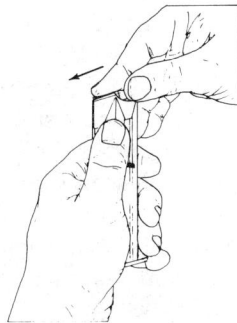

3.4.

Figure 3.4 Step 3

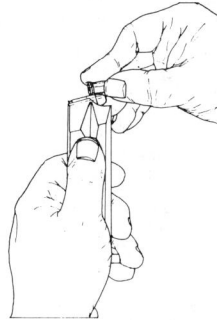

3.5.

Figure 3.5 Step 4

with the back wall against the palm of the support hand, and grasp a cartridge between the thumb, index, and middle fingers of the strong hand, base pointing forward; (2) place the cartridge rim on top of the follower in front of the magazine lips; (3) press down, and slide it back under the lips; and (4) repeat by placing the second cartridge on the first cartridge in front of the lips, and push down and back. Repeat step 4 until the magazine is fully loaded (charged).

Unload the magazine by following these steps: (1) grasp the magazine with the back wall against the palm of the support hand and the thumb on top of the cartridge; (2) with the thumb on the cartridge rim, push it from the magazine while the index finger and thumb of the strong hand grasp the bullet as it comes out (tipping it up slightly will sometimes help with high-capacity magazines); and (3) catch the cartridges in the cupped strong hand until the magazine is unloaded. You should leave the magazine unloaded if it is not to be used for an extended period of time.

3.6.   **3.7.**   **3.8.**

Figure 3.6   Step 1.   **Figure 3.7**   Step 2.   **Figure 3.8**   Step 3.

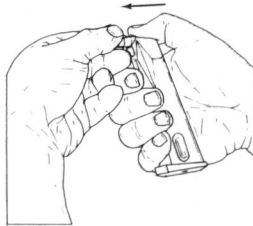

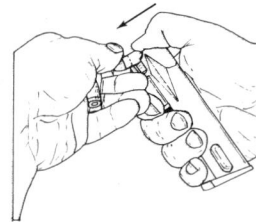

Loading and Unloading Both Autos, a General Description.   *Loading:* Insert and lock home a fully loaded magazine into the auto, pull the slide to the rear and fully release it to chamber the first round from the magazine, push the safety "on" (always "on" for an S-A auto, but either "on or off" for a D-A auto—depending on the method used) and holster the loaded auto. *Unloading:* Remove the magazine from the auto, pull the slide to the rear to eject the chambered round, ease the slide forward and then easily lower the hammer, and safely store the unloaded auto.

Each of the these procedures is accomplished without touching the trigger or hammer (with two exceptions). (*Note:* Depending on the auto, it may or may not have a manual safety to push "on." Many of the newer double-action designs have internal safety mechanisms or a combination of external and internal safety mechanisms that do the job. You must be thoroughly familiar with your auto's safety system and use it.)

Right-Handed Procedures

Right-Handed LOADING of the D-A and S-A Autos

1. Begin by holding the auto in the master grip with the right hand. The trigger finger is out of the trigger guard and straight along the side of the frame. The auto is held slightly above waist level and just in front of the body. The muzzle is pointed in a safe direction.

2. The left hand picks up a loaded magazine, inserts it into the magazine well, and locks it home (fully locking it into the magazine well, with a click being heard). The right-hand wrist cants the top of the auto out to the right to facilitate insertion of the magazine.

3. As soon as the magazine is locked in place, the right hand turns the auto 90 degrees to the left. The slide is gripped by the left hand and pulled completely to the rear. Note that the trigger finger is outside the trigger guard and straight along the frame.

4. The slide is then fully released, to fly forward, chambering the first round from the magazine.

(The ending step 5a is for an S-A auto and the ending step 5b is for a D-A auto.)

5a. For a single-action auto—The right thumb pushes the safety "on." When this is done, the hammer will remain cocked for the first shot in the single-action firing mode. The S-A auto is now cocked and locked. Holster the loaded auto.

5b. For a double-action auto—The right-hand thumb pushes the safety "on" and the hammer will safely decock (fall), striking the rear end of the slide. The safety is either left "on" or pushed "off" (depending on the carrying method used). The first shot will be in the double-action firing mode. The D-A auto is now hammer down and safety either "on or off." Holster the loaded auto.

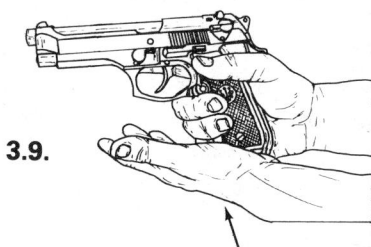

3.9.

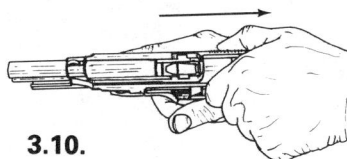

3.10.

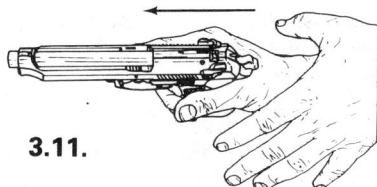

3.11.

3.12.

Figure 3.9 Step 2.
Figure 3.10 Step 3.
Figure 3.11 Step 4. Remember to keep the trigger finger outside
the trigger guard.
Figure 3.12 Step 5b for D-A auto. (*Note:* Several methods exist
to make the auto safe after a round has been chambered,
depending on what S-A or D-A auto you are using.)

A Note on Lowering the D-A Auto Hammer. In step 5b, when the safety lever is pushed "on," the hammer will safely decock, by falling on the rear of the slide. It is completely safe unless the officer forgets and pulls the trigger instead of pushing the safety "on." An extra safety measure can be taken by easing the hammer down instead of letting it fall. The thumb of the support hand is placed on top of the hammer and eases it down when the safety is pushed "on." In reality the auto will not fire when the safety lever is pushed "on" to decock the hammer, but it is just an added safety precaution. The use of reasonable and extra safety procedures can keep an unintentional discharge from occurring when an officer makes a mistake. Also, many officers are uncomfortable with the hammer falling when a live round is chambered. This is just a little bit of extra safety that can go a long way when a mistake is made.

Some modern D-A autos have no external manual safety, but rely on internal safety systems. These autos are even easier to handle, as there is no manual safety to push "on" or "off" and will be discussed later.

A Note on Replacing the Round That Was Chambered from the Magazine. During the process of loading the auto, the first round in the magazine was chambered by the action of the slide. Now the magazine has one less than its maximum round capacity. At this point you can remove the magazine from the auto and replace it with a fully charged magazine. Or you can simply remove the magazine, put one round back into the magazine, reinsert the magazine into the auto, and lock it home. During this process, you never touch the hammer, trigger, or safety lever. Only the magazine release is depressed. Make sure that the magazine is fully locked in place when it is placed back into the auto.

Right-Handed UNLOADING of the D-A and S-A Autos

1. Begin by holding the auto in the master grip with the right hand. The trigger finger is out of the trigger guard and straight along the side of the frame. If the auto has a safety it is "on." The auto is held just in front of the body, slightly above waist level, with the muzzle pointing straight out (away from the body). The muzzle is pointed in a safe direction.

2. The left hand is positioned below the magazine, the right thumb pushes the magazine release, and the magazine falls into the left hand. The magazine is secured—put someplace.

3. The left hand now grasps the rear of the slide on the grooves, to the rear of the ejection port. The thumb can be positioned to push up on the slide stop to lock the slide open when it is pulled to the rear.

4. On an S-A auto the safety is now pushed "off" to unlock the slide. On a D-A auto the safety remains "on" if on the slide. The left hand pulls the slide to the rear and holds it open to eject the chambered round. Also, the slide stop can be pushed up to lock the slide open.

5. Now, visually check the *chamber* and the *magazine well* to make sure that the auto is empty.

6. The slide is now eased forward until it locks in place and the hammer is lowered (the S-A auto hammer is lowered by pulling the trigger, as the left-hand thumb eases the hammer down; the D-A auto hammer will already have been lowered automatically, as the safety was "on"). The auto is now unloaded with the slide closed and hammer down. Now safely store the unloaded auto.

Left-Handed Procedures

When describing the loading and unloading procedures for the D-A revolver, many changes occur between a left- and right-handed officer. These must be shown completely. But with the auto, the hand's functions are simply reversed. There is no need to restate the procedures; simply switch the hands. As already shown with a right-handed officer, the right hand grips the auto throughout the loading and unloading process, with its thumb doing all the pushing and depressing of levers and buttons. The left hand handles the magazine, grasps the slide to pull it to the rear, and eases the hammer down.

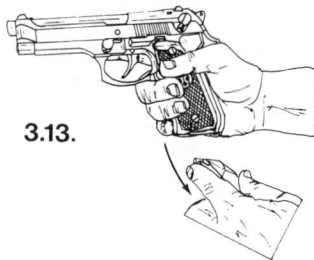

3.13.

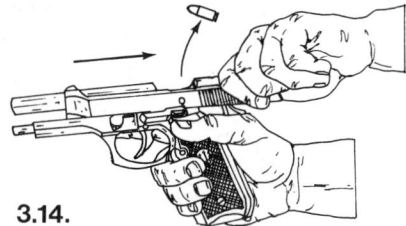

3.14.

3.15.

3.16.

Figure 3.13 Step 2. The magazine is removed from the pistol.

Figure 3.14 Steps 3 and 4. If an S-A auto, the safety is pushed "off" just before the slide is pulled to the rear, with the trigger finger out of the trigger guard.

Figure 3.15 Top View of Step 5.

Figure 3.16 The slide stop can be pushed up to lock the slide open, instead of having to hold the slide back for the visual inspection.

Figure 3.17 Step 6. The slide is eased forward.

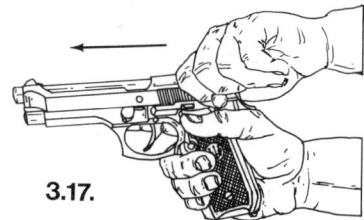

3.17.

With a left-handed officer, the hands are simply switched. The left hand grips the auto throughout the loading and unloading process, with its thumb and trigger finger pushing and depressing all levers and buttons (the trigger finger depressing the slide stop and magazine release and the thumb pushing the safety lever). The right hand handles the magazine, grasps the slide to pull it to the rear, and eases the hammer down. Simply stated: If you are left-handed, the left hand assumes a good master grip and maintains it through all the procedures.

A Note on Safety During Inspection Formations. When a number of officers are gathering for handgun inspection, each officer will unload his or her handgun at a designated "safe area." This is done one at a time until all handguns are unloaded with the slides locked back or cylinders open. Each station should have a designated safe area (an enclosed area with a bullet trap which can safely take an unintentional discharge) where all handguns are loaded and unloaded.

A Note on Ambidextrous Safety Levers. An ambidextrous safety lever is a must for left-handed officers. Automatics without an ambidextrous safety create a dangerous situation, as left-handed officers tend to leave the safety "off," as opposed to having to fumble with it if a situation should suddenly occur. No service auto should be considered if it does not come from the factory equipped with an ambidextrous safety. Obviously, this does not include D-A autos, which have no external safety levers, or the excellent Sig-Sauer D-A autos, with decocking levers on the frame, which are easily activated with the trigger finger. We are referring to two types of safety levers: (1) the safety lever on S-A autos at the rear end of the frame, used to lock the hammer in the cocked-and-locked position, and (2) the safety lever on D-A autos (which is really a decocking lever but provides many safety functions) at the rear end of the slide, used to safely decock the hammer. These two safety levers must be ambidextrous.

By following the procedures shown, you have the ability to safely handle, load, and unload any of the three service handgun design types. We proceed with the readiness conditions used to place and keep the handgun in a condition to respond instantly to a threat(s). These are concerned with the condition in which the handgun will be carried or stored.

READINESS CONDITIONS FOR THE THREE SERVICE HANDGUNS

Each of the three service handgun designs can be placed in several readiness conditions that dictate the sequence necessary to fire the handgun. An example would be a loaded D-A auto, with safety "on" and hammer down. To fire, the safety is pushed "off" and the trigger pulled. But the question is: Was that readiness condition the most appropriate for the circumstances involved and the carrying mode?" Each design type has its own set of readiness conditions, which are most appropriate for the particular mechanical functioning. The readiness conditions thus follow the mechanical workings of each design type. For the service handgun you carry, you must understand and use the particular set of readiness conditions for the various circumstances involved.

The service handgun is either loaded and holstered or unloaded and safely stored as a rule, but loaded and stored may also be required at some point. During your day-to-day functions as a police officer, the service handgun will be either loaded and holstered either on or off duty, or unloaded and safely stored when you are at home. As already stated, day-to-day use follows this rule: If the handgun is loaded, it is holstered; if the handgun is unloaded, it is safely stored; it is never loaded and laid down. A third circumstance may arise where the handgun is loaded and ready to fire, but instead of being on your person, it is stored close at hand. The handgun might be a secondary or backup handgun and a readiness condition must exist for this circumstance. This is sometimes called the "glove compartment carry" or the "bag carry."

In preparation for these three circumstances, we outline the most appropriate readiness conditions for each: the carrying mode (loaded and holstered), loaded storage, and unloaded storage. When preparing for these, we are concerned mainly with placing the handgun in the most appropriate condition for the circumstance: to be able to respond instantly to the threat(s) with the holstered handgun in the carrying mode, or to be able to respond with minimum effort (requiring only one hand) with the handgun loaded and safely stored, or (requiring two hands) for the handgun to be unloaded and safely stored possibly as the household self-defense handgun.

You must know what readiness condition your service handgun is in, at all times, and the steps necessary to place it in the firing condition. At all times, wherever the handgun is, you must know its condition and how to make it fire. The readiness conditions provide you with that knowledge. Study the three conditions for the particular service handgun design type you use.

The Readiness Condition System. To simplify matters, we use a system that gives the three readiness conditions for each of the design types. Each of the design types is given a three-letter designation: DAR, D-A revolver; DAA, D-A auto; and SAA, S-A auto. Behind each of these designations the readiness conditions are given in order: (1) carrying mode, (2) loaded storage, and (3) unloaded storage.

First, a brief outline containing the three design types and their readiness conditions is given to familiarize you with the conditions and their functions. Second, a complete explanation of these conditions will expand and cover all points. These are the only correct readiness conditions for any of the service handguns. The handgun must be in the correct readiness condition for the circumstances involved: loaded and carried in the holster, loaded and stored, or unloaded and stored. Other inappropriate readiness conditions will be examined to show the total range of conditions that are incorrectly used.

A Brief Outline of The Three Service Handgun Design Types and Their Readiness Conditions

Double-Action Revolver READINESS CONDITIONS

DAR 1—carrying mode: Fully loaded cylinder and hammer down. To fire, merely pull the trigger.

DAR 2—loaded storage: Fully loaded cylinder and hammer down. To fire, merely pull the trigger. (The same as *DAR 1.*)

DAR 3—unloaded storage: Empty cylinder that is closed. To fire, open and load the cylinder, close it, and press the trigger.

Double-Action Automatic READINESS CONDITIONS

DAA 1—carrying mode: Round chambered, full magazine locked in place, hammer down, and safety "off." To fire, merely pull the trigger (the same as with a double-action revolver).

DAA 1a—carrying mode: Round chambered, full magazine locked in place, hammer down, and safety "on." To fire, push the safety "off" and pull the trigger.

DAA 2—loaded storage: Round chambered, full magazine locked in place, hammer down and safety "on." To fire, push the safety "off" and pull the trigger. (The same as *DAA 1a.*)

DAA 3—unloaded storage: Chamber empty, magazine removed from the auto, and the safety "off." To fire, the support hand inserts the magazine into the auto, then grasps the slide, pulls it to the rear and releases it (chambering the first round from the magazine), and the trigger is pressed. (A secondary form of safe storage, unchambered storage, can be used with an auto and is explained later.)

Single-Action Automatic READINESS CONDITIONS

SAA 1—carrying mode: Round chambered, full magazine locked in place, hammer cocked, and safety "on." To fire, push the safety "off" and press the trigger.

SAA 2—loaded storage: Round chambered, full magazine locked in place, hammer down, and safety "off." To fire, the thumb cocks the hammer and the trigger is pressed.

SAA 3—unloaded storage: Chamber empty, magazine removed from the auto, and safety "off." To fire, the support hand inserts the magazine into the auto, then grasps the slide, pulls it to the rear and releases it (chambering the first round from the magazine), and the trigger is pressed. (A secondary form of safe storage, unchambered storage, can be used with an auto and is explained later.)

As shown in the outline, each design type has three readiness conditions (numbered the same for each design type), with each condition having a description of the steps necessary to fire the handgun. When describing these conditions, readiness condition 1 is the carrying mode no matter which design type we describe (this also applies for readiness conditions 2 and 3). Now, when we describe readiness conditions 1, 2, or 3, everyone will be talking about the same condition no matter which service handgun design is involved.

Readiness condition 1, the carrying mode, is the proper method for carrying the service handgun when loaded and holstered. In condition 1, the handgun is loaded, safe, and holstered, yet instantly ready to be snapped out and fired. This is the condition the handgun will be in whenever officers carry their service handguns.

Readiness condition 2, loaded storage, is the proper method for storing the service handgun when loaded. In condition 2, the handgun is loaded and safe, yet ready to respond with minimum effort. Only one hand should have to be used to pick up the handgun and fire it. This condition is normally used for storing a loaded backup handgun under certain circumstances. Hidden away, it must be ready for quick action if necessary. This condition is rarely used.

Whenever the handgun is in condition 2, you must have complete control over the area in which the handgun is stored. The area in which the handgun is loaded and stored is always under your control. If the area is left, remove the handgun from the loaded storage condition and either take it with you or place it in unloaded storage, if the storage site can be secured completely by other means.

Readiness condition 3, unloaded storage, is the proper method for storing a service handgun when unloaded. In condition 3, the handgun is unloaded and safely stored. This is the condition in which officers will place their service handguns when at home (with certain exceptions, depending on the situation and the people residing in the home). The unloaded storage condition can be modified when using the service handgun as the home self-defense gun.

We now proceed with a full examination of the three readiness conditions for each of the three service handgun design types. Each design type will be examined individually to cover all aspects. Other inappropriate readiness conditions will also be examined.

The D-A Revolver's Readiness Conditions

Conditions 1, 2, and 3. Only two readiness conditions actually exist for the D-A revolver: either loaded or unloaded, with the hammer down. The loaded revolver is used for conditions 1 and 2. The unloaded revolver is used for condition 3. The D-A revolver is mechanically simple in its function and very easily understood. That is part of the functional beauty of the revolver; it is simple to work. No special consideration must be given. Open the cylinder and either load or unload it and close the cylinder; that is all the mechanical functioning that is required. There are no external safety levers or buttons to fool with or think about. Although simple, it is actually the most difficult service handgun to fire and manipulate.

The D-A revolver has an internal safety attached to the trigger that keeps the firing pin from making contact with the cartridge's primer whenever the trigger is not pulled to the rear. When the trigger is at rest a piece of metal is pushed up underneath the hammer to keep it back, so the firing pin is not protruding through the frame. This can readily be seen on an unloaded revolver with the cylinder closed. Pull the trigger and the firing pin will protrude through the frame; release the trigger and the firing pin disappears back into the frame as the piece of metal pushes the hammer back. The D-A revolver is safe until the trigger is pulled.

The hammer of the D-A revolver is cocked in only one situation: when attempting to place a longer-distance or more precise shot, where you have enough time. Except for this rare situation, the hammer is never cocked. If you find yourself with a cocked hammer, lower it by placing the thumb of either hand on the hammer spur (the rear end of the hammer), pull the trigger, and use the thumb to ease the hammer down. This is not a fast technique, but is done in the three steps outlined, one at a time. Practice this technique with an unloaded revolver until you are comfortable with its workings. The first time you lower a hammer you do not want to be in the middle of a situation with live rounds in the revolver.

The D-A Automatic's Readiness Conditions

Condition 1, the carrying mode, takes advantage of the double-action mechanism by carrying the D-A auto with the safety "off" and hammer down. In this condition you are instantly ready to draw and fire the first shot double-action, just like the D-A revolver; merely draw and pull the trigger.

Condition 1a, a secondary carrying mode, can be used by carrying the D-A auto with the safety "on" and hammer down. This would require the safety to be pushed "off" before the trigger is pulled. The safety is pushed "off" as the auto is snapped up into a locked out two-handed firing stance (the same as an S-A auto). Many feel that this adds an additional safety factor if the auto is removed from the holster by a threat, who would have to figure out the safety, giving an officer time to counterattack and regain control of the situation.

The Difference between the Two.   The main reasoning for the use of condition 1 is the perceived increase in firing speed and the possibility of fumbling with the safety in a stress situation. These are considered a trade-off for reduced in-the-holster safety, but is that really the case? When practiced, both conditions are equally fast when drawing and firing (the difference being negligible), but CONDITION 1a lends itself to increased safety. Another factor, usually left out when considering which condition to use, could become critical: a safety lever which is accidentally pushed "on" while the auto is holstered. In condition 1 you are training yourself just to think trigger. If the safety is accidentally pushed "on" while the auto is in the holster, and you draw and attempt to fire but nothing happens, you will waste a full second realizing that it is "on," pushing it "off," and firing. You may not have that second to waste. By always having the safety "on" in the holster and always having to push it "off" before firing, this will never happen. The safety can be pushed "on" by the action of the holster, some object rubbing against it, or an officer holstering the auto with it unknowingly "on." Pick either condition and make sure that you use it exclusively—no switching back and forth.

Condition 2, loaded storage, is the same as condition 1a, with the safety "on" and the hammer lowered. The D-A auto is now loaded and then safely stored. To fire, push the safety "off" and pull the trigger. It is now readily available in its stored location, with only one hand being necessary to remove the auto and fire it. Remember, you must be in immediate control of the storage area; if not, the auto is removed from the storage area and taken with you, or unloaded and stored.

Condition 3, unloaded storage, is used to store the D-A auto safely when an officer is home. In this condition the D-A auto is unloaded with the safety "off." The auto and magazine are stored separately. To fire, use the support hand to insert and lock the magazine into the auto, then use it to pull the slide to the rear and fully release it (to chamber the first round from the magazine), and press the trigger.

Depending on the situation in each officer's home, condition 3 can be further modified to unchambered storage: a full magazine locked into the D-A auto, with the chamber empty, hammer down, and safety "on." To fire, push the safety "off", use the support hand to pull the slide to the rear and fully release it (to chamber the first round from the magazine) and press the trigger. The auto's slide is very hard to pull to the rear (especially with the hammer down) to chamber the first round; thus making unchambered storage reasonably safe, yet one step closer to being able to fire a shot in a self-defense situation. Every officer must fully analyze the home environment when deciding how to safely store the service handgun.

The S-A Automatic's Readiness Conditions

Condition 1, the carrying mode, correctly utilizes the single-action mechanism by carrying the S-A auto with the hammer cocked and the safety locked "on": cocked and locked. This is the only correct carrying mode for the S-A auto when carried in the holster. In condition 1 the S-A auto is instantly ready to be drawn and the safety pushed "off" as the auto is being brought up into a firing position. The thumb remains on top of the safety once it is pushed "off." If not, as has been demonstrated on a number of occasions, the thumb may push the safety back "on" when firing. Keep the thumb on top of the pushed "off" safety.

Condition 2, loaded storage, keeps the auto loaded and stored. Once loaded, the hammer of the S-A auto is lowered to render the auto safe, though stored in a ready condition. The S-A auto's holstered condition of cocked and locked is never used for the loaded storage condition. This is done to prevent the safety from being pushed "off" accidentally while stored, and then only a small press of the trigger will fire the auto. The hammer is down and safe even though in contact with the rear end of the inertia firing pin. While the hammer is contacting the rear end of the firing pin, the tip is not touching the primer of the chambered cartridge. This occurs as the firing pin is not long enough to touch both, and the firing pin return spring keeps its rear end pressed back in contact with the hammer. Now the S-A auto is stored in a ready/safe condition and the safety cannot be inadvertently wiped "off" during storage. To fire quickly from the loaded storage condition, just thumb cock the hammer and press the trigger.

Lowering the Hammer. Once the S-A auto is loaded, the hammer is lowered by placing the support hand's index fingertip (the side of the finger's tip) covering the rear end of the firing pin as the strong hand's thumb holds and lowers the hammer when the trigger is pressed to release it. As the hammer is gently lowered, it will touch the index fingertip (held sideways into the slot at the end of the slide, covering the firing pin), which slides out of the way to let the hammer rest fully in the down position, the strong-hand thumb easing it down all the way. The thumb of the support hand will be holding "in" the grip safety (directly below the hammer) on any Colt .45 auto or look-alike. If not, the trigger will not move to the rear to release the hammer. Also, the support hand will be cupped overtop the slide, with the other three fingers resting along one side of it.

Remember to keep the trigger pressed to the rear or the hammer will catch on the half-cock notch and not completely lower. If it does, stop, release the trigger, fully cock the hammer (pull the hammer back with the thumb until it will go no farther, putting the fingertip back in place and always keeping the thumb on the hammer), and begin lowering it again.

This hammer-lowering technique must be practiced many times with a unloaded auto until it works easily. Never perform this technique quickly; always proceed slowly and gently to lower the hammer safely.

A blow to the lowered hammer will rarely fire the chambered round, but if dropped muzzle down on a hard surface, from 10 feet or more, it may fire, as the firing pin is instantly brought forward by inertia as the rest of the auto stops when striking the surface. The sudden striking of the muzzle on the hard surface will force the firing pin (whose mass is great enough) against its return spring and strike the primer of the chambered cartridge, firing it. To prevent this from occurring, almost all of the newer manufactured autos have some type of firing pin block that locks the firing pin until the trigger is pressed to the rear. The autos thus equipped cannot fire unless the trigger is pressed to the rear, no matter what else happens.

Condition 3, unloaded storage, is used to store the S-A auto safely when an officer is home. In this condition the S-A auto is unloaded with the safety "off." The auto and magazine are stored separately. To fire, use the support hand to insert and lock the magazine into the auto, then use it to pull the slide to the rear and fully release it to chamber the first round, and press the trigger.

Depending on the situation in each officer's home, condition 3 can be further modified to unchambered storage: a full magazine locked into the S-A auto, with the chamber empty, hammer down, and safety "off." To fire, use the support hand to pull the slide to the rear and fully release it to chamber the first round, and press the trigger. The auto's slide is very hard to pull to the rear (especially with the hammer down) to chamber the first round; thus making unchambered storage a reasonable safety compromise, yet one step closer to being able to fire a shot in a self-defense situation. Every officer must fully analyze the home environment when deciding how to safely store the service handgun.

Inappropriate Readiness Conditions for Both D-A and S-A Automatics

Poor readiness conditions are a result of a lack of knowledge, a lack of commitment to training, and/or various administrators placing extreme safety restrictions on their officers (both military and police). Three examples of carrying conditions (for the loaded and holstered auto) that run from inappropriate to downright foolish will demonstrate just how ridiculous these can be.

The single-action auto "hammer down carry" is used by those who feel it is safer than having the hammer cocked and the safety locked ''on'' (cocked and locked). This just demonstrates a lack of knowledge about the weapon and its mechanism. To fire, the auto is drawn; the hammer then has to be thumb cocked by either hand for the single-action firing mode (as it does not have a double-action mechanism), and the trigger is pressed. Adding an unnecessary step to a function that must work under stress to save an officer's life is nonsurvival oriented. Many people who advocate this feel perfectly all right about carrying a rifle or shotgun around with the hammer (striker) cocked and the safety locked ''on,'' but for some reason the S-A auto is not to be trusted.

The ''military carry'' is used by many armed forces of the world to facilitate the inspection and transfer of weapons and ammunition during sentry duties. It is a further extension of ridiculous readiness conditions. It is often referred to as the half-loaded or partially loaded condition, as no round is chambered but a full magazine is locked into the auto. To fire, the auto is drawn, the slide is pulled to the rear and fully released (chambering the first round), and the trigger is pressed. The military carry is slow, requires two hands, and involves a large fumble factor. Increased time and the possibility of a not fully retracted slide, causing a malfunction, are the main problems. During a lethal encounter none of this can be allowed to occur, as time is always at a premium.

As an interesting side note, it is amazing what can be overcome with training. Many soldiers who are required to carry the auto in the military carry and in a flap holster have developed a drawing and chambering technique and practiced it until their speed is incredible. It just shows that with training you can make almost anything work, but the carrying condition must be correct from the beginning to increase officers' survival advantage.

The ''unloaded carry'' is the true epitome of foolishness. Sometimes called the deadman's carry, the auto is carried completely empty, with no magazine in the auto. To fire, the strong hand draws the auto and the support hand draws the magazine. As both come forward, the support hand inserts the magazine and pulls the slide to the rear, fully releasing it to chamber the first round, and the trigger is pressed. Try performing this during a lethal encounter, where stress and time are working against you. The unloaded carry will dramatically increase both the time needed to place the auto in a firing mode and the fumble factor involved.

These three examples give you an idea of some extremely inappropriate readiness conditions. The proper condition your service handgun is in for the circumstances involved is no small matter. Follow the proper readiness conditions given for each of the design types.

A Note on the Half-Cock Notch. The half-cock notch should not be used as a readiness condition. It is intended as a secondary safety device to catch the hammer if it should slip off the full-cock notch. This can occur if the auto is dropped and either the hammer is jolted off the full-cock notch or if the hammer is hit and knocked off. Leave the half-cock notch to perform its function; do not purposely place the hammer in the half-cocked position.

THE FIRING CONDITIONS

From any readiness condition, the service handgun is snapped up into a firing position. As it is snapped up, the handgun must be in a firing condition, or placed into one, for the handgun to function mechanically (perform the sequence of mechanical events) and fire the round(s). When a handgun is in the firing condition, only the trigger has to be pulled or pressed to cause it to fire. Nothing else has to be done—just pull the trigger.

Firing conditions work hand in hand with the carrying conditions when the handgun is holstered, in hand, and/or when actually firing. When close to firing, or when you need to fire instantly, the handgun is placed in the firing condition. At other times, the handgun is in the carrying condition (holstered or in hand) to be safe, yet ready to respond instantly if a threat(s) appears. The handgun will be in either a carrying condition or a firing condition at all times when carried and used, and you must know the handgun's condition at all times and the procedures necessary to fire it. There is no time for thought; you must already know how to produce the handgun in a firing position and condition and fire it. Placing a handgun in a firing condition may have to be done instantly a fraction of a second before firing, and you must know exactly what to do.

D-A Revolver.   The D-A revolver is simple, as the carrying condition and firing conditions are the same once the D-A revolver is loaded. From the carrying condition, merely bring the revolver out and pull the trigger to fire it, as it is already in the firing condition. When returned to the holster, just make sure that it is completely loaded; there is nothing else to do. (*Note:* The hammer should have not been cocked and must be down before holstering it.)

D-A Automatic.   The D-A auto has two carrying conditions that must be accounted for. Make sure that you use only one of these carrying conditions and return the D-A auto to it once any firing has been completed. The carrying condition you use must be the same every time you holster the handgun.

For condition 1 (hammer down and safety "off"), the D-A auto functions just like the D-A revolver when fired: merely bring the auto out and pull the trigger to fire it, as it is already in the firing condition. Before reholstering, the safety is pushed "on" to lower the hammer safely and then pushed back "off" to return the auto to condition 1 (returning it to the carrying condition). Remember to fully load the auto before reholstering.

For condition 1a (hammer down and safety "on"), the carrying condition differs from the firing condition only by the safety being "on." To place it in the firing condition, push the safety "off." Before reholstering, the safety is pushed "on" to lower the hammer safely and it is left "on" to return the auto to condition 1a (returning it to the carrying condition). Remember to fully load the auto before reholstering.

S-A Auto.   The S-A auto's carrying condition differs from the firing condition only by the safety being "on." To place it in the firing condition, push the safety "off." Before reholstering, the safety is pushed "on" (the hammer will remain cocked and the safety must be "on") to return the auto to the carrying condition. Remember to fully load the auto before reholstering.

THREE UNIQUE DOUBLE-ACTION AUTOS

Of the second generation D-A autos manufactured today, three possess unique mechanisms that must be addressed: the Glock 17, H&K P-7, and Sig-Sauer autos. These excellent autos are covered at this point due to their unique mechanisms and handling procedures. This is just an overview of their mechanisms. Make sure that you check the instruction manual and/or instructions given by your firearms instructor.

Heckler & Koch P-7.   The H&K P-7, commonly referred to as the squeeze-cocker, is unique due to the cocking/safety mechanism built into the front of the grip. From directly below the bottom of the trigger guard to the front of the magazine well runs the "cocking grip" (or squeeze-cocker), which appears as the front of the grip with finger grooves. Its function is threefold: to cock the auto in preparation for firing, to decock the auto and make it safe, and as a slide release when the slide is locked open if the last round has been fired.

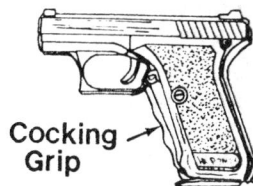

Cocking Grip

Figure 3.18   On the Heckler & Koch P-7, note the cocking grip below the trigger guard.

When a master grip is assumed with full pressure, the cocking grip is depressed rearward, which cocks the striker mechanism in preparation for firing. The cocking grip must be completely held in for the P-7 to fire. When the cocking grip is allowed to come forward, by easing the master grip, the P-7 is automatically uncocked and instantly safe. Squeeze in the cocking grip and you are ready to fire; release the cocking grip and the auto is instantly safe. When fully depressing the cocking grip, the fingers just firmly squeeze it in. When releasing the cocking grip, the fingers do not leave it but just allow it to come forward fully.

There is no external safety or slide release on the H&K P-7. After the last round has been fired, an internal slide stop lever locks the slide to the rear. The ambidextrous magazine release levers (to the rear of the trigger guard, at the top of the cocking grip) will release the magazine. To release the slide, once a fresh magazine has been locked home, merely fully depress the cocking grip, which releases the slide to chamber the first round from the magazine.

In Use. Consider the cocking grip as a safety lever. Whenever you are not ready to fire, the cocking grip is released; whenever you are ready to fire, the cocking grip is depressed. When drawing, the cocking grip is depressed only after the muzzle is well in front of your body. During any loading, unloading, or handling, the cocking grip is fully forward, the only exception being dry firing, only after checking to make sure that the auto is unloaded (check it twice).

Glock 17. The Glock 17 is most noted as being constructed substantially of a special polymer that is stronger than steel while being a fraction of its weight. Our main interest is the unique internal safety system, with no standard safety lever to push.

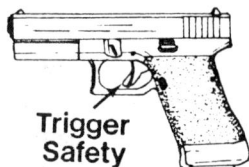

Trigger Safety

Figure 3.19   On the Glock-17, note the trigger safety on the front of the trigger.

The safety system features three internal safety devices that disengage automatically when the trigger is pulled, just before firing. When the trigger is released, they engage automatically. An external safety lever is mounted on the face of the trigger, which prevents rearward movement of the trigger unless completely depressed by the trigger finger resting on the trigger. In effect, firing the Glock 17 is like firing a revolver: Just pull the trigger when it is time to fire. Pull the trigger and it will fire; release the trigger and it is instantly safe. The trigger also serves as a cocking indicator: When the auto is cocked, the trigger moves well forward of its uncocked position. You can tell at a glance if the auto is cocked.

In Use. Once the auto is loaded, the only action needed to fire it is to press the trigger, which breaks very clean at 5 pounds. When firing is finished, as long as the trigger finger is out of the trigger guard and the trigger is released, the auto is safe.

Sig Sauer P-226. Our main focus on the Sig P-226 is the "decocking lever" to lower the hammer safely, and other safety features. The decocking lever is located on the top front of the left grip panel (on the frame) and can either be depressed by the thumb of a right-handed officer or trigger finger of a left-handed officer. Depressing the decocking lever will safely lower the hammer, which comes to rest on the "safety intercept notch" (keeping the hammer back from the firing pin).

Two internal automatic safeties keep the auto safe. The automatic firing pin block locks the firing pin whenever the trigger is forward. The safety intercept notch keeps the hammer from touching the firing pin once the hammer is decocked. These two safeties are disengaged only when the trigger is pulled to fire the auto. If the trigger is not pulled, the auto cannot fire.

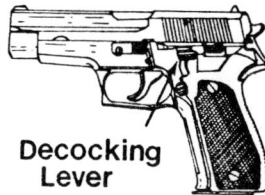

Decocking Lever

Figure 3.20 On the Sigarms P-226, note the decocking lever on the left side of the grip above the magazine release.

In Use. Once the auto has been loaded, the decocking lever is pushed down to lower the hammer safely. Now the auto is ready to fire in the double-action mode, and the only action needed to fire it is to pull the trigger. There is nothing else to press; just pull the trigger. When firing is completed, depress the decocking lever to lower the hammer safely.

SUMMARY

In this chapter we have completely covered the three service handguns and how they function. Mainly, you must learn how to function safely with your service handgun. Study, practice, and restudy the areas that cover your type of service handgun and your strong hand. You must use these handling procedures to build a set of safe handgun handling habits.

4

The Anatomy of the Defensive Stroke: The Holster-to-Stance Reflex

At the moment of truth in a lethal encounter, the service handgun becomes an extension of an officer's will: snapping up and firing to stop the threat(s). After the encounter has ended and the officer is questioned about the action, he or she may have no recollection of the handgun being drawn and brought into a firing position, only that it was suddenly up and firing.

There was no magic involved, although it may have seemed magical at the time. The handgun moved through a reflexive set (reflex) of trained-in movements to place it in a position to fire. This set of movements is called the HOLSTER-TO-STANCE REFLEX: the instantaneous movement of drawing the service handgun out of the "holster" and snapping it up into a locked-out two-handed "stance." As the basis of all defensive handgun use, this reflexive set is practiced until it becomes a subconscious reflex that requires little thought. When the threat appears, the handgun is produced in a position to fire, as you concentrate on the front sight and critical decisions of the lethal encounter.

Chapters 4 and 5 are sister chapters that cover the two reflexive sets that combine to form the most vital ability in defensive pistolcraft: the draw from the holster to the "hit" on the target. This chapter completely covers the holster-to-stance reflex, which places the service handgun in a locked-in two-handed firing stance in preparation for firing (one-handed firing is also discussed). Chapter 5 continues with the firing reflex, used to place "hits" from the two-handed firing stance. They are taught as separate and combined reflexive sets to meet any situation that may occur. For defensive handgun skills, these two chapters are the most important in the book.

AN UNDERSTANDING OF THE IMPORTANCE OF REFLEXIVE SETS

Reflexive sets of trained-in firearm skills are critical to the defensive operation of the service handgun, as during a lethal situation the operation of the handgun must be a trained-in reflexive action. To produce these reflexive sets, the actions of the handgun must be learned and trained-in through constant repetition. Repetitious training produces reflexive actions that occur automatically. During a situation the mind must be clear to concentrate on the critical decisions (tactics, shoot/no-shoot, etc.) while your weapon use skills are occurring automatically.

Reflexive sets are also referred to as task programming, which a person will develop only through repetitious practice. These sets, or programs, are most valuable during stressful situations, where they function automatically at a subconcious level. When an officer is attempting to function under the high stress of a lethal encounter, there can be no conscious thought about which weapon use skill to use. If conscious thought on weapon techniques is needed, you will not only lose valuable time but will reduce your critical decision-making ability. During lethal situations time is extremely important and will always be in short supply. Having to sort out consciously how weapon use techniques work during a situation will, in all probability, produce increased fumbling, which will increase your stress level. If you fumble even slightly, you will perceive yourself as possibly losing the encounter, which will instantly increase your stress and cause you to work faster, in all likelihood causing your fumbling to increase. Under stress, one negative occurrence tends instantly to create others.

There are five main areas where reflexive sets of trained-in skills are a must: the holster-to-stance reflex, firing reflex, manipulation, reloading, and immediate action. All must be trained-in reflexive sets so that they function automatically. Even with minimal repetitive practice these five areas quickly become reflexive actions.

One fact that most officers fail to realize is that all of these reflexive sets can be practiced in the privacy of your own home any time you want to. Actual firing on the range is only a small part of the total practice an officer needs to engage in. With an unloaded handgun, an officer can practice every weapon use skill except actually firing. This is called dry practicing and will be completely covered in a number of locations throughout the book.

Reflexive sets work! The use of one particular trained-in reflexive set has been demonstrated to virtually all officers while driving their cruisers on a midnight shift. While patrolling, most officers have, at one time or another, drifted off slightly while being sleepy or while lost in thought. Suddenly they snap back into awareness, not remembering the last mile or two they have just driven. Even though they cannot remember the last mile or two, they were able to drive it in their semiaware/semiconscious state. How did they accomplish this? Their trained-in driving skills from years of practice while driving allow each officer to maintain control over his or her vehicle although functioning at a subconscious level. It works whether driving your cruiser or defensively using your service handgun.

The Holster-to-Stance Reflex

You must be able to draw and "hit," either one- or two-handed, on demand of the situation at any time. You have no doubt already practiced this set in your live fire training, practice, and qualification. This is nothing new; the holster-to-stance reflex is merely the act of instantly drawing and locking into a position to fire (or firing, if necessary) either one- or two-handed. Although it is true that this is nothing new, the real question is: Are you doing it right? This reflexive set is a combination of many separate parts that create the whole; each will be taken in turn and analyzed for a complete understanding of the techniques involved.

Just so there is no misunderstanding, the "holster-to-stance reflex" is the "defensive stroke" that instantly places the service handgun in a locked-out firing position. These synonymous terms describe the most important reflexive set you will learn with the service handgun.

Holster-to-stance reflex versus holster-to-hit reflex. Many instructors teach a holster-to-hit reflex instead of a holster-to-stance reflex. What is the difference between the two, and why is it important?

A holster-to-hit reflex always ends with the handgun being fired; as the handgun is snapped up, it is fired. Training that incorporates this reflexive set exclusively is suspect in that it is creating officers who are preprogrammed to shoot instantly (reflexively) as soon as their handgun is locked out. Remember, what you do in training, you will do on the street. In any court case involving an officer's use of the handgun, the method of firearms training will be examined closely, especially if an officer shot too quickly before he or she could determine what was occurring.

The holster-to-stance reflex, on the other hand, teaches officers instantly to snap the service handgun up into a firing stance, from which they are ready to fire instantly if necessary. Officers are not totally trained to fire as soon as the stance is locked out, but are trained that producing the handgun in a position to fire and actually firing it are two different reflexes. (*Note:* During training, officers will usually fire as soon as the handgun is drawn and locked out in a firing stance. But they are not trained exclusively to do this.) The situation may call for instantaneous firing as the stance is assumed; if so, the officers will fire instantly.

What supports this method of training is that nothing interferes with the officer's critical/decision-making process during high-stress situations. When the situation occurs, the handgun is snapped up (with no thought taken away from the decision-making process). If the officer decides to shoot, he or she is already looking over the sights and firing. If the officer decides not to shoot, no part of the training takes over to inadvertently fire the service handgun during the high-stress situation.

When an officer trains only to fire instantly at the end of the defensive stroke, he or she may do it on the street. The holster-to-stance reflex does not train this in.

The holster-to-stance reflex.   As with any physical motor skill, the defensive operation of the handgun must be properly learned and practiced until it becomes a reflexive set of movements that happen automatically. When you acquire the target and mentally give the now signal (make the decision to shoot), one fraction of a second later you should be looking over the sights, applying trigger pressure. The reflexive set of movements should occur just that quickly, automatically placing the handgun in a position to fire with virtually no conscious thought. Whether drawing from the holster or snapping the service handgun up from a lowered position, the movements are virtually the same.

The use of the reflexive set allows you to focus all your conscious thoughts on the fight, its critical decision making, and the tactics involved. The service handgun's movements are preprogrammed and function automatically, clearing all your thoughts for critical decision-making during the situation.

The holster-to-stance reflex is broken down into four positions:

Position 1: The grip. The initial movement of the strong hand grips the holstered handgun in a good master grip, the trigger finger is straight alongside the frame, and the thumb has unsnapped the holster's safety mechanism (if one is present).

Position 2: The draw to belt level. The handgun is drawn from the holster and brought forward to the belt-level position, with wrist straight and muzzle pointing at the floor, at an angle well in front of the feet.

Position 3: Support. As the handgun moves forward of the belt-level position and the hands come together for a supported two-handed grip.

Position 4: Locked out. The arms continue forward to lock out the two-handed grip into a firing stance.

These four positions form the holster-to-stance reflex, which produces the handgun in a position to fire—on demand, at any time. Whenever these positions are referred to by number, you will know exactly where along the holster-to-stance reflex we are talking about.

Training.   These four positions, along the holster-to-stance reflex (the line the handgun takes when it is snapped up from the draw to the locked-out two-handed stance), are used when initially training new officers to train in each action. Every officer must understand these four positions that make up the most important reflexive set used in firearms training. Their value lies in the fact that every officer engaged in training can quickly get on track and follow the firearms insstructor. When first training, these positions are slowly followed one right after the other; only then are the positions used together. Also, they should be reviewed during refresher training to sharpen every officer's weapon use skill.

4.1.

Figure 4.1   Position 1: the grip.

4.2.

Figure 4.2   Position 2: the draw to belt level.

4.3.

Figure 4.3   Position 3: support.

4.4.

Figure 4.4   Position 4: locked out.

THE FOUR POSITIONS

The four positions on the holster-to-stance reflex must be analyzed to cover all aspects of the applied techniques. As a defensive weapon user, this set is critical to your performance with the handgun. If only one set of movements for firing the handgun could be learned, the defensive firing stroke is what you would learn.

Position 1: The Grip

The master grip.   The logical beginning of the holster-to-stance reflex is the grip on the holstered handgun. When the decision is made to draw the handgun, the hand instantly moves to the holstered handgun and assumes the master grip—the strong hand's grip on the handgun. The proper master grip is a must before the handgun is drawn, as an improper grip will cause wasted time and motion. This occurs while adjusting the grip as the handgun is snapped up. But further, an improper grip can cause the handgun to fall from your hand as you draw; losing control of your handgun during a lethal encounter may, in all probability, be the last thing you do.

The master grip on the holstered handgun is the same as your firing grip (except that the trigger finger is out of the trigger guard, riding along the side of the frame). No change in the master grip will occur throughout the handgun's use. Remember, the master grip = the firing grip; the only change is the trigger finger, which is outside of the trigger guard until the handgun is coming on target just before firing. The trigger finger is separated from the rest of the hand when assuming the master grip, as it must function independently from the rest of the hand when firing.

The master grip is assumed by the web of the hand (between the thumb and index finger) being placed high on the back strap of the handgun (make sure that the web does not go too high and interfere with the hammer). The fingers then wrap around and grip the stocks, with the trigger finger straight along the side of the frame and the handgun straight in the hand. The master grip is firm but not excessively tight. With practice, the hand will learn to find the handgun and assume the master grip instantly.

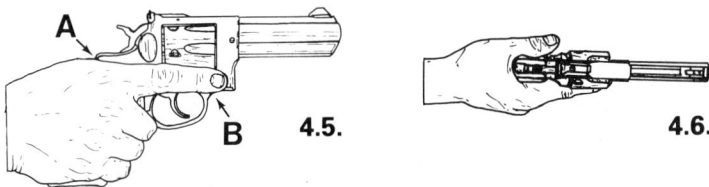

Figures 4.5 and 4.6   The web is high on the back strap (A) and the trigger finger is straight along the side of the frame (B) (Fig. 4.5). The handgun is held straight in the hand (Fig. 4.6).

The master grip is essential and you must work with yours until it feels natural, until your hand knows every curve of the grip. First, you will have to find the best grip for your hand and the particular service handgun you carry. UNLOAD the handgun (check it twice) and hold it in the support hand, Now, open the thumb of your strong hand to form a "V" and place the handgun into it, making sure that the web (the area between the base of the thumb and the index finger) is high on the back strap, and wrap your fingers, except the trigger/index finger, around the stocks. Become used to placing your trigger finger straight alongside the frame whenever gripping the handgun. Now insert your trigger finger into the trigger guard and place it on the trigger. Your trigger finger should be able easily to reach and pull the double-action trigger using the "first joint" (if using a double-action handgun). Reaching a single-action trigger will be no problem. (*Note*: Fitting the handgun into the strong hand is done only to help you find and learn the best grip for the handgun

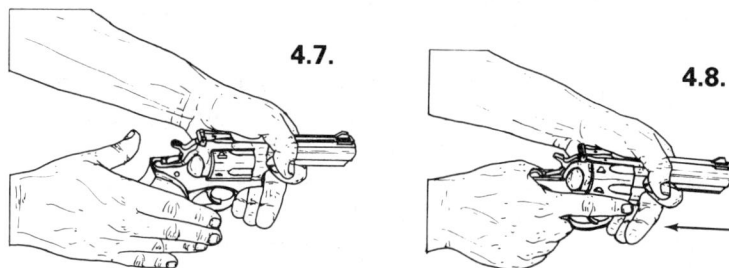

Figures 4.7 and 4.8 The support hand holds the handgun in preparation (Fig. 4.7) and then fits it into the strong hand (Fig. 4.8).

you are using. Once this is accomplished and you have developed your master grip, this technique is not used anymore for this purpose.)

When the handgun is correctly held in the strong hand, it must appear to be a natural extension of the hand. With the elbow bent at 90 degrees, hold the handgun at waist level and look down at the positioning. The handgun *must* be straight in the hand, not canted to either side or up or down. The forearm, wrist, hand, and handgun must form a straight line. As such, the handgun will follow the natural pointability of the hand and index finger. A mirror will also be helpful in checking your positioning.

Readjusting Your Grip After The Draw.   The master grip = the firing grip and ultimately you should not have to readjust your grip after drawing the handgun, but this is not the case some of the time. When quickly gripping the handgun for the draw, a less than perfect grip can occur. As the handgun is drawn and brought up, you can feel the difference in your master grip and usually make the minor adjustments necessary as the handgun is coming up. Sometimes you may have to fire with a less-than-perfect grip; again, this presents no real problem—control the handgun in the two-handed stance and fire. Readjust the grip at the first chance that presents itself, usually after firing the first one or two shots.

A Secure Grip and Your Holster.   As stated before, the grip on the holstered handgun must be secure before you draw. If the handgun is not firmly gripped on the draw, it could fall from the hand. Achieving a good, firm grip takes nothing more than practice with the handgun and holster. With practice, a good master grip can be achieved almost the instant the hand touches the holstered handgun.

Due to the design of certain holsters, a good master grip may not be possible with the handgun still holstered. If you are issued one of these holsters and must use it, practice with it to achieve the best grip possible. The best duty holsters leave the entire grip clear so that the strong hand can instantly assume a firm grip. Also,

4.9.   **4.10.**

   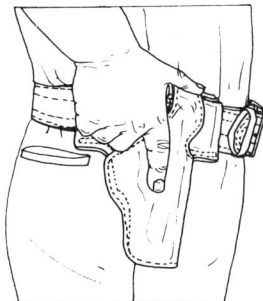

Figures 4.9 and 4.10 On a good security holster, the handgun's grip is exposed, while the trigger guard is completely covered (Fig. 4.9). When the master grip is assumed, the trigger finger is held straight on the outside of the holster, and stays straight along the handgun's frame after the draw (Fig. 4.10). The excellent De-Santis Law-Tech duty holster is shown.

the trigger guard is covered on a good duty holster, reinforcing that the trigger finger is straight along the frame on the draw and when reholstering.

Touch indexing, a trick of the trade.   A good trick that can improve both the speed and accuracy of the strong hand gripping the handgun is to lightly touch the inner forearm or elbow to the grip of the holstered handgun (with the arm held down). This creates a "touch index" that increases your ability to place the strong hand instantly on the handgun's grip. Use it when you practice gripping your handgun to improve your skill. You must also practice with the arm held away from the body, to simulate other positions that your arm could be in when having to draw.

The touch index can be important in a situation that is about to happen. You have perceived that something is not right, that a dangerous situation may occur. To outward appearances nothing about you has changed, as the small movement of touching the inner forearm to the handgun's grip will no doubt go completely unnoticed. But you are prepared and positioned to move instantly should the danger present itself. Through your touch index, the strong hand will be right on target when it snaps to the grip.

Another small variation of the touch index is to bend the elbow naturally and place the thumb of the strong hand on top of your belt close to the buckle. As such, you are instantly ready to make your move—very casual looking, but set like a spring to move instantly. When the strong hand moves from this position, it snaps back to the handgun's grip, the master grip is instantly assumed, and the handgun is out—very fast. This is just one of the touch indexes that will be used.

The strong hand's movement to the handgun's grip.   There are two methods used when the strong hand makes the initial gripping move to the handgun's grip. Either one can be used effectively, try them both and determine which is best for you. You must pick one and stick with it.

Single-Movement Draw.   The strong hand makes a circular motion, coming down behind the handgun, then up under the grip to assume the master grip. With this method, the circular motion of the hand brings it under the handgun and up to the handgun's grip. The fingers are straight as the motion is started and brought down across the holster. As the circular motion continues, the fingers bend (except for the trigger finger, which stays straight) and they first contact the front of the grip. Almost at the same instant, the web and palm wrap over the back strap of the grip. This method is referred to as a single-movement draw (also continuous-movement draw): the circular movement of the hand is a continuous flow, not pausing, or starting or stopping, anywhere along the arc the hand makes as a complete draw.

Double-Movement Draw.   The strong hand goes straight to the grip, placing the hand directly on top of the grip as the master grip is assumed. With this method the hand drops straight to the top of the grip, with the web and palm first coming in contact with the back strap. Almost at the same instant, the fingers wrap around the front of the grip. This method is referred to as a double-movement draw: the first movement of the hand to the grip, and then the second movement of the hand drawing the handgun out and forward.

Either of these movements will continue through the draw. Their beginning, though, is the proper gripping of the handgun. When first starting, practice the movements as separate actions, stopping when the strong hand grips the handgun. With practice, both are very fast. Remember, pick one and stick to it.

Holster Security Devices.   When the master grip is assumed, any holster security device will be unsnapped (usually, a snap and strap arrangement). As soon as the handgun is gripped, all security devices must be cleared in preparation for the draw.

Position 2: The Draw to Belt Level

As soon as the master grip is assumed, the draw clears the handgun from the holster and brings it foward into the belt-level position. The wrist is instantly straightened from the draw as the handgun arrives at the belt-level position. The trigger finger is still out of the trigger guard (it will be kept there until just before the target is acquired).

The action of drawing the handgun and snapping into the belt-level position is very important and will be used extensively by police officers. This is why the draw to belt level is trained-in as one movement. In the belt-level position, the handgun is held at belt level and close to the body. As the handgun comes forward from the draw, it stops at the belt line, with the thumb touching the belt. The barrel is naturally pointing at the floor about 9 feet in front of you; this natural and safe point occurs with the forearm, wrist, and handgun in a straight line. The handgun is not held directly at the side, but about halfway between the belt buckle and pants seam,

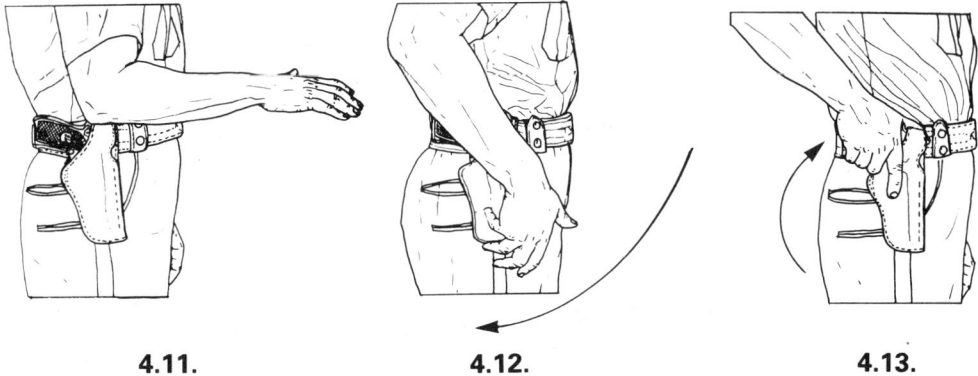

4.11.   **4.12.**   **4.13.**

Figures 4.11–4.13 Begin practice with the strong hand held straight out (Fig. 4.11). The draw is done by the strong hand making a circular motion (Fig. 4.12), going down below the grip and up to assume the master grip (Fig. 4.13). Creating a single movement as the draw continues the circular motion.

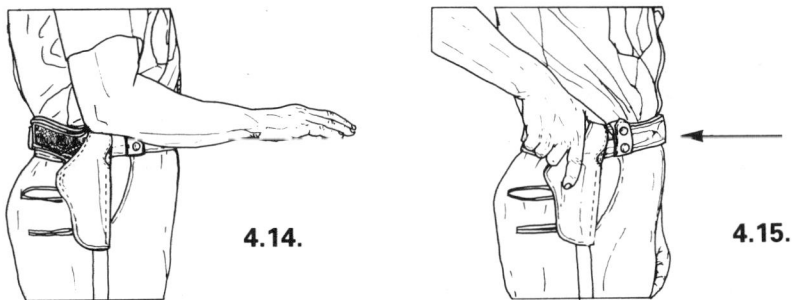

4.14.   **4.15.**

Figures 4.14 and 4.15 Begin practice with the strong hand held straight out (Fig. 4.14). The draw is done by the strong hand snapping straight back and assuming the master grip (Fig. 4.15). Creating a double movement when the handgun is drawn.

achieving a natural feel. This is an extremely important position for searching and defensive handgun work.

The draw will be covered first and then further points on the belt-level position will be given.

The draw.   The two methods of drawing the handgun, the single- and double-movement draws, which we began describing in the preceding section are continued here. (*Note*: We are only examining the technique for the strong side, forward-facing holster, riding straight up and down or with a rearward tilt. Only this style holster should be used for uniform duty on a Sam Browne belt. The "Law-Tech" holster by DeSantis—as shown in the drawings—is one excellent example of this style holster. Concealable drawing techniques are covered in Chapter 15.)

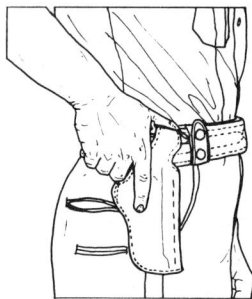

4.16.

4.17.

Figures 4.16 and 4.17   From the master grip on holstered handgun (Fig. 4.16), the drawn instantly places the handgun in the belt-level position (Fig. 4.17).

The drawing techniques.   In the preceding section (on the grip) you were shown the beginning movements for two drawing techniques, the single- and double-movement draws. In both of these the grip and draw are one smooth movement but are broken down into two distinct movements when training new officers how to draw. This is done to make sure that they (1) achieve a proper master grip on the holstered handgun, and then (2) perform a correct drawing movement that completely clears the leather each time (the draw continuing to the belt-level position). Both of these are separate parts of the same technique and instructors training new officers must make sure that each is done correctly. We begin with the master grip already properly assumed on the holstered handgun. (*Note*: When training new officers, the positions are done slowly so that each movement can be seen by the instructors. This is especially true of the draw to belt-level position. Instructors must make sure that the handgun is correctly clearing the holster each time and the wrist completely straightening out when it arrives at the belt-level position.)

From the time the master grip is assumed on the holstered handgun, the actual draw is the same for either drawing technique. The handgun is pulled out of the holster by the hand coming up and forward, with the wrist bending. Once the muzzle has cleared the front lip of the holster, the handgun will then be snapped—or punched—forward. As the handgun is snapped forward, the bend in the wrist is instantly straightened out.

When training new officers, the draw is a continuous one, right through to the belt-level position. When the draw to belt-level position is done slowly, the instructors can see what the officers are doing. The main problem to watch out for is the handgun "canting" to the inside or outside; the handgun must be held straight up and down (the arm or wrist not being allowed to cant the handgun). The handgun is then snapped forward with the wrist instantly straightening out. Make sure that the wrist straightens out instantly as soon as the handgun starts forward.

Tailoring your draw.   There is a large degree of variation in handguns and holsters used by departments; you must work with the service handgun and holster issued to you, developing a draw that is completely appropriate for you and your

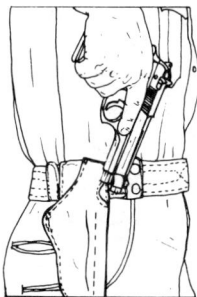 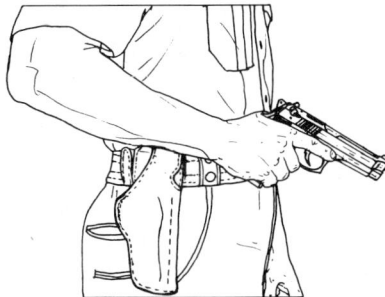

4.18.   **4.19.**

Figures 4.18 and 4.19 When drawing, the handgun is pulled up and forward with the wrist bent so that the muzzle can clear the holster's front lip (Fig. 4.18). As the handgun clears the lip and is started forward, the wrist is instantly straightened out (Fig. 4.19).

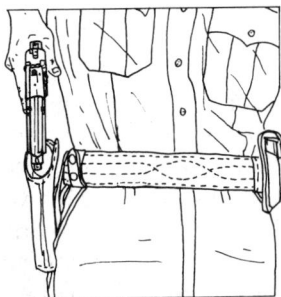

4.20.

Figure 4.20 On the draw the handgun must be held straight up and down and not canted to either side.

equipment. You know what equipment you are issued and you must work with your equipment to find the best way to draw. Also, the configuration of your body must be taken into consideration when developing your draw. Small differences occur between everyone, and what might feel quite appropriate for one person may feel slightly uncomfortable to another. Your draw must feel natural and this is where tailoring helps you work into one that feels right.

Tailoring your draw is fairly easily accomplished. Put your belt and holster on, unload the handgun (check it twice), and you are ready. Begin by drawing the handgun and reholstering it several times using either of the two drawing methods described (you should try both and pick the one that feels right). Right away you will probably notice several "glitches" (small problems) in the method of gripping, use of the holster's snap, smoothness at which the handgun comes out of the holster, placement of your hand or arm during the movement, and so on. Slight changes may certainly be needed: possibly a slight outward movement of the arm, less bend to the wrist, a better angle for the handgun to come out of the holster, and so on. These small changes can really make the difference. Work them one by one until the problems begin to disappear. Ultimately, most can be taken care of, although some may no doubt remain.

Relax the shoulder and arm when working with the draw. Also, hold the arm still until you start the draw. Do not begin developing the bad habit of telegraphing your movements. When the arm moves into the drawing motion, make it a smooth and continuous movement. Use the fewest movements in the shortest distance to the target.

As you work through this process of eliminating glitches, you will notice that your drawing technique is improving. It's beginning to feel better, more natural. Each time you practice and work on the draw, you are improving, getting closer to your optimum drawing technique. This is not a difficult process but one that requires a small amount of commitment. An understanding of three areas—the holster, eyes-off draw, and trigger finger out of trigger guard—will help you establish a drawing methodology.

The Holster.   Three factors are important for a duty holster; it must (1) hold the handgun securely, (2) be tight on the belt, and (3) always be in the same location. These factors are important for a duty holster; the last two are especially important for the draw.

1. It must hold the handgun securely. Far too many officers have experienced the sinking feeling of reaching for their handguns only to find empty holsters: the handgun being left on the seat of their cruiser, sticking up by the barrel in the middle of a field they have just run through, or bounced along the pavement. Of course, an appropriate balance between security and drawing speed is very important and included in any holster selection process. It is better to lean a little more heavily to the security side, as the officer can be expected to struggle with suspects and engage in other strenuous physical activity while the handgun must stay in the holster.

2. The holster's belt loop must be tight on the belt and the belt must be worn snugly on the body. This will stop the holster from flopping around or slipping on the draw. A loosely fitting holster can cause real problems on the draw, as the handgun, holster, and belt may rise up together as you are trying to draw, with the handgun staying in the holster. The holster must be tight on the belt and the belt must be tight on the body. If the holster or belt is loose, this condition will usually cause you to form another bad habit, using your support hand to hold the holster when drawing and reholstering. This must not be done, as the support hand will be needed for other tasks.

3. The handgun and holster must be in the same location every time you go for them. No switching between different uniform holsters; you must know where the holster is each and every time. A problem in this area usually happens when an officer wears two different types of holsters. When a threat occurs, the officer goes for the handgun where he or she thinks it is, but it is in the other location. Now the officer must think, losing time and advantage, and then go to the other location. Officers cannot afford the loss in time that fumbling on the draw will produce.

Eyes-Off Draw.   You must be able to perform your draw without looking at the handgun or holster. In real situations you must keep your eyes on the action/ threat(s) at all times. When it is time, your draw produces the handgun directly in your line of sight with the target, without ever having taken your eyes away from the action/threat(s). To function in this manner, the draw must be done the same way each time and by feel. Find one way of drawing, stick to it, and practice it by feel. Also, when the handgun is reholstered, it must be done by feel.

Trigger Finger Out of Trigger Guard.   Always remember safety when drawing by keeping the trigger finger out of the trigger guard whenever drawing, placing it on the trigger only when coming on target just before firing. This will not only produce a safe draw but will increase the speed of your draw. By training yourself in this way, you will not only avoid unintentional discharges, but with an increased safety level that you can feel, you will increase the speed of the draw, knowing that it is "safe." There will be plenty of time to index the trigger finger as you are bringing the handgun up, just before firing. Remember, we never practice anything we do not use in a real situation. In a real situation the trigger finger is out of the trigger guard until the handgun is coming up, just before aligning on the target.

These three factors will help you develop a safe and fast drawing methodology. Remember, the function of the draw is to remove the handgun from the holster quickly, in a safe and consistent manner. Once a safe draw is developed, use it consistently. Have one way of doing it and stick to it. Practice your draw by doing it slowly; only after becoming comfortable with the draw should you begin to increase the speed.

The belt-level position.   When first assuming the belt-level position, look down every now and then to check that everything is straight, especially the wrist. Some officers have a tendency to bend the wrist inward, wrapping the forearm, wrist, and handgun around the body. Do not let this happen; keep it straight. When coming foward from the draw, the handgun is locked into the belt-level position. This is not a tight lock, but an easy, controlled lock, which is snapped into (the handgun going right into the position).

The belt-level position serves you several ways during real situations as well as during initial training. The truth of all defensive firearms training is: You never train-in anything that will not serve you in a real situation. Three factors show the functioning of this position during real situations.

First, this is an excellent position when searching with the handgun out, from close quarters to much larger areas. From the belt-level position, the handgun is ready for instantaneous use, yet close to the body and not a target for an attacker to try and grab. If instantly attacked at close range, the handgun is positioned to rock-up and/or point out and fire. If the threat(s) is not right on top of you, the handgun is positioned to snap up into a locked-in two-handed firing stance. When searching in this position, the support hand is free to use a flashlight, open doors, move things, climb with, and so on. As such, you are prepared to respond instantly to any threat(s) that appear, while having the flexibility needed during the search.

Second, you are safe with the trigger finger out of the trigger guard, so a startled reaction or slip does not instantly send off a shot. Also, the barrel is pointing to a spot on the floor about 9 feet in front of you. If an unintentional round is sent out of the barrel, it will strike the floor in front of you and not your foot. A hit foot or leg would no doubt occur if trained to hold the handgun down at your side as some still do, giving you the instant "Chester" look.

Third, the belt-level position is ideally located between the holstered handgun and the locked-out, two-handed firing stance. The handgun travels up through this position when drawn from the holster to either point shoot at very close range or snap up into a locked-in two-handed firing stance. This is all one package—the holster-to-stance reflex—and each part of the package complements the other. The holstered handgun or the belt-level position are the two main starting positions to snap into any of the firing positions.

In training and when searching, you will start in the belt-level position and come back to it many times. Do not let the handgun hang down or stick out; do not be sloppy with your handgun. There is no excuse for poor gun handling in training and definitely no excuse during real situations.

Position 3: Support

From the belt-level position, the handgun travels forward less than a foot to where the support hand comes across the body, to support the strong hand and handgun in a good two-handed grip. As the two-handed grip is achieved, the arms continue forward, locking-out into the two-handed firing stance.

The draw to the locked-out firing stance is one continuous, smooth movement, with no hesitation or stopping. As the handgun comes forward, the support hand crosses the body and assumes the two-handed support grip while the handgun is snapping forward into the stance. There is no hesitation as the two-handed grip is assumed. The strong arm makes one continuous movement, from draw to locked-out stance. Many officers make a small hesitation as the two-handed grip is assumed and slightly adjusted, before it is locked out into the stance. There is no need for this, as there will be plenty of time for the support hand to assume and adjust the two-handed grip as the handgun is being locked out into the stance.

Support hand positioning.   As the draw is begun, the support hand is positioned close to the centerline of the body (not over the centerline, which would place the support hand in front of the muzzle), with the inside of the wrist touching the belt and the hand opened and pointing straight forward. In this position it is instantly ready to assume the two-handed support grip as the strong hand brings the handgun past, enroute to being locked out in the firing stance.

The support hand does not comes out in front of the strong hand and handgun. This would place the support hand in front of the handgun's muzzle, which violates safety rule 2 and could get your hand quickly drilled. As the strong hand

4.21.   **4.22.**   **4.23.**   **4.24.**

Figures 4.21–4.24   The draw is begun (Fig. 4.21). The handgun is drawn and brought forward (Fig. 4.22), as the support hand is positioned close to the body's center line but not over it. As the strong hand brings the handgun past the two-handed support grip is assumed at position 3 (only after the muzzle is in front of the support hand) (Fig. 4.23). The stance is locked out at position 4 (Fig. 4.24).

brings the handgun forward, the support hand "meets" the strong hand as it is going past. It meets the strong hand at position 3; it does not chase the strong hand forward assuming the grip past position 3. This understanding is very important to the total grip, as the two-handed grip must be assumed at position 3, to allow the "adjustment space" necessary as the arms are going forward to lock out the firing stance. From the two-handed grip (assumed at position 3) to the locked-out firing stance, some degree of adjustment must occur. This adjustment completely settles in the lock of the grip, wrists, and arms, and occurs as the arms travel from position 3 to position 4 (the locked-out firing stance). The melding of flesh and muscle that occurs as the hands snap up through this adjustment space locks in everything as the two-handed firing stance is achieved. This is not difficult; it will occur automatically, just as the rest of the holster-to-stance reflex occurs.

When practicing, you must make sure that the two-handed support grip is first achieved at position 3. If achieved before position 3, the support hand is in danger by being in front of the muzzle. If achieved after position 3, the adjustment space to lock in the hands is reduced.

The gripping techniques.   Either one of two defensive firing stances is used: the Weaver or Isosceles stances. The two-handed grips used for each of these stances are similar but different, following the differences in the way each stance is assumed and locked in. The complete differences between the stances are discussed later. For now it is important to address these two grips: the Isosceles grip and the Weaver grip.

The Isosceles Grip.   The Isosceles stance is formed with the chest directly facing the target, the arms and elbows locked straight out (forming the two equal sides of an isosceles triangle, hence the name), and the hands locked into a good two-handed grip.

The two-handed Isosceles grip is learned by first assuming the two-handed grip and the stance a number of times to acquire a beginning feel for it. Make sure that the handgun is unloaded (check it twice) and follow these steps:

1. Face straight forward at a target and lock both arms and elbows out directly in front of the chest at eye level, with the handgun held in a proper master grip in the strong hand.
2. Bring the support hand next to the strong hand and line up the thumbs by straightening out the strong-hand thumb (on the handgun) and placing the support-hand thumb next to it.
3. Place the large muscle area (below the support-hand thumb) into the opening on the grip (just behind the tips of the strong-hand fingers forming the master grip) and wrap the fingers overtop the strong-hand fingers.
4. Bend the strong-hand thumb down and lock the support-hand thumb overtop it. Slight isometric pressure is applied to either side of the handgun by both hands, and the fingers and thumb of the support hand lock in the grip. This pressure is firm, but not to the point where the handgun begins to tremble.

4.25.

4.26.

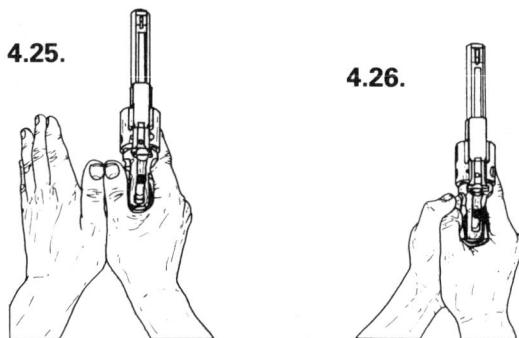

Figures 4.25 and 4.26   The strong hand grips the handgun and holds it next to the support hand with the thumbs lined up and held straight (Fig. 4.25). The support hand wraps around the strong hand, with the support hand's thumb wrapping overtop the strong hand's thumb (Fig. 4.26).

To help the two-handed grip stay locked in, pressure is applied by the thumb and fingers of the support hand. The support-hand thumb locks down on top of the strong hand thumb and applies downward pressure, while the support-hand index finger is applying upward pressure against the bottom of the trigger guard and all four support-hand fingers are applying pressure around the strong-hand fingers. Their combined use locks in the two-handed grip by applying two-directional pressure to keep the two hands together. Both wrists are locked, the body's weight is slightly forward, and the knees are slightly bent (not locked). The position is flexible.

Two variations are sometimes seen: placing the support hand index finger on

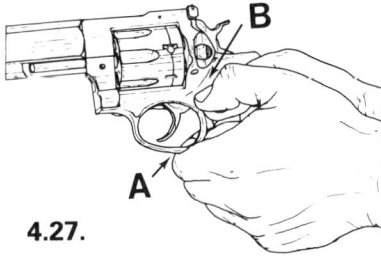

4.27.

Figure 4.27 The grip is locked in by the support hand's index finger pressing up on the bottom of the trigger guard (A) and the thumb pressing down on the strong hand's thumb (B).

the front of the trigger guard or placing the support hand thumb on the rear part of the strong hand directly behind the hammer. Placing the index finger on the front of the trigger guard is really not a large problem, but it can reduce the control exerted on the handgun. Placing the thumb to the rear of the hammer is a competition trick that does not function well in real situations. Assume this grip, stay in it for awhile, and you will see what we mean. Very quickly the stretched-out hand will begin to fatigue. In short, both of these should be avoided. (*Note*: These are separate variations, as the hand cannot stretch to use both of these together.)

The Weaver Grip. The Weaver stance is formed by the officer standing at an angle to the target, as he or she would in a boxing stance with the strong-arm side to the rear at about a 40-degree angle to the target. The strong arm, holding the handgun in a good master grip, is angled across the body, being straight or slightly bent, while the support arm is sharply bent, with the elbow pointing down. The two-handed grip applies isometric pressure by the strong hand pushing forward into the support hand, which is pulling back, on the strong hand.

The two-handed Weaver grip, as with the Isosceles grip, is learned by first assuming the two-handed grip and the stance a number of times to acquire a beginning feel for it. Make sure that the handgun is unloaded (check it twice) and follow these steps.

1. Face forward at about a 40-degree angle at a target (with your strong-hand side to the rear), without moving your body, bring the strong arm straight out and up to eye level and lock it straight out (the arm will angle across the body). The handgun is held in a good master grip by the strong hand.

2. Bring the support hand in front of the strong hand well below the muzzle (the support arm's elbow is sharply bent and the tip of the elbow is pointing down). The support hand forms into a cup by closing and curving the fingers in with the thumb held straight up.

3. Bring the cupped fingers back and place them over the four fingers of the strong hand, with the large muscle area (below the support hand thumb) being placed into the opening on the grip (just behind the tips of the strong-hand fingers forming the master grip).

4. Bend the support-hand thumb down overtop the strong-hand thumb. Isometric pressure is applied by the strong hand pushing forward into the support hand, which is pulling back into the strong hand. The isometric pressure can

4.28.   **4.29.**

Figures 4.28 and 4.29 With the strong arm held straight and angled across the body, the support arm is bent (elbow pointing down) and its hand forms a "cup" that is held in front of the strong hand well below the muzzle (Fig. 4.28). Then bring the support hand's "cupped" finger back and place them over the strong hand's fingers gripping the handgun (Fig. 4.29). Bend down the support hand's thumb overtop the strong hand's thumb.

be exerted very strongly when firing in this grip, greatly improving control when firing.

To help the two-handed grip stay locked in, pressure is applied by the thumb and fingers of the support hand. The support-hand thumb locks down on top of the strong-hand thumb and applies downward pressure, while the support-hand index finger is applying upward pressure agains the bottom of the trigger guard and all four support-hand fingers are applying rearward pressure into the strong hand, which, in turn, is applying forward pressure into the support hand. The strong hand is pushing into the support hand, which is pulling back into the strong hand, forming the isometric lock to decrease dramatically the effects of recoil. Both wrists are locked, the body's weight is slightly forward, and the knees are slightly bent (not locked). The position is flexible.

One variation regularly seen is placing the support hand index finger on the front of the trigger guard. As with the Isosceles grip, this is not a large problem, but it can reduce the control exerted on the handgun. Rarely do you see a shooter place his or her thumb to the rear of the slide. Usually, they do it once, as the reciprocating slide will cut the top of the thumb when it travels to the rear (ejecting an empty case).

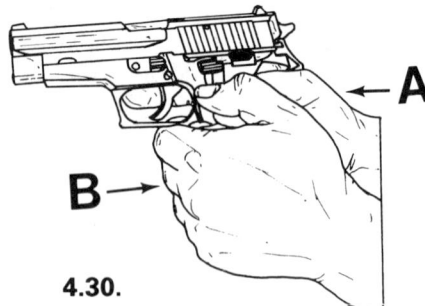

4.30.

Figure 4.30 The isometric pressure is applied by the strong hand pushing into the support hand (A), which is pulling back into the strong hand (B). Also remember, the strong hand's thumb and index finger locks the grip in.

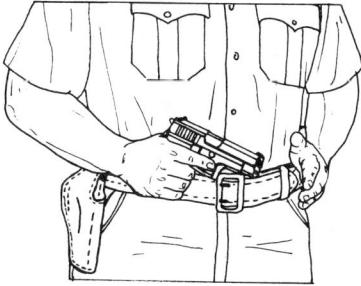 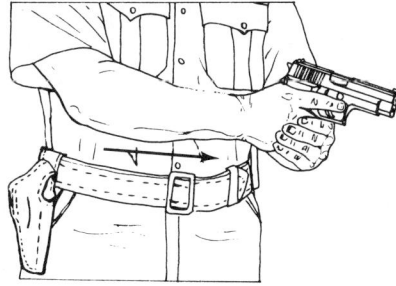

4.31.   **4.32.**

Figures 4.31 and 4.32   When initially practicing, hold the handgun in the belt-level position, with the support hand back from the body's centerline well back from the muzzle, with the inside of the wrist touching the belt (Fig. 4.31). Practice by bringing the handgun forward and assuming the support position at position 3 (Fig. 4.32).

Assuming the two-handed grip at position 3.   Once you have practiced the grip (for the stance you will use) and have developed a feel for it, the time has come to begin assuming the grip at position 3 as the handgun moves forward. Begin by taking a practicing position: hold the handgun in the belt-level position and place the support hand slightly back from the centerline of the body with the inside of the wrist touching the belt. Practice by bringing the handgun slowly forward until the strong hand is almost even with the support hand (the muzzle being well past the support hand). At this point, the two-handed grip is assumed by the support hand moving over slightly to meet the strong hand, which in turn is moving straight forward toward the target. The hands should meet about 8 to 10 inches in front of the body.

Practice until the hands come together smoothly, seeming to lock into each other automatically, forming the two-handed grip. After even limited practice, assuming the grip should begin to flow easily, the two hands flowing together at position 3 to create the grip. Once you feel comfortable, increase the strong hand's speed in bringing the handgun forward. Make sure that you make the catch at position 3 and not before or after it.

Position 4: Locked Out

The locked-out two-handed firing stance is the focal position of defensive pistol-craft, providing a platform from which to fire and control the handgun. As stated before, when using the handgun defensively, only one stance is used, either the Isosceles stance or the Weaver stance. You must select one of these and use it exclusively.

Selecting your stance.   Few techniques in defensive pistolcraft are so hotly debated as the superiority of either the Isosceles or the Weaver stance. Which is best? Talk to a number of experts or shooters and you will hear that each is the superior defensive firing stance. Both are good locked-in two-handed firing stances that will accomplish the task at hand, providing a "platform" from which to fire and control the handgun. We will examine each stance separately to provide a better understanding of these two firing platforms.

The Isosceles Stance.   This stance has been around since the early part of the twentieth century. Its earliest form was developed by W. E. Fairbairn, a British officer in charge of firearms training for the Shanghai police from 1910 through the 1920s. He found that by locking the arms in front of the body, with both hands holding the handgun at eye level, an officer could control and fire the handgun much better. The technique was picked up and used by the New York City Police Department firearms training section, who dubbed it the turret position, as the shooter's upper body will turn like a gun turret when turning to place "hits" on threats positioned around an officer.

The Isosceles stance began proving what many officers thought, that a two-handed firing stance should provide twice the control of one-handed firing, improving the officer's ability to "hit." Over time it has grown in popularity and is the predominant two-handed firing stance used by police departments nationwide.

The Isosceles stance uses a locked-in position where the chest/upper body is facing straight toward the target, the arms and elbows are locked out, and the two hands are holding the handgun at eye level. Generally, this stance is noted as an excellent precision shooting stance to place precise hits with light loads. For that reason it is used almost exclusively during PPC competitions, where precise hit placement is the overriding factor. The Isosceles stance also produces excellent two-hand instinctive and low-light shooting capabilities, as the triangulated, locked-in arms center the handgun directly in front of the body.

The Weaver Stance.   This stance was developed by Deputy Sheriff Jack Weaver of the Los Angeles Sheriff's Department in 1958. While participating in combat pistol matches at the Southwest Combat League in California, Weaver began using a two-handed firing stance and started winning every match he entered. At the time, every other competitor was using a one-handed firing position (usually from the hip or held out, as these were leatherslap-style competitions), but very quickly they began switching to the winning two-handed firing technique.

The Weaver stance was adopted by the practical shooting community for its speed and locked-in controlling features that are required during combat situations. With the birth and growth of the International Practical Shooting Confederation (IPSC) competitions, the Weaver stance was perfectly suited for live-fire matches that were beginning to simulate the handgun skills that are required during real situations. As such, the Weaver stance is used almost exclusively for the speed and control required. The Weaver is the newest two-handed firing stance around and is alrcady making inroads in the law enforcement community, at present being used by the FBI and other law enforcement organizations.

The Weaver stance uses an angled position, much like a boxer's stance, with the strong side to the rear. The strong arm, holding the handgun, is straight or slightly bent and held at an angle across the body, the support arm is sharply bent with the elbow pointing down, and the two-handed grip is applying isometric pressure by the strong hand pushing forward into the support hand, which is pulling back on the strong hand. Generally, this stance is noted for its ability to control heavy loads and stay locked on target for follow-up shots. It does not produce the most precise platform, but it does produce the most solid one. When the stance is properly locked in (which occurs almost instantly as the handgun is snapped up), the trigger can be manipulated as quickly as possible, yet the "hits" will stay in the center area of a combat target at close combat ranges. The Weaver is the most valid stance for the realities of close and quick lethal encounters.

Pros and cons of each stance.   These two firing stances are one of the hottest continuing debates in defensive pistolcraft. Many instructors attempt to muddy up the waters as to which is best. In reality, either firing stance will function just fine if it is practiced enough. Training is the key.

Many arguments are proffered as to which is superior, but both stances are very much alike. In fact, they are more alike than different. Here is a brief look at three of their main similarities and differences.

Three Main Similarities

1. Creating a locked-in firing platform is the most important function the stances perform, and they both do this very well, although the Weaver is far superior in control. Both use a locked-in two-handed grip with locked arms and shoulders. The way the support hand grips the strong hand is virtually the same for either stance. Each stance creates a locked-in platform from which to fire and control the handgun, yet being able to unlock for the realities of the search. When unlocked, the elbows bend and/or the arms pivot at the shoulders to assume ready positions while searching or after having fired on the threat(s). However, the Weaver is much more flexible during the search.

2. Both stances have the ability to be used in virtually any position or with any movement: kneeling, pivoting, traversing, firing around cover, or in virtually any awkward position where both hands are available to fire the handgun. Even though these factors are quite evident, shooters keep trying to show that one or the other cannot accomplish some of these functions. Either stance will work just fine through any of these positions and movements. (*Note*: These positions and movements are described thoroughly in Chapter 13.)

3. Both are used with the body's weight slightly forward and the knees slightly bent (unlocked). Many say that in the Weaver stance the body is straight and the knees are locked (from the original or classic Weaver stance). This is not true today; the knees are always slightly bent and the body's weight is slightly forward, as in a natural boxing stance. The Isosceles stance is far more prone to holding the body straight or leaning slightly to the rear. When either is used correctly, the knees will be slightly bent and the body's weight slightly forward.

Three Main Differences

1. The way the stances are angled to the target and the positioning of the arms are the first readily apparent differences, the Isosceles being straight and the Weaver being at an angle. The first complaint usually noted about the Weaver stance is that the body's side is angled to the threat and the officer's bulletproof vest does not usually protect the side. It is true that in the Weaver stance some part of the side is more exposed than in the straight-on Isosceles stance, but this is very slight. When someone wants to make this point, they show an exaggerated Weaver stance with the side facing almost fully forward for effect. Assume a Weaver stance and stand at a 40-degree angle to a mirror and see how small it is. But remember, this is also a plus when standing in the interview stance, with your gun side facing away from a possible threat (protecting your service handgun). If the threat attacks, no other movement is necessary, just snap the handgun out and fire, as you are already in the angled stance of the Weaver.

The positioning of the arms allows for greater flexibility when using the Weaver stance. In the Isosceles stance the arms and elbows are locked out, while in the Weaver stance the piston action of the arms is far more flexible. Flexibility is very important when dealing with the realities of searching and the obstacles encountered, and the Weaver is far more flexible.

2. The Weaver provides a much stronger grip and stance, with control being far superior. When firing, the Weaver stance will exert much greater recoil control and lock the handgun in position for follow-up shots. This is the main advantage of the Weaver—superior recoil control. Lock into both stances and feel the difference in the two-handed grip around the handgun and the control that can be exerted. You can feel the superior lock of the Weaver stance. Lock into either stance and have another person press down on the strong-hand wrist with a finger; the Isosceles is easily moved, while the Weaver is hard to budge. Press up on the wrist and the same thing will occur.

3. The Isosceles is more natural and easily assumed when training begins. Initially, the Isosceles is the easiest to learn, as it is simplistic in form, but the Weaver is learned quickly and with a slight amount of training feels and functions just as naturally. Some instructors state that the Weaver requires a larger number of bodily locks than the Isosceles, but in reality it is assumed just as fast and easily when trained in, automatically occurring and requiring no thought. With training and practice they function the same, although the Isosceles is easier to learn.

These are three principal ways the stances are similar and different. In reality, both stances will work just fine. At this juncture you must decide which two-handed firing stance you will use exclusively. Outside input may decide which firing stance you will use (usually, in the form of departmental firearms training procedures). If not, work with both the Isosceles and Weaver stances, engaging in both dry and live fire practice, and then make your selection. Once the selection is made, stick to it and do not switch back and forth.

Realities for either stance.   No matter which two-handed firing stance you use, there are realities for both.

1. Pick one of the stances and use it exclusively. Use only one of these two-handed stances and practice/use it the same way each time. You are working to develop a reflexive set that will function automatically with no thought needed. When you repeatedly train-in the same set of movements (producing the two-handed stance), they become a reflexive set that will serve you well when the time comes to use them during a lethal encounter. Movements that you practice repeatedly will turn into the reflexive sets that you will need to survive.

2. A good stance must be natural and comfortable. Once you begin to learn one of these two-handed firing stances, adjust it slightly until it feels right for you. Remember, you will produce the handgun in the same two-handed stance time after time, and the more natural and comfortable it is, the better you will do it. Adjust it until it feels right for you.

3. Keep your balance and be flexible. In the two-handed stance, your balance is centered and slightly forward (depending on the situation). Stand straight or slightly bent forward (to keep the weight slightly forward) and keep the knees slightly bent or unlocked. In a real situation you must be flexible and ready to move instantly in any direction; keep your balance and be ready to move.

When we say knees bent, we do not mean the deeply bent knees of the old FBI crouch firing position, but slightly bent or unlocked. During a lethal encounter, balance and flexibility are extremely important for instantaneous movement. Keep your knees bent and your weight forward.

(*Note*: Knees bent and weight forward will occur almost automatically during a lethal encounter as the body moves to respond. W. E. Fairbairn observed this physical reaction to danger over 70 years ago in a Shanghai alley crisscrossed with clotheslines. During a nighttime gun fight, an alley was moved through quickly. But later, when walking through the same alley after the encounter was over, the officers found that they could not stand straight and walk, as the clotheslines were in their way. What had occurred was a bodily reaction to danger. During the lethal encounter, their bodily response to danger had caused them to crouch enough so that they passed underneath the clotheslines without even noticing them.)

4. Do not add any extra movement into the mix. When it is time to shoot, the handgun is brought up in a straight line, punching it out into the line of sight, with only the arms and hands moving. Bring the handgun up to the head, not the head down to the handgun. When it is time to produce the handgun in a firing position, you see the threat and know where you want to hit; snap the handgun up into your line of sight and place the "hits." Also, become used to bringing the handgun up and firing from whatever position you are then in. Remember, any extra movement slows the process down.

5. You must practice both right and left two-handed firing, as you may need to switch the handgun depending on the situation. This can readily occur in very tight surroundings, or the need may arise when going around different sides of cover to limit body exposure.

THE ONE-HANDED HOLSTER-TO-STANCE REFLEX

The locked-in, two-handed firing stance is the focal point of defensive handgun use, but you must also train for a one-handed holster-to-stance reflex. Once the two-handed set has been learned, the one-handed set is an exact copy, except that the support hand is not used.

Situations may arise where only your strong hand can be used when firing the handgun, as the support hand is occupied performing some task. You must also train for this eventuality, as it is nonsurvival oriented to train only for two-handed use. The two-handed and one-handed sets are the same up through position 2 (the draw to belt-level position). As the strong hand punches the handgun out from the belt-level position, it goes straight up into the locked-out one-handed firing stance.

When locking-out one-handed, try not to hold the arm straight out from the body, but angle it slightly across the body for a better hold. Also, cant the strong arm in just slightly by rotating the whole arm and handgun toward the body side (if you are right-handed, slightly cant the handgun to the left). This will produce a more controlled position. The sights will be slightly canted, but just sight as you normally would. (*Note*: A further understanding of sighting with a canted handgun is discussed in Chapter 8.)

The one-handed holster-to-stance reflex must be practiced to train it in. Do not just practice the two-handed set; also practice the one-handed set.

USING THE HOLSTER-TO-STANCE REFLEX

The truth of speed.   The speed stroke begins with the draw and culminates in a locked-out two- or one-handed firing stance. The term "speed stroke" is used to associate the defensive stroke with the necessary speed in delivering it, as one fact stands out: The faster you snap the handgun up, the more time you will have to align it on the threat and fire. You must work on developing a smooth stroke that reduces all unnecessary movements. These must be reduced as much as possible for the quick, smooth defensive stroke that is needed. Start out slowly, then build speed as your smooth defensive stroke builds into a reflexive set. Only then increase your speed. It must be emphasized that you concentrate on producing smooth, not jerky motions as you practice. Ultimately, the smoother you are, the faster you are. Smooth = fast; fast = more time to shoot. Remember, the quicker you snap into a firing position, the more time you will have to shoot.

When dealing with the truth of speed you must thoroughly understand one fact: The fastest draw is having a handgun already in your hand before the action starts. The closer you are to the locked-out firing stance, the closer you are to the first shot. If you know that the encounter is about to start (and the situation is tactically correct), draw the handgun and become prepared to fire on the threat(s) before it attacks. Always be thinking your way through a situation to produce the survival advantage necessary to come out on top. Be as close to the first shot as possible.

Using the reflexive set. The holster-to-stance reflex minimizes all movements (no extraneous bodily movements), until they are the fewest and shortest between the holster and target. When you decide to use the defensive stroke, your eyes lock on the target and the handgun is snapped up into your line of sight; the head does not move by going up or down to the handgun. Only the arms and hands move, snapping the handgun up in a straight line from the holster to the target. Once the handgun clears the leather, it is not dipped down, then up, or brought up and then down. The handgun is punched out in a straight line to the target, acquiring the two-handed grip along the way. Learn and practice the holster-to-stance reflex slowly and smoothly until you get the feel; only then push for speed. Stay loose and natural (avoid tightening up) and you will be faster. To gauge yourself, par time from the draw until the first shot at 10 yards is 1.5 seconds.

4.33.

Figure 4.33 The holster-to-stance reflex is a fluid movement of all the combined parts.

SUMMARY

In this chapter we have covered the most important reflexive set in defensive handgun use, the holster-to-stance reflex. When combined with the firing reflex, covered in the following chapter, you will be able to draw and hit, either one- or two-handed, on demand of the situation, at any time.

5

Firing the Service Handgun: The Firing Reflex

Once the service handgun has been snapped into a locked-in firing stance, you are ready to apply the firing reflex to place "hits" on the threat(s). In chapter 4 we described the holster-to-stance reflex, which placed the service handgun in a two-handed firing stance in preparation for firing (one-handed was also covered). In this chapter we continue with the firing reflex, used to place "hits" from the firing stance.

THE REASONING BEHIND TWO REFLEXIVE SETS

Producing the handgun in a position to fire (the holster-to-stance reflex) is separated from firing the handgun (the firing reflex), thus producing two separate reflexive sets that can function together when instant shot placement is needed but can also function separately during the search or other defensive handgun use (when the handgun is snapped up in preparation for a threat that has not yet materialized or may be a mistake).

Many will say that this is accomplished by totally training the officer to snap up into a firing stance and fire instantly every time. The problem occurs when a single reflexive set (snapping up and firing, all at once) is the only one you are trained for. As we know, during stress you will revert to your trained-in reflexive sets and use them exclusively. What you were trained to do is what you will do. This is the function of training and it works well as long as the training is correct. If faulty training techniques are taught, faulty actions will occur on the street during lethal situations. The truth behind this statement is readily brought home when a murdered officer is found with empty cases in his pocket. During the lethal encounter, he wasted valuable reloading time by placing empty cases extracted from his revolver into his pocket, just as he had been taught on the range. Faulty training will appear as faulty actions on the street, always causing an officer problems, possibly causing his or her death or the death of an innocent.

The main problem of a single reflexive set is that under the stress of a possibly lethal situation, officers may fire too quickly before they know what they have—generally missing whatever they are aiming at, but sometimes wounding or killing an innocent on the scene. This occurs all too frequently, often with tragic results for both the innocent person and the officer involved. Luckily, most of these snapped-off shots go wild and miss their intended target. If constantly trained to fire at the end of a defensive firing stroke, officers are predisposed to do just that on the street, during the elevated stress of what they assume could possibly turn into a lethal encounter, whether real or not.

The firearms training that officers go through must insert conscious thought between the process of producing the handgun in a position to fire and the process of actually firing it. Two separate reflexive sets must be used, which can be used separately or combined to place an instantly needed shot, with the mind being the functional determinant that occurs between them. As such, officers are not preprogrammed to fire instantly at the end of the defensive stroke.

Improved Shot Placement

Training that incorporates these two reflexive sets will also improve the officers' ability to "hit." By separating the two reflexive sets, officers learn to use them both together and independently. Many shots fail to hit because the officers fired too quickly for the situation. They rushed the trigger, or flinched, or the sights were not properly aligned. In other words, they did not take that small fraction of a second to verify the sights and manipulate the trigger properly, which would have guaranteed a "hit." When the two reflexive sets are learned separately (along with combined use), officers begin to understand that different situations can have different firing speeds. Instead of rushing through firing and possibly missing, they can take whatever time is required for the problem at hand.

There is no reduction in firing speed because the sets are handled separately, but there is an increase in "hits." As will be shown, officers can fire the instant the firing stance is locked out—and firing does not occur any quicker than that.

The Firing Speed Rule

When the reflexive sets are dealt with as separate techniques (along with combined use), this helps officers understand the firing speed rule and train-in the reflexes to help make it work. First the two parts of firing speed must be understood. Presentation speed (the time it takes to present the handgun in a position to fire) + triggering speed (the time it takes to align the sights and manipulate the trigger) = firing speed (the total time it takes to bring the handgun up and fire). What must be understood is that the presentation and triggering speed can be two different speeds. Again, we are dealing with a constant and a variable. Presentation speed is the constant, as the handgun is always produced in a position to fire as fast as possible. Triggering speed is the variable, as it is never fixed (occurring anywhere from as soon as the handgun is locked out to a second or more).

The holster-to-stance reflex is the presentation speed (from the holster) and the firing reflex is the triggering speed. Thus these two sets will at times use two different speeds. The two different speeds are stated in the **firing speed rule**: ''You always snap up fast, but you cannot always fire quickly.'' Whenever you snap up into a firing stance, you do it as fast as possible (everytime), as the faster you snap up into the stance, the more time you will have to shoot. You go as fast as your level of skill safely allows, to snap the handgun up into a locked-in firing stance as fast as possible.

Firing the handgun does not as always work as quickly. If the threat is right on top of you, obviously you must instantly fire to ''hit'' the very close and large target. This has never been a problem if you lock-in your position. The problem occurs when the threat is farther away or harder to hit: behind cover, or farther away, or possibly has a hostage, or it is moving, and so on. You must have the trained-in ability to slow down enough to take the time needed to place your ''hits'' accurately. This is much easier to accomplish when the two sets are handled as separate functions; you learn right from the beginning that each can have a speed of its own.

As a police officer, your triggering speed during the many and varied situations will no doubt be instant to short, but it is a variable and dependent on the situation. Many seem to feel that all firing must be done as quickly as possible. To some degree they are right, but it must also be done as carefully as needed to place the ''hits.'' Everyone wants to be able to shoot fast, but quick and a miss is no good. You must condition yourself to take the time necessary to ''hit'' with every round and not let time pressure cause you to fire too quickly. This does not mean that you have to go slowly. You will still be firing from instantly to very quickly, but slowing down enough to verify the sights and manipulate the trigger properly. With training, you will fire faster than you have ever fired before, but carefully enough to get the ''hits.''

The key is knowing the amount of time needed to solve the different shot placement problems (situations) that occur and not letting time pressure cause you to go too fast. Different shot placement problems run the gambit from an instant-attacking threat 2 feet away, to a threat behind cover at 25 yards. Obviously, a different firing speed is needed to solve these two very different problems. These two are at opposite ends of the time scale. You must know the amount of time you will need to align the handgun and fire during any situation that may occur. This can be accomplished only by practicing for different situations and finding out how much ''time'' you will need. With practice, you will begin to understand how much time to use for each situation.

Time pressure becomes a very real problem during a lethal encounter. Even though you may have enough time to place the ''hits'' easily, the stress factor will cause you to go very fast, at times firing much too quickly. When the encounter occurs, you must instantly get down to the job at hand in a matter-of-fact manner, placing your "hits." Get to work; do not let time pressure you into missing. You must shoot as carefully as necessary to place the "hits" on the threat(s). If time pressure gets the better of you, you will in all probability begin fumbling and missing, with the time needed to place the "hits" increasing. When the situation is overpowering and time appears to be critically short, think of two actions when firing, front sight/squeeze or lock out/squeeze (the first for aimed fire and the second for unaimed fire). Get down to your firing to place your "hits." Let the threat(s) worry about the time pressure as you are accurately placing your "hits."

Let me state right now that the two reflexive sets are intertwined, part of each being part of the other. They are addressed separately to produce complete awareness of all the tenets employed in their use. The mind is the determinant, the functionary, the controlling link between these two sets. Let there be no mistake: The mind separates the sets or instantly combines them, depending on what the situation dictates.

Training That Incorporates Both Sets

Firearms training must use the two reflexive sets together and separately, training them in as separate and combined functions. You must not only train to fire as the two-handed firing stance is locked out, but incorporate part of the training to locking out into the stance without firing. This is accomplished by practicing the holster-to-stance reflex, snapping the handgun into the two-handed firing stance, with the handgun aligned on the target, without firing. This will reinforce what officers will be doing many hundreds of times throughout their police careers, snapping the handgun up in response to a perceived threat (obviously not firing when the stance is locked out). Officers must train for both separate and combined use, not just for combined use.

Departmental live-fire training. When departmental live-fire training is engaged in, virtually all of it must be devoted to firing the service handgun and qualifying with it. The main reason for this is the limited time set aside for firearms training by most departments. Most officers receive firearms training only once a year and it must be devoted to the very necessary live-fire practice. During live-fire training, 90 percent of the training must involve firing the service handgun. The firearms instructors must use this time to detect and clear up any bad firing habits that officers exhibit. In reality, little time exists on the firing line to do anything else. This translates into combining the two sets into one. When the handgun is produced in a position to fire, it is fired.

A small amount of the training during live fire can be devoted to the separate use of the reflexive sets. This mainly revolves around (1) drawing and snapping into a locked-out ready position (just below the line of sight), then at the signal engaging the target(s); (2) drawing and going to the belt-level position, then at the signal locking out and engaging the target(s); or (3) moving several steps forward with the handgun locked out into a ready position before engaging the target(s).

Away from the firing line, another instructor can have officers (not then on a live-fire relay) demonstrate their holster-to-stance reflex (defensive stroke) by engaging in dry practice. The handguns will be unloaded first, as dry firing will be engaged in during dry practice. The instructor will tell the officers whether or not to dry fire at the end of the defensive stroke, then watch as they snap into their firing stances. While observing this, the instructor can correct any faulty habits observed in both reflexive set and dry firing.

Individual Dry- and Live-Fire Practice and the Two Reflexive Sets

In both your individual dry- and live-fire practice, make sure that the holster-to-stance reflex and the firing reflex are trained in as both separate and combined use. During dry practice with an unloaded handgun, this is usually no problem and the sets are practiced both ways, as the temptation to fire a loaded handgun does not exist. During live-fire practice, though, avoid the tendency to combine the two reflexive sets to the virtual exclusion of their separate use. When engaging in both dry and live-fire practice, the sets are practiced in their combined form 70 percent of the time, separate use making up the remaining 30 percent. You must practice both ways; do not forget this.

When engaging in either form of practice, study your own form when snapping into the defensive stroke. Look for any improvements that will produce a smoother, quicker defensive stroke. Remember, smoother is quicker. Always work to improve your defensive stroke, eliminating any unnecessary movement and producing a smoother reflexive set of movements, both combined or separate in use. Constantly work to improve your defensive stroke; it will get better with time.

THE FIRING REFLEX

The ability to place "hits," by using the firing reflex, must become another one of your trained-in reflexive sets. When it is time to fire, the four parts of the firing reflex function together automatically to place the "hits." The four parts are: the locked-in firing stance (both one- and two-handed), combat sight picture, trigger manipulation, and follow-through. Each part must be performed correctly to place your "hits" accurately.

Locked-In Firing Stance

The techniques involved in locking into and using a one- or two-handed firing stance were covered in Chapter 4. These centered on the holster-to-stace reflex, which ended in a locked-out Weaver or Isosceles two-handed firing stance. Several of the points are reinforced in this section. (*Note*: The firing reflex will be described with all references to the two-handed firing stance. One-handed firing is almost an exact reflection of two-handed firing, except that only one hand holds the handgun.)

The locked-in firing stance produces a steady platform from which to control and fire the handgun. The locked-in two-handed grip and arms, creating the platform, are reproduced exactly the same way each time the stance is assumed, thus consistently producing the handgun in the same position every time it is snapped into. This is the key factor in using any firing stance: Use it the same way each time. Once a stance is picked (either the Weaver or Isosceles stance), it is used exclusively. Do not switch between the stances; use only one.

Balance must be maintained when using your stance. The body's balance is slightly forward, with the knees slightly bent. When balance is maintained, the platform can turn a maximum of 135 degrees to each side (from aiming at a target directly to the front), forming a 270-degree firing arc without moving the feet or being off balance. As such, fire can be brought to bear on almost any area around you, except the 90 degrees directly to the rear. (*Note*: It is true that you can contort your body to fire completely around the circle, but this is foolish, as you are not properly balanced and are not flexible. A simple and small movement of one foot will easily turn you to cover that area, while being balanced and flexible.) Balance and flexibility are very important when searching with the handgun and/or firing it. Only through being properly balanced do you also maintain the flexibility necessary to move instantly in any direction. Make sure that the platform is properly balanced, weight slightly forward and knees slightly bent. You will know when the balance is right.

The firing stance must be practiced extensively by engaging in "dry practice." Only by repetitive practice will you train-in the two-handed firing stance. With the handgun unloaded (check it twice), use the defensive stroke to produce it in a position to fire, either dry firing at the end or not. Your main concern is to train-in the platform so that it becomes second nature, becoming a very familiar, comfortable position. If it is not, work on adjusting it until the stance feels proper. A little work can really make a difference here. Everyone is different; fit the stance to your unique bodily configuration.

The grip must be correct and firm. The two-handed grip must be firm, but not to the point where it causes the handgun to tremble slightly; if it does, the grip is too tight. The wrists are locked and the hands are pushing into one another, applying isometric pressure. Make sure that both hands fit together properly, with as much contact on the grip as possible, leaving no open spaces on the handgun's grip. The support-hand thumb is locked down on top of the strong-hand thumb and applying downward pressure, and the support-hand index finger is applying upward pressure on the bottom of the trigger guard for a very strong grip. This will create a locked-in two-handed grip that the arms will lock into position.

The platform must be locked in and steady, to control the handgun when firing. A locked-in platform prepares you for the next two parts, sight picture and trigger manipulation.

Combat Sight Picture

The sights on the handgun are used to align the handgun's bore on a precise point on the target. When using the sights, you must use a correct sight picture, which is the proper alignment of three things: rear sight, front sight, and target. The front sight will be the most important to you and will always be "in focus." The front sight is the key to a correct combat sight picture.

You strive for a correct sight picture (proper alignment) for each and every shot, but at normal encounter distances this is not always possible. Snapping up into your trained-in firing stance at the target will place the handgun generally on target, then verifying and/or correcting the sight alignment will show that the handgun is exactly on target before firing. Accuracy (which is relative to the problem at hand) will depend on a correctly aligned sight picture. Given enough time and distance from the threat, the manipulation of the trigger should fire the handgun only when the correct sight picture is attained. Sight picture and trigger control are the two most important factors in attaining "hits."

When discussing and describing sight picture, we use today's predominant handgun sight design . . . the Patridge sights. The sight was designed by E. E. Patridge, a notable American handgun shooter of the 1880s and 1890s. The sights consist of a square post front sight and a square notch rear sight. When aligned, the square post will fit within the square notch. The correct sight picture is achieved when the top of the front and rear sights are level and the front sight is centered in the rear sight, with an equal amount of sidelight on either side of the front sight when viewed through the rear sight. Virtually every service handgun has this style of sights or a close variation. The correct sight picture is shown here, with several examples of incorrect sight pictures.

5.1.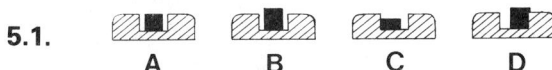
A   B   C   D

Figure 5.1 Four sight pictures are shown with the black front sight and shaded rear sight. A correct sight picture (A) shows the top of both sights level and equal sidelight. The other three are incorrect sight pictures, with bullets striking: high (B), low and left (C), and high and right (D).

Sighting shift from threat to front sight.   While engaging in dry fire practicing, you must practice your sighting shift with the sight alignment. When the handgun is brought up into your line of sight with the target, the sighting shift occurs as you stop focusing on the target and shift your focus to the front sight. As in a real situation, you focus on the target (exactly where you want to hit) before the sights are brought up. The "sighting shift" occurs the instant the sights come into your line of sight. At that moment, the eye shifts its focus from the target to the front sight, which now appears sharp and clear (the target and rear sight are blurred, although easily recognized). The sighting shift is the first thing done when the sights are snapped up and is critical to placing your "hits" effectively, as you must concentrate on the front sight when firing.

This is very difficult to train-in, as the overwhelming urge is to focus on the threat(s) during a lethal encounter. But training will give you the ability to focus on the front sight as you revert to your trained-in reflexive sets during the encounter.

The Key Is the Front Sight.   The key to a correct combat sight picture is to focus on the front sight. With the front sight in focus, it will appear very sharp and clear, the rear sight and target being out of focus and appearing slightly blurred or fuzzy. When the action begins and while it is occurring, you should be thinking of two things for every shot: front sight/squeeze. The front sight must be in focus and you are squeezing the trigger.

How Quick Is the Human Eye?   During close encounters, the sights may or may not have been used; often, the officer does not even know for sure. It is rather amazing that the officer, after the encounter is over with, does not know. But so many things occur instantly during a very quick, stress-filled encounter that this can easily happen. The officer may have used the sights or looked over or through them, but may not remember. At the officer's maximum speed, even though he or she does not remember, the human eye may have accomplished the task.

As amazing as it sounds, the human eye can attain an accurate image in the small time of one one-hundredth of a second. Your eye can verify the sight picture much more quickly than you can fire. Obviously within this extremely fast fraction of a second, there is not enough time to correct the sight picture, only to verify it.

The instant the sights snap up into your line of sight, the sighting shift occurs and you are verifying and/or correcting the sight picture very quickly as the trigger finger is squeezing the trigger and the handgun fires. This can be done very fast. Your locked-in stance has no doubt produced the handgun on target or almost on target and verification and/or slight correction of the sights can be accomplished almost instantly as the front sight is focused on. It occurs very quickly.

Is One Eye or Two Better When Firing?   Some officers keep one eye open to sight with when firing, and some officers keep both eyes open when firing. Either method will work equally well in daylight with nothing else happening, but what about low-light firing or if a malfunction occurs? For the majority of encounters in which a police officer may be involved, only one eye should be used to aim with. When actually firing, the nonaiming eye is closed and opens instantly when you stop firing. At all other times the nonaiming eye is open.

You should close the nonaiming eye when firing for three reasons:

1. When firing in low-light conditions, the service handgun's muzzle flash can cause you to be blinded for several seconds while your eyes readapt to the surroundings. By closing the nonaiming eye when firing and instantly opening when the firing is finished, the nonaiming eye is not affected by the muzzle flash and can see fine. Even if the aiming eye is momentarily blinded, the nonaiming eye can take over. Remember, the nonaiming eye is closed only when actually firing; at all other times it is open.

2. In case a cartridge malfunction occurs and something is blown back into your face, the nonaiming eye is somewhat protected and may not be hurt. On the firing range everyone wears safety glasses when firing, to avoid such an occurrence. On the street this is impractical, but the nonaiming eye can be protected to some degree by closing it when firing.

3. When the nonaiming eye is closed, you tend to concentrate more fully on the front sight and the firing that is occurring. Fully concentrating on stopping the instantly occurring lethal threat is, at that moment, vital to your survival. Many say that action will cut down your peripheral vision and that you may miss another suddenly appearing threat. In reality you reduce your peripheral vision by only about 45 degrees when one eye is closed, with about 135 degrees still visible (of the 180-degree arc seen when both eyes are open). Try it and see: Look straight ahead and close one eye, then see how much of the 180-degree arc you can still see.

As soon as the exchange is over, the nonaiming eye is instantly opened to include the 45 degrees that was left out. In reality, the firing will usually be over with in 1 to 2 seconds as you stop the threat(s) and instantly expand your vision to include the whole encounter zone. Taking all the information into consideration, it is clear that the nonaiming eye should be closed when firing.

Combat Sights. When setting up a service handgun for defensive use, the sights should be set up as combat sights, where the point of aim/point of impact are the same (where you aim is where the bullet will "hit"). Thus the part of the target that is in the middle of the front sight will be "hit." Target sight settings, which use a 6-o'clock hold, should be avoided. The 6-o'clock hold is where the sights are aligned on the bottom of the bull's-eye to hit the center of the circle (holding directly under the target—hence a 6-o'clock hold).

The sights should also be zeroed (set) for 25 yards, which will mean they will be virtually right on from 0 to 25 yards. When sighting in, use sandbags on a shooting bench (placing the hands on them), or a good locked-in prone position, to steady the handgun and produce the tight groups necessary for you to sight in. Always be in the shade when sighting in. If in the sun, the shadows can throw off the sight picture and bullet strike. Fire a three- to four-shot group and then make the necessary adjustments. When firing make sure that the handgun is steady, straight up and down, and use the single-action firing mode for the smoothest let-off (a surprise break every time). Continue this process until the hits are grouped in the center of the target, then fire three more groups of five or six shots to make sure that the handgun is sighted in.

If your handgun has adjustable sights, the rear sight will contain all the adjustments for windage (to either side) and elevation (up and down). Adjusting the rear sight is simple: Move the sight in the SAME direction that you want your group to move. For elevation: If the group is low and you want to raise it, raise the rear sight; if the group is high and you want to lower it, lower the rear sight. For windage: If the group is left and you want to bring it to the right, move the rear sight to the right; if the group is right and you want to move it to the left, move the rear sight to the left. If your revolver has fixed sights, they are usually part of the milling cuts in the frame and nothing is adjustable. If your automatic has fixed sights, the rear sight is set in a dovetail cut in the slide and windage is adjustable by drifting it either right or left in the dovetail. For elevation adjustments, only the front sight can be filed. All sight settings should be done at the departmental range and verified by the range instructor.

Trigger Manipulation

The main shooting problem each officer must solve is the smooth and timely manipulation of the trigger. There is quite a bit to learn about proper trigger manipulation, more than you think. Once you know how to manipulate the trigger, improved manipulating skills will come only through extensive practice—both live- and dry-fire practice. Trigger manipulation can make or break any shot and is the most important factor in placing "hits."

The process of manipulating the trigger seems simple: The handgun is brought up and locked into position as the sights are aligned, with the front sight being in focus, and increasing pressure is applied to the trigger until the handgun fires. The trigger finger manipulates the trigger by taking up the slack and applying a smooth, increasing pressure until the handgun fires. This increasing pressure must be smoothly applied in a timely manner, without "jerking" the trigger.

Proper trigger manipulation is a combination of three factors: (1) correct trigger finger placement for the firing mode used, (2) smoothly applied increasing pressure by the trigger finger, and (3) applying the pressure in a timely manner for the situation. In other words, the trigger finger is placed on the trigger correctly and smoothly applies pressure, yet quickly enough for the situation, until the handgun fires. The first two work together whenever the trigger is pulled, while the last one depends on the situation.

Trigger-finger placement for the firing mode used.   Two areas of the trigger finger are used when pulling or pressing the trigger, the "first joint" and the "pad." Each of these goes with a firing mode: the first joint with the double-action mode and the pad with the single-action mode.

The "first-joint" position places the bend of the first joint on the outside edge of the trigger. When the trigger finger enters the trigger guard, the bend will be placed on the first edge of the trigger, with the area directly forward of the bend (toward the tip) wrapping over the face of the trigger. [*Note*: The bend can be placed in the center of the trigger, but two things can occur: (1) for a small hand, the trigger finger may not reach and/or the master grip will have to be changed for it to reach; or (2) for a large hand, the tip of the trigger finger may make contact with the opposite side of the trigger guard, directly to the rear of it, and obstruct a smooth pull.]

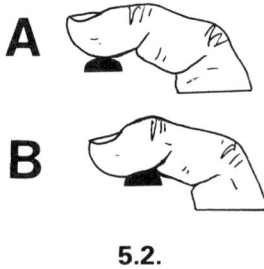

A

B

5.2.

Figure 5.2 The pad position, with the pad directly centered on the trigger (A). The first-joint position, with the joint positioned at the edge of the trigger (B).

The "pad" position places the center of the fingertip directly on the face of the trigger—centered on it.

In all double-action firing, the first-joint position is used for the increased leverage necessary for the longer and heavier double-action trigger pull. The longer trigger travel and increased trigger weight require more trigger-finger engagement and leverage to overcome the greater weight of the trigger. The bend and more of the trigger finger's tip wrapped across the face of the trigger improve leverage.

In all single-action firing, the pad position is used for the shorter and lighter single-action trigger press. The shorter trigger travel and lighter trigger weight require less trigger-finger engagement and leverage to press the trigger.

Smoothly applied increasing pressure. For each of the two firing modes, there is also a method for manipulating the trigger: the double-action pull and the single-action press. Both are basically the same, one smooth continuous motion of the trigger, building up to a surprise break (you are not precisely sure when the handgun will fire during the pressure buildup), but they are slightly different.

The Double-Action Pull. In the double-action firing mode, the distance the trigger travels is longer and the amount of pressure that must be applied by the trigger finger is greater. When pulling the trigger, you take up the slack, then pull the trigger directly back as one smooth, continuous motion to fire the handgun (which will mechanically cock the hammer back and drop it). A smooth continuous movement of the trigger, with no stopping or slowing down, is required to help overcome the heavier double-action trigger pull.

Once the slack is taken up, the trigger is pulled smoothly through its travel arc, the mechanical arc of the trigger as it is pressed rearward. The arc can be felt as you are pulling it through and the hammer can be seen coming back before it drops; as such, the surprise break is not as dramatic as with the single-action trigger press. But still remember not to rush the trigger, possibly "jerking" it. The trigger pull is still a smooth, fluid movement, with no interruptions throughout the pull (either slowing down or going faster). Sometimes the tendency is to rush the trigger at the end of the pull; do not let this occur in your practice. At first, the sights may move a little too much, but with practice a smooth, fluid, straight-through pull will come.

Once the shot has been fired, the trigger must be released to travel forward and reengage for the next shot. If the trigger is not fully released, it will not engage the hammer cocking mechanism or it will only rotate the cylinder of a D-A revolver, without firing it. The trigger finger maintains contact as the trigger is instantly released; just do not let the trigger go. The trigger release must be controlled or this may "jerk" the handgun and cause problems. Control is exerted by keeping the trigger finger on the trigger when releasing the trigger forward (controlling it forward). This is done very quickly in preparation for the next shot; there is nothing slow about it. When the trigger stops (as it is all the way forward) the trigger finger stays on it and does not continue forward, leaving the trigger. The trigger finger is instantly ready for another pull.

The Single-Action Press. In single-action, the trigger travels only a very small distance and the pressure applied is a third to a half that of the double-action trigger pull. When using the single-action firing mode, you take up the slack (only in the S-A auto, not in the single-action mode of a D-A revolver, as there is no "slack"), then press the trigger directly to the rear by increasing the pressure smoothly until the handgun fires (by disengaging the sear holding the hammer cocked and it falls). The press is a very short, smooth increase in pressure on the trigger, which suddenly drops the already cocked hammer, for the surprise break.

Once the shot has been fired, the trigger finger pressure must be released slightly for the trigger to reengage. This will almost occur by itself when the handgun fires, as the trigger comes forward only a very small distance. Just release the trigger finger pressure while maintaining contact with the trigger.

(*Note*: In the foregoing, we were referring to the S-A auto and its single-action firing mode. When using the single-action firing mode of the D-A revolver, there is no slack to be taken out. The trigger manipulation begins when it is pressed directly to the rear by smoothly increasing the pressure until the surprise break occurs. Also, after firing the D-A revolver in the single-action mode, the trigger must be fully released and the hammer thumb-cocked for another shot in the single-action mode.)

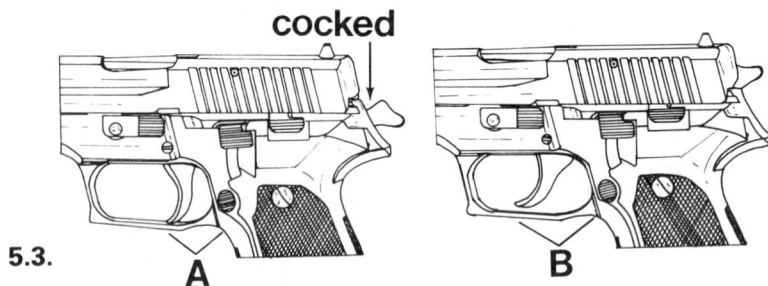

Figure 5.3 The single-action press, for the shorter trigger travel and lighter trigger weight (A). The double-action pull, for the longer trigger travel and increased trigger weight (B).

Trigger Manipulation to This Point.   Up to this point the trigger manipulation factors combine into two separate sets, one for double-action and the other for single-action.

1. Double-joint pull. Whenever using the double-action firing mode, the trigger finger's "first-joint" position is used, and the trigger manipulation is a "pull" for the longer/heavier trigger.
2. Single-pad-press. Whenever using the single-action firing mode, the trigger finger's "pad" position is used, and the trigger manipulation is a "press" for the shorter/lighter trigger.

These factors are used every time you fire the handgun. They do not change but are used together every time. (*Note*: The DA/SA switch is the one exception and is covered later in this section.) Once they are practiced together, they become trained-in and function smoothly. Continual practice with both dry and live fire is needed to maintain your trigger manipulation skills.

The last remaining factor is manipulating the trigger in a timely manner. The question is: How fast will you have to pull or press the trigger? This is answered by the situation and what is occurring.

Manipulating the trigger in a timely manner.   Timing the trigger, or how fast you will have to shoot, is very important and depends on the situation. It will depend mainly on the size and distance of the target, with the trigger manipulation being either a slap or a squeeze.

The Slap.   If the target is close and large enough, a slap is used to manipulate the trigger quickly. Trigger pressure will begin as soon as the muzzle comes on any part of the target, although the sights are not locked up, verified, and/or corrected to place your "hit." As the handgun is coming up, you are instantly prepared to slap the trigger when you lock on the target. At this close distance, you need to fire as quickly as possible. The slap is not a jerk, but a very quick squeeze. A precise sight picture is not needed at these close ranges, merely placing the front sight on the threat or using stance-directed fire.

The Squeeze.   If the target is farther away and/or smaller, a squeeze is used to manipulate the trigger. The sights are snapped up, verified and/or corrected as the squeeze is begun, and the squeeze continues to a surprise break, firing the handgun.

You must "hit" with the first bullet and every one after it. When the threat(s) is very close, a very quick slap of the trigger is required, but if the threat(s) is farther away, a more deliberate squeeze of the trigger must be used to get a "hit." Time is almost always working against you during an encounter and you must time the trigger for the situation at hand. You must learn to judge the speed of your shots depending on the situation and structure.

Trigger manipulation for the three service handguns.   Trigger manipulation is separated into the techniques for double- and single-action handguns. The following outlines the trigger manipulation for each of the three service handguns.

D-A Revolver.   The "double-joint pull" is used for the longer/heavier trigger of the D-A revolver. Just smoothly and continuously pull the trigger directly to the rear. Virtually all defensive use will be in the double-action mode; if the single-action firing mode is used, simply cock the hammer and use the trigger finger's pad for a single-action press (this is rarely used).

Also, make sure that the trigger release is smooth and controlled. Many officers just release the trigger and allow it to fly forward. The trigger must be controlled, both when pulling and when releasing. If not controlled, it may affect the next shot. Once fired in the double-action mode, the trigger is controlled forward (the trigger finger always maintaining contact with the trigger) and then the slack is taken up in preparation for the next shot (this is not slow at all, but a very quick action). When the sights are aligned, the pull again fires the revolver. Immediately reestablish the sight picture after each shot.

(*Note*: When firing, all trigger manipulation is one-stage: The trigger is pulled back in one smooth continuous movement until the revolver fires. A competition trick is the two-stage triggering technique, in which the trigger is pulled back in two stages: The trigger is pulled most of the way back so that the hammer stops and appears to be cocked as the pressure is maintained, the sights are then aligned precisely, then a finishing press of the trigger brings the hammer back a very short distance and drops it. Basically, these competitors are trying to make the double-action act like a single-action. Two-stage triggering has no place in any police firearms training.)

D-A Automatic.   A unique triggering situation occurs with the D-A auto, due to the DA/SA switch. The first shot for the D-A auto will be the same as a D-A revolver, the longer and heavier trigger pull. For the first shot in the double-action mode, the double-joint-pull is used. Once the first round has been fired, the remainder of the rounds fired will be in the single-action mode (the hammer being cocked back by the action of the slide every time the automatic is fired). But for the remainder of the "initial" shots (before the first lull in the action), the trigger finger placement will still be the first joint even though firing in a single-action mode. Though continuing to use the first joint, much less trigger travel and pressure will be used for the single-action mode. In other words, maintain the same trigger-finger relationship until the initial exchange is over with. Once the initial string is over with and a lull occurs in the action (the firing stops), the trigger finger can then be instantly adjusted to the single-pad-press for the remaining action. The double-joint-pull must be used exclusively for the initial string of rounds fired, usually during the opening ceremonies of a lethal encounter.

Many shooters mistakenly shift their trigger finger placement after the first shot is fired, for DA/SA switch. They correctly use the double-joint-pull for the first shot, then for the second shot they switch to the single-pad-press midstream during the firing. Switching in midstream causes problems. The DA/SA switch should occur after the initial exchange is over with and there is a "lull in the action." The first-joint trigger-finger placement should be maintained for the initial string of rounds fired, just exerting lighter pressure for the single-action trigger manipulation. Once the initial exchange is over with, the switch to the single-pad-press can be made.

When firing the D-A auto, keep the thumb clear of the slide release, which could be either pushed up, locking the slide back while you are firing, or held down, keeping the slide from locking back after the last round (run dry).

S-A Automatic. The S-A-auto is the simplest to describe, as all firing will be in the single-action mode. As such, the single-pad-press is used for the shorter-lighter trigger press.

The trigger finger does not touch the trigger before the safety is pushed "off." This can easily send off an unintentional discharge as soon as the safety is pushed "off." Only after the safety is pushed "off" does the trigger finger come in contact with the trigger to take up the slack in preparation to fire (of course, they may occur almost as one, when a quick shot is needed). When firing the S-A auto, the strong-hand thumb remains on top of the safety lever it pushed "off," keeping downward pressure on it. This is done to keep the thumb from accidentally knocking the safety back "on" when firing and stopping the auto from firing the next round.

The trigger finger as a separate function from the hand. When firing the handgun, the hand functions in two ways: to hold the handgun in a controlled/stable position and to fire it. To perform these two functions, we separate the trigger finger from the rest of the hand. Always think of the trigger finger as being separate from the rest of the hand when firing. As such, the whole hand remains stable, with only the trigger finger manipulating (pulling or pressing) the trigger. Many officers milk the handgun by moving and squeezing the other fingers of the hand when firing. This must not be done, as it will make the platform unstable and cause misses. Remember, only the trigger finger moves when firing.

When practicing, train in the separate movement of the trigger finger while the rest of the hand remains steady (not moving at all, just maintain the master grip). The support hand must also remain steady when firing, as it supports the strong hand. Once the hands are locked together in the two-handed firing grip, only the trigger finger moves when firing. This must be accomplished to "hit" with the handgun consistently.

The surprise break and "jerking" the trigger. Firing the handgun should be a surprise every time; do not anticipate when the handgun will fire or you will probably jerk the trigger, causing a miss. Keep the handgun steady, with sights aligned, and apply smooth continuing pressure "until it happens." The surprise break is that easy; let it happen by itself and do not try to force it. Most of the forcing comes at the very end of the trigger manipulation, as officers become impatient and want the shot to be fired *now*. You must resist the temptation to force the handgun to fire. Forcing the handgun to fire will not increase your firing speed, but it will greatly increase your chances of a miss. Focus on the front sight, increase trigger pressure, and let the handgun fire; let the surprise break happen. Take the time to practice this technique and use it mentally whenever engaging in dry- and live-fire practice (especially important when first practicing and training in trigger manipulation). Also note that the surprise break can be done very fast; it can be applied however fast you are firing.

Jerking the trigger or flinching occurs in anticipation of firing the handgun and the associated recoil and noise. They can only be lessened or removed with practice. Try not to anticipate the precise moment of discharge, but let the surprise break happen by smoothly increasing the pressure on the trigger until the handgun goes off. You must train-in the proper trigger manipulation, while the hands, arms, and shoulders exert the proper control and hold the handgun steady.

A sloppy or jerked trigger will cause you to miss your intended target. You may "hit" the threat, but you will certainly not hit it where you want to. This is critical, as you are trying to produce fight-stopping "hits" on a threat who is trying to shoot and kill you. "Hitting" the threat only somewhere (not in a vital area) will in all probability not produce enough shock to its system to render it incapable of firing on you. Just "hitting" the threat is not enough; you must stop it. Remember, you must "hit" with the first bullet and every bullet after it.

Taking Up Trigger Slack.   Trigger slack is the initial, and extremely small, first movement of a trigger from its rest position. When the trigger finger first touches the trigger, the slack is taken up by a very small amount of rearward pressure until you can feel it stop. Slack is found in all three service handguns and their firing modes, except one combination: No trigger slack is present when a D-A revolver is used in the single-action firing mode. Do not attempt to take up any slack when using the D-A revolver in the single-action firing mode, as the first movement of the trigger will fire the revolver.

When taking up the slack in the trigger, there is a definite pressure wall (increased pressure level) that is reached when the slack is taken up. Unload your service handgun (check it twice) and practice taking up the slack by touching the trigger and pulling it slightly back until it stops at the pressure wall. The trigger will move rearward an extremely small distance until it stops and only greater trigger-finger pressure would make it continue rearward, firing the handgun. Practice this by taking up the slack at position 4, at the end of your defensive stroke. Continued trigger-finger pressure at this point is all that is needed to fire the handgun.

(*Note*: If using the S-A auto, when unsure if you are going to fire, the trigger finger touches the trigger but does not take up the slack. Once you are sure you are going to fire, the slack is taken up just before you fire.)

When the Trigger Finger First Makes Contact with the Trigger and Trigger Timing

When first to touch the trigger. At what point do you put your trigger finger into the trigger guard, on the trigger, in preparation for firing? The rule is: The trigger finger enters the trigger guard and makes contact with the trigger only once the handgun's muzzle is pointed at any part of the threat's body or in its general direction and the handgun is beyond position 3, with the muzzle well in front of your body. Two factors must be present before the trigger finger enters the trigger guard: The muzzle must be pointing at the threat or in its direction and the handgun must be in front of your body. There is only one exception to the rule: using the speed rock to stop an extremely close threat, with the handgun being fired while held close to the body.

Both factors must be present before the trigger finger enters the trigger guard. You must first identify the threat and the need to stop it. The handgun is now brought up toward the threat. As soon as the muzzle is pointed at any part of the threat's body or in its general direction (as the threat may have moved behind cover), a fired bullet would "hit" the threat or be directed toward its location and not a danger to anyone else. By the time the muzzle is up, the handgun would be at least in position 3 and well in front of your body. This keeps you safe from your own handgun, as the trigger finger enters the trigger guard only after the handgun is in front of your body and pointed away from it (only after position 3). The first part of the rule places you on target before touching the trigger, while the second part of the rule keeps you safe from your own handgun.

At no time does the trigger finger enter the trigger guard before position 3 (with only one exception, the speed rock). This also includes any one-handed firing and point shooting techniques, as the trigger finger enters the trigger guard only after the handgun is out at position 3, in front of your body. After position 3, the trigger finger enters the trigger guard and touches the trigger in preparation for firing. The trigger manipulation from then on depends on the situation: how close the threat is and what size target is presented.

The speed rock is the only exception to placing the trigger finger into the trigger guard before position 3. If the threat is extremely close (arm's length or touching distance), the handgun will have to be fired from waist level, with the handgun held very close to the body, referred to as the speed rock. When firing from the speed rock, the support hand would be held up to fend off the threat and is well away from the handgun's muzzle. This is the only time the handgun is fired while held close to the body. At all other times, the trigger finger enters the trigger guard only when the handgun is out in front of the body after position 3.

Trigger timing. The handgun is brought up and held in position, with the sights aligned, and increasing pressure is applied to the trigger until the handgun fires. The trigger finger enters the trigger guard and touches the trigger as the handgun is coming up, after position 3 and before the front sight comes into view at position 4. Once the front sight comes into view the trigger slack is taken up, the sight picture is verified and/or corrected (properly aligned on the threat), and continued pressure is applied to the trigger until the handgun fires. The question is: How do you time the trigger, using the slap or the squeeze, and when do you start the trigger pressure?

We begin with the firing speed rule: "You always snap up fast, but you cannot always fire quickly." The rule is divided into two distinct timing parts: (1) snapping the handgun up as fast as possible, and (2) manipulating the trigger as fast as the situation allows. Timing the trigger is also divided into two parts: (1) inserting the trigger finger into the trigger guard and touching the trigger, and (2) taking up the slack (if appropriate) and applying the trigger pressure to fire the handgun. The first parts of each are combined: As you snap up the handgun as fast as possible the trigger finger enters the trigger guard and touches the trigger (between positions 3 and 4). The second parts of each are also combined: As position 4 is reached and you see the front sight the trigger slack is taken up and you continue the trigger pressure to fire the handgun, or stop the trigger pressure not to fire the handgun (depending on the situation). Whether or not you fire depends on the situation and what may instantly occur.

Once locked out in your two-handed firing stance at position 4, with the trigger finger on the trigger and the slack taken up, you are instantly ready to respond to the situation. Remember, your conscious decision to fire or not fire can be made and then changed up to the point where the handgun fires; a split second before you fire you can stop and not fire. In most cases you have already decided to fire before the handgun comes up, as the threat is a real and continuing one, but if the situation instantly changes, you can stop and not fire the handgun. (*Note:* There will also be times when you are locked out at position 4 and the trigger finger is just lightly resting on the trigger, without the slack being taken up.)

The remainder of trigger timing is the trigger manipulation at position 4. The situation will dictate how much time will be needed to make the shot(s). When position 4 is reached, focus on the front sight and fire as carefully as needed to place the "hits." Generally, the closer the threat is, the larger the target area and the faster the shot(s) can be fired: conversely, the farther away the threat is, the smaller the target area, and more time must be taken when firing the shot(s). Obviously, situations can occur where a very close threat has a very small target area, due to being behind cover, and the firing speed may not be as fast. You must be able to judge the firing speed necessary for the problem at hand and "time the trigger" for it.

When firing at a very close threat, with a large target area, the firing speed can be extremely fast, with only the briefest focus on front sight and/or locked-out stance to align the handgun on target, and the trigger is slapped. When firing at a threat farther away, with a smaller target area, the firing speed will not be as fast, as the sights must be more critically aligned and the trigger more carefully squeezed to keep the sights aligned when firing.

Trigger timing can be learned only by practicing and finding out how much trigger manipulating time is needed for the many different shooting problems (depending on whether the threat is close or farther away and whether the target area is large or small). Learn your trigger timing beforehand.

Trigger Manipulation for a Very Close Threat. When the threat is very close (from arm's length out to 10 feet), an instantaneous shot will be needed exactly as position 4 is reached (just as the two-handed firing stance is locked-out). Just as before, the trigger finger is placed in the trigger guard and touches the trigger after position 3. But instantly, the trigger slack is taken up and the trigger-finger pressure continued before position 4 is reached, usually firing the handgun the instant the sights come up to eye level and relying on stance-directed fire to place the "hits." As such, you are firing the instant the two-handed firing stance is locked out. What also may occur is that the handgun will fire midstroke, just before position 4 is reached. If that occurs, the bullet will still "hit" the threat, as the muzzle is well up and pointed out. At such close proximity, instantaneous "hits" must be used, at or slightly before position 4.

Speed, Grip, and Trigger Manipulation. An understanding of the relationship between speed, grip, and trigger manipulation is important. When a lethal situation occurs and the service handgun is quickly presented in a position to fire, trigger manipulation is one of the key factors. When the handgun was quickly drawn and snapped up through the holster-to-stance reflex (speed being one of your main concerns when dealing with a life-threatening situation), an improper grip can easily occur. But if the trigger is manipulated properly, even while the handgun is held improperly, the shot(s) will "hit" the target. It is two halves of the same truth: If the trigger press is proper, a poor grip will cause little problem; if the trigger press is poor, it matters little if the grip was good. When we say poor grip, the strong hand is not gripping the handgun properly (usually due to a faulty initial grab on the holstered handgun), but still maintains control over the handgun.

An excellent demonstration can be given with any handgun to prove that even with a poor grip (from less-than perfect to downright bad), the handgun can be fired effectively if the trigger press is proper. Hold a handgun, either revolver or automatic, only with the thumb and second finger, then aim at a target 7 yards away and fire one shot by pressing the trigger properly with the trigger finger. It seems amazing to many officers that with this exceptionally skimpy grip, the handgun can be fired effectively, placing center "hits" on the target. When the officer firing is comfortable firing one shot, go to two and three shots in a row, all to prove that even with an improper grip on the handgun, a proper press of the trigger will effectively place the "hits." Many will also be amazed that the handgun does not fall out of the officer's hand when firing with this skimpy grip. The ultimate amazement to many will occur when the demonstration is done with a Colt .45 auto, which everybody somehow thinks kicks like a mule. Holding and firing it with two fingers will instantly put this falsehood to rest.

(*Note*: Complete control must be exerted over any officers engaged in this demonstration. In reality, only the range officer need demonstrate this.)

With regard to speed, speed is always strived for, but the trigger is not rushed. When working to increase your firing speed, practice speeding up the defensive stroke, but do not rush the trigger.

Trigger creep and overtravel.   The trigger action should be slicked up to take care of any creep or overtravel. Creep is any motion or an irregular feel in the trigger as it is pulled to the rear (after slack is taken out) just before or on the break. You will feel something that is not right (a little grab or roughness) instead of the smooth let-off you should feel. Overtravel is any excessive movement of the trigger after the sear breaks and the hammer falls to fire the handgun, or a double-action mechanism cocks and drops the hammer. Obviously, some degree of overtravel must exist for the handgun to function reliably, but excessive overtravel can cause a slight jerking of the handgun. A crisp, smooth trigger is the desired end of a trigger job by a gunsmith and a delight when manipulating the trigger.

On any work involving the trigger, care must be taken not to lighten up the engagement too much or misalign it, which could cause a service handgun to mal-function and drop the hammer unintentionally. This can cause problems especially with an auto. If an improper engagement between sear and hammer is produced, the hammer can follow the slide as the latter goes forward to chamber the next round from the magazine. As the slide goes into battery, the hammer will fall to half-cock and stop or interrupt the firing process. Remember, reliability is the first requirement of a service handgun.

Trigger Face.   Service handguns with have either a smooth or a grooved trigger face—the front of the trigger with which the trigger finger comes into contact. In reality, it makes only a small difference in a service handgun, but here is the reasoning as to which is more appropriate. On a D-A auto or D-A revolver, the trigger's face should be smooth, as the trigger finger, when it pulls the trigger rearward, will slide very slightly across the trigger's face. A grooved trigger will cause a very slight movement of the handgun when the trigger is pulled. On a S-A auto, the trigger's face can be smooth or grooved, as the trigger finger does not slide across it. In reality, it is of little consequence in defensive shooting.

Trigger Weight.   Any service handgun must have enough trigger weight (the amount of weight required to pull the trigger back) to allow the trigger finger to be placed on the trigger and take up the slack without firing the handgun unintention-ally. During a number of circumstances, the officer must be able to touch the trigger and take up the slack, while the trigger must have enough trigger weight (when the pressure wall is met, after the slack is taken up) to keep the handgun from firing until the officer decides what to do.

When using the double-action firing mode this is no problem, as the trigger has plenty of weight and trigger travel for the trigger finger to touch and take up slack. Problems can arise when using the single-action firing mode, with the lighter trigger weight and much shorter trigger travel. Your margin of error will be much less with the S-A auto and the slack should not be taken up until just before you are actually going to fire. If there is no question that you will be firing, take up the slack as would be normally be done in the defensive stroke. But if unsure as to whether you are going to fire, do not take up the slack; only touch the trigger. (*Note*: When using the D-A revolver in the single-action firing mode, there is no slack; do not attempt to take up the slack. The D-A revolver is used only in the single-action firing mode for longer and harder shots, and this use is very rare.)

An officer must be able to touch the trigger and take up the slack as the handgun is coming up, in preparation for a possible threat; then, if the situation suddenly changes and the officer decides not to shoot, the handgun will not unintentionally go off due to too light a trigger weight. When tracking a moving threat, the officer must be able to touch the trigger and take up the slack in preparation for firing, being able at the last second to make the decision to shoot or not to shoot. Also, when confronting an armed threat, the officer must be instantly ready to fire by touching the trigger (not taking up the slack), yet know that the handgun will not fire until he or she wants it to. At other times, when the handgun is held on a possible threat (unknown if it is a threat or not), the trigger finger should be out of the trigger guard and straight alongside the frame (safe, yet instantly ready to insert the trigger finger and manipulate the trigger).

The trigger weight on double-action service handguns is usually 7 pounds or greater and presents no problems, as this is more than enough trigger weight. The problem usually occurs with single-action service handguns, where the trigger weight can be made very light. Under no circumstances should a trigger weight be lighter than 4 pounds on a single-action auto. We again note that on a D-A revolver the single-action firing mode is used only rarely, to place "hits" on threat(s) which are a good distance away and/or presenting a small target. Do not use the D-A revolver's single-action firing mode except during these very rare situations. Remember, double-action is the D-A revolver's defensive firing mode.

Dry-fire practice for improved trigger manipulation.   You must practice trigger manipulation by engaging in both dry- and live-fire practice. Everyone understands that live-fire practice is essential to training in proper trigger manipulation. What most officers neglect is dry-fire practice, which is of greater importance than life-fire practice for the maintenance of proper trigger slap and squeeze.

Dry-fire practice should be engaged in a minimum of 10 times a month and live-fire practice should be engaged in no less than once a month. (*Note*: If you fire on the range only once a year for your department, you must then engage in live-fire practice on your own, at least once a month to confirm your skills.) Dry-fire practice must be engaged in to maintain and sharpen your trigger manipulation skills a minimum of every three days. This is simple to engage in and can be accomplished away from the range, as no live firing is done. Live-fire practice, even engaged in minimally, will show that your dry-fire practice is working to maintain and improve your skills.

To engage in dry-fire practice, find a room in your house and go there to practice by yourself. When selecting a room, the wall you will be practicing against (pointing the muzzle at) should be capable of safely absorbing an unintentionally fired bullet. You are going to be safe and use good common sense, but it is always better to have a safety buffer. To increase this safety buffer further, all ammunition is completely away from you and out of your gun belt—if you are wearing it to practice the defensive stroke. The best area is in a basement with cinder block walls below ground level. As targets, place a few aiming points or half-sized combat targets on the wall.

Make sure that you and your equipment are ready. Again, you must be alone to concentrate completely on the practice at hand, as any distractions can influence your practice. Full time and attention should be devoted to improving your trigger manipulation. The same concentration should be used for dry-fire practice as for live-fire practice.

Make sure that the handgun is unloaded (check it twice before starting) and begin the practice. Pick one of the targets on the wall and snap up into your locked-in two-handed firing stance. Place the trigger finger on the trigger and take up the slack as you are aligning on an aiming point on the wall (or a precise point on the combat target). Manipulate the trigger for both the slap and squeeze, simulating different firing speeds. Make sure that you lock up into the firing stance as fast as possible every time.

While holding the handgun in a two-handed firing stance, concentrate on the front sight and squeeze the trigger until the hammer falls. Work for a surprise break. You must press or pull the trigger straight to the rear in one smooth motion while the sights remain aligned. Concentrate on the front sight and practice holding the handgun and sights steady throughout the trigger manipulation. An interesting test of your steady hold during the trigger manipulation is the nickel test. Put a nickel on top of the handgun's barrel or slide. Now manipulate the trigger and if you jerk or flinch, the nickel will fall off. Practice with this until the nickel remains steady throughout your trigger manipulation. Practice will create a smooth trigger manipulation. Remember, the trigger finger functions separately from the rest of the hand, which holds the handgun steady.

One of the main purposes of dry-fire practice is to train in trigger manipulation. Also, this is one of the best methods for lessening jerking or flinching of the trigger. Dry-fire practice not only trains in trigger manipulation, but also trains in the grip and positions of the arms and shoulders when firing from your two-handed firing stance.

Each dry-fire practicing session is ended after a reasonable number of trigger presses have been accomplished or until the hand or trigger finger become uncomfortable. With the proper mental attitude toward your practice, only a limited number of trigger presses are needed to accomplish this practice.

Follow-Through

When the handgun fires, you must stay in position and instantly reestablish your sight picture; do not bring the handgun down immediately after firing. Once a second or two has passed, lower the handgun to just below the line of sight while staying locked in your firing stance (accomplished by the arms pivoting at the shoulders to slightly lower the locked-in unit). You must get in the habit of holding the service handgun in position immediately after firing, ready to fire again instantly and then going to a "ready position" (by slightly lowering the handgun, with the stance still locked out), to be ready to respond instantly to the same threat or another one in the immediate surroundings. The handgun is already in place when you fired the first shot(s) and you are still in position, ready to fire again instantly if necessary. Do not go soft; stay in position, ready to fire again.

This is used in conjunction with cover and concealment (C&C) considerations. If caught in the open during the opening ceremony (when the encounter starts), you will probably have to fight in the open initially. As soon as the opening ceremony is over with, you must move to a C&C position for the remainder of the encounter, moving between and fighting from behind C&C. When initially moving to C&C, get behind it fast and stay in a ready position in case the threat(s) attacks again. Staying in a ready position (there are several) keeps you instantly prepared. If no C&C is available, you may have to stay where you are for the moment. Keep in a ready position with the handgun held in a locked-in firing stance.

Almost all shooters develop the bad habit of firing their string of five or six shots during live-fire training or qualification, then bringing the handgun down when finished firing. This is an entirely wrong, nonsurvival-oriented habit that you must not form (or change if it is already formed). Sometimes you will see shooters fire one or two shots, bringing the handgun down and then back up to fire one or two more shots, and so on, until they are finished shooting—again, a completely nonsurvival-oriented habit. When you finish firing a string, bring the handgun down to a "ready position," ready instantly to snap up the 6 to 10 inches and fire. Be ready for the action to start again. Obviously, if you have to reload, the handgun is brought down instantly and reloaded. Always remember, C&C is part of your consideration at all times.

Once you "hit" the threat and it goes down, keep the handgun in position ready to fire; do not think that the emergency is over. The threat may be playing dead or there may be more than one threat. Maintain the two-handed firing stance in position after the shot(s) are fired by lowering the handgun slightly below the line of sight for a better view of the threat.

When engaging in dry-fire practice, follow-through by maintaining the sight picture a second after the hammer falls. Hold the handgun steady, in-position, throughout the whole trigger press, making sure to follow-through at the end (maintaining the sight picture for 1 second).

When engaging in live-fire practice, follow-through by instantly reestablishing the sight picture after every shot. When the handgun fires, you will lose the sight picture due to recoil; this cannot be prevented. What you must immediately do is reestablish the sight picture. This is aided by a proper, firm grip that fights the handgun's recoil. When it is time to fire, lock in (grip, arms, and shoulders are locked, forming a locked-in unit) and fire; you will be surprised how steadily and strongly you can hold the handgun in place during firing. Do not allow the handgun to rise up out of the support hand. If your hands are coming apart when firing, strengthen your grip. This will reduce the time needed to realign the sights on the target and speed up your next shot.

When the handgun is lowered to the ready position, take your trigger finger off the trigger, with the fingernail touching the front of the trigger guard (another touch index). This will make you safe. If the action begins again, merely touch the trigger and take up the slack as the handgun is coming up to align on the threat. When the encounter began, stress dump occurred instantly and you still are under the influence of stress. With the trigger finger held less than an eighth of an inch away from the trigger, you will not send off an unintentional round. Use the touch index of the fingernail touching the front of the trigger guard to stop the forward movement of the trigger finger and hold it ready and safe.

When you move to another position, the trigger finger is taken out of the trigger guard and held straight alongside the frame. This must be done to keep you from firing an unintentional round if the trigger finger accidentally pulls the trigger—if you are startled, or you slip, or your hand hits against an object.

Notes on Particular Automatics. When a right-handed officer holds the trigger finger along the frame of a Colt .45 automatic, the tip of the finger must not rest on the slide release pin that is protruding through the right side of the frame. The tip of the finger can push this slightly out and cause the auto to malfunction. Also, the Colt .45 automatic's safety should be pushed "on" whenever moving. When using a H&K P-7, the squeeze-cocker, the master grip is relaxed, which decocks the auto and makes it safe. This should be done whenever moving. If the auto needs to fire, a full master grip is taken as the auto is coming up into a firing position. Also, other D-A autos should be decocked before moving.

Moving Targets

Most officers usually feel confident that they can "hit" a stationary target, but when it comes to a moving target their confidence level is greatly reduced. The moving target seems to add some strange extra factors that make it extremely difficult to hit. "Hitting" a moving target is not that difficult, especially close ones, which will be the vast majority of those encountered. But it takes an understanding of three factors to place the "hits."

FTM (Follow the Movement). To "hit" moving targets during lethal encounters, you must use three factors: (1) concentrate on the front sight, (2) track the moving target, and (3) smoothly manipulate the trigger. Follow the movement:

front sight, track, manipulate. If any one of those three is missing, you will probably miss the target.

Two of those factors—front sight and smooth trigger manipulation—are already part of your firing relfex. The third factor—tracking the moving target—is merely moving your locked-in two-handed firing stance with the target. Many believe that tracking causes the main problem, but improperly using any one of the three factors can cause the miss.

Do Not Lead a Moving Target.   Aim at the center mass of a moving threat. Many will find this statement interesting, as virtually everyone thinks that some lead is necessary on a moving target. During a lethal encounter, and under the stress dump, you will not be able to take the time to figure out how to lead the threat. When the threat moves, it will be moving quickly, at any angle to you—away from you, toward you, sideways to you—and it may quickly change directions. All of this at an unknown speed and range. If you try to lead the threat, you will only have problems.

Usually, the moving threat will be 10 yards and under and posing a deadly threat to you—much of the time 5 to 20 feet away. If the threat is a greater distance away (over 15 yards) and especially if running away from you, deadly force may not be justifed. Rarely would a shot be beyond 15 yards. But at the close ranges that lethal encounters usually involve, just aim for the center mass, track the target, and smoothly manipulate the trigger, squeezing off your shots.

At ranges of 15 yards and beyond, leading the target must start. A good index for leading targets 15 yards to 25 yards, is to hold the front sight on the leading edge of the threat. In whatever direction the threat is running, just hold on the leading edge. At longer ranges, front sight and smooth trigger manipulation must be more exacting. Again, during a lethal situation, you must not have any complicated ways of figuring lead. When the situation happens, you must know what to do.

Tracking.   Tracking is accomplished by locking the upper body into the locked-in two-handed firing stance and turning at the waist. When firing on a moving target you must be stationary. If you are trying to move and shoot, you will no doubt miss. The upper body and handgun must become one unit as the upper body turns at the waist to track the moving target. Concentrate on the front sight, which is on the threat, and keep it there as you turn your upper body at the waist. As you are tracking, smoothly manipulate the trigger for the shots while following through.

Multiple Targets

In any lethal encounter, there is a good possibility that you will have to engage multiple targets. When engaging multiples you must place one "hit" on each target first, one right after the other. (*Note*: Obviously, each has a gun and is trying to shoot you.) You do not have the time to place two "hits" on each of the threats, as the last one may shoot before you are able to "hit" it. Once fire has been placed on each target, get behind cover and continue the fight from there.

Engaging multiple targets, unlike moving targets, requires you to rotate (by traversing and/or pivoting) your stance, lock in, and then fire. When any lateral movement is needed to engage targets located around you, you will traverse and/or pivot to turn, then instantly lock in and engage the target. Your body must be positioned to move by having your weight slightly forward and knees slightly bent, ready to move in any direction. When detecting targets, your eyes will move to the target first, a microsecond before the body begins to direct the handgun toward the target. The length of the microsecond will be determined by how far the targets are apart; when engaging close multiples, eyes and handgun move together.

When moving the handgun you will use traversing and/or pivoting to turn the firing stance. Most of the time the targets are close together, and merely traversing, by turning the upper body and its locked-in firing stance at the waist, is all that is necessary. If a further turn is needed, pivoting will be used to turn the whole body and center it on the target. (*Note*: Traversing and pivoting are discussed in Chapter 13.)

The main idea is that you must **lock in** before firing, unlike tracking a moving target. Turn to the target, **lock in**, and fire. If you do not lock in before firing, you will probably swing past and overshoot the target. Turn, lock, and fire are the keys when firing multiples.

SUMMARY

In this chapter we have described the firing reflex that you must use when placing your shots. In the beginning, practice slowly and "hit" the target. When the defensive stroke becomes faster and you can "hit" the target consistently, start increasing your firing speed. You must start "hitting" right from the beginning, with the first round and each one after it. If you find yourself having a problem "hitting," slow down your firing speed just slightly to begin "hitting" consistently again. Only then begin increasing your firing speed.

All four parts of the firing reflex must function smoothly to place the "hits." The four parts—locked-in firing stance, combat sight picture, trigger manipulation, and follow-through—must become a trained-in, smoothly functioning reflexive set, by engaging in continual dry- and live-fire practice. Problems with any one of these will cause misses. The two most important ones to concentrate on are the combat sight picture and trigger manipulation; work extra hard on these.

With the completion of Chapters 4 and 5 you now understand the two most important reflexive sets in defensive pistolcraft. They are trained-in as separate and combined sets, functioning together when instant shot placement is needed, or functioning separately during the search or other preparatory defensive handgun use. These two sets provide you with the ability to present the handgun and fire it instantly.

6

Weapon Use Skills: Manipulation and the Holding and Firing Positions

The holster-to-stance reflex and firing reflex are the basic abilities needed to present the weapon and fire it. During a lethal encounter, when suddenly attacked, these skills will give you the ability to draw instantly and place "hits" on the threat(s). But these are only a part of the weapon use skills needed by a police officer. When engaged in searching or other defensive use, the handgun must be safely and effectively manipulated in response to the ever-changing situation, yet instantly ready to respond to a threat(s) that may occur.

The real question is: How do we translate the holster-to-stance reflex (defensive stroke) into the fluid handgun manipulation that is needed during any searching or defensive handgun use? The answer lies in your understanding of how to manipulate the handgun in the holding and firing positions during the search, to place it in a position to respond instantly to a threat(s). When manipulating the handgun, you are maneuvering it in the holding and firing positions in response to the changing situation and structures of the search. It sounds complicated, but it is not. Using the holding and firing positions is very simple and very effective. Once handgun manipulation is learned, it is applied to the search by using it in conjunction with search tactics. Do not skip or glance over this chapter; it is vital to your defensive weapon use skills.

The holding and firing positions are easy to learn, as there are only three holding and three firing positions in all, and by using them, you are ready instantly to respond to a threat(s) while searching. The main difference between the holding and firing positions is how and where the barrel is pointed. In the holding positions, the barrel is pointed down in a nonthreatening position and used to maneuver the handgun safely around other officers and obstacles during the search. In the firing positions, the barrel is pointed at the threat or the possible threat location, ready to fire instantly if necessary. With a little practice they begin to flow automatically with the search, making you safe and effective.

Once manipulation is learned and trained-in, it functions automatically while searching. It becomes second nature without having to think about it; thus leaving all your thoughts clear for the critical decisions at hand. You are responding instantly to the realities of the search without having to think about how to maneuver the handgun. Remember, the free and uncluttered mind, needed to concentrate fully on the critical decisions and make them instantly, must be bought and paid for with practice and preparation.

A beginning understanding of manipulating the handgun in the holding and firing positions.   Manipulation is easy to learn and use, but the initial understanding of how it works is sometimes hard to grasp. Basically, manipulating the handgun in the holding and firing positions allows you to place the handgun in the best tactical position to respond to whatever is occurring at that moment.

Holding positions are used to increase your safe in-hand use of the handgun and to maneuver it around objects when searching. Firing positions are used to keep you ready to fire instantly. Manipulation simply moves the handgun between these positions (only six altogether), as determined by the situation and structure of the search—what is occurring and what objects are around you.

These two sets of positions are applied directly to searching. General searching is a combination of two modes, searching and approaching. Searching is concerned with the larger, total area you are moving through, with no precise location to focus on. Approaching is concerned with moving toward a precise location where a threat(s) could be hiding. Each flows into the other throughout the search, as you continually move through and clear all areas. As a rule, the holding and firing positions correlate to searching/approaching, by using the holding positions when searching and using the firing positions when approaching.

When searching, watching the total search area with no precise location where the threat(s) is possibly hiding, use a holding position to keep the handgun ready for a threat(s) that could appear anywhere around you. As such, you are flexible: ready to move and/or snap into a firing position if the threat(s) appears (no matter where it is around you). When approaching, going toward a precise location where the threat(s) could be hiding, use a firing position to direct the handgun at that precise location as you approach it. As such, you are instantly ready to fire if the threat(s) presents itself. As searching and approaching flow into one another, so do the holding and firing positions. (*Note*: This is explained more thoroughly in Chapter 10.)

The area or structures you are searching in/through dictates the majority of manipulation. Your movement through the area and its channelization (hallways, doorways, fences, etc.), create a maze that has to be passed through when conducting a search. When searching and approaching you must use the most appropriate handgun manipulating positions to flow with the realities of the total search, yet be prepared if the threat(s) suddenly attacks. You must know exactly how to manipulate (or maneuver) the handgun in a professional manner. This is the art of manipulation. It is not hard to do once the holding and firing positions are learned and you understand the search concepts given here. Once that is accomplished, the handgun moves automatically in the most effective, fluid way as you are searching.

THE TOTAL PICTURE OF WEAPON USE SKILLS

Weapon use skills comprise reflexive sets of trained-in skills in the three areas of handgun use: handling, firing, and manipulating. An officer first learns handling and firing as the basics of the handgun's defensive functioning. Manipulating is learned last (it is almost never taught) and is a set of proven methods to maneuver the handgun while searching, to keep in the best position to be safe, yet instantly ready to respond to a threat(s). For an officer to progress beyond just a basic ability to position and fire the handgun, he or she must know how to manipulate the handgun while searching or engaged in other defensive handgun use.

Handling and Firing

Handling and firing are the basics of any handgun use. Handling is the safe operation of the handgun: loading, unloading, reloading, drawing, reholstering, and so on. Firing is the method of producing the handgun in a controlled firing position, aligning the sights, manipulating the trigger to fire the handgun, and following through after the shot(s) has been fired. In defensive handgun use, handling and firing are taught to produce officers who are safe and can place effective/timely "hits" on a target. In other words, the question is: Can the officer perform basic defensive functions with a handgun?

Manipulation is the last step (and rarely taught) to produce the total package of defensive handgun use. Manipulation is the smooth and precise operation/direction of the handgun when searching, which responds to all the realities of the search, while being instantly ready to fire. Instead of a hodgepodge of methods or none at all, manipulation provides a set of proven methods to maneuver the handgun through the many obstacles, tight places, corners, and so on, encountered when searching, all the while keeping the handgun in a position to respond instantly and effectively to a threat(s). Manipulating the handgun is nothing more than maneuvering the handgun in the holding and firing positions when searching, to be as prepared as possible for a threat(s).

As a police officer you have gone through firearms training at the academy that covered the handling and firing functions. If properly presented, these two functions produce officers who are safe in their basic handling of the handgun and can fire in an effective/timely manner and "hit" the target. The first chapters covered these skills with an explanation of the most modern handgun handling and firing methods. Manipulation is the professional polish of an expert weapon user and goes a long way to creating the total package of weapon use skills that are vital to police officers.

Manipulation

When searching, manipulating the handgun is used to direct it throughout the search. When changes occur in the situation and structure while searching, you respond with the best handgun operation/direction to meet these changes. Your handgun manipulation flows with the search so that you are instantly ready to produce the handgun in a position to fire at all times. That is the question and also the secret of how to **manipulate the handgun** when faced with the many different situations (approaching an unknown trouble call, searching on a B&E in progress, etc.) and structures (houses, warehouses, stairs, doorways, hallways, etc.) you'll find, while staying safe, yet instantly ready to fire.

Manipulation answers this question with a set of procedures to clean up your handgun use on the search and always keep you safe and yet positioned to fire instantly. You must have pre-thought-out and trained-in **manipulation** procedures so that you know what to do without having to decide what to do during the search.

The starting points of manipulation. When beginning **manipulation**, there are three starting points that need to be covered: tactical safety, in-hand or holstered, and the draw. Once these points are understood, we move right into the holding and firing positions.

Tactical Safety. This was covered in Chapter 2, but needs to be restated in conjunction with manipulating the handgun.

The safe handling and manipulating of the handgun are critical during police searches, as safety is coupled with an instant readiness to fire. When officers are searching, they are going in ''hot''—high stress and a loaded handgun. During these times, you must have trained-in manipulating procedures to maneuver the handgun safely throughout the search, while being ready to fire instantly.

Tactical safety is one of the signs of a professional weapon user and part of his or her reflexive sets. The holding positions are used as part of your tactical safety package, by manipulating the handgun in the holding positions, so that the muzzle is pointed away from other officers or innocents when searching. The holding positions are also used to maneuver the handgun around obstacles during the search.

The holding positions, with their safe direction of the muzzle, become the trained-in function of basic safety rule 2: Keep the muzzle pointed away from other people, except the threat or the possible threat location. These positions make this rule a trained-in function, by holding the muzzle down in a nonthreatening and nondangerous position when searching around other officers or innocents. (*Note*: The muzzle is held down, never up.) By holding the muzzle down, you make sure that it does not cross any part of another officer's or innocent's body. Remember, the search is always fluid, with officers (and sometimes innocents, found when searching) moving around each other; during these times, officers cannot let their handgun's muzzle cross anyone's body. Manipulating the handgun in the holding positions accomplishes this.

The second basic safety rule that is always followed is rule 3: Keep your trigger finger out of the trigger guard while searching, only indexing it in preparation for firing as you are coming on target. Disregarding this rule causes 95 percent of all unintentional discharges.

These two basic safety rules are always followed for the tactical safety needed when searching. These are both common sense rules, but you would be surprised how many officers do not follow them. Make sure you always follow them to be professional in your use of the handgun and tactically safe.

In Hand or Holstered.   During the search the handgun is in either one of two places at all times: in hand or holstered. It is never any other place; never lay it down. When holstered, the handgun is there for one of two reasons: (1) you are not engaged in a function where the handgun should be out, or (2) you have holstered the handgun while both hands are used to accomplish a task.

Do not forget this, as it is very important: The handgun is never any place other than in hand or holstered. If the action starts, you must know instantly where to go for your handgun (if not in hand) and not have to fumble for it or leave it if you have to move instantly when fired upon. Do not disarm yourself by laying your handgun down. Many times you will see an officer lay his or her handgun down to relax the strong hand at some stopped place during a search, or lay the handgun down while he or she is using two hands for a task. You must control your handgun at all times. Never lay your handgun down.

The Strong-Hand Relaxing Technique.   At some point in long searches, you may want to very briefly relax your grip on the handgun. This is done to shake the hand out from its continuous grip on the handgun and not allow a fatigued condition to continue. When doing this, make sure you have completely secured the immediate area and that you are behind cover. This relaxing technique will take only 5 to 10 seconds, but make sure that you are safely positioned before you start. Hold the handgun directly in front of the body with the insides of both forearms touching the sides of the body. The support hand grips the handgun around the barrel (slide for an auto) and front part of the frame, keeping well back from the muzzle, and supports it (make sure that a S-A auto's safety is "on"). The strong hand opens up and leaves the grip, only going about 4 inches directly back from it, and is gently flexed and the fingers moved back and forth to restimulate the strong hand, thus reducing fatigue. The support hand holds the handgun in position, exactly as the strong hand left it. Held in such a position, the strong hand can instantly regrip the handgun if something should occur. After 5 to 10 seconds the strong hand regrips the handgun and the search continues. Relaxed, the hand is better able to perform its functions.

Drawing and Reholstering.   You begin the search with a draw, end it by reholstering, and during the search may perform these again several times while needing two hands for some task. Dry practice your drawing and reholstering techniques (with an unloaded handgun) by picking out an aiming point on a wall and looking at it throughout your dry practice. Both of these must become smooth movements and have to be done eyes off and without the support hand touching the holster.

The draw will end in either one of two actions: the handgun stopping in the belt-level holding position or going out into one of the firing positions. The belt-level holding position is the most often used position when searching, to keep the handgun in a controlled position that is very useful when dealing with search realities.

THE HOLDING AND FIRING POSITIONS

Defensive handgun skills are transferred to the search by the process of manipulating the handgun through the holding and firing positions. These positions keep you prepared to respond effectively to the threat(s) while you are responding to the realities of the search: instantly ready for the threat(s), while maneuvering through, around, over, and under all the obstacles of the search.

The handgun is drawn and manipulated through these two types of positions to be ready to fire instantly on the threat(s) while searching, and yet be safe and able to respond to the realities of the search. These positions work easily and follow the holster-to-stance reflex that you have already learned. Once trained-in you do not have to think about these positions when searching; they take over to manipulate the handgun almost by themselves.

The two groupings of positions.   There are two groupings of positions that the handgun is held in and manipulated through during the search: the holding and firing positions. The main difference between the two is where the barrel is pointed. In the holding positions, the barrel is pointed down in a nonthreatening position and used to maneuver the handgun safely around other officers and obstacles on the search, yet the handgun is instantly ready to snap up into a firing position if a threat(s) appears. In the firing positions, the barrel is pointed at the threat or a possible threat location, and is used when approaching possible threat cover (PTC) and when firing on the threat.

The task of manipulating the handgun on the search is to maneuver the handgun safely and effectively in response to changes in the situation and structure, while being ready to fire instantly. The three holding and three firing positions (only six positions altogether) are used to accomplish this.

Why six positions? The reason six positions are used instead of two or three is to be able to respond in the most effective manner to all the realities of the search. One main reality in handgun use is: You will not always be able to have two hands on the handgun when searching and firing. Sometimes you can have only one hand on the handgun, as the other hand is occupied with climbing, carrying something, holding something open, using a flashlight, and so on. To train just for two-handed searching and firing is nonrealistic and nonsurvival oriented. Therefore, it boils down to training in one- and two-handed use.

THE THREE HOLDING POSITIONS

1. *The belt-level position.* The handgun is held at the belt line with the strong-hand thumb touching the belt. This is a close-in, controlled position at belt level and is the most used position when searching.

2. *The support position.* The handgun is again held in a close-in, controlled position at belt level, but slightly in front of the body, with both hands holding the handgun in a two-handed grip.

3. *The lowered position.* The handgun is held in a two-handed grip, with the arms locked out and lowered just below the line of sight.

(*Note*: These holding positions are *not* one-right-after-the-other positions but completely separate holding positions to be used in conjunction with the firing positions while searching.)

Figure 6.1 Belt-level position.

Figure 6.2 Support position.

Figure 6.3 Lowered position.

THE THREE FIRING POSITIONS

1. *The point position.* The handgun is held anywhere between two points: at belt level with the elbow bent at 90 degrees, to midway out (between belt level and held straight out) with the elbow bent at about 130 degrees. This follows the point shooting firing technique for very close-quarters searching and firing.

2.. *The one-handed stance position.* The handgun is locked out in a one-handed firing stance at eye level.

3. *The two-handed stance position.* The handgun is locked out in a two-handed firing stance at eye level.

(*Note*: As with the holding positions, these are *not* one-right-after-the-other positions, but completely separate firing positions to be used in conjunction with the holding positions while searching.)

6.4.

Figure 6.4   Point position.

6.5.

Figure 6.5   One-handed stance position.

6.6.

Figure 6.6   Two-handed
stance position.

The Holding and Firing Positions' Relationship to the Holster-to-Stance Reflex

All six positions are found along the line the handgun travels when using the holster-to-stance reflex, which is basic to all defensive handgun use. This reflexive set is merely the instantaneous drawing and snapping up into a one- or two-handed firing position, usually in response to a quickly appearing threat(s). As the basis of all defensive handgun use, the sets (both one- and two-handed) are practiced until they become subconscious reflexes that you do not have to think about. When the threat(s) appears the handgun is produced in a position to fire as you concentrate on the front sight and the critical decisions during the encounter.

You must be able to draw and "hit," either one- or two-handed, on demand of the situation at any time. This is nothing new. When using these reflexive sets, the handgun is brought up in a straight line from the holster, into either a one- or two-handed firing stance, with all the holding and firing positions falling along that line. These positions that you are learning follow exactly the basic holster-to-stance reflex that you have already trained-in.

As we view the following outlines of both the one- and two-handed holster-to-stance reflexes, the holding and firing positions will appear as positions along those sets (the holding and firing positions are designated in parentheses).

THE ONE-HANDED HOLSTER-TO-STANCE REFLEX

1. Holstered handgun.
2. The draw brings the handgun up into the belt-level position (the belt-level holding position).
3. The handgun is brought forward with the elbow bent at a 90-degree angle (the point firing position).
4. The handgun continues forward until the bend in the elbow is about 130 degrees (the point firing position).
5. The handgun is locked out in a one-handed firing stance at eye level (the one-handed-stance firing position).

6.7.   **6.8.**   **6.9.**

6.10.   **6.11.**

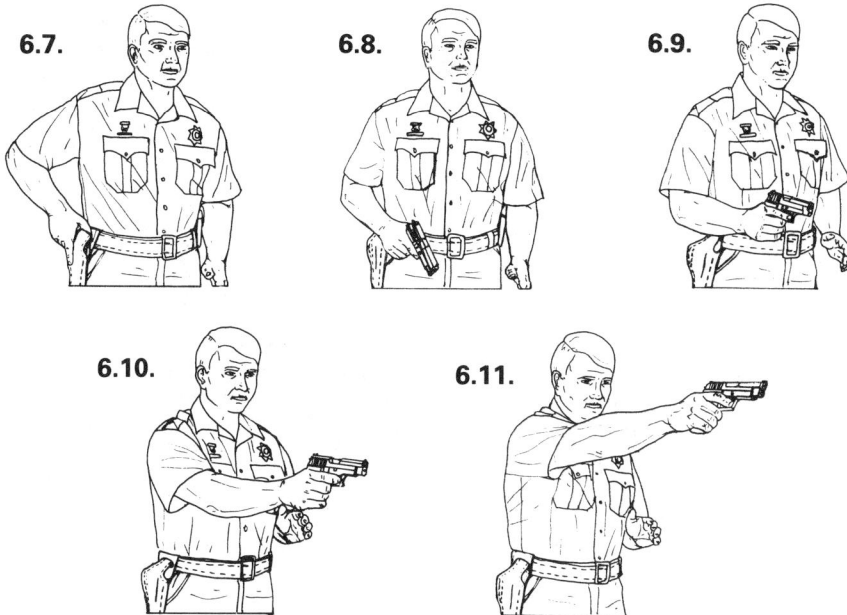

Figures 6.7–6.11   The line the handgun travels through during the one-handed holster-to-stance reflex: The holstered handgun (Fig. 6.7). The draw to the belt-level position (Fig. 6.8). The handgun continues forward with the elbow going through the 90-degree bend (Fig. 6.9). The handgun continues forward with the elbow going through the 130-degree bend (Fig. 6.10). Finally, the handgun is locked out in a one-handed firing stance at eye level (Fig. 6.11).

(*Note*: The point firing positions in 3 and 4 are considered just one firing position that goes from a 90- to a 130-degree bend in the elbow.)

THE TWO-HANDED HOLSTER-TO-STANCE REFLEX

1. Holstered handgun.
2. The draw brings the handgun up into the belt-level position (the belt-level holding position).
3. The handgun is brought forward with the elbow at about a 90-degree angle as the support hand comes across the center of the body and wraps about the strong hand for a two-handed grip (the support holding position).
4. The handgun in the two-handed grip is locked out just below the eye level (the lowered holding position).
5. The handgun in the two-handed grip is locked up at eye level in the two-handed firing stance (the two-handed-stance firing position).

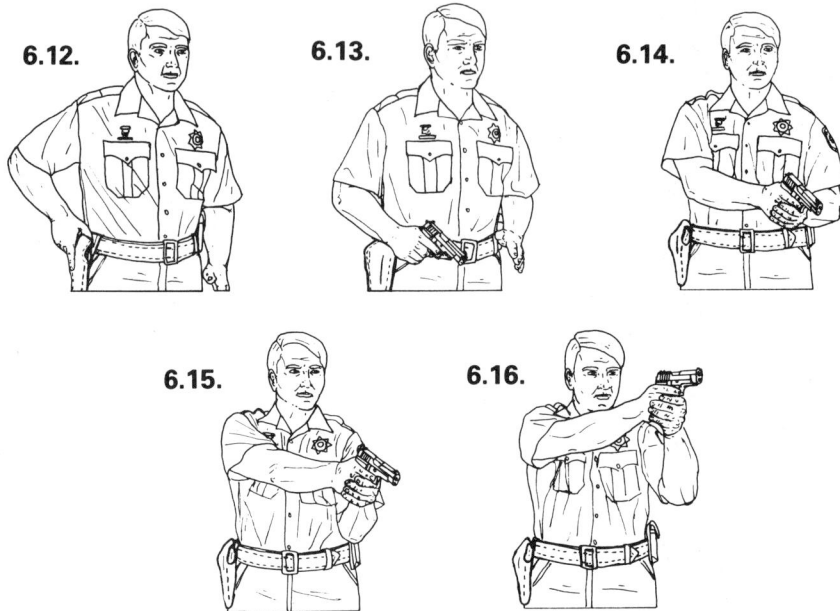

Figures 6.12–6.16 The line the handgun travels through during the two-handed holster-to-stance reflex: the holstered handgun (Fig. 6.12). The draw to the belt-level position (Fig. 6.13). The support position is assumed (Fig. 6.14). The arms are locked out just below eye level (Fig. 6.15). Finally, the handgun is locked out in a two-handed firing stance at eye level (Fig. 6.16).

(*Note*: The lowered holding position is used in conjunction with the two-handed stance firing position, so the handgun is lowered out of your field of vision while searching, but can be instantly locked up into the two-handed firing stance.)

A Note on the Belt-Level Holding Position. Both the one- and two-handed sets are the same up through number 2, up through the belt-level holding position. This is a very important position that leads into all the other holding and firing positions—the base position that can instantly snap up into any of the others. Being held close to the body, it is a very important position to control the handgun while searching.

The whole idea is to practice and train-in your techniques so that they become reflexive sets. These six positions fall along the one- and two-handed holster-to-stance reflex that you have already trained-in. You are not using something new, you are merely incorporating into your searching the separate parts of the most common reflexive sets that you already use. What could be more natural and effective? These six positions are already trained-in; now use them to manipulate the handgun through when responding to changes in the situation or structure during the search.

A last note on the reflexive sets. During any search the handgun will be in-hand virtually all the time and holstered only when both hands are needed for a task. If the threat(s) presents itself when the handgun is holstered, you must have these trained-in reflexive sets to snap the handgun out instantly and fire. Remember, we train for the ultimate breakdown in a situation, which invariably comes at the worst time.

EACH HOLDING POSITION IS EXAMINED

When the handgun is held in any holding position, the barrel is not held level but is pointing downward in a nonthreatening position. The holding positions are used to (1) maneuver the handgun around obstacles while moving through the search, (2) maintain safety when searching with others (making sure that the barrel is pointed *down* when moving around others), and (3) snap into a firing position in response to a threat(s).

The Belt-Level Position

This is the first and most often used of the holding positions. Its main function is to place the handgun in a close-to-the-body, controlled position after a draw or between other positions. From the belt-level position, all the other holding and firing positions can readily be snapped into.

It is the first position arrived at after the draw and the same for either the one- or two-handed reflexive sets. In this position, the elbow is bent at about a 90-degree angle and the handgun is held at belt level with the thumb touching the belt (about halfway between the belt buckle and the side of your body, until it feels natural). The wrist, forearm, and handgun are held in a straight line (no bending the wrist in or wrapping the wrist and forearm around the body). The muzzle is pointing at a spot about 9 feet in front of you. Also, the handgun's butt can be slightly canted out (away) from the body, so the arm is more naturally positioned. Work with your positioning and make it feel comfortable and natural.

The handgun is held close to the body and excellently controlled; as such, it is not a target for a threat to try and grab. Its use also eliminates the poor practices of letting the handgun hang at the end of your arm pointed at the feet or held up along the side of the head (always seen on TV). If improperly positioned by being held up or down, and a threat suddenly attacks, you have got problems, such as (1) the handgun must travel a longer distance to swing up or down to fire, (2) it is much easier to grab and fight over, and (3) if an unintentional round goes off, you will either perforate your foot or temporarily (maybe permanently) lose your hearing and sight on at least one side of your head, or possibly do worse.

In this close, controlled position, if the threat(s) attacks, you are ready. You can instantly use the speed rock at touching distances merely by rocking the handgun's muzzle up and firing, or point it out for quick point-shooting fire out to 5 yards, or snap up into a locked-in two-handed firing stance whenever possible at whatever distance. When firing on a very close threat, the handgun is very difficult to grab for and especially hard with bullets coming out of it. From this holding position, the handgun is instantly ready to snap into any of the firing positions.

As everyone knows, the quickest draw is the handgun already in the hand. But you cannot always walk around with the handgun in hand. Therefore, at the first inkling that you should have the handgun in hand, it is drawn out of the holster and placed in the belt-level position, from which you are instantly ready to respond.

The Support Holding Position and the Lowered Holding Position

These two-handed holding positions are used to keep you as close as possible to a locked-out, two-handed firing stance, by already having both hands locked together in a good two handed grip with the handgun lowered. In these positions you merely have to instantly lock out or raise the arms to snap into a two-handed firing posi-tion—extremely quick and effective. These positions put you as close as you can be to a locked-out two-handed firing stance and thus closer to the first shot. Remem-ber, a locked-out two-handed firing stance should be used whenever possible.

The question is often asked: Why not just stay in a locked-out two-handed firing position while searching? The answer is: You cannot search in that position, as changes that occur demand flexibility. The flexibility needed comes from these two-handed holding positions. From the two-handed position close to the belt line (where the two hands initially come together) to the locked-out two-handed firing position, you must have the flexibility to manipulate the handgun along that line while searching.

These two holding positions give you that flexibility when searching or ap-proaching. Often, physical objects encountered when searching will not allow the handgun to be held in a locked-out two-handed stance, as you maneuver around, over, or through them. The handgun must be brought down or into the body as they are passed. Also, you may want to bring the handgun into the body to conceal yourself as you hide behind an object. Flexibility is an important part of searching and you must be able to maneuver the handgun in a flexible manner.

These positions start with the support holding position, where the support hand first assumes the two-handed grip. As you are searching, you suddenly per-ceive that a threat may be close but are not sure where (no exact location). Now the hands come together for a two-handed grip at position 3, at waist level just in front of the body. By the hands having already assumed a two-handed grip, you are now closer to a locked-out two-handed firing stance and close to the first shot. If some-thing does not feel right, assume a two-handed grip for the support holding position and/or locked it out in a lowered holding position. Now you are prepared if the action starts, and you merely have to lock the arms out or rotate them up for a locked-in firing stance.

The lowered holding position is often referred to as the ready position, where the locked-out arms and handgun are lowered just below the line of sight. This is done by locking the arms out in the two-handed firing stance to form a locked-in unit. With the arms forming this locked-in unit, it is rotated down from the shoulders, about 8 to 10 inches below the line of sight. In this holding position you are as close to a locked out two-handed stance as possible. If the threat(s) appears, simply rotate the arms back up, lock in, and fire—very fast and effective. If using the Weaver stance, the locked-out arms are lowered until the support arm elbow touches the side of the body, another touch index.

The level of the barrel in the holding position. One of the main reasons for using the holding positions is to increase search safety by holding the barrel down in a nonthreatening position, thus keeping officers from inadvertently pointing their handguns at each other while searching. In all the holding positions, the level of the barrel has been shown as angled downward, pointing down at the floor. But when moving around other officers on the search, it will become necessary, at times, to lower the barrel further to keep it from crossing another officer's body. This is especially true if a very close area is being searched.

When another officer is close and starts to cross in front of your handgun's muzzle, you must lower the barrel further until the other officer is clear and then bring it back up once the officer has passed. Sometimes the muzzle must be held almost straight down until the other officer is clear, but it is never pointing down at your feet. This is usually done very quickly as the two officers pass. Also, when you are turning past another officer, the muzzle must be held down further, until it clears the other officer. This is just common sense and being safe when searching with other officers.

In the belt-level and support positions, lower the position slightly and bend the wrist(s) downward to lower the barrel and muzzle. When the officer is clear, bend the wrist(s) back up and slightly raise the position—very easily accomplished. In the lowered position (which forms a locked-in unit), the arms pivot at the shoulders to lower the barrel and muzzle. While still keeping the arms and grip locked in, simply rotate the locked-in unit downward from the shoulders. When the officer is clear, just rotate the locked-in unit back up.

Once the holding positions are worked with, they begin functioning almost automatically. Remember, the search is a fluid function, with officers moving around each other. Usually, as you and other officers begin to search, a pattern will develop and officers will rarely cross each other's line of fire, especially when a two-officer search team is conducting the search. But some crossing is unavoidable in the fluid search.

EACH FIRING POSITION IS EXAMINED

When the handgun is held in any firing position, the barrel is held level, pointing at a threat or a possible threat location. The firing positions are used when you know/feel a threat may be close and/or are approaching a possible threat location.

Usually, there is a precise location where the possible threat(s) may be—as a rule, some piece of possible threat cover (PTC). With the barrel leveled in a firing position, you are ready to fire instantly if the threat presents itself. In the firing positions, you are as close to firing as possible.

The Point Firing Positions and the One-Handed-Stance Firing Position

These firing positions are used mainly when only one hand is available to hold the handgun, as the other hand is performing some other task. Point firing positions are also used when approaching possible threat cover that is very close and restricted— virtually no room to maneuver. With the handgun held in a firing position close to the body, you are ready to fire instantly if the threat attacks at this very close range and very tight area, which would preclude using any of the two-handed stances.

No Time to Switch.   At many points in the search, you will need to use one hand to perform some task, and only the strong hand will be on the handgun. If a threat(s) suddenly attacks, you will have to fire one-handed, as there will be no time to switch instantly. The initial exchange, in all probability, will have to be fired one-handed. As instantly as possible, the other hand drops what it was doing as you improve your position and switch to a two-handed firing grip. You must train to fire one-handed, as the situation may occur where you will have no choice but to use one-handed firing.

The point firing positions are taken directly from the point-shooting method described in Chapter 14. At very close range, from 0 to 12 feet (from touching distance to the length of a medium-sized car), point shooting is very effective if you have trained-in the pointing movement. These firing positions are excellent for searching very tight and/or awkward areas, where much of the time the other hand is required to aid in your movement. The point firing positions allow you the most freedom of movement and flexibility in tight/awkward areas such as these.

If forced to use one hand when firing, always try to lock the arm out in the one-handed stance firing position at eye level. This will enable you to align the handgun by sighting along the barrel or to use the sights for aimed fire (if you have the time). This will be dictated by the situation—how close the threat(s) is and how quickly it is occurring. The one-handed stance firing position is a locked-out one-handed firing stance in your line of sight. This is used the same way as a two-handed firing stance except that only one hand is on the handgun. Follow the methods of the firing reflex when aiming and firing.

The Two-Handed-Stance Firing Position

As you know, the locked-out two-handed firing stance should be used whenever possible, whenever the situation allows. Not much needs to be said about how it functions, as it was discussed in detail in Chapter 5.

The two-handed-stance firing position is used mainly when approaching a piece of possible threat cover (PTC). While you are searching in a holding position, a particular location appears as a good place where a threat(s) could be hiding. You now snap into a two-handed-stance firing position and begin approaching that location, ready to fire instantly if the threat(s) presents itself. With the handgun locked up into a two-handed firing stance at or just below eye level, you are as close as possible to the first shot. You are positioned to respond instantly.

Once the firing positions are worked with, they begin functioning almost automatically. They are used in combination with the holding positions when searching, both flowing with the search.

SUMMARY

This chapter is very important to building your weapon use skills. Manipulation is the most neglected part of firearms training, yet must be part of a professional weapon user's total package of skills. Many other parts of this book will involve these skills.

Manipulation is nothing more than maneuvering the handgun in the holding and firing positions when searching, to be as prepared as possible for a threat(s). It provides you with a set of proven methods to maneuver the handgun through the many changes that occur when searching, while keeping you ready to respond instantly to a threat(s). You must study and learn these holding and firing positions (only six positions altogether), as they will improve your gun-handling abilities and increase your survival advantage.

7

Your Mental Set and Survival Response

The survival skills that you will use to stop a lethal threat(s) successfully are founded in four factors: (1) mental set, (2) weapon use skills, (3) encounter tactics, and (4) preparation. All four work in concert to produce the total package necessary to stop a threat(s). Lack of preparation of any of these will greatly reduce your chances of survival. Many consider your mental set to be the most important of the four, although we handle them equally.

This chapter covers the methods and reasoning behind the mental set that all officers must produce within themselves. Failure to develop this skill properly will dramatically limit their ability to recognize the threat(s) before an encounter begins, engage it effectively during the encounter, and make the correct critical decisions throughout the encounter. Officers must develop a proper mental set long before an encounter takes place.

The mental set is a preset state of mind that is produced when officers mentally condition and prepare themselves for the realities of lethal encounters. This is accomplished by facing encounter problems that could occur, establishing pre-thought-out decisions as to how these problems will be handled and engaging in survival reinforcement exercises. The realities of lethal encounters MUST be faced squarely by every officer, who must mentally condition himself or herself to what will/may occur. This might sound far too psychologically inclined to many readers, but read on; do not skip this extremely important chapter.

Your mental set follows one simple rule.   The mental set factors described here follow one simple rule: You must eliminate as many of your decision-making processes as possible before a lethal encounter occurs. Once that is accomplished, by pre-thinking them out and deciding what you will do beforehand, you are preset (or pretuned) to the realities you will face in an encounter and how you will handle them. Now you can focus the greatest amount of your decision-making process on the lethal encounter at hand.

When one of these realities takes place within the encounter, you have already decided your response long beforehand. With no time lost and virtually no thought taken away from the critical decisions at hand, you respond correctly. By utilizing this process, there is no time lost trying to figure out what to do and the mind is free to make the instantly occurring critical decisions during the encounter. It is nothing more than mentally preparing yourself before a lethal encounter occurs.

THE FIRST DECISION THAT YOU MUST MAKE

We begin the development of the mental set with the first critical decision you, as a police officer, must make. Failure to make, or come to grips with, this decision can cause your death or the death of other officers at a future date. The decision must be made before you go on the street for the first time.

Hopefully, while you were in the academy or before, you made one of the most important decisions toward your survival. The decision will answer the use-of-deadly-force question: Will you use the weapon when the time comes to defend youself and/or others? The answer to this question is vital; you must make the decision to shoot long before a lethal encounter occurs. Confusion can be fatal, as there will be no time to think through your feelings when the bullets start flying.

If you have not done this, do it now before you are faced with a lethal encounter, trying to figure out what to do. Get your brain work done first. Find out what level of threat is necessary to constitute the use of lethal force and think through your own emotions and moral stance. Simply stated: What will cause you to fire at another person, and will you do it? Stop right now and reflect on this for just a few seconds. If you have to think about it at all or you are not quite sure of the total answer, do a rethink right now. Rethink this primary critical decision right now!

If you cannot come to grips with this decision, you will need to rethink quite a bit more than just this one decision. As an officer, a situation may unfold where your inability to fire could jeopardize not only yourself, but other officers or innocents involved. Think carefully about your position in this matter. You are a sworn police officer with vested authority and an issued service handgun. The inability to use that service handgun, or not use it quickly enough, could very easily cost lives and negate the function you are entrusted to perform.

(*Note:* For all people—officers and civilians alike—who carry or keep a firearm for personal protection, Massad Ayoob's book *In The Gravest Extreme* is required reading. It provides a complete understanding of the role of the firearm in personal protection. You must read this book.)

YOUR REACTIONS UNDER STRESS
AND YOUR SURVIVAL RESPONSE

When a lethal situation occurs, changes take place in your mind and body to increase your ability to cope with the situation. In effect, a number of changes occur: Your body enters into the fight-or-flight reflex, causing a whole series of physical changes as your mind becomes overloaded with stimuli in the form of high-level stressors, reducing reasoning ability and increasing emotions which will make critical decisions harder. On the positive side, you become stronger, faster, and more physically able to survive, but on the negative side, your decision-making process is greatly reduced, your emotional response is greatly increased, and certain mechanical functions are limited. When these changes occur, you will revert to your conditioned response (the physical skills that you have trained-in through practice and preparation) and mental preparation (critical decisions that have been pre-thought-out and prepared for). If you have not prepared either of these, you will be relying on whatever other skills you possess and luck. As everyone knows, luck can be very cruel!

Your Survival Response = Conditioned Response
(Physical Skills/Practice) and Mental Preparation
(Pre-thought-Out Critical Decisions)

Conditioned response and mental preparation are the two halves that combine to form your survival response. When a lethal encounter occurs, you will revert to a response based on what you have practiced and prepared for your survival response.

The conditioned response half is the weapon use skills and practice that produce a skilled defensive weapon user. With sharpened skills, your manipulation of the handgun in response to the threat(s) becomes second nature, without having to think about it consciously. The mental preparation half is produced by making pre-thought-out decisions beforehand. These decisions are based on facing the realities of lethal encounters and deciding what you will do beforehand. When one of these occurs during an encounter, you will already know what action to take. Thus your mind is as free as possible to concentrate all your thoughts on the critical decisions at hand.

When a deadly situation occurs both halves function together, producing your *survival response*. Suddenly the threat(s) appears and as you instantly make the critical decision to shoot, the handgun is already in position, front sight in focus and slack taken up as the sear breaks, firing it. Your mental preparation enabled you to decide instantly what response was warranted and, as if by magic, the handgun was already in your line of sight, placed there by your conditioned-response functioning on a subconscious level. The two halves that form your survival response can function together smoothly only if both halves are properly trained-in and maintained. If either half is neglected, your survival response will be reduced.

The freedom of mind needed to make the right critical decision and the trained-in physical skills needed to function instantly and effectively to stop the threat(s) must be bought and paid for with practice and preparation. In the remainder of this chapter we analyze the conditioned response and mental preparation that every officer must develop within himself or herself to deal effectively with an encounter.

CONDITIONED RESPONSE

The conditioned response is the weapon use skills and practice that produce a skilled defensive weapon user. Repetition, through practice, produces trained-in reflexive sets of weapon use skills that are vital to your survival. As these skills become trained-in, they become second nature: When you know that it is time, the weapon is there, front sight in focus, and you are firing. These skills must be deeply programmed through repetition (training-in the sets). As such, when the conscious mind knows that it is time to fire, that is all the decision it must make to produce the handgun in a position to fire, and to fire it. The physical mechanisms used to accomplish this function at the subconscious level, in response to the conscious mind's recognition of the need.

Under the tremendous stress of the encounter, the conscious minds of some officers become overwhelmed by the weight of events and the many decisions that need to be made. In this overwhelmed state, their minds will be unable to focus— at the conscious level—on the tactics and techniques that can save their lives. If unable to function subconsciously (by not having trained-in reflexive and mental sets), these officers will be in real trouble. If weapon use or mental skills have not been trained-in but require conscious thought to make them work, these officers may not be able to function at all and possibly may not survive the encounter.

When the reflexive and mental sets are trained-in, officers can tap into their subconscious abilities to call forth these sets when needed, almost without any conscious thought. When the encounter happens suddenly, the officers find themselves responding tactically, while the handgun is being manipulated automatically, with the conscious mind fully concentrating on the continuing encounter and critical decisions being made. Many areas of weapon use skills will be covered in this book. Here we are outlining the conditioned responses that occur during a time of increased stress. How will your body and mind react to stress, and how can you use this to your advantage? The correct conditioned responses that will serve most effectively during a high-stress encounter must be developed within each officer.

Stress

Knowing the reactions that stress produces in the body provides us with the ability to develop training methods and techniques that compensate for their occurrence. We must train for the radical physical and mental changes caused by stress during a lethal encounter.

Most known is the fight-or-flight reflex that manifests itself when a human being perceives a deadly threat. During this alarm reaction, high-level stressors instantly activate the body in preparation for fight-or-flight. This involves both electrical and hormonal signals that work to mobilize the energy output necessary for the emergency. Adrenalin (norepinephrine and epinephrine) and cortisol are released into the body to aid in preparation for the strenuous physical action to come.

The Physical Machine Prepares

In reality, the body becomes a physical machine, preparing for a physical war. The dump of adrenalin and noradrenalin into the bloodstream instantly begins preparing the body for the impending encounter. The physical animal, produced by eons of evolution, begins to surface as the body is physically geared up for the encounter. A true metamorphosis takes place as the body mobilizes its inner strength and mechanisms in response to the age-old appearance of danger.

The total changes in the body as it gears up are truly amazing. The heart rate and breathing become faster to provide more blood and oxygen to the brain and muscles. To aid in this process, the nose and throat openings are widened as saliva and mucus dry up, providing increased air to the lungs. Muscles begin to tighten up in preparation for the strenuous physical action to come. The body's physical strength increases as it becomes stronger for the physical effort that may occur (fight or flight). Pain will become a secondary consideration, and if pain occurs it will be sublimated until after the danger has passed. Just under the surface of the skin, blood vessels contract, reducing the chance of increased blood loss if wounded. Also, clotting time is now faster, the body having the ability to close any wounds faster. With reduced blood at the skin surface, a pale appearance and cold hands are observed. To keep the body cooler, perspiration increases. Your ability to see is improved as the pupils dilate, increasing the body's ability to locate the danger with its main sense. Also, bodily stores of energy (sugar) are released to supply the upcoming need. Truly an amazing engineering feat—the human animal can prepare almost instantly for an all-out survival fight.

The Mental Side of the Physical Machine Also Prepares

While the physical machine is gearing up for war, the mental part of the physical machine is switching to its own survival mode. Mentally the human animal switches to its survival-first mode, with all the mental processes being geared up and altered for the encounter to come. Mentally gearing up produces its own special strengths and weaknesses (just as physically gearing up does). The mind experiences dramatic changes: judgment and reasoning ability become very limited, emotional responses increase, the decision-making ability is reduced, and focusing too much on a single object or event becomes a problem.

The first mental reaction is some level of anxiety at the unfolding encounter (triggering and then continuing to trigger the bodily responses). Anxiety will increase as the encounter progresses. At some point the conscious mind may become overloaded, with input and information coming in so fast that the mind cannot handle it. Faced with the overload, the mind will degress to a simpler response level based on past training, experiences, or courses of action. An officer's survival will now rely on his or her trained-in reflexive and mental sets. The key is training-in these sets to function at the subconscious level.

Without these trained-in sets, the officer will have nothing to rely on. He or she will not be able to create during mental overload (decide on some innovative course of action or invent a new way of responding), but will do one of two things: either make some move that is inappropriate and will have little chance of succeeding, or make no move at all. Making no move at all (freezing) is the worst response that can occur. You become stationary, immobile, and easy to take.

During the encounter, the officer will have to cope with a number of limiting mental factors: reduced or faulty reasoning, increased emotional responses, reduced decision-making ability, tunnel vision, and distorted perceptions. These will be discussed in this chapter.

Understanding the bodily and mental responses to stress can help us lessen negative bodily responses by providing training methods to offset these effects. Through eons of evolution the human animal has trained for a particular type of dangerous encounter: a close encounter with an animal or enemy, usually involving bodily contact, or running as fast as possible to escape. The body works exceedingly well for these encounters, where no technical skill is required. But with the advent of weapons that dramatically increased the user's striking distance, a new set of bodily skills and responses are demanded. There is no time to evolve these skills and responses, they must be trained-in, with training methods that offset any negative responses. Your weapon use skills must hold up under the effects of stress. Remember, when stress occurs, you revert to your conditioned response and mental preparation—your survival response. Both the bodily and mental responses to stress must be taken into consideration when training.

Bodily Responses to Stress

These appear as an increase in muscular strength (gross movements) and a decrease in fine coordination (finite movements). With the increase in muscular strength, the muscles tighten up and your ability to perform finite tasks with the hands decreases. You become stronger to meet the threat, but you also become clumsier in your movements. Many times, trembling of the extremities and a partial loss of control are also noted. Therefore, techniques must be taught that reinforce gross movements (dependent on larger, sweeping movements) and physical strength instead of finite movements (dependent on small, more precise movements).

In high-stress situations, gross movements work well under the pressure. As you are using gross movements with the handgun, you see that they are working. You become assured that what you are doing, here and now, right in the middle of an encounter, is working to save your life. This reassurance increases your confidence in your ability to survive. If trembling of the extremities is occurring, this will also help reduce it. If, on the other hand, you rely to some degree on finite movements and they start to break down, your negative responses to stress will increase dramatically. You will perceive yourself fighting a loosing survival battle, which will heighten all the negative responses, as you now feel that you are struggling to catch up. Gross movements must be used as the training base to develop effective techniques that will hold up during an encounter.

Use one set of techniques and do everything "by feel". For your conditioned response, you must use one set of techniques and perform these "by feel." Along with using techniques that employ gross movements, you must select and use only one set of techniques. Obviously, you must have a number of techniques to cover all the necessary weapon use skills, but for each particular function, use only one technique and train it in completely. No switching back and forth between techniques; select the techniques you are going to use and train them in. You must also practice the techniques the same way every time, so that they become the reflexive sets that function automatically when needed.

Everything must be practiced by feel, reducing and/or eliminating the need to look at what you are doing. Although there are times that you must glance at what you are doing, you must reduce this to a minimum, and in many of the techniques it can be eliminated altogether. Your main concern is the action/threat(s); you must keep your eyes on this throughout the encounter.

A constant and a variable. In effect we are dealing with a constant (the body's conditioned responses when employing weapon use skills) and a variable (critical decisions during an encounter). You must improve the constant to maximum efficiency in order to derive the greatest advantage when it interacts with the variable. Weapon use skills (the constant) must be maximized by knowing exactly how your weapon functions, fires, reloads, how to handle malfunctions, and so on, and using techniques that incorporate gross movements are practiced the same way each time and done by feel. Improving your weapon use skills, the constant, will free up your mental processes for the critical decisions of the encounter, the variable. This constitutes the bodily responses to stress; all others (although bodily in nature) are covered under mental responses.

Mental Responses to Stress

These appear as a general degrading of the mental processes, especially the ability to make decisions. You enter into a condition where a reversal usually takes place: instead of sublimating your emotional responses and being controlled by your reasoning ability, a reversal usually occurs, placing your emotions in the controlling position and lowering your reasoning ability. In this reversal condition, you will find it hard to use reason, make decisions, instantly think of what to do, and you will be on an emotional high (overreacting to everything). Fear itself will also be a major limiter and must be overcome. Once you know what is going to take place and prepare for it, the negative effects of these reactions can be greatly reduced.

Reduced decision-making ability.   This is one of the largest negative effects. Your mind will be overloaded with stimuli during the encounter, but will still have to make many critical decisions—most of these having to be made very quickly or instantly. Your main focus in preparing for this is to eliminate as many of the decision-making processes as you can from the mix, thus reducing the number of decisions that have to be made instantly during an encounter. This allows the majority of your decision-making processes to center on the critical decisions of the continuing encounter.

Your weapon use and tactical skills must become trained-in reflexive sets forming your conditioned response. When you need them, the skills are there. No conscious thought or decision making is needed. When it's time, you must not have to think about how to use the weapon or what tactic to use. These skills have to become second nature, functioning subconsciously. Your weapon use and tactics must function almost automatically, clearing your mind for the critical decisions that must be made during the encounter. Mental preparation also reduces many of the decision-making processes, as you have already decided what you will do when faced with many of the realities of lethal encounters.

Reduced or faulty reason.   These can cause your death very quickly. During stress-filled encounters, officers who are trained and experienced will sometimes engage in actions that place them in unnecessary danger. They will seem to forget their training and common sense completely and engage in foolhardy risktaking.

Your number one priority during an encounter is the safety of you, other officers, and innocents. During the encounter you will have options to select from and you must not pick the wrong option due to faulty perceptions or faulty reason. Too many officers feel the need to get the threat(s) no matter what, causing them to leave cover to get a shot at a threat(s) or to approach a downed threat that may be faking. The superman syndrome or uncontrolled anger can cause officers to take foolish or reckless chances. Faulty reasoning, attitudes, or perceptions can become much harder to control during an encounter and have killed many officers.

One example points this out: A suspect, having just robbed a liquor store, is walking to the rear of the shopping center when a marked cruiser pulls into the parking lot and heads toward the suspect. The officer is completely unaware that a robbery has taken place. As the cruiser begins to pass, the suspect suddenly panics and fires three shots pointblank into the car, missing the officer. Stunned, it takes the officer several seconds to radio out and begin pursuing the suspect, who ran up a bank at the edge of the parking lot and disappeared behind a church. At the rear of the church, the suspect is nowhere in sight, but there are several dark areas and recessed doorways. The officer hears the suspect, puts his handgun back in the holster, and rushes in. Immediately the officer begins fighting with the suspect. Luckily, the suspect had lost his revolver while running. This foolish and reckless act could easily have caused the death of the officer, who acted out of uncontrolled anger. Other responding officers arrived just seconds later.

You must come to grips with possible attitude/ego problems that you think may occur to you during an encounter. You know your own ego needs and what you may do during an encounter. Understand that you must control your own emotions, which may cause you to select options that are reckless. With police work comes a certain amount of unavoidable risk; there are a certain number of chances that must be taken and certain dangerous tasks that must be performed. Obviously, a certain amount of danger/risk comes with the job, but you must not engage in foolhardy actions that will place you and possibly other officers in "needless" danger. The job has enough danger; do not add to it needlessly.

Tunnel vision.   This is another problem caused by stress. It can cause you to focus totally on the perceived danger facing you and to black out other vital sensory input around you. As you focus on the threat, you exclude just about everything else. This concentration of focus, or tunnel vision, is fine when placing your "hits" on the threat(s) to stop it, but the problem occurs when your focus remains in one place for too long. You must be able to expand your focus throughout the encounter: picking up your 360-degree scan and hearing, to begin including, not excluding, all the sensory inputs in the encounter zone. This is accomplished by training yourself to use expanded focus to increase your sensory input, expanding your senses into the larger environment through the encounter! This is not easy, as tunnel vision will work to keep you focused only on the danger. You must fight to expand your focus between the exchanges of fire, to take in the entire encounter zone. Remember to keep your main focus on the action/threat(s), while expanding your focus by taking quick glances around you, and pick up your hearing.

One of the best ways of ending tunnel vision is the simple act of turning your head for quick glances to one side or the other. This will cause you to expand your vision physically by looking away from the main source of danger. Also, make sure that you expand your sense of hearing to include, not exclude, the sounds around you. During the action, your concentration will be so intense that you will exclude even the loudest noises—shouts from other officers next to you and even their gun shots. Now, during the lull you must fight to expand both your vision and hearing. Remember, always make sure you keep your main focus on the action/threat(s) while expanding your senses.

Tunnel vision also works to your advantage during an encounter by helping you concentrate your abilities totally on the precise task at hand, such as watching the FRONT SIGHT and manipulating the trigger to stop each threat. The problem occurs when tunnel vision remains locked in and fixed. You must train yourself to expand your focus to cover the larger environment for additional threats. If you do not, fixation will occur and your focus will be locked on one object or area. Don't fixate; pick up your 360-degree scan and hearing. You must practice and constantly remind yourself to use expanded focus. Remember, what you do not notice can very easily kill you!

Also note that your focus will be changing from tight to expanded throughout an encounter. Whenever engaging a threat(s), tight focus will automatically occur to help you concentrate completely on the dangerous task at hand and exclude much of what is occurring around you. This helps you concentrate your skills when firing the handgun, especially front sight/squeeze. Once the exchange of rounds has stopped and a lull in the action occurs, instantly begin expanding your focus into the entire encounter zone. Think of it as a camera focusing: Suddenly, the threat(s) attacks and tight focus is used to concentrate your skills when firing the handgun; then the shooting stops and you must instantly expand your focus into the larger encounter zone. Tight focus when the bullets are flying to stop each threat and expanded focus when the shooting has stopped, like a camera focusing in and out. Tight focus is simple and you have nothing to do as your body takes over to switch automatically to tight focus when the shooting starts. Expanded focus will take training and you must work to make it occur. Once the exchange of fire has stopped, immediately expand your focus while keeping your main focus on the action/threat(s).

Distortions in perceptions.   These will manifest themselves as distortions in time and space relationships and the ability to keep track of the fast-moving encounter. They will occur as the norm. It seems incredible that an encounter that may last for only a few seconds seems to have lasted much longer and can cause you to lose track of the events within the encounter. When high-level stressors (generated from an instantly occurring life-threatening encounter) are dumped into the body, the body focuses on what is instantly important at that moment. All else seems to be unimportant to the body's first consideration—survival. As such, distortions in perception occur.

A very unique distortion experienced by most officers during a lethal encounter is the slow-motion effect. While engaged in the encounter, it seems to be moving in slow motion, even though moving very fast. The encounter may have started and ended instantly (taking only several seconds), but it seems to have moved much slower and lasted much longer. The events moved slowly, so much so that very small details will later be recalled by officers, the classic one being reports of seeing a bullet flying through the air and striking the threat.

Far from a negative problem, mentally increased time segments provide an officer with an increased chance to process all of the incoming information. In reality, time is of course running the same; only the officer's increased mental ability to follow the events and choose an appropriate course of action speeds up. This will allow the officer to process information and select a course of action instantly, at a speed much faster than normal. Once an instantly occurring encounter is over with, officers can tell everything about the source of danger, but almost nothing of any other events occurring around or beside the source of danger. This is due to tight focusing while instantly processing information.

Your ability to keep track of what took place, how long it took, and the distances involved will be a problem. Now that we have defined this problem, how do you lessen its impact? The answer lies in reducing things you have to keep track of or think about during an encounter. Keeping track of things wastes your time and reduces your decision-making process.

The classic example of this is counting the rounds that you have fired. Many instructors still teach their students to count the rounds they have fired. In real situations, this has been found to be an error in technique. First, any officer counting the number of fired rounds in a gunfight will in all probability be wrong, as there are many more important occurrences taking place that the mind is trying to control. Second, there is no need to count the rounds fired if you use modern tactical reloading procedures. But many still feel it necessary to clutter up their mental process with this minutia. The mental process must be as free as possible from unnecessary distractions during an encounter.

Your conditioned response must be made up of weapon use skills that are trained-in reflexive sets, to keep you firing almost automatically. Whether instantly firing on a threat, manipulating the handgun on a search, tactically reloading at the proper time, instantly clearing a malfunction that has occurred, using the flashlight at the right times on a search, or any of the other weapon use skills. These techniques must be trained in and must function on a subconcious level, with no thought taken away from the critical decisions occurring during an encounter.

MENTAL PREPARATION

In preparing for lethal encounters, you, the police officer, must make certain mental preparations. These preparations are based on a two-step process: first, knowing what realities can occur during lethal encounters, and second, mentally engaging in pre-thought-out decisions as to what you will do if these realities should occur. You have already made some of them, the most important of which is: ''I may have to kill someone to defend myself and/or others.'' This is definitely one decision that you must not have to sort out at the moment of truth. You must know that you will shoot if necessary. When the time comes and you must do it now, you must do it just that quickly. If not, you may be dead.

You must have confidence that you will survive. When you bought this book you took a definite forward step toward increasing your survival advantage. You are making a commitment to do what is necessary to be a survivor. With that attitude alone your survival rate has already greatly increased. Your confidence will increase with the skills contained here. Within yourself, you have the ability to perform phenomenal tasks to survive. You can survive if you want to! You have already made the decision that you want to be a survivor—that you will survive! That goal will be enhanced as you study this material.

One of the first to realize that mental factors must be addressed in training was Jeff Cooper, who developed and coalesced these factors as part of defensive firearms training. When preparing for the possibility of lethal assaults, officers must understand the mental factors they must use to stop the threat(s)—before, during, and after the encounter.

The following five mental elements for surviving lethal encounters are steps in mental preparation to improve your instant reaction and ability to carry your actions through to stop the threat(s).

Mental Elements for Surviving Lethal Encounters

There are five mental elements for surviving lethal encounters. These elements form a set of "mental cues" that are used together, throughout lethal encounters, to carry you through it. As mental cues they keep you "cued up" to what you must do to survive.

1. Awareness. You must cultivate an aware attitude toward life, as outlined in the assets model. Awareness did not just begin with the encounter; you were using it long before the encounter started and will use it long after the encounter has ended. Awareness is used continually. You must be aware to recognize the danger signs in order to react to them. At any time you should know what is going on behind as well as around you.

Once a possible danger sign is recognized, keep a close eye on it and/or find out what is not right. As soon as a danger sign is recognized, begin planning your moves (to be prepared if the possible threat materializes) and checking out the danger sign. Do not disregard or rationalize it as something else: Check it out. This is not done in a conspicuous manner, drawing attention to yourself, but is handled subtly as the danger sign is checked out. Remember, danger signs must be explained satisfactorily.

Whatever else you are doing, you are prepared if the action starts and formulating a quick course of action. Remember, your reactions to possible danger sign(s) are not overt or conspicuous, but very subtle and virtually undetectable.

Awareness Progression. The concept of awareness progression is important to your ability to respond to the threat(s). This term refers to your increased awareness from the first recognition of a danger sign until the threat(s) presents itself. Its truth is simple; the more aware you are of the existence of a threat(s) and the longer you have been aware of it, the better prepared you are to handle it. You progress through stages of awareness by observing continuing danger signs that an encounter is at hand. The more aware you are of the possibly increasing danger, the more prepared you become. At the first danger sign, you become aware that something might possibly be wrong; as more danger signs come in, you know that something is definitely wrong and have already become prepared (planning a course of action and improving your position). Now, when the threat(s) presents itself, you already have a course of action and are effectively positioned to implement it.

Danger signs take you up the awareness progression ladder; as they increase, you become more prepared. The main problem in awareness progression is missing, disregarding, or misinterpreting the danger signs. Danger signs are usually something out of place, something that does not feel right, someone looking nervous, someone following you, a bulge in a pocket, and so on. All of these and quite a few more constitute danger signs that your awareness picks up. Something is not right. If unaware, you will miss them. You must be able to spot something that is not right. People, for example, generally have a "normal" look, but when they are engaged in an illegal or dangerous act, they change; you must be able to spot the change.

The first danger sign must be spotted, not just the second or seventh. The first danger sign you see may be a gun in the threat's hand, but more than likely that was not the first danger sign given. If you miss the danger signs and the action starts, it will catch you unaware and unprepared, playing a catch-up game. If the situation happens instantly, it will appear to go by instantly. But if you have time and are prepared, it will be experienced much more slowly. The reality is: If you are aware and prepared, your chances of survival go up dramatically. You will be aware and prepared only if you catch the danger signs.

The Color Code System.   Many instructors use a color code system for threat progression. The system describes four or five colors that you progress through during an encounter, describing levels of alertness, readiness, or the action taking place. This system was introduced by Jeff Cooper, who modified a military color code system and applied it to defensive weaponcraft. The main advantage of this system is training people to become aware in the first place. Colonel Cooper brought this directly to the forefront, making civilians and police officers understand that awareness and a prepared state of mind are critical for survival.

The color code system generally in use today involves four levels of awareness of danger and responses to it:

Condition white. The officer is unaware of the immediate surroundings and thus is easily taken if the threat(s) presents itself.

Condition yellow. The officer is aware of the immediate surroundings. The officer is casually, though completely aware of what is going on around him or her. A police officer must never go below this condition. There is no perceived danger sign yet.

Condition orange. The appearance of the first danger sign alerts the officer that something may be wrong. The officer is now planning, watching for other danger signs, and checking his or her surroundings (finding out what is going on). This is commonly referred to as nonspecific alert—something may be wrong, but the officer may not be sure what it is.

Condition red. The officer has now confirmed that a threat exists and he or she becomes completely ready to respond to it. If possible, the officer will position himself or herself more effectively to respond to the threat(s) when it occurs, usually involving a covered position. This is commonly referred to as specific alert—something is wrong and you know exactly what it is. Whatever occurs after this point, the officer is completely ready to mentally and physically respond to it.

The color code system is used to increase your awareness and preparation throughout a situation. Four main truths are fundamental to it:

1. The first truth is: Being in condition white at the start of a lethal encounter will greatly reduce your chances of survival. If you are in white, you are completely unaware and easily taken.

2. The second truth is: Being in condition yellow is a lifetime commitment for a police officer. You must be aware, and yellow is a relaxed state of awareness that is easy to stay in during all waking hours.

3. The third truth is: The more time you spend in orange and red, the better prepared you are when the threat(s) occurs. Once your awareness tells you that something may be about to happen, the time you spend in orange and red preparing and planning (both mentally and physically) will pay off dramatically when the threat(s) occurs. You are instantly ready and prepared, reducing your reaction time to virtually nothing.

4. The fourth truth is: The situation can instantly switch from white to red. Nothing says that a situation has to work through all of the conditions. It can readily skip any of them. Your total awareness, by being in yellow, will be your only defense if a situation suddenly occurs (with no previous danger signs) and you find yourself in condition red.

These color code systems were used originally (and still are) by the military as a mechanism to bring a group of people to the same level of alertness at the same time. Their main value in defensive handgun use is teaching officers to be aware in the first place and to instantly prepare (both mentally and physically) for the threat.

Awareness progression is very simple. You MUST live your life in a state of eased awareness, being aware of the people, places, and events around you. When a danger sign is recognized, you flow with the situation by rising and falling with it. You will know what to do whether the danger signs increase or if the danger sign turns out to be nothing. The main factor is your awareness and ability to recognize danger signs. The longer you know a threat is about to occur, the better prepared you are when it does occur.

2. Self-control.   Awareness recognized the danger signs and prepared you for the threat(s). Now your self-control will be needed to function correctly when the threat(s) presents iteself and throughout the encounter. You must control yourself and the handgun during the encounter to stop the threat(s) successfully. You can control your environment only if you are under control.

Self-control is the basic factor that holds the other four elements together, yet it is nothing more than keeping your head during the encounter. When the encounter begins, self-control is exhibited by your ability to get to work instantly to place your "hits," employing the techniques to fire quickly and effectively on the threat(s). You must attend to your shooting techniques in a matter-of-fact manner, while making the critical decisions throughout the encounter. During these encounters, you do not need precise marksmanship, but you need to use correct techniques to place your "hits." When the bullets start flying, use self-control to get down to work by concentrating on your tactics, shooting skills, and critical decisions.

Self-Control and Fear.   During an encounter, especially one that you know is about to occur, fear may become the predominant emotion. If fear is left unchecked, it can slow down or blunt your reaction to the threat(s). When this occurs, use your self-control to overcome fear. When that strange empty feeling in your stomach begins, stop right there and control yourself. Get down to the work at hand. If you let fear grow and feed upon itself, it will become a debilitating problem. Do not allow fear to grow. You are a police officer and knew this would probably occur on the job, and you have been trained to handle it. Now, get down to the work that you have been trained for and handle it—stopping the threat(s) and making your immediate environment safe. Self-control is the key to controlling fear and will help you control the situation at hand.

If the threat(s) presents itself instantly, fear will probably have little or nothing to do with the encounter, as fear needs time to build up. If you were aware and recognized the danger signs early on, fear can build between the time you recognized the first danger sign until the threat(s) occurs. It is during this time that fear will do its worst, if you let it. At the first sign of fear, control it.

You must have confidence in your ability to keep your head during an encounter. With improved weapon use skills and an understanding of encounter tactics, you will have confidence in your ability to control the encounter. Once you have confidence in your abilities, you will have self-control.

3. Quick course of action.   Hopefully, your awareness has placed you one step ahead and you have already choosen a quick course of action to implement if the threat(s) occurs. If unaware, you will be caught flatfooted with fewer options open. If the threat(s) instantly appears and you are caught unaware, you will just as instantly have to select a course of action and implement it, carrying it through completely. When it is time to move, do not hesitate—do it. Once a course of action is started, carry it through completely. How quickly you are able to decide on a course of action will be based to a large part on practice. Once the course of action is selected, you must have confidence in what you have selected and your ability to carry it through.

Practice selecting courses of action by engaging in "scenario imaging." Form a mental image of a possibly pending encounter and quickly select a course of action. No matter where you are, scenario imaging can and should be practiced. Imagine sitting in a restaurant when two armed men come in the front door and announce a hold up. Imagine standing in a bank line when someone begins unwrapping a package and starts to take out a sawed-off shotgun. Imagine that you are about to unlock the door of your car when two men start moving toward you, split up, and are now coming toward you from different sides. Imagine sitting in a diner when somebody walks by with a gun in his pocket and sits down. The idea is that you must quickly plan a course of action to use, whether an armed threat suddenly appears or danger signs are recognized that a threat may possibly occur. With practice, your decision-making process will speed up and your confidence will increase.

Hesitation can be fatal. Once a course of action has been selected, it must be carried out. Do not hesitate, stop part way through, or change the plan midstream (unless instantly changing circumstances dictate that you must). Many hesitate too long and lose their chance or start to carry it out and stop halfway through. Half-measure tries will not work and may possibly get you killed. When it is time to move, you must do it instantly, with full force, and carry it through completely. Usually, a counterattack that follows these truths will work even if it is not the best course of action. At times the course of action is less important than the speed and force with which it is carried out.

Surprise is also a factor. If carried through properly, your course of action will probably catch the threat completely by surprise as it is in all likelihood not expecting you to attack. Once the threat is off balance, never let it recover. Keep "hitting" until the threat is stopped.

4. Aggressive speed in action.   Often the most important factor in winning an encounter is the aggressive speed you use when you make your move. Your response must be aggressive in nature and fast in action. If either of these are less than full force, your move may fail. When you make your move, you must move hard and fast, and not stop until the threat(s) is stopped. This will take a very aggressive and fast attack on your part and the attack must continue until the threat(s) is stopped. Understand that one of your best defense mechanisms is an instantaneous aggressive attack on the threat(s).

There is no holding back until the threat(s) is stopped. In all probability you are fighting for your life. Use all the power you possess and then some, to win. There is no second chance; you must win for yourself and your family.

5. Follow-through.   Once the encounter begins, you must follow it through to the very end. Even though an encounter seems ended, it may start up again. You must maintain your action and follow-through to the very end. Do not go soft just because one threat is down and appears to have been stopped: the threat may only have a minor wound and be faking it until you approach, or there maybe another threat you did not see in the initial exchange, or a crowd may become ugly. Stay on top of it until help arrives and the encounter has ended completely. Maintain cover and your 360-degree scan. Many officers have gone soft before the encounter has ended completely and been killed by a threat they presumed unable to attack them further. Play it safe; follow through.

These five mental elements for surviving lethal encounters cue you throughout the encounter to what you must do. Learn these and they will serve you well.

When caught up in a lethal encounter fighting for your life, your mental set is probably the most important factor to your survival. It involves all your decision-making processes, your self-control, and guides you through the encounter. Without the proper mental set you will be depending on luck to survive.

SURVIVAL REINFORCEMENT

The mind can be a tremendously restricting force that does not allow the body to use its full potential and resources. The most striking examples of this are officers with flesh wounds, who died because they decided they were going to. They died of wounds that, in and of themselves, would not cause death. These officers allowed shock to overcome and kill them. Examples also exist of officers shot many times in vital zones, yet they survived. How can you increase your ability to survive if shot? The main answer is: You must develop a tough mental attitude and decide that you are going to survive at all costs.

Do not let your mind restrict what your amazing body can do. Use your mind to strengthen your body and bring forth the hidden resources that your body possesses. There is a much greater chance that you will survive if you decide to survive no matter what happens. Just because you are shot, possibly shot in a vital zone, does not mean that you are going to die. You would not stop fighting the threat(s) if you had half a chance, so why would you stop fighting to survive just because you are wounded? Your chances of surviving are probably very good if you tell yourself you are going to survive and fight back the shock.

Survival reinforcement techniques can help you deal with the problems of lethal encounters long before they occur. In a lethal encounter you want to win, to survive. You begin preparing to survive by mentally engaging in survival reinforcement techniques to reinforce that you will survive. Basically, you mentally create simulations of many and varied lethal encounters, working through every aspect of these encounters, always reinforcing that you will survive. Akin to self-hypnosis, it provides you with an easily used method of facing the realities of lethal encounters, working through all aspects (both negative and positive) and always reinforcing that you will be a survivor.

This is usually accomplished while you are sitting quietly in some room away from all distractions. It is not something that has to be planned for. Say that you just sat down in your favorite chair to relax. In that quiet period, with your eyes closed while you are relaxing, think through some lethal encounters, with you as the main player. Simulate, work through, and visualize everything that will occur: how you would quickly plan a course of action, what would be the best covered location for you, watching the threat(s), what happens when the threat(s) attacks, your aggressive and fast counterattack, focus on the FRONT SIGHT, how you would react, how the threat(s) would react, you shooting the threat(s), you getting wounded, how you would follow-through (though wounded) until the encounter is completely ended, and so on.

Visualize many lethal encounters (especially anything that bothers you) and work through your actions, reactions, and decision-making processes during them. You are facing and working through lethal encounter problems beforehand. For this to be effective, realistic simulation is the key; reproduce the exact conditions of each encounter and feel it, as though it were really happening. Make it as real to you as you can by visualizing: the noise, the feeling of pain, the blood, the front sight as you pull the trigger, and so on. In short, visualize it all: anything involved with the lethal encounter. This is very important, as you must face and deal with these problems long before an encounter occurs. Visualize your mistakes and things that can go wrong. When working through each encounter, use the total encounter from beginning to end: before it occurred, during its occurrence, and after it has ended. Always visualize yourself as surviving no matter what.

When working through these encounters, you will find rough spots, areas that bother you or cause you to hesitate. These are problem areas to which you must give extra attention. Set up similar problems in other encounters and work through them a number of times. When these problems surface and are recognized, take care of them before they are faced on the street. For survival reinforcement to work, you must deal with these problems now. Do not wait for the encounter to deal with them. After awhile these rough spots will start to smooth out as you confront and deal with your problem areas. Survival reinforcement, by working through many different situations, will actually improve your skills when dealing with any situation.

Always end with a positive survival experience. Do not allow negative throughts to pervade this process. You can survive; there is no question of that. Officers are surviving all the time through the deadliness of encounters. Always work through these situations to a positive survival ending, reinforcing your survival advantage.

This process of survival reinforcement is used to strengthen your ability to survive by working through all aspects of lethal encounters: directly facing any problem areas that you have and setting yourself mentally to survive. With improved skills you will have greater confidence in your ability to handle any encounter, thus increasing self-control and reducing anxiety and fear. This process will also toughen you to any other crisis that you may have to face, creating a more prepared officer who is ready to deal effectively with any situation.

You have the ability to survive. Make a commitment to your survival by using this process. The survivor can be you.

SUMMARY

Throughout this chapter you have seen how your mental processes and bodily responses can help or hinder you when faced with a lethal encounter. As shown, the mental set is a preset state of mind used throughout lethal encounters. Every officer must develop it within himself or herself long before an encounter begins. When an encounter does occur, officers will revert to their survival response, based on what they have practiced and prepared for. This chapter covered the methods, techniques, and reasoning behind both the mental set and survival response necessary to survive an encounter. These are important parts of your total response to lethal threats, to increase your survival.

8

Cover and Concealment

The proper awareness and use of cover and concealment (C&C) is one of the most important tactical considerations that a police officer can make. Whether engaged in searching or during a lethal encounter, the officer's ability to survive may be based on his or her timely/effective use of C&C. To be aware and prepared to use cover, an officer must be aware of it, be positioned close to it, and be tactically ready to move behind it. The tactical awareness and use of cover must be developed as one of your premier tactical habits. Get in the habit of deciding on the closest available C&C options, considered close if you can get behind it in 2 seconds. Condition yourself to think cover and always be prepared to take advantage of it. Remember, C&C is not just an initial consideration when the action starts, but is always planned for and used before, during, and after a lethal encounter. Your ability to survive may depend on the correct use of C&C.

Cultivate an awareness of all the C&C options available to you, by noting them during your day-to-day movements. Obviously, this must become an on-duty habit, but also make this part of your off-duty habits; make it a life habit. By training in C&C option awareness, you are now one step ahead if the action should start, as you already know where the best C&C is and are instantly prepared to move to it. No thought is necessary—you know where to go without using precious seconds trying to find it. If you know that an encounter is about to start, position yourself behind cover before the threat(s) presents itself.

144

The main reason for using cover is to place you in a safe position to help you stay alive. All other reasons are secondary: being able to return fire, apprehending the threat(s), and so on. The main reason you are using cover is to stay alive. When effectively using cover during an encounter, move behind it, stay behind it, and fire from behind it. All secondary considerations can be addressed when you are safely behind cover as the bullets are flying. Obviously, there will be times when cover cannot be taken before you must engage the threat(s) and it would be foolhardy to attempt to move to cover under such circumstances, but if at all possible, cover is to be used during an encounter.

THE DIFFERENCE BETWEEN COVER AND CONCEALMENT

First, you must cultivate an awareness of the C&C options available to you. This begins with an understanding of the differences between cover and concealment. Cover is any object that will conceal part or all of the body and provide significant protection from projectiles (from slowing down a projectile to stopping it altogether). Concealment is any object or effect (shadows at night) that will hide part or all of the body but does not provide significant protection from projectiles. Both conceal the body (either the whole body or part of it) but only cover provides protection from incoming bullets. Cover's main function is to provide protection against bullets. Concealment's main function is to separate you from the threat(s) and hopefully provide the time needed for you to exit the immediate encounter zone or move to a covered position.

The importance when choosing between cover and concealment becomes obvious. If you have a choice, always select cover. If no cover is close at hand, concealment will have to do. At times, neither a cover nor a concealment option is close at hand—can be reached within 2 seconds. If that is the case, the encounter may have to be fought without the luxury of C&C. The hierarchy of C&C is: covered position first, concealed position second, in the open almost never.

In the street, examples of cover and concealment can be found everywhere. The first ability you must cultivate is being able to identify an object correctly as cover or concealment. Examples of excellent cover are brick walls, large trees, engine blocks of cars, telephone poles, fire hydrants, ditches, large rocks, mailboxes, earth rises, large metal dumpsters, the corner of almost any building, and so on. Examples of fairly good cover are cinderblock and some wooden walls, doorjambs, smaller trees, remainder of the car's body, and so on. For an object to be cover, it must be constructed substantially of solid material. If cover is close at hand, always use it. The problem is that cover may not always be close at hand when you need it. The next best object may only provide concealment, but that may have to do initially. Examples of concealment are walls in most houses, furniture, bushes, certain fences, store counters, and so on. Amazingly enough, although not considered cover, many will slow down or stop a goodly number of bullets, especially small pocket handgun rounds. But this cannot be counted on.

When getting behind a concealed position, it is only used very temporarily. Always consider a concealed position to be a temporary position. It is taken initially, as nothing better is around. Once a concealed position is taken, you must locate a covered position and make your move to it. Of course, the closest covered position may be too far and cannot be reached safely without subjecting yourself to extended threat fire. But if cover is close, move to it and get behind it.

The only reason to get behind a concealed position instantly is the hope that the threat(s) will not know the difference and stop shooting at you when you disappear. But also remember that it will not take the threat(s) long to figure out that it may be possible to shoot through the concealment you are behind. A concealed position must only be used very temporarily, affording temporary protection by hiding your movements.

C&C options awareness.   As stated first in the beginning of this chapter, the reality of selecting C&C must begin with an officer's tactical awareness of the C&C options available to him or her. If unaware of the C&C options available and the action suddenly starts, an officer may have to select instantly what he or she thinks is cover and move to it, and the move may be wrong. In your daily movements, be aware of C&C options and choose between them, all along the way, to be prepared when the action starts. This will reduce just one more of the decision-making processes, by having already selected the best C&C option before the encounter started.

C&C is a two-way proposition.   As you search through an area, C&C are available to both you and the threat(s) hiding. You will use C&C for protection and to hide the progress of your search while moving through an area. The threat(s) will use C&C to hide from you until it either attacks you or tries to make its escape. As such, C&C works both for and against you: You must use C&C throughout the search, yet you must be constantly aware of the C&C options available to the threat(s) and how it may use them against you.

The Hidden Perspective Effect.   Often the different perspectives of the officer and threat(s), as they face each other across some intervening cover, can lead to the officer being exposed without knowing it. Beware of this hidden perspective effect. An officer may think that he or she is fully hidden behind cover, but in fact the threat's angle of view (perspective) may allow it to see the officer, even though the officer does not see the threat. Officers must watch out for this and try to position themselves out of the threat's view. Always take this into consideration by trying to stay covered from areas where possible threat(s) could be located.

INITIAL THOUGHTS ON USING COVER

Be Behind Cover Whenever Initiating Any Action

Whenever you initiate the action, make sure that you are in a covered position and ready for the instant action that may occur. When you recognize a possible threat and decide to stop it before it presents itself (you have correctly read the danger signs and know that an encounter is pending), you must be positioned properly behind a good covered position before taking action. Only then make your move. Whatever the threat does, you are safely positioned and instantly ready to fire. You have the advantage and can usually maintain it during the encounter.

When you have the time and ability to select a proper covered position, you may want to do so away from the area you are then in. Too many innocents (a gunfight may kill or wound a number of them) or other considerations may be present that require you to move to an adjacent area to challenge the threat when it leaves the scene. If you can, exit the immediate area and take up a covered position in an adjacent area the threat will have to go through when leaving. Always try to keep in visual contact with the threat if possible. Engineer the situation to your advantage and wait for the threat. Your ability to use cover correctly will be your greatest advantage at this time.

Moving From C&C Position to C&C Position During an Encounter

Hopefully, during the initial stages of an encounter you have taken up a covered position. If you were aware and read the danger signs correctly before the encounter starts, you should be behind cover when it starts. If not, you may instantly have to move behind whatever C&C is closest during the opening ceremony (the initial exchange of gunfire). Do not try to shoot and move at the same time. Either remain stationary and shoot (which sometimes is the only option open to you) or move to a covered position and then fire. Do not engage in both at the same time, with the possible exception of laying down suppressive fire under extremely rare circumstances.

Once behind cover, you may be staying there throughout the entire encounter or moving to more appropriate cover, depending on the encounter and what is occurring. You are now planning one or two moves in advance and selecting C&C options that may be moved to. Always select the next C&C position before leaving your present one. Make sure that you know where you are going before you move. Plan all your moves in advance of executing them.

When you decide to make your move, put everything you have got into it.

Under no circumstances, slow down, stop, or change midstream. If you do, you will increase your exposure to direct fire, improving the threat's chances of "hitting" you successfully. You must quickly follow your movement through. You have decided where you are going before you made the move, now execute the move quickly. The next covered position should not be very far away, as you will probably have to move through an open area to the next position. Move only short distances each time. When moving a short distance (20 feet and under), spring up and run fast, bent forward at the waist, with your weight going forward. When moving a larger distance (20 feet or more) break up your movement by zigzagging back and forth, making it harder for the threat to "hit" you. Hopefully, before the threat is able to track you successfully, you are safely behind the next covered position.

Never move with a partially depleted handgun; reload before you make your move. If reloading is necessary, reload before moving. When you hit the next covered position, quickly assume a firing position. With the handgun in the strong hand, use the support hand to slow your contact with the cover; you will be running to it and the support hand will absorb the shock of the abrupt stop. As soon as you are at the next covered position, you should be ready to fire. Be in a good flexible position, with the handgun held in a two-handed firing position at least 1 foot behind the cover. In preparation, you may want to holster the handgun, as you may need two hands for climbing and it will lessen the chance of dropping your handgun if you slip and fall. Judge the area you will be crossing and the cover you will be going behind. Having the handgun holstered will also speed up recovery from a fall, as two hands are available to help you spring up with. If moving only short distances, there is no need to holster the handgun.

Allow nothing to telegraph your intention to make a move. Any visual or audible preparation will signal your intention to make a move. When it is time, spring into your move.

If you are in a good covered position, stay there unless forced to move, usually because your position is outflanked. A strong covered position is good, but flexibility is also important. If you become locked into a position and the threat(s) wants you, they will eventually get around to flanking your position to eliminate you. You must have enough flexibility to change locations if needed. Remember, flexibility in an encounter or on a search is extremely important.

Preplan your move from cover. You must know where you are going and the best way to get there. Depending on where your next covered position is, you will want to run the shortest possible distance until you have cover between you and the threat(s). Running directly from your position to the next one is not necessarily the shortest possible distance until intervening cover is between you and the threat(s). If the next covered position is laterally to the rear of your present one, you can back up from your cover, still keeping it between you and the threat(s), and then make your move. If the next covered position is diagonally in front of your present position, instead of running directly to it, run to the side until the cover is between you and the threat(s), and then finish running up to it. Move the shortest possible distance until intervening cover is between you and the threat(s).

APPROACHING, TURNING, AND SHOOTING AROUND COVER

On any search, officers will be moving through an area clearing it either by finding nothing or locating and controlling the threat(s). During these clearing operations many corners with hidden sides will be encountered. These corners must be turned in a safe and effective manner to find out what is on the hidden side—a threat(s) waiting to fire or just an empty area.

Two methods of turning cover are used: the glancing technique and the controlling technique. They are used separately and together, depending on the search problem and will increase your survival advantage if a threat(s) is waiting for you to turn the corner. When engaged in the clearing operations, officers must approach, turn, and sometimes shoot around these corners. We begin with the close approach of possible threat cover.

The Close Approach

As you approach possible threat cover, you must be in a firing position and mentally prepared to fire if necessary. Close approaching always stresses two of the basic search rules: Always be in a position to respond to the threat(s) (always in a firing position) and planning one or two alternative courses of action (options) if changes occur in the situation or structure. Obviously, you must use all the basic search rules (covered in Chapter 10), but these two are highly concentrated on during the close approach of possible threat cover (especially the last several seconds until the edge is turned).

If the threat(s) presents itself you can fire on it, but you must also have preplanned one or two options (in advance) that you can instantly take. There will also be times when you can get to the corner only by crossing an open area. We again stress that you must always be in a firing position and planning one or two options in advance. You must be prepared to fire and/or move instantly if attacked. When the edge, with its hidden side, is finally approached to be turned, you must be as prepared as possible, as you are very close to danger if a hidden threat(s) is there. You must quickly prepare to turn cover and expose the hidden area.

Approaching and preparing. Whenever you are approaching a corner, you must be in a firing position and preparing to turn cover. When turning cover we refer to checking the hidden side of some physical object where a threat(s) could be hiding. As such, there is some edge to be turned (whether to the side or above) with a hidden area behind it. Usually, you will move down a wall or some intervening surface [between you and a possible threat(s)] until the corner is reached. At that point you will then turn cover by using one of the two techniques to safely and effectively check out the hidden area. Approaching the corner, you must be in a position to fire and mentally ready to do so if necessary. Remember, cover is a two-way proposition; as you move closer to the corner and/or are ready to turn it, the threat(s) may come out from behind that corner and attack you. On the approach always be in a position to fire. Once close to the corner, you prepare by getting into position before actually turning the cover. As such, you approach the corner, position yourself beforehand, and only then turn the cover to see if a threat(s) is around the corner.

Your Reaction Area When Approaching.   The approach will end as the corner is reached and you position yourself to turn the cover. You are now extremely close if the threat(s) decides to attack. Watch for it and be ready to respond to it. On the last part of the approach, make sure that you stay away from the cover (the wall or surface you are moving along) and do not hug it. You must stay away from the cover as much as possible—by no less than an arm's length in preparation for turning the cover.

Staying away from the cover and corner as much as possible will afford you a larger reaction area in which to maneuver if the threat(s) attacks, giving you the distance needed to react in. If the threat(s) were to attack suddenly and you were hugging the wall, there would be no distance to counter it. The farther away from the cover and corner you are positioned, the better your chances of surviving an attack. Conversely, the closer you are to the corner, the better the chances the threat(s) has to attack you successfully. Turning the cover wide has the advantage of increasing your reaction area and making you harder to attack, especially with blunt or edged weapons. With many structures, it will not be possible to be very far back from the corner (if at all), but if you can increase your distance from the corner, do it.

The firing position is maintained through the whole process of turning cover: while approaching the corner, during preparation at the edge, and when actually turning the cover. As you closely approach the corner, the handgun will be in a

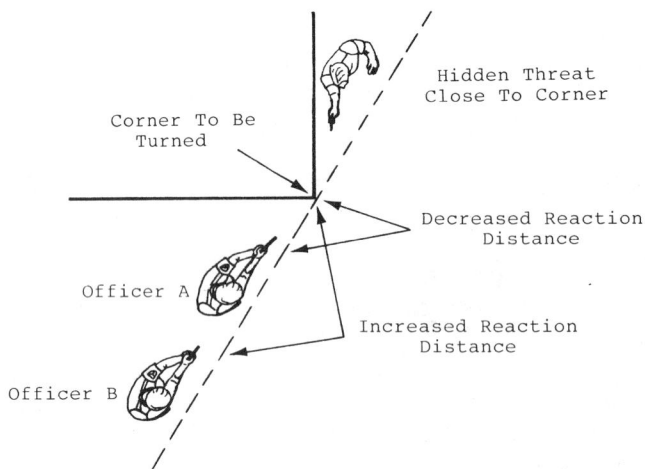

8.1.

Figure 8.1 Officer B has a much greater reaction distance than Officer A, who is too close to the corner.

firing position and you are ready to fire instantly. Being right on top of the corner to be turned is a critical time as you are the closest you will be to a threat(s). Be prepared to respond instantly. The threat(s) can use the corner to hide behind and shoot at you, just as you will use the corner against it. Turning the corner (finding out what is on the hidden side) is always coupled with an instant readiness to shoot (you are always in a firing position). This is also where a deadly mistake can be made, as there may be an innocent on the hidden side of the corner. By using the proper methods for turning cover, the chances of making a mistake such as this are greatly reduced. Remember, you must identify the threat before you can respond.

Positioned back from the edge.   When the approach ends and you are at the edge, you must position your body before turning cover. Positioning includes your relationship to the corner, placement of the legs and upper body, holding the handgun in a firing position, and how it all functions together (completely covered with the techniques).

The Edge.   There is an edge to any corner, where a small movement beyond that edge will show the hidden side. You step into position (position your body) and become ready just back from the edge. Then a small movement of head and handgun is all that is needed to clear the edge and see the hidden side. The same edge will present itself whether positioning yourself 3 feet away from the corner to be turned or 30 feet away from it. Stop just back from the edge to position yourself before turning cover.

Consider the edge as a line extending from the corner out as far as it will go. The side you approached and prepared on is the covered side and the other side of the line, when the edge is turned, is the exposed side. You can prepare to turn cover anywhere along the edge while you are on the covered side.

Turning Cover

Two methods for turning cover.   When turning cover several problems exist, and to solve these, two methods of turning cover are used: the glancing technique and the controlling technique. The glancing technique is used to take a very fast look into the hidden area and then instantly go back behind cover. The controlling technique is used not only to look into the hidden area, but to remain there, controlling it with the handgun. Using these can be tricky, as there are several problems involved, but they can work very well, especially showing you the mechanics behind turning cover.

The Problems.   Problem 1: If you take a glancing look by popping out and back, you will get a fast look into the hidden area, usually not seeing everything but definitely seeing a threat positioned at the corner ready to attack and staying under its reaction time (if the threat attacks, you are already back behind cover). If instantly attacked, you have avoided it successfully, which is the main purpose of this technique. By popping out and back, though, you have no control over the area

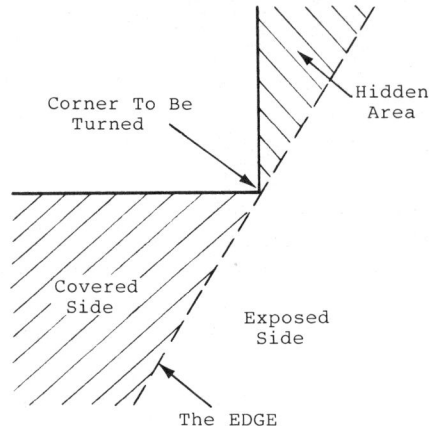

Corner To Be
Turned

Hidden
Area

Covered
Side

Exposed
Side

The EDGE

8.2.

Figure 8.2 The edge is a line that must be broken for the officer to see into the hidden area or the threat to see into the covered area.

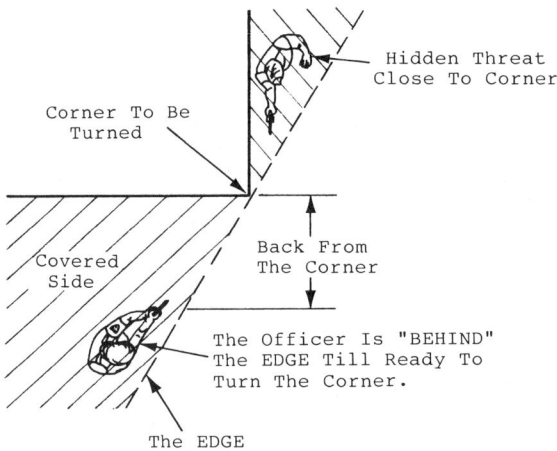

Hidden Threat
Close To Corner

Corner To Be
Turned

Back From
The Corner

Covered
Side

The Officer Is "BEHIND"
The EDGE Till Ready To
Turn The Corner.

The EDGE

8.3.

Figure 8.3 Before turning the corner, the officer should increase the reaction distance as much as possible and be in a prepared position, ready to break the edge.

(you are back behind cover) and you have not really had a good look into the area [you may not see a hidden threat(s)]. Problem 2: If, instead, you use the controlling technique by popping out and staying, you will completely see the area and control it, but may be attacked instantly at the corner or targeted by a well-hidden threat. When you are out to stay, you can control the area with the handgun in a firing position, but may initially be vulnerable to attack (especially in being unable to locate a hidden threat immediately). There are two different controlling techniques that improve its function.

In the final analysis, these techniques are used separately and together when turning cover. Just using these will give you a decided advantage, by showing you how to position yourself properly and turn cover correctly.

The glancing technique. The glancing technique is a method for turning cover safely and effectively to accomplish two tasks: to check the other side of cover for the threat(s) and stay under its reaction time. The technique was developed to fill the need for a safe and effective method of turning cover, which gave the officer the advantage if an armed threat(s) was waiting on the other side at (or close to) the corner. When used, the glance will place you in a prepared position, instantly ready to fire if necessary, and under the threat's reaction time if it attacks instantly.

The technique hinges on three factors to turn the corner successfully: (1) you must be in a position to fire, (2) expose as little of your body as possible, and (3) stay under the threat's reaction time. This is done by popping out in a position to fire, with only a small part of the head, hand, and forearm showing, and popping back instantly: out and back, just that fast. What you see around the corner and what the threat(s) does will dictate your next reactions.

The glance will give you an initial look into the hidden area. With the handgun ready, you pop out for the glance with as small a part of your head and body as possible and then pop back (head and barrel go out together as a unit and go back in together). The time lapse was less than a second and you should be able to take in all the hidden area and see any noncovered threat(s). The whole idea is that you are popping out for a glance, knowing that you are popping back instantly: instantly out and back. If a threat(s) is there and tries to attack, you are well under its reaction time and any attack will find you safely back behind cover. If the threat(s) charges out to attack you, it will get the muzzle of your handgun. When using the glance correctly, you are ready to find out what is in the hidden area and ready to respond to it.

Positioning Behind the Edge. Once you have approached the edge, you must position yourself before turning cover. (*Note:* The close approach has placed you just behind the edge. Now you must position yourself and your firing stance before turning the edge.) Just behind the edge, you "step into position" (correctly positioning your body and firing position) for the glance. You are away from the actual corner by at least an arm's length (if at all possible, much farther), with the end of the handgun's barrel, when held out in a firing position, being away from the corner by at least 5 or 6 inches (if only an arm's length away from the corner). Try to be back from the corner as far as possible. When preparing, you face the corner to be turned, with the firing stance pointing at the corner and muzzle well back from it. Once properly positioned, the glance is made.

Positioning for the glance is natural and quick as you step into position. After you learn and practice it a few times, it begins to flow right with the search. The placement of the feet, body, and firing stance are the same for both the glancing and controlling techniques. There is only one method of positioning yourself when turning cover. (*Note:* The bodily positioning will be described for the glancing technique, although it also applies to the controlling technique.) We begin with placement of the feet.

Foot placement is important not only for balance, but also for the glance to function smoothly. When turning a corner, you will turn it either to the right or left and the front leg (closest to the corner when facing it) is the main one used to rock your upper body out and then back. [*Note:* To a threat(s), you appear to pop out and back instantly, but the movement is described more correctly as rock out and back, to reflect the way the legs rock the upper body out and then back.] The upper body is slightly bent toward the side to be gone around, but the front leg's knee is slightly bent directly toward the corner. This is very important, for when the knee bends a little to rock the upper body out and slightly forward, the knee must not go beyond the edge of the corner and be exposed.

If turning the corner to the right, the right leg is the front leg (the rear leg, the left leg, is to the rear of the body) and the body is bent slightly to the right side. The whole upper body is locked into a firing position before the glance. When time to glance, the front-leg knee bends slightly forward directly toward the corner and the waist bends slightly more to the side. The movements cause the upper body to rock out and slightly forward, with only part of the head, handgun, and hands clearing the edge. Then instantly the legs and waist rock the upper body back, bringing the head, handgun, and hands back behind the edge: out and back, just that fast. (*Note:* The front leg's knee bends slightly, as this is not a deep stance but just enough to rock the upper body out and back.)

We refer to positioning yourself as "stepping into position," because it is that easy and quick. It has to function smoothly and quickly in order to flow with the search. The front leg steps into position with the upper body locked into the firing stance, and you are ready.

Stepping into position behind the edge is accomplished quickly and easily and the glance is done very fast during the continuing search. There is nothing hard about this. Once the positioning is practiced a couple of times you will know what to do. Only two firing positions are used, either a one- or a two-handed firing position.

The One- and Two-Handed Firing Positions.

There are only two firing positions used: one for one-handed firing and another for two-handed firing. Both of these allow for the most limited exposure of the body when glancing. Two firing positions are used, as the realities of the search may require one-handed use, where one hand may be needed to perform some task (opening doors, holding a flashlight, moving an object at the corner, holding a small extendable mirror around a corner), or the area is so close that a two-handed firing position cannot be used. As such, only one hand can be on the handgun. A two-handed firing position is preferred and used whenever possible, but many times this is not possible and you must train for one-handed use.

One-handed. You close-approached the corner with the handgun held in a firing position (approach with a two-handed firing position if possible, even though a one-handed firing position may have to be used to turn the corner). Once at corner and just back from the edge, you step into position, with the handgun held in a one-handed firing stance pointed directly at the corner (with a 90- to 135-degree bend in the elbow). As the upper body is rocked out, the head pops out, with the

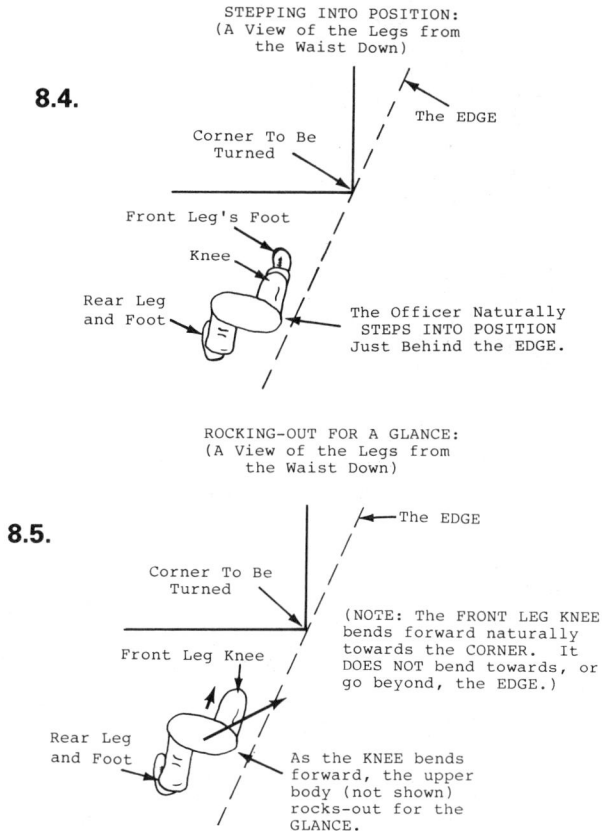

STEPPING INTO POSITION:
(A View of the Legs from
the Waist Down)

8.4.

The EDGE

Corner To Be
Turned

Front Leg's Foot

Knee

Rear Leg
and Foot

The Officer Naturally
STEPS INTO POSITION
Just Behind the EDGE.

ROCKING-OUT FOR A GLANCE:
(A View of the Legs from
the Waist Down)

8.5.

The EDGE

Corner To Be
Turned

Front Leg Knee

(NOTE: The FRONT LEG KNEE
bends forward naturally
towards the CORNER. It
DOES NOT bend towards, or
go beyond, the EDGE.)

Rear Leg
and Foot

As the KNEE bends
forward, the upper
body (not shown)
rocks-out for the
GLANCE.

Figures 8.4 and 8.5 Step into position with the leg closest to the corner (Fig. 8.4). When turning the corner, the front leg knee bends forward, directly toward the corner, and the body weight rocks out overtop of that knee (Fig. 8.5). Make sure that the knee stays behind cover. (Note: Drawings not to scale.)

arm simultaneously bringing the handgun out about 1 foot below the head, then both go back—out and back together. A threat(s) hiding there would see only part of a head and the handgun about 1 foot below it. If you need to fire instantly as the threat(s) attacks, use the pointing method to align the handgun and pull the trigger, which will present no problem, as the threat will be close.

Two-handed. You close-approached the corner with the handgun held in a two-handed firing position. Once at the corner and just back from the edge, you step into position, with the handgun held in a two-handed firing stance barely below eye level (so you can have a better view as you pop out) pointed directly at the corner. As the upper body is rocked out, the head and handgun popout together, then both go back: out and back together. A threat(s) hiding there would see head, aimed handgun, and part of forearm. If you need to fire instantly, the handgun is brought up to eye level and fired.

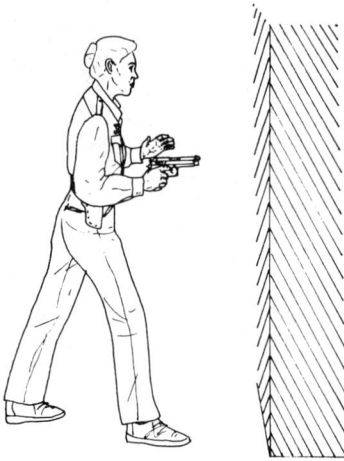  

8.6.   **8.7.**   **8.8.**

Figure 8.6 Step into position, behind the edge.
Figure 8.7 Rock out.
Figure 8.8 What the threat would see—part of the head and handgun about a foot below it.

  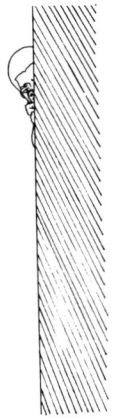

8.9.   **8.10.**   **8.11.**

Figure 8.9 Step into position, behind the edge.
Figure 8.10 Rock out.
Figure 8.11 What the threat would see—part of the head, handgun, and forearm.

THREE COMMON MISTAKES WHEN TURNING COVER

1. Too close to cover. If the threat(s) is right there, the officer has no chance to maneuver.

2. Turning cover while not in a position to fire instantly. The handgun must be held in a firing position and ready to fire whenever turning cover.

3. Too much exposure of the body. Only a small amount of the body need be exposed when turning cover. Make yourself the smallest target you can. Commonly referred to as the "jack-in-the-box" mistake—popping out with almost all of the body.

8.12.   **8.13.**   **8.14.**

Figure 8.12   Too close to cover.
Figure 8.13   Turning cover when not in a position to fire.
Figure 8.14   Turning cover with too much exposure of the body.

Prime examples of these three common mistakes can be seen during any TV police show. Whenever TV police officers are about to turn cover, it never fails that they have their handguns held up, next to their heads, with their backs laying along the wall directly at the corner. When it is time to move, they turn the cover by jumping completely away from the cover they could have used, legs spread, and only now bringing the handgun down to try and find the target. Very dramatic, yes; very realistic, no! You must be completely ready and prepared before you turn cover. If you are not, you may get caught.

The controlling technique.   The glancing technique is used to pop out and back instantly, while the controlling technique is used to come out and stay out. This technique is used to establish and maintain control over an area while looking over your sights. You come out in a position to fire and establish and maintain control. The main problem in its use is being attacked immediately by either a threat located right at the corner or a well-hidden threat that you do not see initially. Often, glance is used first to take care of a possible threat at the corner, then coming back out (at a different level) to control the area.

There are two controlling techniques—locking out and angling out—that can be used, depending on the situation. Locking out is the quicker of the two and accomplished exactly as the glance, except that you do not pop back behind cover; when you pop out, you stay out. Angling out is a process of sectioning the hidden area, one section at a time, to clear and control each section. In both, you step into position and prepare yourself the same as when using the glancing technique. Always be in a firing position when turning cover.

Controlling techniques can work well to control a threat(s), with you in a good covered position and looking over your sights. But these controlling techniques are not meant to be interpreted as stay-out-at-all-costs techniques. If the hidden area is not controllable, get back behind cover. When trying to control a hidden area, you may suddenly find yourself confronted by more than one threat and/or a threat(s) with superior weapons. If the control problem is too large, instantly move back behind cover. Do not forget this. These techniques can give you the ability to control the hidden area, but if you find a much larger control problem, move back behind cover.

Locking out.   This controlling technique is nothing more than the first half of the glancing technique. In the glance, you pop out and back, and when locking out you pop out and stay out. Everything is done exactly the same as in the glancing technique, except that you do not pop back. You pop out and stay out to establish and maintain control over the hidden area. Follow all of the preparatory steps for the glancing technique.

This technique is much quicker than angling out, but in doing so presents the problem of having instantly to take in, visually understand, and control the entire hidden area. This may present a real problem if there is more than one threat and/ or the threat(s) has superior weapons. If confronted by a control problem, instantly move back behind cover. Locking out is used after first glancing, to take a quick look into the hidden area. Once the glance gives you a glimpse of the hidden area, locking out (at a different level) can be used to control it.

Angling Out.   This controlling technique, although slower, allows the hidden area to be cleared and controlled a piece at a time instead of coming out and trying to control all the hidden area instantly. It is accomplished by angling around the corner one section at a time, which takes longer, but exposes only small sections of the hidden area to clear and control, one at a time. It trades speed for an improved ability to establish control, by reducing the area to be controlled. Basically, the hidden area is controlled one step at a time.

To understand this, consider the corner to be the center of a circle, with you being anywhere along the edge (on the covered side). As you angle around the circle, moving slowly a half-step at a time, your eyes and muzzle of the handgun will take in a small section of the hidden area each time you move. When each section is viewed, you can see much more readily what the small section holds and control it. Each small section is cleared and controlled until the whole hidden area is revealed. If a threat is found, the officer is in a firing position to respond instantly if necessary. When done correctly, the officer can often see some part of the threat before the threat sees the officer (especially a threat at the corner).

The angling-out technique is prepared for exactly like the glancing technique, before the edge is turned. Once in position, the technique uses small half-steps for each section. The half-steps are done by the front foot taking a half-step to the side and then the rear foot taking a half-step by moving over toward the front foot. The front foot then continues the process by taking another half-step. Each foot movement is a half-step, which will reveal another section. The technique works like this: half-step (front foot), scan/control; half-step (rear foot), scan/control; half-step (front foot), scan/control; and so on. Remember to keep the feet about shoulder width apart and maintain your balance and flexibility. If you are very close to the corner (an arm's length), the half-steps will have to move only 6 to 10 inches to reveal a large enough section; if you are 10 feet away from the corner, to cover the same area, the half-steps will have to move twice the distance and more. The farther away you are, the larger the half-steps will have to be. When half-stepping, you move around the circle as if on a ring of the circle. The name is derived from the angling around the circle.

Angling out is usually done by itself as a single technique; nothing precedes it. When it is time to turn cover, the angling-out technique performs the task methodically. It takes longer than the locking-out technique, but not that much longer.

Using any of these techniques when turning cover is tricky but gives you a decided advantage if you use them correctly. Whenever using them, always be flexible and ready to move back behind cover.

Glancing and controlling, used separately and together.   When turning cover, the angling-out technique is always used by itself to locate and control a threat(s), but the glancing and locking-out techniques are used together much of the time, and their combined use must be understood. Most of the time, glancing is used first to locate a very close threat that may be waiting to attack the instant you appear. Once glancing initially indicates what is in the hidden area, you either control it or move back to a covered position.

Generally, you use the glancing technique and pop out and back to locate the threat(s) and stay under its reaction time if attacked. If a threat is there and attacks, you are under its reaction time as you instantly disappear behind cover. Once the glance has located a threat (whether it attacks or not): you can now lock out at a different level and control and arrest, or shoot if the threat begins or continues an attack. Always make sure that you use the corner's cover (by using the edge), both when glancing out and when locking out.

A secondary option, especially if more than one threat or superior weapons are involved, is to move rearward to a covered position from the corner. Your other search team members(s) should be in a backup position(s) covering you as you turn the corner. Now, as you move rearward to the backup's position, the backup(s) will cover your movement. If the threat(s) suddenly comes out to attack, the back-up(s) will engage it.

If the glance reveals no threat(s), fine. Pop back out and stay locked out to control the area and check it out again, double-checking to make sure that a threat(s) is not there. Once cleared, go around the corner and continue the search. Whenever glancing or locking out at a corner, you must use a different level each time. This usually means higher or lower than the last position you came out at, as your previous location may be targeted (the threat is aiming directly at the last position where you appeared).

Turning cover more than once.   When you pop out and back for the initial glance at the hidden side, if you found a threat, you can come out again either to control and arrest or fire as it attacks or continues an attack. Whatever else you are doing, you must come out at a different level. Once you have popped out and back at a level (a certain point along the side of the corner), the threat has located you and may be concentrating/aiming at that point. Surprise the threat by coming back out at a different level (either lower or higher). Do not come back out at the same point. Usually, only one side (corner) is available when turning cover, but if another side is available (usually when the cover is a large object) it can be used to surprise the threat by appearing at the different side. Also, limited use can be made of the top of an object, although as a rule any cover should be turned at its side, not over its top.

[*Note:* When turning cover and you find more than one armed threat or the threat(s) has superior weapons, the best option is to return to the backup officer(s) position and if necessary call in the troops. Just because you have located a threat(s) does not mean that you have to engage it at that precise moment or in that location, which may not favor you. If the threat(s) attacks, there will be no choice. But if the threat(s) does not attack, the option is yours. If you have the option, use it correctly.]

Three levels for turning cover.   There are three levels used when turning cover, and each level has a shooting position associated with it: high/standing, medium/crouching, and low/kneeling. You must be able to move quickly into another shooting position to come back out at a different level (higher or lower). Say that you glanced at a high level in a standing position and located a threat; now you drop quickly into a kneeling position (a different level) and lock out at a low level.

Flexibility is an important factor in any encounter situation. When turning cover, flexibility is vital, as you must have the ability to move quickly if necessary. The standing and crouching positions provide the most flexibility, as the officer can quickly move from either. The kneeling position is fairly flexible, as the officer can rise quickly from the one-knee-down position and move. The prone position is not used when turning cover as it takes too long to assume and is the slowest to move from (although many people would be surprised just how quickly an officer can rise and move from it). Also, the setting position is never used in any defensive firing; completely disregard this position.

To be used quickly and with flexibility, all the positions must make use of the same feet placement and upper body lock. When it is time to change your position and come back out quickly at another level, the feet remain in the same position, as only the legs and waist bend to lower or raise the body. Whichever one- or two-handed firing position you have decided upon can be used at any level.

High/Standing.   This position was covered in the initial explanation of how the body was positioned behind the edge. The front leg's foot (closest to the corner) is in front of the body with the knee slightly bent directly toward the corner and the rear leg's foot is behind the body. When stepping into position, the front leg takes a normal step (either forward or to the side) and plants the foot, with the feet being about shoulders' width apart. With the stance facing forward (directly toward the corner), the body is balanced between the feet and slightly bent at the waist toward the side to be turned, and the upper body is locked into a firing position directed at the corner. When rocking out and back from behind the edge, the strength and balance of the stance rests on the front leg, the upper body rocking out and back at an angle, directly over top of it. Make sure that no part of the front leg is exposed, by keeping it back from the edge. The feet do not have to move when quickly assuming the other two positions; only the bending of the knees and waist is used to lower the stance.

As you arrive at the corner, you "step into position," by the front leg stepping forward or sideways and planting that foot just back from the edge. Easily and naturally, just step into position. The upper body was already locked into the firing stance as you approached. By stepping into position and bending slightly at the waist toward the side to be turned, you are ready to turn cover instantly.

Medium/Crouching.   With the feet in the same positions, merely bend both knees farther to lower the body and bend the upper body slightly farther to the side for the medium/crouching position. This will lower the upper body to a halfway point between standing and kneeling. Rock out and back by bending the waist and using the knees.

Low/Kneeling.   With the feet in the same positions, come to a kneeling position with the rear leg's knee touching the ground. Rock out and back by bending the waist with the lower body and knees almost not moving at all. Make sure that the front leg's knee is held in and not allowed to move out from behind cover when rocking out. (*Note:* The front leg, with the knee up, allows the quickest and surest method of instantly rising and pushing away from the corner if you need to move quickly.)

Which level to use first.   The order in which these positions are used is dependent on the backup officer(s) positioning, as the officer(s) must be able to fire at an attack threat(s), while the point officer may be positioned forward of the backup officer(s). Two situations occur: (1) the point officer is in between the backup officer(s) and the corner (usually a tight area), or (2) the point officer is to the side of the backup officer(s) (usually an open area).

8.15.

8.16.

8.17.

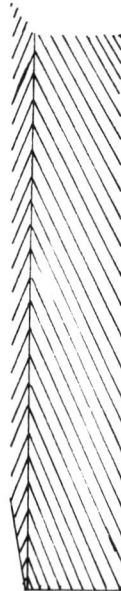

8.18.

Figures 8.15–8.18 The high/standing position is assumed, still behind the edge: side and front views (Figs. 8.15 and 8.16). The corner is turned by rocking out: side and front views (Figs. 8.17 and 8.18).

8.19.   **8.20.**

8.21.   **8.22.**

Figures 8.19–8.22 The medium/crouching position is assumed, still behind the edge: side and front views (Figs. 8.19 and 8.20). The corner is turned by rocking out: side and front views (Figs. 8.21 and 8.22).

8.23.

8.24.

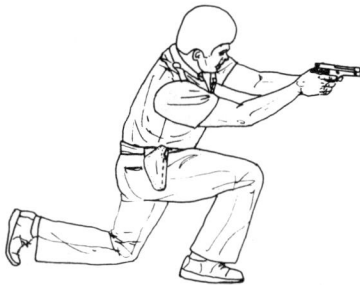

8.25.

8.26.

Figures 8.23–8.26 The low/kneeling position is assumed, still behind the edge: side and front views (Figs. 8.23 and 8.24). The corner is turned by rocking out: side and front views (Figs. 8.25 and 8.26).

The Point Officer in Between.   When turning cover in tight areas, the point officer may have to be in between the corner to be turned and the backup officer(s), who will have a clear firing area only if the point officer is low (in a kneeling position). As such, glancing is first done in a medium or high position to discover the threat, so when the point officer comes back out again when locking out to control and/or fire, he or she will be in a "low" position if the firing occurs. (*Note:* If glancing is first done in a low position, the point officer would have to come back out again when locking out at a higher level, reducing the backup officer's firing

8.27.

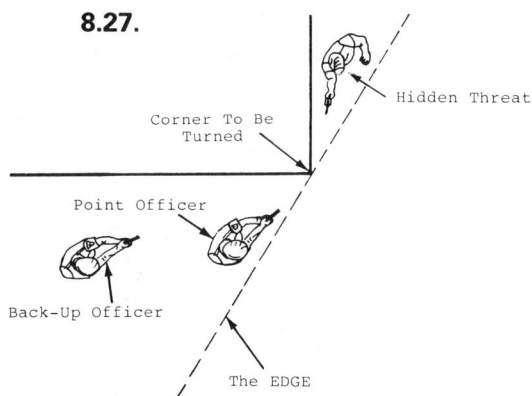

Corner To Be Turned

Hidden Threat

Point Officer

Back-Up Officer

The EDGE

8.28.

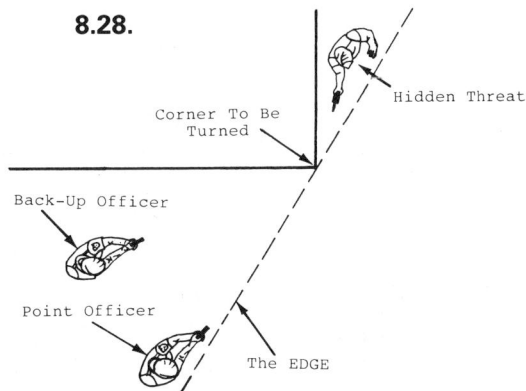

Corner To Be Turned

Hidden Threat

Back-Up Officer

Point Officer

The EDGE

Figures 8.27 and 8.28   The point officer in between (Fig. 8.27) and the point officer to the side (Fig. 8.28).

area.) Also, if a backup officer is to advance and take up a closer support position at the edge, he or she just steps into a high position, back from and over top of the point officer, to add a secondary control element to the area.

When the point officer turns cover for the first time, he or she must be in a medium or high position. If turning cover the first time reveals a hidden threat(s), the point officer quickly drops down to a low position when coming back out again to either control and arrest or fire if necessary. When the point officer drops into a low position, this bodily movement (no verbal communication needs to be made) alerts the backup officer(s) that a threat(s) has been located and gives the backup(s) a clear firing area with the point officer in a low position. If the point officer decides to backoff from the corner, he or she will maintain a firing position and quickly back away from the corner. Again, this bodily movement will alert the backup officer(s) that the threat(s) has been located and the backing-away point officer will give a clear firing area. (*Note:* The only time a medium or high position would not be used when turning cover the first time is if the cover itself was low and only a low position could be used.)

If the point officer needs to take a second glance, or comes back out again to lock out and control an area where no threat was found, he or she would use either a medium or a high position—opposite from the first one used. The low position is saved for when a threat(s) is located or if cover itself is low.

The Point Officer to the Side.   Usually, when the point officer can be to the side, the area is more open. The backup officer(s) now has a clear firing area, as the point officer is away from the corner. The point officer should still use a medium or high position for the first glance, going to a low position if the threat is located, thus providing the same bodily movement cues for the backup officer(s). Also, backing off should be done the same as in the first method.

Many will say that you should initially turn cover from a medium or low position, not a high, eye-level position, especially when you know or think a threat(s) is close. An officer's head at eye level is what most threats will expect to see first and if a gun is being aimed, you can bet it will be at eye level. This is true especially if the threat(s) knows you are close, but as long as the glance is used correctly whenever initially turning cover, you will be well under the threat's reaction time if it fires. If a threat(s) is found, the high/low combination is very effective, due to the large difference in the levels at which the officer appears. The threat first sees the officer pop out high and if it prepares to fire, there is quite a surprise when the officer suddenly pops back out low. In fact, if the threat is aiming the gun, it may not even see the officer pop back out low. If a crouch/low combination is used, the threat may adjust by lowering its position to match the officer's first crouch position and be closer to the low position that the officer will use next.

Be very careful on your approach and positioning before the corner is turned, as noise, light, or reflections can tell the threat(s) if you are going to pop out high, medium, or low. Light splash is a real problem when turning cover and can quickly give your intentions away. Use the flashlight carefully and always be aware of light sources around you.

Once the first glance surprises the threat, keep surprising it by coming back out at a different level or location. When surprising the threat, also remember the rule of three. By the third time you have popped out and back at several points up and down the corner, the threat may begin to figure things out. The threat may now be aiming not at the last point you came out, but at one of the other two where you may appear, with a 50/50 chance that you will come back out where the threat is aiming. Never continually pop out and back along the same corner more than three times. In reality, you will rarely get past two times. Instead of continuing, back off to the backup officer's covered position and with sufficient officers present, contain and control the threat(s). Also, when more than one armed threat is present and/or the threat(s) has superior weapons, back off to the backup officer's covered position and proceed only when sufficient officers are present.

When turning cover, tools such as mechanics mirrors are available and will allow you to stay behind cover for the initial look into a hidden area. The techniques shown here are used when no other tool is present to check out hidden areas. Also, the situation may dictate the use of other methods.

Shooting Around Cover

An understanding of how the two firing stances function.   When discussing methods of firing around cover, we again have to involve the two-handed stances: the Weaver and Isosceles firing stances. Each of these works well when turning cover, but you must understand how to make them work while staying covered. The main purpose of turning cover and/or firing from a covered position is the protection the cover provides from incoming bullets. To use cover effectively the least amount of body must be exposed when turning cover and/or firing the handgun. When firing around cover, only a part of the head, the hands holding the handgun, and a small portion of the forearm need be exposed. There is no need to expose any more of the body. Especially make sure that no part of the front leg or its foot is exposed.

The Strong and Support Sides of Cover.   A quick note on the strong and support sides of cover is important to the following explanation. As you are facing cover, you will either be turning or shooting around "your" strong or support side of cover. When we refer to the strong side of cover, it is your strong side: If you are right-handed, the right side of cover is your strong side; if left-handed, the left side of cover is your strong side. Strong and support sides of cover do not refer to which is best to shoot around, but are used when explaining the techniques you will use to fire around cover. Remember, whenever we refer to the strong side, we are referring to your strong-hand side (if you're right handed, your right side); similarly, whenever we refer to the support side, we are referring to your support-hand side (if you're right handed, your left side). The opposite will be true for left-handed officers.

Use your trained-in firing stance and cant it when firing around cover.   When firing around cover you will use your trained-in firing stance without much change. The limited body exposure will be accomplished by canting the handgun and stance toward the side to be turned. Canting is done by slightly turning the wrists and arms while slightly bending the entire upper body at the waist. Neither the master grip on the handgun nor the two-handed firing grip is bastardized when canting. The angled position of the Weaver stance is perfectly suited to fire around the strong side of cover, with virtually no canting required. But when the Weaver is used to fire around the support side of cover, the stance must be canted quite a bit. The Isosceles stance must be canted quite a bit on both sides or it would expose too much of the body.

Canting the Firing Stance and Handgun.   Canting reduces the amount of upper body exposure when firing around cover by tilting the firing stance and handgun toward the side to be turned. This is not an exaggerated tilt, but a slight one, with the handgun being tilted between 20 and 30 degrees from the perpendicular (from straight up and down), but not tilted more than 30 dgrees. Most of the tilt is accomplished by slightly bending the waist, which tilts the entire upper body and handgun. The wrists and arms are slightly turned to make any fine adjustments to the mix. Everyone differs a small amount bodily and you must find out what is most comfortable and workable for you.

When canting the handgun, its sights will be slightly tilted. How does this effect aiming? At close ranges, 10 yards and under, there will be little realistic change in the point of impact; just aim where you normally would and fire. After 10 yards and/or if a very small target is presented, you can compensate for the canted handgun. If you are canting the handgun to the left, compensate by aiming slightly high and to the right. If canting the handgun to the right, compensate by

 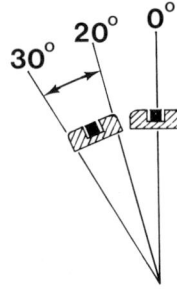

8.29.   **8.30.**

Figures 8.29–8.30   The stance is canted from the waist
(Fig. 8.29). The sights are canted between 20 and 30 degrees, but no more than 30 degrees (Fig. 8.30).

aiming slightly high and to the left. A rule for this would be: Always aim slightly
high and slightly opposite from the cant.

You Must Switch the Eyes.   Firing around the strong side of cover presents
no problem; just use your strong-side eye. Switching to the support-side eye when
firing around the support side of cover is a little harder to get used to. When firing
around the support side of cover, you must use your support-side eye to expose less
of your head. If you use the strong-side eye, almost all of your head will be exposed
beyond the cover. The support-side eye will function very well to align the sights;
use it.

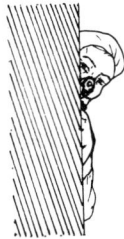 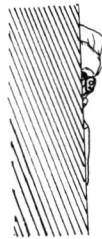

8.31.   **8.32.**

Figures 8.31 and 8.32   When firing around the support
side of cover, if using the strong eye, too much of the
head will be exposed (Fig. 8.31). You must use the support eye when turning the support side of cover, for less
head exposure (Fig. 8.32).

Switching the handgun.   When the support side of cover is turned, some
say to switch the handgun from the strong hand to the support hand, then assume
your firing stance on the opposite side of your body. This is usually done when
using the Weaver stance, as switching the stance to the support side makes it fit

perfectly (just like it does on the strong side). If you practice and use it, it will work very well. In reality, switching should not be done, with one exception, as officers will not practice it or use it in stress situations. Most officers will not practice it enough to make it part of their reflexive sets and during real situations they will not use it. Just keep the handgun in the strong hand and cant it when turning support-side cover, unless too tight to maneuver the handgun properly.

There is only one need for switching: when actual space limitations at the corner to be turned require that the handgun be in the support hand. If a tight corner must be turned on the support side, the handgun must be in the support hand, as your strong hand and arm will have trouble maneuvering the handgun when turning the corner. When close and tight, the handgun must be in the strong hand for a strong-side corner and in the support hand for a support-side corner. Test this yourself in a small closet doorway, for instance, and you will see what we mean.

The Quick Switch. If switching is called for, it must be performed quickly and easily. The technique for switching the handgun is called the quick switch and is done by following these steps:

1. Bring the support hand exactly opposite the strong hand gripping the handgun (with the trigger finger out of the trigger guard). The support hand is held ready to accept the handgun's grip by the fingers being partially closed, with the thumb held straight up and the index finger held away from the other fingers.
2. The strong hand's thumb releases the grip and is held straight up, as the joints where the fingers join the hand pull the fingers slightly back while the fingers are still wrapped around and holding the front of the grip. This will cause the handgun grip's backstrap to tilt out from the strong hand toward the support hand.
3. The support hand now begins to grip the handgun by the web (between the thumb and the index finger) going high on the backstrap as the thumb and the index finger grip either side of the frame. Keep the trigger finger straight along the side of the frame.
4. Instantly, the strong hand releases the handgun as the support hand fingers wrap around the front of the grip. The handgun is switched.

During the switch, control of the handgun is always maintained. Practice the quick switch with an unloaded handgun, by switching it back and forth several times until the technique works easily. Hold the handgun directly in front of your body when practicing—about 8 to 10 inches away from it. When first learning, practice over top of a bed or other soft surface in case the handgun is dropped. Whether revolver or automatic, it works the same, but with a S-A auto, push the safety ''on'' before making the switch. Also note that the trigger finger is always out of the trigger guard throughout the quick switch. Make sure both index fingers are straight alongside the frame when making the switch.

8.33.

8.34.

8.35.

8.36.

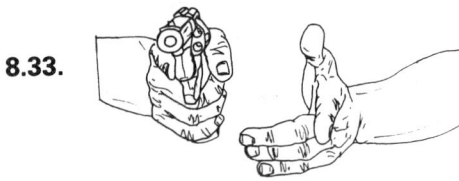

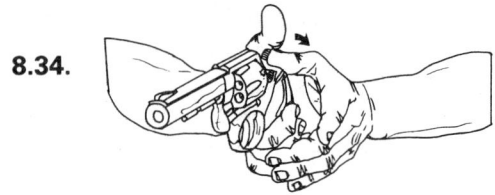

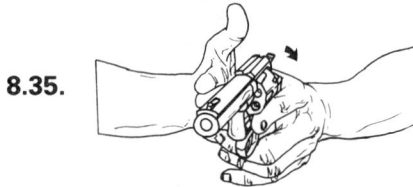

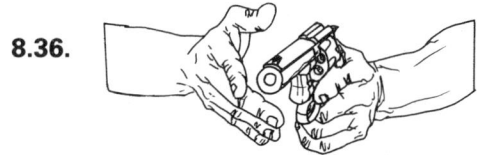

Figure 8.33 Step 1.
Figure 8.35 Step 3.

Figure 8.34 Step 2.
Figure 8.36 Step 4.

Firing around or over cover.   Turning cover and/or firing around it is much safer when using the sides of the cover as opposed to the top. Turning and/or firing over the top of cover exposes the entire top of the head to both direct and ricochet fire. But there may be circumstances where you must turn cover and/or fire overtop of it. During those circumstances, the same methods apply as when glancing around the sides of cover.

If turning and/or firing over the top of cover, do not support the handgun on top of the cover. You will be using a rock-up-and-down method when coming up from behind cover to fire.

The technique for rocking up and down over the top of cover follows the same procedures as those for rocking out and back around the sides of cover: close-approach in a firing position, step into position (becoming prepared) with the handgun's muzzle at least a foot to the rear of cover, and then rock up to look overtop of cover at the hidden side and instantly rock down: up and down, just that quick.

Bodily Positioning.   Only a crouching or a kneeling position can be used when turning the top of cover. (*Note:* If standing behind cover that is higher than your head, it is too high for you to turn the top of cover without being able to step on some object.) Depending on how high the top of the cover is, you will assume the appropriate crouching or kneeling position behind it in preparation for rocking-up from behind it. The positioning of the feet is exactly the same as the three levels for glancing (or for any of the techniques used when turning cover). Lock into your firing position behind the cover, and when the turning cover is done, use the knees and the waist to raise and lower the upper body. It does not matter whether you are using a crouching or kneeling position; bending the knees and waist works the same for both. Bending the knees raises and lowers the body straight up and down, while bending the waist brings the upper body forward and back (toward and away from cover). Both of these actions work in conjunction to make the precise height positioning behind the cover. When it is time to rock up, the actions of the waist and the knees work together to rock the upper body up and forward.

The positioning of the head when rocking up is very important. Never rock up with the head held straight up. Bend the neck toward the strong side so that the head comes up at an angle or on its side. This will keep most of the brain closer to cover and well below any glancing or ricochet bullets which may otherwise strike it. Always use the support-side eye by turning the head sideways and laying the strong-side cheek on the strong-side shoulder. Work with it until you find a comfortable position. If you cannot completely bend the head to the side, bend it as much as possible; the more you bend it down, the more you are protecting the brain.

This will also keep you from prematurely exposing the top of your head before turning cover. Often officers do not know that the top of their head is slightly exposed while positioning, before turning the top of cover. They do not realize this, as the eyes are several inches (3 to 5 inches) down from the top of the head and can rather easily misjudge the level of the head in relation to the top of the cover. Misjudging is far less likely to occur when turning cover to the side, as the lead eye, with the head turned slightly, is much closer to the side of the face (about 1 inch). Turning the head to the side helps you to judge properly the relationships involved when going over the top of cover.

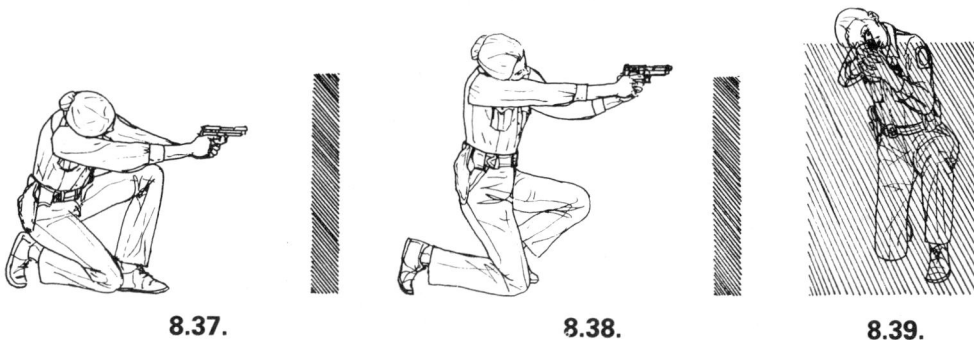

8.37.   **8.38.**   **8.39.**

Figures 8.37–8.39 Behind cover, with the waist and knees bent and in a firing position, the officer is hidden and ready (Fig. 8.37). When time to rock up, the knees and waist straighten up, bringing the firing position up to clear the top of the cover (Fig. 8.38). To reduce the head's exposure, turn it to the side, by resting the cheek on the strong arm's bicep and sighting with the support side eye (Fig. 8.39).

When and how to fire from a rested position.   When should you use a rested position (resting the hands on cover for steadier firing) to fire from, and how is it used? Generally, if the situation is 15 yards and under, a rested position is not used, no part of the hands touching the cover. If the situation is over 15 yards and/or the target is small, a rested position can be used, the back, front, or bottom of a hand being firmly held on the cover, with no part of the handgun touching the cover.

15 Yards and Under.   With a closer target there is no need to use a rested position to aid firing. It is much faster to just pop out in the two-handed firing stance and fire. You must make sure that the handgun's muzzle is kept well back from the cover to be able to pop out and fire. At this close range there may be no time to pop out, assume a rested position on the cover, and then fire.

Over 15 Yards and/or a Smaller Target.   With a further and/or smaller target, the sight picture is more critical and a rested position can improve "hits." To take a rested position, you lock into a two-handed firing grip and place the back, front, or bottom of a hand firmly on the cover. When doing this, make sure that no part of the handgun makes contact with the cover, as recoil may bounce it off the cover and cause the shot to go wild or cause a malfunction with an automatic. When using a rested position around the sides of cover, two methods can be used: back-hand support and front-hand support.

The back-hand support position places the back of one of the hands against the cover. When firing around the strong side of cover, the back of the support hand is placed on the cover. When firing around support-side cover, the back of the strong hand (actually, the tips of the support-hand fingers that are wrapped around the strong hand) is placed on the cover. Be careful of the fingertips, as they are very tender. Do not slam them into the cover. The handgun and hands are extended past the rear corner of the cover for the back of a hand to be placed on the cover. This means exposing more of the hands and body when firing.

The front-hand support position places the front of the support hand against the cover (directly on the corner) with only the front part of the handgun sticking out beyond the corner. This means much less exposure for the hands and body. The front of the support hand is used for both sides of cover. To accomplish this, the handgun must be canted for the front of the support hand to be firmly rested on the cover, while the barrel (or slide) will extend beyond it. Make sure that the cant is enough so that the trigger finger is not interfered with when firing.

When firing overtop of cover, the front or bottom of the support hand is placed on the cover. Mostly the bottom of the hand is used, but where the corner is appropriate (car fenders, embankments, tree limbs, etc.), the front of the hand can be used. Again, bending your neck will expose less of the head, especially the brain area. If a rested position is not used correctly—too exposed and/or too long in the position—it can make you an easy target. In such a position you are very vulnerable and exposed, as a rule. Usually, this is used when firing from a prone position or types of cover where you are more hidden.

When using a rested position, you may have to pop out, rest the handgun, and fire all very quickly. Prepare yourself the same as you would for the glance, except that the handgun's muzzle is just several inches back from the cover. When time to pop out, rest the handgun and fire; the body rocks out, with the hand being placed on the cover, the shots are fired, and then the body rocks back behind the cover again. Use different levels when coming out more than once.

The one-cover-back option.   At various times during a lethal encounter, an officer may have to, or want to, back off to a C&C position behind his or her original position. This can occur if the covered position the officer is then occupying becomes untenable or if it is tactically advantageous to move. When planning, always make sure that you know where the next cover to the rear of your position is.

We use the one-cover-back option either to surprise the threat(s) and/or to provide reaction distance for you to respond to the threat(s). The secret of the move is to perform it without the threat(s) seeing you move from your present covered position to the one-cover-back position. This can really be a surprise to the threat(s) if it thinks you are just hiding at your original covered position. If the threat(s) tries to flank or attack your previous position, you are not there but safely one cover back, now firing on the threat(s) who is at your previous position.

By moving one cover back, your reaction distance to the threat(s) has increased and can provide you with a buffer, especially when more than one threat is present. If you have managed to move without being seen and can surprise the threat(s), you will have more of an advantage. But even if you are seen moving one cover back, you have still improved your reaction distance to the threat(s).

Always keep the one cover back option in your planning during an encounter, as it will always improve your reaction distance and may really improve your advantage by surprising the threat(s).

COVER AND CONCEALMENT: NOT REMEDIES FOR ALL ENCOUNTERS

Many officers mistakenly feel that C&C are remedies for all encounters. This could not be further from the truth, as the improper use of C&C can quickly get you killed.

Cover cannot always be your first thought.   Encounters are broken down into initial and subsequent exchanges. The initial exchange is usually the quickest and deadliest time during a lethal encounter, much of the time deciding the outcome. If not behind cover, in all probability you will have to get on target and "hit" until the threat(s) is down. When the threat(s) attacks, immediately engage it and keep "hitting" until the threat(s) is down. You must then immediately seek cover, as the threat(s) may still be capable of firing or there may be additional threats. Stay covered while checking all areas of the encounter zone.

If caught flatfooted by the initial exchange (opening ceremony), you must snap up to speed by drawing and firing instantly if the threat is close. Diving for cover and then instantly returning fire can work if the threat is far enough away and/or in a covered position. But you must not "just think cover" when caught unaware and the bullets start flying. Turning from the threat and diving for cover may get you shot in the back several times before you reach the cover.

[*Note:* We are describing a no-choice situation; the threat(s) is trying to kill

you right now and only you can stop it. During different circumstances other options could be used. Here, we are dealing with no-choice situations, where your
survival depends on your ability to stop the threat(s) instantly.]

Very Close Cover.   Generally for cover to be considered very close, a covered
position must be 10 feet or less away (10 feet away is pushing it), and you must be
able to be behind cover in a second or less. The only time you would consider moving behind cover if caught flatfooted is with a piece of very close cover available
that you have already selected (no time to look around for cover). When moving
behind cover, you would be in the process of drawing your handgun to return fire
the instant you are behind it.

C&C penetration problems.   A cover or concealment position you are behind does not stop the situation and the deadly attack on you; it merely interrupts
the attack (sometimes not even doing that) by the threat(s) actually not being able
to "hit" you or thinking it cannot "hit" you. If the threat(s) possesses a weapon
that can penetrate your cover, it will eventually get around to shooting through your
cover if it does not do it to begin with. If the threat(s) have been watching too much
TV and stop firing once you are behind concealment, given a small amount of time,
the threat(s) will figure it out and shoot right through the concealment.

When selecting C&C options in your daily movements, you must learn to recognize the best cover options available. You must also learn to recognize what the
threat(s) is using against you, as it may radically change the ability of cover to stop
the projectiles coming your way. The main problems occur when the threat(s) is
using either a rifle or a shotgun (with rifled slugs). Projectiles from either of these,
especially high powered rifles, can penetrate an amazing variety of tough objects.
Often, the best option when facing a threat(s) so armed is to back off until more
troops and/or a specialty unit can solve the problem.

Do not stay hidden behind cover.   Cover is used as protection from incoming bullets during the encounter. But cover has to be used correctly so that you can
be an active participant. If you become a passive participant and stay hidden behind
cover, you may become completely passive if the threat(s) takes the advantage and
kills you. If you stay hidden behind cover, the threat(s) is now in control of the
encounter and can either escape or attack you. At the least the threat(s) can escape;
at the worst the threat(s) can flank, or directly attack your covered position and kill
you if you are unaware that it is coming.

You must not only know what is going on during the continuing encounter,
but you must take steps to control the threat(s) and/or engage it if it continues
attacking. This can be accomplished only by being an active part of the encounter.

Cover and concealment must be used intelligently to be used correctly. You
must control the encounter or at the very least control your ability to survive. C&C
will greatly improve your survival advantage if intelligently used.

USING THE CRUISER AS COVER

The cruiser you drive is an excellent, mobile piece of cover. It is initially at hand as you drive it to the scene and you have learned how to position it—on felony stops and at situations in progress—to increase effectively the protection it can afford. It can provide you with a means of instantly exiting the encounter zone. The cruiser has a lot of potential as cover, although there are a few ins and outs to its use. As such, you can use the cruiser to increase your advantage, whether responding to dangerous situations in progress or if suddenly attacked.

The first consideration is flexibility when using the cruiser's cover options. With the cruiser, flexibility translates into two methods: quickly exiting the encounter zone by driving out of it, or once you and the cruiser are committed to the area, effectively using the cruiser as cover.

Exiting the encounter zone.   The cruiser's cover options begin with its use as an effective covered escape module. If you can use the cruiser to escape the encounter zone effectively, that is the first option that should be taken. Lay partially across the seat by bending sideways to the right, with your head low and peering over the center of the dashboard, and use your cruiser to exit the encounter zone.

When initially arriving on the scene of a call, two precautions should be taken as normal procedures before the cruiser is shut off and you are committed to the area: taking the time to smoke over the scene, and placing the cruiser in the rod mode (reverse or drive, whichever way leads out). You are as alert and prepared as possible if the shooting starts. Many officers pull up to the scene too preoccupied with picking up whatever equipment they are taking, placing the cruiser in whatever condition they are going to leave it in, and communicating on the radio. All this takes attention away from the area around the cruiser for several seconds. Also, the gearshift is instantly rammed into park as soon as the wheels stop rotating and the cruiser is shut off—wrong initial moves if you need to leave quickly.

Instead of limiting your options, as the cruiser comes to a stop, keep your foot on the break and move the gearshift into the rod mode (either reverse or drive). Now smoke over the scene for several seconds. You are stopped and concentrating all your attention on the area before shutting the cruiser down and exiting it; thus you are keeping open a survival option if the action starts instantly.

Many attacks take place as soon as the cruiser is stopped or as the officer is beginning to exit it. If an attack is launched, you can lie across the seat and hit the gas to exit the encounter zone. Stay low, just peering over the dashboard or to the rear, enough to see where you are going. Using these procedures keeps open a survival option that would otherwise be closed if you instantly put the cruiser in park and shut it off. The first cover option available to you is getting low and driving out of the encounter zone. The cruiser can take a surprising amount of punishment at times; at other times, though, bullets seem to find their way into it easily. This is your first option and best bet if initially attacked.

Using the cruiser as cover.   What are your cover options once you are committed to the scene (the cruiser is shut off and you are just starting to exit it or you have already exited it). These are broken down into two areas: before and after exiting the cruiser.

Before Exiting the Cruiser.   If attacked while inside the cruiser, you may not have time to try and start the cruiser to exit the encounter zone without first assuming a prepared position and responding to the attack. The cruiser can still be used to drive you out of the encounter zone once restarted, but first you will have to respond to the attack. Your initial response to an attack is to drop instantly into a prepared position inside the cruiser and draw your handgun. This position is assumed instantly by laying down across the front seat and turning to the right so that your back lays on the seat; the left leg must be bent at the knee. (*Note:* Hopefully, you do not place large gear/report holding boxes on the front seat; these only limit your options if attacked.) As this position was executed, your service handgun was drawn and is now held in a two-handed position ready to fire instantly. Laying on your back, with the handgun in a two-handed position, you have the best chance of meeting an attack successfully wherever it comes from. If the attack does not continue, the next survival option will be either to start the cruiser and exit the encounter zone or exit the cruiser and take up a covered position outside it.

Driving out of the encounter zone was covered previously in this section. When exiting the cruiser, you must first know from which side the attack is coming. Attempt to get a visual on the threat(s) attacking you. You will usually have a good indication of where the attack is coming from if bullets have hit the cruiser's windshields and windows. Once the area where the attack is coming from is located, exit from the opposite side of the cruiser and take up a covered position. If you exit the cruiser into the threat's guns, you may not last long. You must exit the cruiser with some part of the cruiser between you and the threat(s) if at all possible. Once outside the cruiser, immediately move to a covered position behind one of the wheels and locate the threat(s). Keep up your 360-degree scan, covering all areas around you, until the threat(s) is located (there may be only one, but keep *scanning* to be sure). The threat's position can change instantly and you must change to meet it. Do not decide to stay at the cruiser; your best option will be to find better cover away from the cruiser. Keep flexible during the changing encounter.

After Exiting the Cruiser.   Once the cruiser is stopped, you must have flexibility in your use of cover. To be flexible when using the cruiser as cover, do not stay inside the cruiser. If you stay inside the cruiser, you become boxed in, with no movement options if flanked or attacked from different angles. Also if boxed in, cover becomes whatever is then between you and the threat(s) and it may be virtually no cover at all. By being flexible, you can continually position the best available cover between you and the threat(s). During the continuing encounter, you must be able to use other cover besides the cruiser and you can do this only from the outside.

Begin Thinking Cover When Arriving on the Scene.   When you arrive on the scene of certain calls that could potentially be trouble or during hours of darkness, always think of the cruiser's cover potential and use it when arriving on the scene. Once the cruiser is stopped at the scene (or close to it), exit the cruiser, take up a position with the cruiser between the scene and you, and smoke over the entire area for a small amount of time. Only then leave the protection of the cruiser and proceed on foot to check out the call. No matter how the cruiser is parked, you stand on the side of the cruiser opposite to where you think the scene (the danger) is located, but you always keep up your 360-degree scan, as a threat(s) can be anywhere. If something should occur in the initial few seconds of your arrival, you are already behind cover and thinking.

How to Use the Cruiser's Cover. The best-covered position on the cruiser is that of being crouched down behind one of the front wheels with the engine block between you and the threat(s). Not only will the engine block stop just about anything, but the tires will protect you from any ricochet coming from under the cruiser. The second-best position is crouched behind the rear wheels. Do not crouch between the wheels, as ricocheted rounds can easily come under the cruiser. Do not use any of the windshield or window glass as cover.

The felony-stop braced firing position (with the driver's door open, the left foot braced against the door hinge, and a two-handed firing grip holding the handgun just over the spotlight) works well on felony vehicle stops with the threat(s) located directly in front of the cruiser. During any other type of encounter, this position with the cruiser between the scene and you, and smoke over the entire initially when firing on a threat(s) in front of the cruiser, but once that exchange is over with, assume a more flexible covered position, away from the cruiser.

The cruiser is an excellent, mobile piece of cover, but it has its limitations. Use it to take you quickly out of the encounter zone as a first cover option. As a second cover option, use its cover potential during an initial attack to survive it, then get away from it and find a better covered position.

SUMMARY

During lethal encounters, cover and concealment can be vital to your survival. As part of your daily movements, learn to evaluate continually the cover options available and always know where the closest covered position is. Make this one of your life habits. If an encounter should occur, effectively use cover by moving, staying, and firing from behind it. The intelligent use of cover is one of the premier tactical habits toward increasing your survival advantage.

9

Encounter Tactics: Before, During, and After a Lethal Encounter

Encounter tactics deal with the three time frames of a lethal encounter—before, during, and after—and your actions throughout them. Before an encounter begins, will you be aware of the presence of a possible threat(s) and prepared to move into action instantly should it present itself or be completely unaware that anything is about to occur? When the encounter begins and during it, will you be caught unprepared and several steps behind the action trying to catch up as it is occurring, or will you be in a position to react to it and be on top of the action, stopping the threat(s)? After the initial threat has been stopped, will you still maintain your tactics, or foolishly think that it is over and rush in? What will you do during the three time frames of a lethal encounter: before, during, and after?

In this chapter we analyze these three areas, covering all the salient tactics and techniques to keep you ahead of the game: before it occurs, during its occurrence, and after it has ended.

THE THREE ON-HAND FACTORS THAT YOU WILL BE ABLE TO RELY ON DURING AN ENCOUNTER

Usually, a lethal encounter instantly begins, is quickly over with, and you will be able to use only that which you have on hand: mentally, physically, and equipment-ally. Let there be no mistake: When the situation begins, whatever you have in you

178

and on you will be the major determinants of your survival! The only other factor that may aid you is luck, and luck is often a cruel mistress. When all is said and done, you are the one ultimately in charge of your own survival and you must have the tools—mentally, physically, and equipmentally—to save yourself during a lethal encounter.

These three on-hand factors must be understood and prepared for. Make them a part of your life and you will be prepared whenever an encounter occurs. Most lethal encounters are decided long before the first bullet flies. Your understanding of these tactics and techniques will prepare you for all phases of its occurrence. The three on-hand factors are:

1. *Mentally:* Your mental set, level of awareness and preparedness, your preplanning, survival reinforcement, and your ability to carry out the plan aggressively.
2. *Physically:* Your degree of physical training and conditioning, and your weapon use skills.
3. *Equipmentally:* The weapons and equipment you have in your possession: Are they appropriate for the situations that could reasonably occur (do you have what you should have for the location and conditions that exist) and in good working order?

Mentally

In Chapter 7 we described the mental preparations that must be made by an officer before an encounter occurs. Of all the information that chapter contained, the five mental elements for surviving lethal encounters (forming a set of mental cues to keep you cued up during an encounter) are extremely important to your mental performance when engaging the threat(s). They are briefly restated here, as they are extremely important to your understanding of encounter tactics.

1. Awareness is quite possibly the most important mental cue as you must be mentally aware to recognize the danger signs in order to respond to them. When a danger sign is spotted, do not misinterpret it; disregard it or rationalize it as something else—check it out. When danger signs are recognized and properly prepared for, you are prepared if the action starts, as you have no doubt been formulating a quick course of action to implement when the encounter begins. Remember, the longer you are aware of a possible threat, the better prepared you are to respond to it. If the danger signs are not followed up or disregarded and the action starts, you will be caught flatfooted and several steps behind the action, playing a catch-up game.

2. Self-control is the basic factor that holds the other four elements together during the encounter. You must control yourself and the handgun during the encounter to stop the threat(s) successfully. Remember, you can only control your environment if you are under control. If you lose control, you probably will lose the encounter. Control is exhibited by getting down to the job at hand, using your shooting skills and tactics in a timely/effective manner, while making your critical decisions to stop the threat.

During an encounter, correct shooting techniques are used to place your "hits," precise marksmanship not being nearly as important. This is accomplished by getting down to the job of your own shooting in a matter-of-fact manner. Control yourself and get down to work by letting your trained-in reflexive sets accomplish what you decide to do. You are trained—allow your training to work for you. Do not restrict your trained-in abilities by losing control.

Do not leave fear unchecked, as it can slow down or blunt your reaction to the threat(s). Use self-control to overcome fear. Get down to the work you have been trained for and work to stop the threat(s) and make your immediate environment safe.

3. A quick course of action must quickly be formulated in preparation for the threat occurrence. Once the course of action is selected, you must have confidence in what you have selected and your ability to carry it through.

Your ability to decide quickly on a course of action will be based in large part on practice. Practice by engaging in scenario imaging. You must practice to increase your ability to plan a quick course of action—whether an armed threat appears instantly or danger signs are recognized that a threat may possibly occur. With practice, your decision-making process will speed up and your confidence will increase.

The factors of hesitation and surprise must also be understood. Hesitation can be fatal. Once a course of action is started, do not hesitate, stop part way through, or change the plan midstream (unless circumstances require it). Do it now, carrying it through instantly. If done this way, your course of action will catch the threat(s) completely by surprise, which can set it off balance. Once the threat(s) is off balance, keep hitting until it is stopped.

4. Aggressive speed in action—when making your move—is a critical factor. Your response must be aggressive in nature and fast in action: in other words, all out. Use all the power you possess, and then some, to win. The encounter we are describing is lethal in nature and your survival may well depend on a violent, aggressive attack on the threat(s). There may be no second chance; to survive, you may have to stop the threat(s) the first time.

5. Follow-through from the time the encounter begins until it completely ends, by maintaining your action until the encounter is completely over with. Many officers go soft, thinking the encounter has ended, and are surprised when it starts up again—sometimes fatally surprised. Allow the encounter to run its course fully and then some; do not go soft halfway through or at the end. Stay on top of it until help arrives; always maintain cover and your 360-degree scan. Play it safe—follow through.

When caught in a lethal encounter fighting for your life, your mental set is probably the most important factor to your survival. It involves all your decision-making processes, your self-control, and guides you through the encounter. Remember, you will think your way through an encounter, mentally selecting every course of action, and mentally bringing about every physical action, all toward stopping the threat(s) and securing your immediate environment. You must practice and improve your mental set, as the most important on-hand factor that you possess when the encounter starts.

Physically

This on-hand factor covers all of your physical abilities: (1) your degree of physical training and conditioning, (2) your trained-in weapon use skills, and (3) your ability to perform in the environment in which the encounter occurs. All three will dictate your response level when it is time to perform whatever physical tasks are necessary during the encounter. If any of these are found lacking, your ability to accomplish the physical tasks required will be greatly reduced. You must make the commitment and effort to improve your physical abilities to build and maintain your survival advantage.

1. Physical training and conditioning are reflections of your fitness. Are you fit enough to perform the physical tasks that may be required during the encounter: running, good cardiovascular fitness, and muscular endurance? In other words, will you have the physical ability and stamina to withstand the possibly prolonged physical and mental strain of a highly stress-filled lethal encounter? It boils down to performance and staying power.

During a lethal encounter, a tactical option may be open to you, and you may hesitate because of a lack of confidence in your physical abilities. These tactical options are often quick to appear and quick to disappear and they must be taken advantage of quickly. They can sometimes make the difference in an encounter and you must have the physical abilities to take advantage of them.

A commitment must be made toward your physical health, getting back in shape (if not already there) and maintaining it. Many officers approach improving their physical health as a prolonged and arduous task involving strenuous workout sessions. It does not need to be this way. One-half hour every other day is all that it takes to start. The main problem is getting officers to start in the first place. Once started, getting back in shape seems to feed on itself. You can see and feel the improvements taking place within your body and how easily it can be accomplished, increasing your desire to continue improving. In a surprisingly short amount of time, even while not exercising extensively, the body begins to tighten up and becomes better prepared for the physical exertion and dump of high-level stressors that will occur to the body and mind during an encounter.

Many departments provide their officers with regular workout sessions or sports activities to keep them physically fit for the job. If no activities are readily available to you, the information on how to proceed is easily found. You know what shape you are in and it is up to you to institute change to improve your physical condition. Improved physical condition can only improve your ability to survive.

2. Weapon use skills must be practiced until they become a trained-in reflexive set that occurs automatically. This is a reoccurring theme throughout this book. Your physical ability to manipulate and fire the service handgun must function automatically. Once you make the decision to fire, the next instant you should be looking at the sights as the handgun is firing, having been automatically produced in a position to fire virtually without conscious throught, thus leaving your mind free for the critical decisions being made throughout the total encounter.

These weapon use skills are physically trained in by repeatedly practicing the reflexive sets. Only through repetition can the muscles, tendons, skeletal structure, and nerves of the body develop the feel and positioning of these sets. Repetition, repetition, repetition is the key to building the reflexive sets of weapon use skills. It is not that difficult and does not take much time, but it does take a commitment.

You must not have to slow down or stop during an encounter to figure out how to make the weapon work or function. All your weapon use skills must be trained into your body long before you need them. When you mentally decide to use the handgun, your body should be physically accomplishing it—the instant the mind decided it should be done, with no thought needed as to how to do it. This can be done only by physically training in these sets of weapon use skills.

3. The ability to perform in the encounter environment is important. Performing in the encounter environment must not be a new experience, but must also be included in your training and practice. Wherever the encounter occurs (the encounter environment or encounter zone), you must be able to respond effectively to the threat(s) at that location and within whatever conditions exist. Be it constructed or natural areas, during the day or at night, and so on, you must be able to function very effectively in any environment or condition present. The only way to prepare for this is to get out and search some of these areas and become familiar with them and their unique problems.

You must have confidence in all of your physical abilities. With improved physical fitness and trained-in weapon use skills, your confidence in your ability to function during a lethal encounter will improve.

Equipmentally

This on-hand function takes into consideration the weapons and equipment you will use when a lethal encounter occurs. The weapons and equipment that you carry and use must be appropriate for the situations that could reasonably occur and in good working order. Many officers do not carry the right equipment, let their equipment become unserviceable, and carry none at all. Your equipment must be appropriate and properly working whether on duty or off duty, whenever and wherever you carry a handgun and a badge.

When you are on duty, everyone expects you to be a professional police officer, with all your equipment in place and in proper working order. Usually, the police department dictates what service handgun will be carried and the minimum number of extra rounds for it. Equipment problems usually involve the equipment's functioning. Service handguns can have an out-of-time mechanism, can be uncleaned with a heavy lead buildup, parts broken, and so on. Extra ammunition can be defective due to exposure to weather and certain types of lubricants over a period of time. Holsters can become worn and not hold the handgun securely, or the stitching can rot or break. All these and more can occur. If police officers do not take care of their equipment or allow a known problem to go uncorrected, they can find themselves loosing a survival battle very quickly.

These quick three examples show what equipment problems can occur. Example 1: A police officer with over 15 years of service always carried a 2-inch revolver as an off-duty handgun, all the while knowing that the firing pin was broken off. Example 2: Another officer returned to the firing range for annual requalification. When he attempted to fire the first six rounds from his revolver, the first three would not fire. Apparently, excessive lubrication had caused the primers to malfunction. Example 3: Another officer had been having problems with his duty holster, allowing the service handgun to fall from it without the snap being unsnapped. The handgun had been left in the seat of his cruiser several times and had fallen to the ground once. When chasing an "assault with attempt to murder" suspect through the woods, the officer and others finally lost the suspect. Only then did the officer realize that his holster was empty. The handgun was never found. Any one of these could have caused the death of an officer; luckily, they did not. Problems such as these are not uncommon; in fact, how many of you know at least one officer who has shown up at roll call without his handgun or with it unloaded?

When you are off duty, you have a greater latitude in what you may carry. The problems arise when officers carry partial equipment, improper equipment, or no equipment at all. When off duty and carrying your service handgun or off-duty handgun, you must have at least one extra reload for the number of rounds in the handgun: a speed loader or six (or five) loose rounds for a revolver and a magazine for an auto. It is essential to have an extra magazine for an auto, as the magazine already in the auto may malfunction, rendering the auto incapable of firing more than one round at a time. The handgun must be carried securely in some type of holster or pocket, so that strenuous physical activity will not cause it to fall out. Stay away from underpowered handguns as your first off-duty weapon. Nothing below a .380 auto should be carried, and a .380 is rather low as a defensive round. Make sure that you know exactly how your off-duty handgun functions and fires, and make sure that you have fired it enough to be completely familiar with it. You must carry an off-duty handgun if you carry an off-duty badge. If you do not want to carry a handgun off duty, do not carry a badge off duty.

You must have the proper functioning equipment for the job at hand. Make sure that you have the proper handgun and equipment; continually check and practice with your equipment to ensure proper functioning, and immediately correct any problems found. Ultimately, you are the one in charge of your survival; make sure that your equipment is proper and functioning correctly.

Remember, lethal encounters are always a "come-as-you-are" affair. There will be no chance to call "timeout" to become better equipped or better trained. When the lethal encounter begins, what you have in you and on you will be the major determinants of your survival!

THE ASSETS MODEL AS APPLIED TO ENCOUNTER TACTICS

The ASSETS model provides an understanding of the continuing process that you will use long before the encounter occurs, throughout the encounter and long after it has ended. The model applies especially to early threat recognition (recognizing danger signs) before the encounter occurs.

As outlined in Chapter 1, the ASSETS acronym stands for "assessing the situation and structure for the most effective tactics selection." The acronym is initially broken down into its two main parts: ASS and ETS. ASS is the continual process of always assessing the situation and structure. This is done on a daily basis, every day; it just did not begin with the threat. You were using it long before the situation started, while the situation was occurring, and you continued using it long after the situation ended. The ASS part especially applies to early threat recognition, by constantly assessing what is going on around you.

Once you have decided that a weapon use response to the situation may be required to stop the threat(s), the ETS part comes into play. ETS is the most effective tactics selection and covers all the tactics and weapon use employed during the situation. Both processes are inseparably linked, one to the other. Assess what is occurring and where you are, and then select the appropriate/timely tactic and/or weapon use to respond to it. This process is a continual one during an encounter, as the situation and structure may change instantly. As it does, you must modify your tactics and/or weapon use to fit it.

This system is in constant use throughout the three time frames of the encounter: before, during, and after. Using it will place you one step ahead throughout the total encounter.

The ASS part and early threat recognition.   The use of the first part of the ASSETS model keeps you in an aware and prepared state of mind. The ASS part is used continually, all the time, as part of your daily life. It is used to tell you everything that is going on in your immediate surroundings, by heightening your perceptions and awareness of people, places, and events around you. You are continually assessing everything around you, all situations occurring and the structures you are then in and around. It did not just suddenly begin with the first recognition of a danger sign that an encounter is about to occur, but it was always there, so you could catch that first danger sign, not just the second or seventh. Its use improves your observation powers by cultivating that hidden talent within each of us and enhances life itself, especially when you catch that first danger sign.

For a more complete understanding, we view the ASS part as a continuum: a line stretching from our past through the present and into the future and the possible occurrence of life-threatening encounters as points along that continuum. A lethal encounter—from beginning to end—appears as only one small moment on the continuum of life that the ASS part flows with. When you use the ASS part, you are always aware and prepared—the essence of the ASS part. When an encounter occurs, you are ready to respond to it—having caught the danger signs and positioned yourself to respond effectively.

This system has relevance to all people, but to you—a police officer—its use may be critical to your survival. As a police officer you must be in a position (at all times) to detect the presence of an impending threat. The moment you became a police officer, you entered into a very demanding profession that requires you to be more than the average person. Not only on the job, but also during your off-duty hours, you must be more aware of and prepared to face the existence of possible danger. This can be accomplished only by cultivating an aware and prepared state of mind as the ASS part outlines.

FROM THREAT RECOGNITION TO DEFENSIVE RESPONSE: CHARTING THE CRITICAL TIME REFERENCE

Along the continuum line, introduced in the ASSETS model, fall the three time frames of the encounter: before, during, and after. Together they may take several seconds or quite a few minutes. The critical time reference occurs throughout the moments before, and just after the threat presents itself, during what we call the opening ceremony, where the initial exchange of gunfire usually takes place. Although designated as the opening ceremony of a lethal encounter, it can occur anytime: during the middle of any call you are on, or at the end of any call you are clearing, or out of the blue. In reality, it can occur anytime, anywhere—often times when least expected.

The critical time reference runs through all of the before time frame and into the first part of the during time frame. We refer to it as the critical time reference, as whatever occurs during this initial exchange often decides the outcome of the encounter. Encounters are usually quick to start and quick to end and the beginning is always a critical time. You must be on top of the situation before the threat(s) presents itself, thus positioned to respond instantly and effectively to stop the threat(s).

You must understand the three time frames of the entire encounter and your

9.1.

The Relationship of the CRITICAL TIME REFERENCE
to the Three Time Spans of An Encounter:

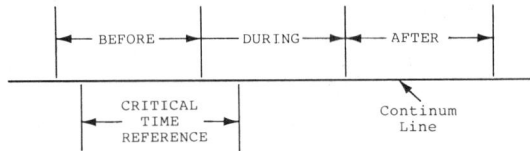

```
       |←— BEFORE —→|←— DURING —→|←— AFTER —→|
       |            |            |           |
       |            |            |           ↖
       |←— CRITICAL —→|          Continum
            TIME                 Line
          REFERENCE
```

responses during them, but you must especially understand and prepare for the critical time reference. The CTR occurs from the first danger sign you could have recognized and correctly interpreted, to the threat occurrence (when the actual threat presents itself), and finally to your defensive response.

When working with lethal encounters, we need to define the time factors and time points occurring within the CTR—for both the threat(s) and the office. By doing so, an understanding of CTR dynamics begins to form. Do not misinterpret what is trying to be accomplished by these terms and the charting device. No one is trying to force-feed a chart system down your throat. What is vitally important is your understanding of the critical beginnings of lethal encounters and how you can improve your advantage. Visually presenting the critical time reference in chart form can graphically increase your understanding of the dynamics involved and how you must use them to your advantage. (*Note:* These terms will be referred to throughout the remainder of this chapter. Learning them in this section will improve your understanding of encounter dynamics.)

The CRITICAL TIME REFERENCE Dynamics Chart:

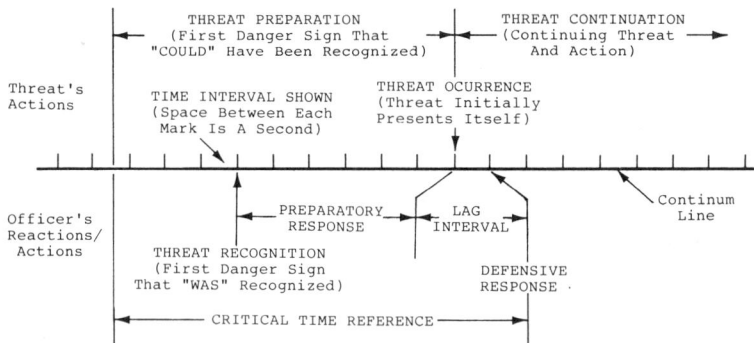

9.2.

```
                    THREAT PREPARATION                    THREAT CONTINUATION
                  (First Danger Sign That                (Continuing Threat
                  "COULD" Have Been Recognized)              And Action)

Threat's
Actions          TIME INTERVAL SHOWN          THREAT OCURRENCE
                 (Space Between Each          (Threat Initially
                 Mark Is A Second)            Presents Itself)

————|—|—|—|—|—|—|—|—|—|—|—|—|—|—|—|—|—|—|—|—|—|—|—|—|————————
                                                                Continum
                           PREPARATORY        LAG               Line
Officer's                  RESPONSE          INTERVAL
Reactions/
Actions         THREAT RECOGNITION                    DEFENSIVE
                (First Danger Sign                    RESPONSE
                That "WAS" Recognized)

                |←———— CRITICAL TIME REFERENCE ————→|
```

NOTE: All TIME INTERVALS for the factors shown will
change depending on the situation and AWARENESS/ACTION
of the officer(s) and threat(s).

Explaining the CTR Chart. All of the factors shown on the critical time reference chart outline both what the threat will do (above the continuum line) and what your responses will be (below the continuum line). The continuum line is the flow of daily life—a line stretching from the past, through the present, and into the future—with the possible occurrence of life-threatening encounters as points along that line. The CTR begins with the before time frame (at the first danger sign that could have been read and correctly interpreted) and continues into the very first part of the during time frame. As these time frames usually occur very quickly, the continuum line is divided into one second segments by the small vertical lines running along it. Each encounter is different, being formulated by what the threat(s) does and what the officer will do in response. As each encounter is different, each CTR chart will be different, showing the advantages for either the officer or threat(s).

The purpose of the CTR chart is to graphically present what is occurring during the critical initial stage of an encounter. You must understand all aspects of the critical time reference and how you have the ability to change the factors to your advantage. If you have the knowledge and can take the appropriate action, you can swing the advantage in your favor.

Time factors and time points from the CTR chart.   First, all the time factors shown on the CTR chart vary depending on the situation and the actions of threat(s) and officer. Their actions will be occurring simultaneously: As the threat(s) is creating the situation, the officer is responding to and modifying it. For the threat(s) and officer, each will be involved with several time factors and time points during the initial exchange, which may quickly decide the outcome.

The Threat's Time Factors.   The threat's time factors are shown above the continuum line. The threat will begin the encounter with threat preparation that for our purposes begins with the first danger sign that could have been recognized. (*Note:* Threat preparation is the before time frame, both beginning with the first danger sign and ending with threat occurrence.) Obviously, the threat's preparation was occurring long before that first danger sign could have been read, but any preparation before the first danger sign is a hidden variable that is not known to the officer. The encounter starts with the first danger sign that could have been recognized (the beginning of the before time frame). Threat preparation will continue from the first danger sign until the threat occurrence point is reached, when the threat(s) presents itself (announces and/or takes physical actions to start the physical threat—such as draws a handgun and announces a hold-up). Once the threat occurrence point is reached, threat continuation will occur until the threat ends, either by the officer stopping it or by the threat accomplishing its purpose and escaping.

The Officer's Time Factors.   The officer's time factors are shown below the continuum line. The officer will enter the encounter at threat recognition when his or her awareness first spots and correctly interprets a danger sign that a possible threat could exit. If the officer was very aware, this may be the first danger sign given. If less aware, it could be the second, third, or seventh danger sign given. Once the officer spots and correctly interprets a danger sign (threat recognition), he or she enters the preparatory response time factor, which runs from that first recognized danger sign until the threat presents itself (threat occurrence). During that time factor the officer will have to snap up to speed as to what is about to occur and tactically assume the best possible position to respond to the threat(s) or stop the threat(s) before it presents itself. As soon as a danger sign is read, planning a quick course of action begins.

Threat recognition and preparatory response may not be available for the officer to use to his or her advantage if the threat instantly occurs (such as a threat coming through a door with gun out—no prior danger signs). The vast majority of the time, though, danger signs do occur before the threat presents itself, especially when the officer is responding to, or on the scene of, an incident. The officer's preparatory response must be increased by catching the danger signs early, giving the officer time to prepare.

Once the threat occurrence point is reached, the officer's preparatory response ends (all planning and preparing) as his or her defensive response instantly takes over to stop the threat(s). Hopefully, the officer's preparatory response has provided enough time to plan and prepare for the initial defensive response—making this response quick and effective, with no lag interval. Also, with enough preparatory response, the officer's defensive response can occur even before the threat(s) presents itself, stopping the threat before it happens. One of the main problems with this is making sure that you locate all the threats involved, not just the obvious one. Secondary threats can radically change the encounter, and these must be located.

The lag interval will appear between the threat occurrence and the officer's defensive response. Generally, it occurs when the officer did not know the encounter was about to happen and is caught flatfooted as the threat appears. If the officer is completely unaware as the threat presents itself, the lag interval can be long. On the other hand, if the officer has recognized the danger signs and is prepared (by having worked through the preparatory response, even though maybe only several seconds long), the lag interval can be reduced to zero. The lag interval must be kept to the barest minimum and preferably reduced to zero.

Working with the CTR chart.   Now that you have an understanding of the seven time and point factors that can occur during lethal encounters (three for the threat and four for the officer), how do they work to your advantage or disadvantage? There are two major truths outlined in the CTR chart.

The first truth of the CTR chart is simple: The first danger sign must be recognized to increase an officer's preparatory response time as much as possible. A simple truth, but a vital one. Awareness is the key, as you must be as aware as possible to catch the first danger sign. The following CTR chart shows the danger signs recognized early on: an increased preparatory response factor, eliminated lag interval, and an instantaneous defensive response.

The second truth of the CTR chart is: If caught unaware or unprepared and the threat suddenly occurs, you must instantly respond to reduce the lag interval to a minimum and begin your defensive response. Even if completely unaware when the action starts, instantly snap up to speed and begin your defensive response, reducing the lag interval as much as possible. If you stop or freeze, you will become

EARLY RECOGNITION Chart:

9.3.

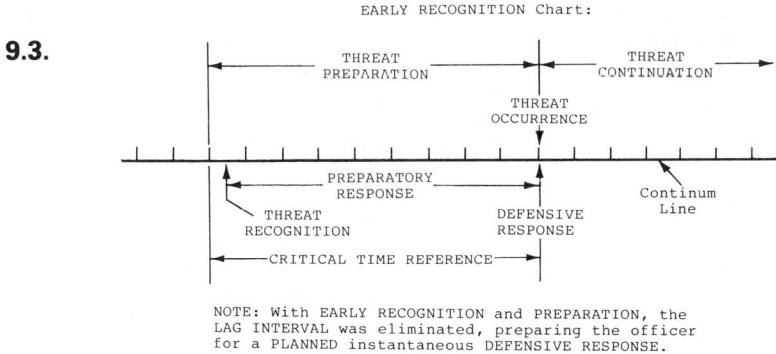

NOTE: With EARLY RECOGNITION and PREPARATION, the
LAG INTERVAL was eliminated, preparing the officer
for a PLANNED instantaneous DEFENSIVE RESPONSE.

NON-RECOGNITION Chart:

9.4.

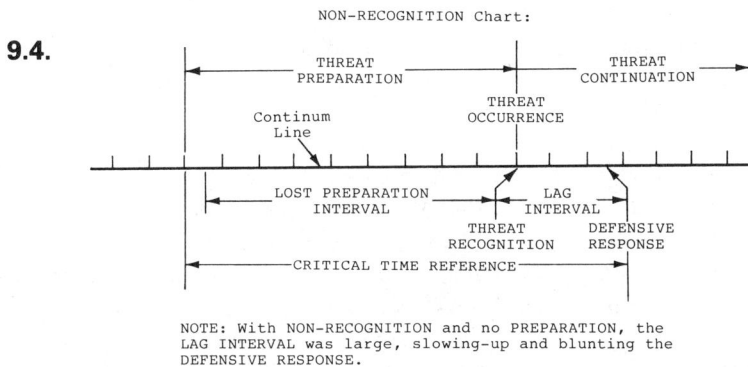

NOTE: With NON-RECOGNITION and no PREPARATION, the
LAG INTERVAL was large, slowing-up and blunting the
DEFENSIVE RESPONSE.

an easy target. The following CTR chart shows threat occurrence and threat recognition occurring as the same point (the officer was completely unaware of the threat's presence when it occurred): no preparatory response was available, the lag interval is greatly increased, and the defensive response is delayed.

Both of these charts show the opposite ends of the awareness and response spectrum. All these factors aside, one point stands out: No matter when you become aware of a lethal threat, you must instantly get down to the work at hand—your survival.

Keep this understanding in mind as you continue through this chapter on encounter tactics.

ANALYZING THE LETHAL ENCOUNTER: LOOKING AT THE AVERAGES AND BEYOND

What is the average lethal encounter, and how must it affect realistic firearms training? As with any researchable subject, data are compiled, patterns begin to form, and averages surface. With lethal encounters it is no different. Over the years data have been compiled on lethal encounters: how quickly they occur, how many shots are fired, what the lighting conditions are, how many assailants there are, where they take place, and so on. Most of these data are derived from shootings involving police officers in the performance of their duties. Although this information does not give us all the answers, it does give us basis when attempting to increase our information on the dynamics of lethal encounters. The study of this information improves our ability to develop and design the most modern and up-to-date training methods available.

Although this information shows the average lethal encounter that can be expected, you must not fall into the trap of training only for the average lethal encounter. True, most defensive firearms training must reflect what the averages show us, but training must also be extended to the nonaverage types of lethal encounters that may occur. Police officers must train for the total spectrum of lethal encounters to increase their survival advantage.

Lethal encounter averages and information. From the FBI statistics and other information, the statistically average lethal encounter shapes up like this:

1. Over 80 percent of the time, the distance will be 7 yards or less, the largest percentage occurring from 0 to 10 feet. At the opposite end, handguns are almost never fired farther than 15 yards away.

2. The average handgun fight will be over in slightly less than 3 seconds, and during the fight, the average number of shots fired by "all participants" is less than three rounds. As can be seen, time is usually very short and the majority of encounters will be decided by the initial exchange of fire. Firing speed (the ability to get on target and instantly place "hits") will be critical to the outcome of the majority of encounters.

3. Almost 70 percent will occur during low-light conditions (hours of darkness or in locations with dim light).

4. An increasing number of assaults on officers will involve more than one threat. Criminals (especially dedicated ones) are increasingly working in teams of two or more.

5. About 70 percent of officers killed will die from handgun wounds (many will be killed with their own handguns).

6. The threat who shoots will usually have two initial advantages: It will usually start the action (being the first to fire, with the officer reacting to the attack), and its mind is made up to shoot the officer before it pulls the trigger. Also, the threat will usually be interested in only two things: survival and escape. The officer, on the other hand, must consider many more factors before he or she fires, all requiring some degree of time. This initially gives the threat an edge that must be countered by early threat recognition and an aggressive, instantaneous defensive response.

7. Many of the threats that shoot will have spent time practicing and probably decided on a method of firing, usually simply involving getting close to the

officer, then quickly producing the gun and shooting as fast as possible. The threat understands that you have been trained in firing your handgun, and in order to win the encounter, the threat must be close to the officer.

Statistics and information: what average encounter do they form?   The average encounter will be close, quick, and in low light. The majority will be surprisingly close and quick, as the threat(s) knows that it will have to be close for the attack to succeed. When the threat(s) attacks, it will usually make the first move, fire first, and attack ruthlessly, holding nothing back. During such attacks, your aggressive, instantaneous defensive response is your best defense, quickly getting on target and "hitting" to stop or counter the threat(s). The outcome of the initial exchange of gun fire, during the opening ceremony, will often decide who wins and who loses. During many of these encounters, more than one threat will be involved.

This is the average lethal encounter that will occur. How you respond to the threat(s) and the attack will depend on a variety of trained-in factors. Today's firearms training must reflect these realities and concentrate on them, but also train officers for the total spectrum of encounters.

THE LETHAL ENCOUNTER: BEFORE, DURING, AND AFTER

The total lethal encounter is involved with three time frames: before it occurs, during its occurrence, and after it had ended. All three of these have their own unique tactics and techniques to keep you one step ahead during each part of the encounter.

Before the Lethal Encounter Occurs

The before time frame is concerned with three recognition levels and your responses during the initial stage of a lethal encounter—during the critical time reference. These three recognition levels are (1) early threat recognition, (2) late threat recognition, and (3) nonthreat recognition. The ideal situation is early threat recognition, providing you with a preparatory response time to plan and prepare so that you can place yourself in the most favorable position to respond when the threat occurs. The worst situation is nonthreat recognition, which allows you NO time to plan or prepare and dramatically increases the lag interval, slowing or blunting your defensive response. All three recognition levels will occur in the before time frame and you must know how to handle each situation, as any one of them can occur. No matter how tactically aware and prepared you are, any of these three recognition situations are possible and you must know how each is handled and what your options are.

Early Threat Recognition.   Ideally, you will recognize the danger signs early, that a possible threat may occur which will increase your preparatory response time to plan and prepare, thus optimally positioning yourself if it should. By having the time to become prepared, you have time to develop a plan (quick course of action) and position yourself to respond most effectively to the threat(s). You have "snapped up to speed" with the unfolding encounter and know exactly what you will do to stop it, either before it starts or when it starts. This is the ideal situation during the initial moments of a lethal encounter, as you know it is coming and are prepared for it. Tactical positioning and increased awareness are the best methods for spotting the danger signs early on.

Late Threat Recognition.   Even if you have missed the first one or more danger signs, you may catch one occurring just before the threat presents itself. This will provide you with a very small amount of preparatory response time to get ready and is far preferable to having no time. You will not have the luxury of a number of seconds to a half-a-minute or more to plan and prepare, but you may have a second (maybe even several seconds) to snap up to speed (become aware that an encounter is about to occur). Planning a quick course of action and preparing to implement it will have to happen within an extremely short time span—sometimes a second or less, but at least you have that time to snap up to speed with the unfolding encounter. Even a second will greatly decrease the lag interval, speeding up your defensive response.

Nonthreat Recognition.   If caught completely unaware and flatfooted, you will have to respond to the instantly occurring threat while you are still trying to figure out what is going on. Unaware, you were not up to speed with the unfolding encounter (unaware that the encounter was about to occur), but now, to survive, you have to begin your defensive response instantly. When caught flatfooted, an increased lag interval will occur while you are snapping up to speed and slow down or blunt your defensive response, which may be your only means of survival. If caught flatfooted, you must still formulate a quick course-of-action and follow it through—no matter how instantly.

Which ever situation you find yourself in will depend mainly on your tactical positioning, awareness, and to some degree the luck of the situation. These three elements will ultimately decide when you will first recognize that a threat is about to occur or is occurring. Approach life tactically and use tactical positioning in your everyday movement. The most common example is the old setting with your back to a wall or being positioned so that you can see what comes in the door. This is merely positioning yourself so that you can easily see what is going on. Once tactically positioned, maintain a high awareness level so that you can spot the danger signs.

Luck is the third element of the mix and will play a large or small role, depending on how the first two elements are used. If not tactically positioned and aware, luck will play a much larger role if a threat occurs. You must use the first two elements to relegate luck to its lowest level.

Preparation when you see it coming.   Once you have correctly interpreted the danger sign(s), before the threat presents itself, how do you prepare for threat occurrence. Time and your ability to maneuver within the encounter zone are the critical factors that determine how much preparation you will be able to make.

Time Frames.   From threat recognition (when you correctly interpreted a danger sign, not necessarily the first danger sign) to threat occurrence you may have a time frame of anywhere from half a second to a half a minute or more. During this preparatory response time you must become as prepared as possible for the threat occurrence, possibly being able to stop the threat before it occurs. Even if given only a second's notice, you will be able to reduce greatly the lag interval (the time between threat occurrence and your defensive response), by having that second to snap up to speed, so you are not caught completely flatfooted. Usually, the more time you have to prepare, the better your defensive response will be.

Ability to Maneuver.   The encounter zone will dictate, to a larger part, your ability to maneuver or take up a good position to respond from. Are you standing or setting, and/or have you been made (has the threat identified you as a police officer yet—whether in uniform, plain clothes, undercover, or off duty)? Even if the threat has not made you yet, you may not be able to maneuver or create movement that would possibly draw attention to yourself. At other locations, though, you have a much greater ability to maneuver and position yourself to respond effectively to the threat(s). This is especially true if outside the immediate encounter zone, viewing what is going on inside the zone.

Preparation Steps.   When you correctly interpret a danger sign, you must instantly snap up to speed with the unfolding encounter and start preparing for it. You may have caught the encounter early on with plenty of time to prepare, or it is a second away from happening. Most of the time you will not know until it occurs. Remember, the threat may present itself at any time. You cannot precisely control that aspect of the encounter, even though you may take the initiative and try to stop the threat before it occurs.

During your preparatory response, four things must be done while following the preparatory response rule: From first recognition, instant weapon response must always be available. All preparation is undertaken with this in mind. For the most part, the initiative is with the threat(s), as its actions (which can occur at any time) will demand your instant response.

[*Note:* We are dealing with lethal assaults, where the threat(s) is trying to kill you. If the encounter instantly deescalates, with the threat(s) giving up or running— fine, do not fire. But if it goes all the way, with the threat(s) shooting it out, you must be ready to respond and stop the threat(s). Remember, as stated in Chapter 1, this book is dealing with lethal assaults, where the threat(s) is trying to kill you. If the situation changes and other control options are available, use them.]

A Possible Threat or Not.   Many will ask: "Why not immediately stop the threat?" The answer is simple: "It may appear as a threat about to occur, but it may also not be a lethal threat at all." Danger signs have been read that a possible threat may very quickly occur, but what if there is no real threat? Often, situations which indicate that a lethal threat is about to occur in reality are just some suspicious-looking people acting inappropriately. They bear watching, and preparation is begun if danger signs are read, but if nothing happens and the possible threat dematerializes, no further action may be required. Although possible, further investigation may be required if probable cause exists that the suspects are possibly engaged in an illegal act. Pick your place to confront them with sufficient back up to control the situation if one occurs.

    Four things that must be done.   During the preparatory response, when preparing for the unfolding encounter, four things must be done in the following order:

    1. Weapon Preparation.   Now that you have a second or maybe half a minute to prepare, you must position your handgun to be ready to respond instantly. The level of positioning (from touching holstered handgun to holding it out in a firing stance) will depend on the situation and what is occurring. This can mean anything from touching the holstered handgun with your hand or forearm to drawing the handgun surreptitiously (stealthily) and locking into a two-handed grip held low or to completely locked out in a two-handed firing stance behind cover. Remember, the quickest draw is having the handgun already in hand. Weapon preparation is nothing more than positioning the handgun as close as possible to the first shot. You know the threat is coming, so position the handgun in anticipation of the first shot. Then, when the threat occurs, your handgun may be up before the threat's handgun is.

    Be certain of what is going on before committing yourself to a weapon use response. You cannot take your handgun out at every danger sign, but when a threat is obviously going to occur, be as close to the first shot as possible. Always take into consideration the situation and surroundings, but be prepared. Touching your holstered handgun to establish a touch index is the appropriate response before you are certain that a threat is about to occur. This is done easily and no one is the wiser.

    This must be accomplished first to follow the preparatory response rule: From first recognition, instant weapon response must always be available. You are now instantly prepared to fire, from the moment you first recognized the threat until it occurs. This preparation can be accomplished in less than a second by easily touching the holstered handgun (either with forearm or hand) for the touch index and is done while you are assessing what is occurring. That may be all you have time for until the shooting starts.

    Touching the holstered handgun is the first preliminary positioning that will be made. This is not a quick, fast movement to the holster, which can draw attention to you (unless the gun fight starts), but an easy movement, with the hand slipping smoothly to the holstered handgun. Now your hand is on the holstered handgun, one step closer to a firing position. The hand only has to touch part of the handgun's grip and the elbow can be bent in more to look more natural. The inside of the forearm can also be used to touch the holstered handgun. By touching the handgun with either, you have created a touch index that tells the body exactly where the handgun's grip is located, greatly increasing your ability to draw the handgun quickly. Before further positioning the handgun by removing it from the holster, number 2 is accomplished.

Your planning at this moment, if the threat(s) instantly attacks, would be to draw the handgun and stop the threat(s) (initially just that simple, obviously depending on the sitaution), then move to the nearest covered position and follow the post-exchange rules (outlined later in this chapter).

2. Assessing the Situation and Structure.   You must find out everything you can about this unfolding encounter, especially the location of any other threat(s). While doing this you are also scanning the location again (of course, you scanned the location as you first entered it and have been maintaining your scan ever since), rechecking for available cover, exit routes, general layout, and other people present. You are assessing the situation (what is going on and who the players are) and structure (what the location can do for you). As the answers come in, you are preparing to take up the best position possible to respond to the threat(s).

3. Tactical Positioning.   If you have the time, select the best position from which to fight. The best position is a covered postition that will not only provide protection, but an exit route, if possible. When selecting a tactical position, if possible choose one that can provide you with the flexibility of movement to other positions. Try not to restrict your flexibility by being in a closed-in position, as the fight may become extended and/or more threat(s) may appear.

4. Planning.   You must formulate a plan (quick course of action) no matter how quickly you must do it, whether or not the encounter is about to occur or is occurring at that moment. You must plan for the threat occurrence—what you will do when the threat presents itself. Planning is also very fluid, as a plan you made 4 seconds ago may now have to be changed to respond to changes in the situation and structures (other threats appearing, innocents arriving on the scene, etc.). For these changes you should have advanced contingency plans—one or two plans (or moves) that you have decided on in advance if the first plan does not work or if a change occurs. These contingency plans can be life savers when the initial plan goes bad for some reason.

You must have an initial plan to respond with when the threat occurs, with at least one (hopefully two) contingency plans to back it up. Mainly you must have a plan and be following it. When the threat occurs, instantly use your plan and follow it through. Once you start the plan, follow it through completely. Also, you must have the flexibility necessary to instantly change plans and formulate new ones.

One fact about planning stands out: It is far better to have a plan and not to have used it than to need a plan instantly and not have one to use! A plan with no need is fine; a need with no plan can kill you.

During and After the Lethal Encounter

The before time frame will abruptly end when threat occurrence happens, with the threat(s) presenting itself. At this point the during time frame begins and you must be ready instantly to implement your defensive response. This time frame will continue until the threat(s) is stopped, when the after time frame begins as the officer must follow through until the encounter is completely over with. At times it is hard to separate where the during time frame ends and the after time frame begins. This will occur, as the encounter will often appear to have ended, but suddenly start up again. As such, we cover them together.

The initial exchange of gun fire.   When the initial exchange of gun fire occurs, you will either be prepared (having correctly interpreted the danger signs) or be caught flatfooted. If you are prepared, you have taken steps to meet the threat(s). The main factor is that you are prepared and instantly ready to respond to the threat(s). If caught flatfooted you must instantly snap up to speed, either drawing and firing instantly or diving for cover and returning fire instantly. Which of these will depend on the proximity of the threat(s)—how close it is and its precise location.

Prepared and Ready.   Having seen the threat(s) coming, you have hopefully positioned yourself to respond effectively to the threat(s) and have a plan (with one or two contingency plans to back it up). Remember, the best position is a covered position. When you are prepared, you have many more options open to you, which will dramatically increase your survival advantage.

When the threat(s) occurs, immediately engage it and keep "hitting" until the threat(s) is down or going down. Then move instantly to a covered position. If more than one threat, place one "hit" on each threat first and then move instantly to a covered position. Once behind cover, use the post-exchange rules: Maintain cover, pick up a 360-degree scan, reload, and plan.

Unaware and Caught Flatfooted.   How you respond will depend on the proximity and location of the threat(s). If the threat(s) is very close, your only option may be to get on target as fast as possible and "hit" until the threat(s) is down and/or stopped, then instantly move to cover. If the threat is farther away or its location is not instantly known, go to cover immediately and/or exit the encounter zone and take up a covered position outside it. Once behind cover, draw and engage the threat(s) if its location is now known. Now, if the threat's location is still unknown, your covered position may not be safe, as the threat(s) may be in a position to fire on you or may flank your position. Back off by a covered route, in the direction opposite from where you think the attack came, to the next cover back (the one-cover-back option). Once behind that cover, use the post-exchange rules.

The post-exchange rules are used after any exchange of gun fire.   Here is where the during and after time frames become intertwined. When any lull occurs in the action, after an exchange of rounds has taken place, you must use the post-exchange rules to follow through in case the encounter suddenly starts up again.

Using the post-exchange rules is exactly the same for the during or after time frames. If the encounter starts up again, you are still in the during time frame, and if the encounter has ended, you have now entered the after time frame. You will not know which time frame you are in until time passes.

Whenever the shooting occurs, be it the initial exchange or any subsequent exchange during a continuing fight, an exchange of rounds takes place and there is a lull in the action, no matter how brief. In the exchange, you must respond instantly when fired on and return fire or go for cover (especially if unsure of the threat's exact location). (*Note:* In the next section we discuss firing during the encounter.)

During the exchange, tunnel vision will set in as you focused on the threat(s) while returning fire. Now the lull in the action occurs (no matter how brief). Your tunnel vision must instantly be expanded from being tightly focused on the threat(s) to the entire encounter zone—still keeping a definite watch on the action/threat(s). You are now going to take action reference your location, scan, reloading, and evaluation by using the post-exchange rules.

POST-EXCHANGE RULES:

1. Seek "cover" if not already there and stay ready to fire.
2. Pick up your 360-degree "scan" and use expanded vision to cover the entire encounter zone.
3. Take advantage of the lull in the action to "reload," always keeping your eyes on the action/threat(s).
4. Take advantage of the lull in the action to "plan," rethink, and evaluate.

Your next set of moves will depend on what the threat(s) may do and/or how quickly other officers can assist you. Whatever else, you are in a covered position, ready to fire, reloaded, and "thinking."

1. *Seek cover and stay ready to fire.* This is the primary survival rule. You must stay behind cover to use its protection and check for additional threat(s) and to reengage the first threat(s) if need be. Stay ready to fire. Keep the handgun in a firing position; do not relax or let up. Resist the strong urge to approach a downed threat(s); it may still possess the ability to fire on you. You are not behind cover thinking that the situation is over with and relaxing, but you are, if anything, working harder to be ready for the threat's possible continued attack. If you are in a good covered position, remain there unless the situation forces you to move. If not in a good covered position, move to one.

2. *Pick up your 360-degree scan.* While behind cover you must keep your eyes on the action/threat(s), but you must also pick up your 360-degree scan, which will check the whole encounter zone and reveal any additional threat(s). You must use your expanded vision to include all areas around your location. Along with picking up your scan, pick up your hearing. Stay on top of the encounter. Do not let up or go limp thinking that you have survived; more challenges to your survival may be at hand. You have survived the initial exchange; you may not survive the next ex-

change if you do not know what is going on around you. What you do not see can kill you.

3. *Reload during the lull.* Once the initial exchange is over with, reload at the first chance you get during a lull in the action. Follow the reloading rule: Reload at the first available lull after you fire; do not wait and run dry. Reloading during the lulls so that you will not have to during the action. You must keep a constant flow of ammo going into the handgun.

4. *Plan, rethink, and evaluate.* Behind cover and ready to fire, you are planning your next set of moves. Whatever else is occurring, you are thinking. Get your brain working and plan your moves: what you will do if attacked, the next piece of cover you can move to, and so on. Plans do not need to be extensive, but they need to be made. You also now have a quick chance to rethink and evaluate exactly what is occurring and your options. Remember a thinking officer is much harder to kill.

Whenever an exchange of rounds takes place, you must use these post-exchange rules to be ready if a subsequent exchange occurs. Using these rules helps you stay on top of the encounter.

Be careful of the crossover between the during and after time frames. What you think is the end of an encounter and the after time frame may still be the during time frame if the threat suddenly continues the attack. Just because a threat is "hit" and down, it may still be capable of attacking you. The threat may not be wounded as badly as you think; even though well "hit" in the chest area, the human body will still take time to shut down. There is also the distinct possibility that secondary threats are close. Maintain your covered position and stay ready to fire.

FIRING THROUGH THE ENCOUNTER

Two distinctly different gun fire exchanges may occur during an encounter: the initial exchange and any subsequent exchanges. The encounter may be over with after the initial exchange or it may continue through a number of subsequent exchanges. Each has its own style of fire and realities, which you must understand.

(*Note:* When covering firing techniques and tactics, we are referring to a live-fire situation then in progress. The threat(s) is at that moment trying to shoot the officer to death. The officer will use these firing techniques to save his or her life in a live exchange of gun fire, whether the initial or subsequent exchanges. As stated in Chapter 1, this book deals with lethal encounters; other control options cannot be used or have already been used.)

Firing during the Initial and Subsequent Exchanges

The initial exchange is uniquely different from the subsequent exchanges that may follow it. It is the quickest and deadliest time during a lethal encounter and can catch you completely unaware when it begins. The threat(s) usually begins the encounter and fires first, initially placing you at a disadvantage if you do not respond instantly. Your plan for an instantly occurring initial exchange is simple: Get on target and "hit" until the threat is down or going down.

Most initial exchanges are very close and quick, with virtually no option open but to get on target instantly and fire until the threat(s) is down or going down. During these exchanges you must "hit" the threat(s) fast and repeatedly, making your shots count. Do not panic at the suddenness of the attack, but get down to work quickly and place your "hits" rapidly. If you just start firing as fast as you can (machine gunning), your shots will be all over the place, probably most missing the threat(s) altogether.

Only "hits" count; misses waste valuable time and ammo and do little to stop the threat(s). Place solid "hits" on the threat(s) as fast as you can. It is not the first shot you fire that is important but the first "hit" on the threat. "Hits" count, misses do not, no matter how fast they were fired. You must understand how fast you can hit and do not try to shoot any faster.

Police officers, virtually every single one, do not know how fast they can accurately fire because it is not taught. Usually, strings of fire during training and especially during requalification have exceedingly long time limits, giving officers plenty of time when firing. When a close/quick lethal encounter occurs, they will instantly fire as fast as possible by "spraying and praying," as they feel they will lose if they do not fire as fast as possible. The results are usually many misses and a few hits. They have been taught to fire slowly and now under the stress of a real encounter, pull/jerk the trigger as fast as they can, spraying bullets all over the place. Control is the key factor in firing. If taught to fire fast and control the handgun, officers will do just that and know they can do it. If only taught to fire at a slower rate and control the handgun, they will not control it when firing fast. Officers must find out how fast they can accurately fire the handgun and have confidence in their abilities to do so during a lethal encounter.

You must maintain first-shot priority by making the first shot fired "hit" the threat. Do not throw the first shot away because it was fired too quickly; make it count. The difference in firing time between a first shot that misses and one that "hits" is usually a quarter- to a half-second. This is a small amount of time to take for a first-shot priority "hit." Also, follow-up shots are quicker and far more likely to "hit" when control is exerted and the first shot "hits." A large part of the problem of missing at very close quarters is speed and time pressure. During a situation, time pressure can cause you to fire much faster than you need to, not slowing down enough to fire controlled shots. Control is the key; get down to work by controlling your handgun and not jerking the trigger.

The initial exchange will decide the outcome much of the time. Stay on your feet and keep firing until the threat(s) is down or has stopped firing due to being "hit." If more than one threat, make sure that you place one round on each threat first. This will be the first few seconds (usually 2 to 3 seconds). Now, instantly increase your distance from the threat(s) and move to a covered position. Remember, if you are caught in the open, the initial exchange will no doubt have to be fought in the open (depending on the threat's proximity), but all subsequent exchanges must be fought from behind cover if at all possible. The initial exchange is one time where cover may not always be taken before you fire (if not already behind cover before the action starts). And, if you turn to move toward cover instead of firing, the threat(s) now has an open target to fire on.

All subsequent exchanges will be fired from cover, using all the advantages that a covered position offers. Once the initial exchange is under way or over with, instantly move to cover for the remainder of the encounter.

Plan A, B, and C (the ABCs of Hitting)

Placing the "hits" on the threat involves three plans. Plan A is used when initially engaging one or more threats. Plan B is a contingency resorted to instantly in case plan A does not work. Plan C is used for the continuing engagement. They are divided into two sets, for one threat and two or more threats.

The ABCs when facing one threat.   When faced with only one threat (one known threat, others may appear), you have only one threat on which to concentrate.

Plan A. Two very fast center-mass "hits." If the threat is not stopped, go to plan B.

Plan B. One or two "hits" to the head or pelvic area. The main reason for contingency plan B is the use of body armor by criminals. More and more we are seeing threats wearing body armor. If the two in the chest (plan A) do not work, immediately switch your point of aim either to the head or the pelvic area (Plan B) and keep "hitting" until the threat is down. The pelvic area is excellent, as it will usually put the threat down and reduce its fighting and moving ability.

Plan C. During the continuing engagement, place your "hits" into vital areas or into any part of the threat that appears, to stop the threat outright or reduce its ability to continue the fight. During a lethal fight, concentrate on placing fight-stopping "hits," but if any part of the threat appears, "hit" that part. This is no game; you "hit" the vital areas or anywhere you can, to stop the threat and save your life. If the threat presents any target, you take it. Any bullet wound on the threat is better than none at all and will reduce its ability to continue the attack. Hit the threat any place you can.

These three plans (the ABCs of hitting) provide you with a ready-made set of plans that you mentally and physically train in with the reflexive sets. They will provide lifesaving direction if caught flatfooted and no time to formulate a plan instantly as the bullets are flying. The ABCs are ready-made plans to increase your chances of survival. Suddenly you are under fire use plan A—two center mass "hits"; if the threat is not stopped, use plan B—one or two "hits" in the head or pelvic area (in case of body armor and/or to put the threat down); and if the engagement continues use plan C—"hit" the vital areas or any part of the threat that appears (to stop the threat outright or to reduce its fighting ability).

Note on Hitting the Head or Pelvic Area. The head is included, as a solid "hit" to it will stop the threat outright and this is all you may see if the threat is behind cover. The head is a very hard target to hit, though (as it can move very quickly back and forth), and even what appears to be a good hit may sometimes fail to stop the threat. The head is a hard target, but a good hit to it will stop the threat instantly. The pelvic area provides a larger and not so mobile area to hit and will usually take the threat down. The threat may not be stopped, but its fighting ability and movement are now limited.

The ABCs when facing two or more threats.   When faced with two or more threats, you must place one "hit" on each of the threats first, one right after the other. You do not have the time to place two "hits" on each of the threats, as the last one may shoot before you are able to "hit" it.

Plan A. One very fast center mass "hit" on each of the threats.

Plan B. Continue firing by placing one or two "hits" to the center mass, head, or pelvic area on any threat that has not been stopped. Plan B is a continuation of plan A, as you never stopped shooting. Again, the head and pelvic area are included in case body armor is being used and/or to take the threats down.

Plan C. During the continuing engagement, place your "hits" into vital areas or any part of the threat(s) that appears—to stop the threat(s) outright or reduce its ability to continue the fight.

Move to cover when "hitting".   When an initial exchange occurs, it may initially have to be fought in the open, but at the first opportunity, get behind cover and fight from behind it. During the initial exchange you must stop the threat(s) by instantly firing on it, but do not remain in the open once this is accomplished. Often, you can move to cover after plan A has been accomplished (whether firing on one threat or two or more threats). Always move behind cover once plan B has been accomplished, and continue with plan C from a covered position if necessary.

The incapacitating and terminating factors.   These two factors center on the ability of the threat to continue the lethal assault. They are markedly different: The incapacitating factor is anything that reduces the ability of the threat to continue the fight, and the terminating factor is anything that increases the possibility of the threat's death. Your goal is to stop the lethal threat as safely and effectively as possible. Killing the threat is not any part of your goal, but the end result may be the threat's death. As such, we are concerned with the incapacitating factor from the standpoint of decreasing the threat's ability to continue the fight, ultimately stopping the threat, which is the goal of your defensive weapon use. We are not concerned with the terminating factor (the threat's death), which is not part of any goal.

Your goal is to stop the threat, but often this is not as easy as it would seem to be. Threats rarely fall down dead when "hit" but often keep on functioning for a period of time, sometimes short and sometimes very long. During these times, the threat may still possess the ability to strike a lethal blow. Unlike TV, where once the threat is shot, the game is over with, real encounters tend to continue and you must follow through during the lethal fight until it is ended.

Whenever in a lethal fight, you must maintain and if possible improve your fighting ability while decreasing the threat's ability. If this is done, you will control the situation. When firing on the threat, good solid "hits" anywhere will reduce its ability to continue the fight (some "hits" stopping it completely, while others will reduce its ability by some degree).

The Incapacitating Factor.   Where to place the "hits" and how many it will take must be understood. Do not be surprised if the threat does not go down and out with the first one or two "hits" and at times quite a bit more. Even though hurt very badly, the threat will often be capable of continuing its attack. Many factors can play a part in how fast a threat is stopped, including bullet placement, the round's effectiveness, how badly the threat wants to survive and/or continue assaulting you (its mental set), any drugs taken, the threat's build and clothing, and so on. It may take a surprising amount of time for the threat's body to shut down enough, so it stops the attack. Do not expect an immediate stop, although it may occur.

Bullet Placement Is the Key.   No other factor is as important to stopping a threat as bullet placement. To use your bullets efficiently, you must place them where they will do the most damage. You must quickly begin working to place your rounds and "hit" the threat.

Where to "Hit".   As the ABCs of hitting outline, center mass is the first target area, then either the head or pelvis, and in the final analysis any target that is presented. The main goal of "hitting" is to shut down the threat's nervous system. When a solid "hit" has been placed in a vital area, the nervous system will begin shutting down within several seconds, stopping the threat from continuing its attack. For this to occur, certain target areas are imporant.

Center Mass (thoracic cavity) is the first target, as the area holds the largest concentration of vital organs in the body and thus provides the greatest chance of placing a fight-stopping "hit" (even if not exactly on target). "Hits" into this area will transmit a lot of shock to the nervous system, especially if one or more vital organs are "hit." Go for center mass first.

The head and pelvis provide secondary target areas that can be resorted to, especially if the threat is wearing body armor. The head is a harder target to hit, not just due to its size but also its mobility. If a good center "hit" to the head is placed, the threat will be stopped instantly. Many times, though, bullets show a tendency to glance around the skull and not enter it and stop the threat. Shoot for the central area, from the middle of the forehead to the middle of the nose and keep it centered. The pelvis, on the other hand, is meant to decrease the threat's ability to continue the attack, by making the threat go down and decreasing its movement. This is the second-largest target area of the body and much less mobile than the head. If the spinal cord is also "hit," this will produce quite a bit of shock and usually make a quick stop.

The base of the skull and the spinal cord will produce instant to quick stops. The best area to produce an instant stop is the area where the base of the skull and top of the spinal cord meet. A "hit" here will produce an instant stop, as the body will no longer respond to the brain's commands. This is a very difficult target to hit. A "hit" to any part of the spinal cord will produce instant to quick stops (whether severed or not). Both of these targets are hard to hit, as these areas are usually not presented.

More Than One "Hit." As stated, shock to the nervous system is what is required to stop the threat. When a bullet "hits," it causes a certain level of bodily shock. When the body is "hit" by a second bullet, the shock is at least double that of the first bullet. By increasing the number of times the body is "hit," you dramatically increase the shock to the body, causing it to shut down more quickly. Multiple "hits" can improve your chances of quickly stopping the threat. These are commonly referred to as doubles, double-taps, and pairs and are used whenever possible. (*Note:* We are not refering to machine gunning a large number of rounds into the threat or excessive multiple shots, but to controlled "hits" of 2 to 4 rounds. Controllable hits are the key.)

One center-of-mass "hit" from a service handgun (a full-powered police service handgun with appropriate ammunition should have the threat off its feet within 2 to 5 seconds about 60 percent of the time. Two center-of-mass "hits," fired within 1 second, should have the threat down within half the time—1.5 to 2.5 seconds about 75 percent of the time. The threat may be stopped instantly or may still be capable of attacking from the ground.

(*Note:* Knockdown power does not exist. Any bodily movement when "hit," such as being thrown backward, is just a reaction to being "hit," not derived from the power or energy of the bullet. This is usually the result of shock to the body or a mental reaction to being "hit.")

The whole idea when placing your "hits" is to stop the threat as quickly as possible, thus stopping its lethal attack. Bullet placement is the key, and knowing where to "hit" is part of that key.

Reloading During the Initial and Subsequent Exchanges

Reloading during the initial exchange. If forced to reload in the middle of the initial exchange, the situation has gone bad. When forced to reload during the action, you have either fired all the rounds in the handgun or a malfunction has occurred. You are in a bad situation, especially if the handgun malfunctioned in the beginning with the threat(s) not being hit. You must now do two things instantly: move and reload. You cannot stay stationary in the open and reload, or worse, try to clear a malfunction. The term "sitting duck" applies very well if you allow this situation to occur.

In the first place, do you really know what you have? The handgun is not firing, but which is it: empty or malfunctioned? You cannot remain stationary to find out. You must move while reloading, increasing your distance from the threat and/or moving to a covered position. When the handgun does not work (either empty or has malfunctioned), move and reload, increasing the distance and/or moving to cover. In the process you become a harder target to hit while moving, and even if hit, you are farther away and can hopefully make it to cover.

The reload must be accomplished while moving, as the threat may be closing the distance to assure hits by point-blank fire. Even if the reload cannot be completed while moving, it can be started, with the remainder being accomplished behind cover or at least with an increased distance from the threat(s). Usually, the reloading process will be completed as you stop behind cover. This is a far more difficult procedure with a revolver than with an auto. With either handgun, standing stationary and reloading only presents the threat(s) with a tempting target. Sidestepping out of the line of fire, then moving rearward is very effective, while you instantly reload. Quickly move behind cover if at all possible. Movement and increased distance (even a small increase can be important) will not give the threat(s) the target it wants and improve your chances of surviving the initial exchange.

When reloading during the initial exchange, you must reload as quickly as possible, dropping the empty magazine or speed loader. The handgun must be returned to action with the utmost speed.

If you ran the handgun dry by firing all the rounds, you no doubt have "hit" the threat(s). Increasing the distance and your movement will have a greater chance of working when the threat(s) is "hit."

Reloading during subsequent exchanges.   Increase the distance between you and the threat(s) when taking a covered position. It will afford you a better view of the larger area, hopefully improving your chances of locating any other threat(s).

When a subsequent exchange of gunfire occurs, get on target and fire quickly to handle the exchange. Once a lull in the action occurs, reload your handgun to keep it fully charged. Even if you think you have fired the handgun only two or three times, reload it. Two reasons for this: First, in all probability you may have fired more than the two or three rounds you think you have and may only have one or two rounds left in the handgun, and second, the handgun must be fully loaded for the next exchange. Use partial reloading to keep the handgun fully loaded—no need to drop your magazines or live rounds. (*Note:* Reloading between every exchange is a more important consideration when using a revolver. With a high-capacity auto it is not nearly as important, but do not run your gun dry.)

What if you are hit?   No matter if you are hit or not, you cannot stop fighting. Even if hit solidly, continue "hitting" the threat. Many say that the first one down will be the final loser. That is not necessarily the case. In all probability, the first one that stops working will be the final loser. Keep working to place your "hits" and be covered. Do not stop working no matter what occurs.

If hit, you also have to fight back shock, which will try to creep up on you insidiously. Use your self-control to fight it and not let shock take control. Remain conscious; concentrate on what is going on around you, not your wounds. Concentrate on doing your job and following through with the situation. Your wounds may seem bad, but in reality they are probably not life threatening. If you think they can kill you and allow yourself to slip into shock, you can die from flesh wounds. People have died from flesh wounds by allowing shock and the feeling they were going to die take over, while other people, with wounds that should have caused their deaths, hung on, never gave up, and survived. The difference is in your determination to survive.

One thing is for certain; you will not survive if you allow the threat to kill you by not stopping it first.

SUMMARY

In this chapter we covered the salient information necessary when engaged in the three time frames of a lethal encounter: before, during, and after. From the beginning you must be ahead of the game and stay on top of it in order to survive. Learn these tactics to increase your survival advantage.

10

Search Tactics

One of an officer's primary responsibilities is responding to the scene of unknown or dangerous situations and ascertaining what, if anything, has occurred there, and if a threating situation still exists, to stop or control it. This will often require a search to make sure that the threat(s) has left the scene or area. To search and clear areas safely, officers must be well versed in all aspects of weapon use and search tactics. In this chapter we deal with the search tactics that are used for the twofold purpose of safely negotiating the search environment, where a possible threat(s) may be located, and applying the weapon use techniques to the search.

The roll of the first responders. When a call goes out, the first responders on the scene—usually two officers but sometimes only one—will initially approach the scene and determine what has occurred or is still occurring. It will be their responsibility to determine if the crime is still in progress, and depending on what they find, whether they can handle it themselves or require further backup and/or speciality units to respond to the scene (K-9 or SWAT). Many times these situations will give no indication to the first responders of the lethal threat hiding inside, or appear to be just another B&E, robbery, and so on, where the threat(s) is probably gone. On scenes such as these, the vast tendency of first responders is to check it out themselves. Often, with no readily apparent threat, there does not seem enough justification to call in further backup or specially trained units. There are also times when an obvious threat exists, but there is no specially trained unit to respond and somebody has to search it. At these times the first responders and sufficient backup must do just that: search the area (woods or constructed area) and clear it, controlling and apprehending any threat(s) found there.

The question is: When faced with an area to search, how is it safely and effectively conducted? The answer begins with an understanding of two basic areas: weapon use and search tactics. These are individual skills that all officers must develop within themselves and provide the basic skills necessary for the team function (two or more officers working together). Every officer must develop his or her individual skills as the basis for searching and the team function. Also, make no mistake, you do not search alone at any time, as the risk is too great, but circumstances may place you as a single unit and you must be able to function as such. With trained-in individual skills and confidence in them, you will be able to function individually. You must understand that your own individual skills are critical to your survival. We train for the worst breakdown in a situation; then, if it occurs and you find yourself as a single unit, you can function alone safely and effectively until backup arrives. Ultimately, you are the one responsible for your survival and the time will no doubt come that you must function by yourself during an encounter. With trained-in individual skills, you will be able to function.

THE SEARCH: A BASIC STATEMENT

The search should be viewed as an unfamiliar environment of many hiding places (close-quarters to warehouse size) where a threat(s) can easily secrete itself. Officers must enter this unfamiliar environment and safely/effectively locate, control, and apprehend the threat(s). Many obstacles and problems will increase the danger of this undertaking.

Usually, all searches are accomplished in unfamiliar surroundings (unless you have searched there before) and you get one chance to search it—right or wrong, safe and effective or not—you get one chance. If the threat(s) is hiding, it is already one step ahead of you; the surroundings are familiar to the threat(s). The threat(s) has been through them and picked a hiding place that is best suited for its purpose (to hide from detection or to ambush you). The threat(s) will know when and where you are coming from 95 percent of the time (in buildings). If you think you can sneak up on it, you are kidding yourself in almost every case, as the smallest noise you make will give you away—and you will make a lot of noises.

No two searches will be alike and each is never understood fully even after you have completed it: many areas, some very large, are missed or overlooked on almost every search (especially in commercial buildings). All searches will have a myriad of physical obstacles to your safety (doors to go through, boxes stacked in warehouses, steps to go up or down, large clumps of vegetation that obscure the view, tightly placed trees that are easily climbed, and so on) that you must surmount to complete the search.

How you accomplish it safely begins with the basics: weapon use skills and search tactics. A good foundation in these will attune you to searching procedures in general and lessen the impact of mistakes that you will invariably make along the way.

Search tactics compromise three areas:

1. The *basic search rules* keep you alert, prepared, and ready if action starts.
2. An understanding of the *search and its environment* provides direction for the weapon use techniques (including flashlight use).
3. The *use of cover* lays out methods for approaching and turning those dangerous, close-range obstacles.

These three areas are used as one package throughout the search—every step of the way, all the time while searching. They provide direction for your search by establishing an understanding of the search environment, tactics to be used, and methods for negotiating obstacles, all of which dictate weapon use. Each area will be covered in detail, providing a total picture of searching.

THE BASIC SEARCH RULES

The basic search rules increase your survival advantage by training you to be aware and prepared when searching. You are aware of the locations around you where a threat(s) could be located and prepared to react if the threat(s) presents itself. Being aware and prepared on the highly stressful search is vital from the obvious standpoint of your safety, but it can also keep you from making a tragic mistake. These mistakes often occur when innocent people arrive on the scene suddenly and unexpectedly. When the unaware and/or unprepared officer is startled by an innocent, he or she may react (under the stress of the situation and/or sudden fear) before knowing what he or she has, and kill the innocent. Following the basic search rules will increase your survival advantage if attacked and increase the survival advantage of an innocent who suddenly blunders onto the scene.

These rules provide a set of mental cues, employed during searching, to increase your tactical awareness of the search environment surrounding you. Properly used, they will place you several seconds ahead when the threat(s) presents itself— not several seconds behind trying to play a catch-up game. In order to stay several seconds ahead on a search, you need the advantage that is provided by early threat(s) location and enough time/space to react effectively to the threat(s). Usually on a search, you can use search tactics to provide the time/space necessary to react to the threat(s). But you must always be aware and prepared when the threat(s) presents itself, and the basic search rules will keep you cued up and ready through-out the search.

Early threat location is very important during the search, as late threat location may be just that—too late. A knife thrust in your side is a prime example of very late threat location. When followed, these rules not only increase your ability to locate the threat early, while you still have enough time/space to react effectively and safely but greatly increase your ability to respond to it instantly.

SPECTR: the learning key.   As a learning key for the basic search rules, we use the acronym SPECTR to identify the key words of each of the six rules: scan, plan, expect, cover, trouble spots, and respond. All six rules function together throughout the search to place you at least one step ahead when the action starts. Their order is arbitrary, but you must fully understand and employ all of them when searching.

1. Scan.   During any search, you must maintain a 360-degree scan around you and also above you (around you takes care of any below-ground-level areas). Many officers fall into the habit of continually scanning at eye level and below—their normal viewing area while walking. This habit makes it hard for them also to scan to their rear and above them. To reinforce this, use the mental picture of a large dome with you in the center. Your scan must cover all parts of that dome as you are searching from ground level up.

Keep your eyes moving (by keeping your head moving), your ears open, and all your senses totally committed to the search. Look, listen, and feel your through the search every step of the way. Do not just walk through an area looking around (using only part of your senses), but keep all your senses attuned to the search at hand. It will take concentration on your part to force all your sensing abilities to the surface, not just sight and sound, but feeling your way through the search. This may sound strange at first, but those who search a lot know what it means: If it doesn't feel right, watch out. There are times when certain bodily mechanisms or senses can feel that something is not right. It may possibly be subliminal or precogni-tive in nature, but some mechanism is alerting you that something is wrong. You may feel it first and not know what is wrong, just that something feels wrong. Go with your feelings and take more precautions as you begin to search through this area where something feels wrong. Take more time and be extra careful.

When scanning, keep the head moving, but do not turn the body and handgun with the head. The body and handgun are pointed in the direction you are searching, but keep the head and eyes moving in a constant 360-degree scan around you. Do not lock the head and body together; keep the head moving. You must search and scan systematically. When scanning systematically, always keep up a 360-degree scan around you while searching, constantly checking out all areas. This type of scanning is nothing more than quick glances around you.

When scanning an area visually, use the visual two-step to cover the area completely. Always make sure that you scan from behind cover. Your first step is to quickly scan the entire area for an obvious threat(s) or indications that a threat(s) could be close. Once satisfied that no obvious threat(s) or indications are present, go to the second step. The second step is a methodical scan of the entire area, using one of three scanning methods:

1. *Horizontal strip method.* Start with the closest strip to you and scan left to right, then scan the next strip right to left, and continue until the whole area is scanned (in horizontal strips out from your position).

2. *Longitudinal strip method.* Start on one side or the other, scan out (away from you) by focusing your eyes on the closest area and then focusing on out completely covering the longitudinal strip, then shift the eyes over a bit (to the next strip) and reverse the process by focusing on the farthest area of the strip and then focusing in to the closest area. Continue until the whole area is scanned.

3. *Area method.* Select certain areas that need to be scanned and scan them thoroughly until the areas are covered. The area method can be much quicker if large parts of the area need not be scanned (when it is obvious that no threat is located in these parts).

When scanning, always clear the closest areas first, as a close threat(s) is usually much more of a danger to you than is one farther away. Clear the areas closest to you first; then clear the areas farther away. Also remember to look up when scanning and searching. Higher areas are the most overlooked places in a search. People are generally used to looking from eye level to ground level, taking in all that lies in between. You must train yourself to look up continually when searching.

2. Plan. Plan your search and select options every step of the way. As you move through the search, you must plan your moves. You are not just walking around looking; you are planning the search every step of the way. Planning will be done from two standpoints: plan how you are going to search through an area, and plan what your options (several things you can do) will be if the threat(s) presents itself.

Planning *how* you will search is used to determine which way you will go and your tactical movement: moving down which side of a hallway, how to approach a door, what cover to use along the way, and so on. This is your decision-making process with regard to what area you will move through (the direction to go) and how you will tactically move through the area.

Planning *reactions* to a threat is used to decide what you will do if attacked: your best cover options, where you will instantly move to, and so on. This is your option-selecting process, usually one or two options that can be acted upon instantly if attacked. You must know long before an attack occurs what action you are going to take [option(s) you have selected in advance] if the threat(s) suddenly attacks. Basically you are planning one or two moves to implement immediately if attacked.

At any time during the search you should be able to say: "I'm following my search plan and have selected options to use if the threat(s) appears.'' Most of the time this planning is done instantaneously as you are searching and sizing up the search environment. But that does not mean that you always have to plan while moving; take the time you need to plan properly. If you need time to smoke over a particular part of the search, take the time. In doing so you are using time to your advantage.

3. Expect.   Always expect the threat(s) to be there; make it real each time. If you expect trouble, you are better prepared for it. No half-measure searches or falling into the habit of deciding that any search is a false one before you carry it out (which is decided only when the search is over and everything has been checked). Expect the threat(s) to be around every piece of cover you check. If you do not, and find the threat(s), a startled reaction may occur that can slow down or blunt your defensive response. Many officers have been startled into inaction (freezing for a second or two) or overreaction (killing an innocent who blundered onto the scene). You will be much better prepared to react if you expect the threat(s) to be there. There will always be some minor startle effect as the threat(s) is suddenly viewed, even if you are prepared, but it will be small in comparison to the major startling effect that occurs when nothing is expected to be there.

Also, if you find one threat, there are two; if two threats, there are three; and so on. The extra-threat rule: No matter how many threats you find, there is always one more to be found—keep looking for the next threat. Of course, there will not always be one more threat, but until the area has been cleared completely, the search is continued for the next threat. Do not break off or ease up the search simply because you have found and arrested one or more threats. If anything, double your search efforts for the possibility of other threats. Many times a secondary threat(s) has escaped or injured or killed other officers who figured that only one threat was involved. Do not go tactically soft; maintain the search until it is complete.

4. Cover.   Constantly use cover throughout your search: Be aware of it, position yourself close to it, and be tactically ready to move behind it. Stay out of the open and move from covered position to covered position as you search. Many times there will be no cover, but if anything is there, use it. Develop this as one of your primary tactical habits.

The proper selection and use of cover is one of the most important tactical skills that you will develop. When speaking of cover, we include concealment. Cover has the dual advantage of concealing part or all of your body, while being able to slow down or stop incoming bullets. Concealment can only conceal part or all of your body. You must be able to select the best cover and use it effectively throughout the encounter.

(*Note:* Chapter 8 will give you a complete understanding of all the techniques and tactics involved to use C&C effectively.)

5. Trouble Spot(s).   Locate trouble spot(s) (a place you are searching toward where a threat could be hiding) as a continuous process while searching. You must orient your search toward the trouble spot(s), keep cover and concealment between you and it, approach carefully, clear it, and pick the next trouble spot(s). As you are searching, trouble spot(s) will appear as the most likely places a threat(s) could be hiding. Make sure that you orient yourself and your cover toward them. There will often be more than one; remain aware of them all as you are searching.

Try to check everything you pass to keep a possible hidden threat(s) from coming out from behind you. There will be times when you will not always be able to check everything, as you cannot break open locked doors while searching (unless you have sufficient cause to believe that a threat is behind it). Make sure that you search systematically and thoroughly, trying to check everything. Attempt to keep your back to what you have already checked, while always maintaining a 360-degree scan.

6. Respond.   Always be in a position to respond to a threat(s) and ready to make a shoot/no-shoot decision. This is accomplished by manipulating the handgun in the holding and firing positions during the search to be ready to fire instantly (especially when close-approaching possible threat cover) and having pre-thought-out your critical decisions before you have to make them. There is no time to think about what you are going to do; you must do it.

Your trained-in weapon use skills will provide you with the ability to fire instantly if necessary, especially when they are used in conjunction with search tactics. Your worked-through mental set has hopefully gotten your initial brain work out of the way long before the first lethal encounter occurs. In other words, you have the skills and are mentally set to function during the encounter.

The basic search rules must be followed to keep you as aware and prepared as you can be, cued-up to what you must do to increase your survival advantage. These are the basics of any search and must be used. (*Note:* The order of these rules is arbitrary; be equally aware of them all and use them in your searching.)

THE SEARCH AND ITS ENVIRONMENT

You must understand what the search entails, and the environment in which it takes place, to apply your search tactics appropriately and effectively. This is not a long, involved process of defining and describing a myriad of searching techniques and search areas, but lays down an understanding of how the search tactics function in the two basic search areas: natural and constructed. Search tactics are a combination of three areas: (1) always using your basic search rules, (2) keying your weapon use techniques to the search and its environment, and (3) using cover and concealment effectively. The first and last are extremely important, but the secret of searching is to key your weapon use techniques to the search and its environment. Once this process is learned, the rest is easy.

The secret of applying the weapon use techniques to the search is easily stated: Weapon use techniques are keyed to the search and its environment by properly manipulating the handgun in the holding and firing positions during the search. The holding and firing positions are trained-in reflexive sets through which you will manipulate the handgun, actually directing the handgun so that it is positioned most effectively while searching. These trained-in reflexive sets will occur automatically when needed. (*Note:* You should already be very familiar with these positions, as Chapter 6 covered the holding and firing positions in which the handgun is manipulated. These techniques are vital when searching.)

The difference between the two positions is in where the barrel is pointed. In the holding positions, the barrel is pointed down in a nonthreatening position and used to maneuver the handgun safely around other officers and obstacles on the search, yet instantly ready to snap into a firing position if the threat(s) appears. In the firing positions, the barrel is pointed at a possible threat location or the threat itself and will be used when approaching possible threat cover (PTC) and when firing on the threat(s). Their use will place you in the best position from which to react while searching around all the obstacles involved (down hallways, around corners, through warehouses, up stairs, in small areas, while climbing, etc.) and yet keep you in a position to fire instantly at all times while searching. There are only three holding and three firing positions used, for a total of only six positions.

The weapon use task while searching is to manipulate the handgun effectively and safely in response to changes in the situation and structure, while being ready to fire instantly. These trained-in positions will allow you to respond in the most effective manner to all the realities of the search.

Searching and Approaching Are Keyed to the Holding and Firing Positions

General searching is a combination of two modes, searching and approaching, which are used throughout the search, depending on the location of the possible threat(s) and/or area to be searched. Searching is concerned with the larger, total area through which you are moving, with no precise location on which to focus. Approaching is concerned with moving toward (approaching) a precise location where a threat could be hiding. Each flows into the other throughout the search as you move through and clear all areas.

For example, you are searching through an area, watching all locations as you move through and clear it, concentrating on the larger search area. While you are searching (concentrating on the larger area), you are also picking smaller areas, or precise locations, where the threat(s) may be hiding and are watching those areas more carefully. If one merits your attention more than the others (a good place the threat could be hiding, noise, movement, it does not feel right), you now approach that location very carefully (concentrating a major part of your attention on that precise location). Obviously, you do not just disregard the larger area, but this one location is where a major part of your attention is focused. Once you have successfully approached and cleared the area, you go back to searching until another possible threat location needs to be approached.

As a rule, the holding and firing positions correlate with searching/approaching by using the holding positions when searching and using the firing positions when approaching. When searching, watching the total search area with no precise threat(s) location, use a holding position to keep the weapon ready for a threat(s) that could appear anywhere around you. As such, you are flexible: ready to move and/or snap into a firing position if the threat(s) appears (no matter where it is around you). When approaching, going toward a precise location where the threat(s) could be hiding, use a firing position to direct the weapon at that precise location as you approach it. As such, you are instantly ready to fire if the threat(s) presents itself. As searching and approaching flow into one another, so do the holding and firing positions.

The size of the search area can vary tremendously, from the passenger compartment and trunk of a car to large warehouses. Smaller searches, such as houses, will be accomplished almost entirely by approaching all areas in a firing position (except when holding positions are used as officers are moving around each other). This is necessary, as so many corners, closets, doors, and angles can hide the threat(s). Also, when searching smaller areas, each must be cleared as you continue the search (moving through one room after the other), thus keeping all possible threat cover (PTC) in front of you as you clear each area and go the next.

Flowing with the total search.   As can readily be seen, searching and approaching flow into one another throughout the total search. As you are searching the larger area, holding the handgun in a holding position, you notice a piece of possible threat cover (PTC). You snap into a firing position, then *approach* and clear the possible threat cover (being instantly ready to fire if the threat is there and attacks). Once the possible threat cover is cleared, you return to the *searching* mode, with the handgun returning to a holding position. You are ready to respond to a threat(s) anywhere around you. As you continue searching, a noise is heard; you instantly snap into a firing position and begin approaching the area to check it out. Once cleared, you return to the searching mode again: back and forth, moving one into the other throughout the search.

The total search follows no hard-and-fast method, but an understanding and use of the holding and firing positions when searching and approaching will give you the flexibility and instant readiness necessary to accomplish any search effectively and realistically. You will note that searching and approaching flow into one another and become almost inseparable at times. With a small amount of practice, each flows effortlessly and smoothly into the other. In a short amount of time, each will function automatically as you move through the search.

The search must be flexible. If you try to use one method of searching, you will find that it cannot be done that way all the time—and at times cannot be done that way at all. The problem is that people build buildings that throw all the pet methods out the window. You must have a good set of flexible basics to use when searching.

Search Environments: Natural and Constructed

Search environments are divided into two areas: natural (woods, fields, swamps, etc.) and constructed (houses, warehouses, alleys, etc.). These areas involve different realities and are handled differently. When searching for a hidden threat(s), you must safely crack the nut that is the search. You must safely enter the search area, safely and effectively conduct the search, and control/apprehend the threat(s). From the beginning of this task many factors will work to increase the problems of performing it.

Natural areas are a mixture of cover and concealment that is broken up and provides many avenues to search/approach. Searching through natural areas, you usually have many ways of approaching possible threat cover and the ability to increase your distance (to some degree) from the possible threat(s) while clearing it. Natural = open (in most cases).

Constructed areas, on the other hand, provide cover and concealment coupled with very restricted avenues to search/approach. Searching through constructed areas, you usually have only one approach way available to move toward and clear possible threat cover, giving the threat(s) waiting at the other end an advantage by knowing where you will be coming from. Constructed = constricted (in most cases).

Natural Areas Search Techniques. Start by following the basic search rules. Natural areas provide a multitude of places surrounding you that can be used as cover and concealment [for both the threat(s) and you; remember, cover is a two-way street] and many avenues for searching/approaching any location. These areas require a searching technique that will best enable you to respond to a threat(s) located at any position around you. Also, you can cut a wide path around any possible threat cover, to check it out from the back, and you can enter or exit wherever you like.

Generally, the handgun is in a holding position as you search natural areas, ready to go into a firing position to meet an attack from any side. If you perceive that you may be approaching a precise location where the threat(s) may be hidden, the handgun is snapped into a firing position. Once the location is passed you go back to a holding position.

In natural areas there is a much greater chance that the threat(s) can be at any location around you and it is much easier for you to pass the threat(s). You must be in a flexible position to respond to any area around you. To accomplish this, the handgun is held in a holding position as you search, ready to go into any of the firing positions to meet an attack anywhere around you.

Natural area search techniques usually allow you more freedom of movement when searching. This freedom allows you to approach possible threat cover from virtually any direction that you wish or to circle it completely, checking all sides first. These areas are no less dangerous, just obstacles you must search around, and the manner in which you accomplish the search is different. At times, many of the techniques described in searching constructed areas will have application in natural areas. These will become obvious as you work with them.

Constructed Areas Search Techniques.   Again, you must start by following the basic search rules as the basis of your search. Constructed areas provide cover and concealment (for both you and the threat) coupled with very restricted avenues when searching/approaching. You must usually approach places of possible threat cover one way: You come down a tunnel, approaching places where a threat(s) could be hiding. Constructed areas are where the real handgun manipulating problems occur. Most of the problems stem from this channelized approach and the close distances involved when clearing possible threat cover.

On the approach, you usually have only one way (or possibly two) in which to move toward and clear the possible threat cover, thus allowing a threat(s) at the other end of the approach way (tunnel) to catch you in the open and fire. When approaching a piece of PTC, you usually cannot find out what is behind it until you are right on top of it. Once there, you are precariously close if a threat(s) is waiting with a weapon. You must be ready instantly at these close ranges which generate short time frames. A hiding threat(s) has the advantage in these situations if it knows how to use the advantage—most do not. The techniques shown here are used to lessen the threat(s) advantage.

As you can see, searching in a natural area allows much more freedom of movement and approach, while searching in a constructed area restricts your movement and approach virtually all the time. You must understand the advantages and disadvantages of each area. When conducting a search, if you are searching the larger area, manipulate the handgun in the holding positions to be ready for a threat(s) anywhere around you; if you are approaching a possible threat location and/or suddenly know/feel the threat(s) may be close, snap up into a firing position to be ready to fire. You must flow with the search and be flexible in order to respond effectively to the many changes in situation and structure that may occur. Manipulating the handgun in the holding and firing positions when searching and approaching allows you the necessary flow and flexibility.

THE USE OF COVER AND CONCEALMENT

Cover and concealment are examined in detail in Chapter 8, but a very brief look at C&C and close-approaching those dangerous obstacles adds to the understanding of searching.

Move from one C&C position to another throughout the search.   As we know, the term "C&C position" is used to designate either a covered or a concealed position. Use a covered position if available; if not, use a concealed position. Always use a covered position first, if available. C&C positions are very important when searching, to protect you and hide your movements. Avoid moving through open areas if you can. Situations will occur where movement must be made through open areas, with no way to avoid it. When encountering an open area, move quickly and smoothly through it to a covered position.

When searching, you are also planning the search every step of the way. Plan from two standpoints: (1) tactically plan which way you will go and the use of C&C along the way, and (2) plan reaction options to use if attacked. At all times, you should be following a plan and have selected options to use if the threat(s) appears. With a little practice, this is accomplished quickly and easily as you move through the area.

The use of C&C throughout the search will be involved with both of these planning areas. First, you will plan your route through the actual search area: which way you will go and the C&C you will select along that route. Whatever route you decide on, your decision will usually be based on the available C&C along it. With no other factors present, you will select the route with the best C&C along it. When time to move along the route, move from C&C position to C&C position. While moving from one C&C position to the next, always select the next C&C position before leaving your present one. Make sure that you know where you are going before you move ahead. This is what you will be doing anyway, planning all your moves in advance of executing them. When you do move, move quickly and smoothly to the next C&C position. Make sure that you do not slow down or stop in the open, as you become a much easier target.

When moving from one C&C position to another, try to select positions that are close enough so that only a short movement in the open is required. Larger distances tend to leave you too open and possibly too far from a C&C position if the threat(s) presents itself. At each new C&C position, take up a ready position, stop, listen, and observe. You move again only after checking the forward area for any sign or indication of threat presence and finding none. Even after you check ahead properly, the threat(s) may still be there. There is no guarantee, as the threat(s) may be well hidden.

Reaction options must be used to prepare you for this possibility. As you are proceeding with the search, you must plan for reaction options: one or two options available to you if attacked. This is nothing more than deciding what you will do and where you will go if attacked. It is just like defensive driving, where you are constantly aware of what you would do if a car suddenly swerved in front of you: what is around you and how would you avoid it. It is really nothing more than planning one or two moves in advance, knowing where you will go if you suddenly have to.

The close approach.   As you approach possible threat cover, you must be in a firing position and mentally prepared to fire if necessary. When close-approaching possible threat cover, two of the basic search rules must be stressed: (1) Always be in a firing position to be ready to respond instantly to the threat(s) (rule 6), and (2) plan one or two reaction options (quick courses of action) if changes occur in the situation or structure (rule 2). Obviously, you must use all the basic search rules, but these two are concentrated on during any close approach of possible threat cover (especially when right on top of it, during the last several seconds until the cover is turned). If the threat(s) presents itself you can fire on it instantly, but you must also have preplanned one or two reaction options, in advance, that you can take instantly.

When approaching, there will be times when you can get to the corner only by crossing an open area. We stress again that you must use these two basic search rules. You must be prepared to fire and/or move instantly if attacked. When the corner is finally close-approached to be turned, you must be prepared before turning cover to make this as safe and effective as possible.

Cover and concealment positions are vitally important when searching. Plan for their use and take advantage of them, to stay protected and hidden when clearing the search area.

POLICE TACTICS FOR SEARCH OR ENCOUNTER

Police tactics.   We use the term police tactics to denote the tactical considerations generally faced by police officers, either individually or in teams of two or more officers, when searching or encountering threat(s). Police tactics must be used continually by officers as part of their daily routine. These tactics were in use long before the search or encounter occurred, but are stepped up and expanded during the occurrence of a threatening situation. Once either occurs, police tactics are concerned with the continual planning process of your approach, maneuvering and placement throughout the situation, and when the threat(s) presents itself, the process used to employ your weapon use skills to stop the threat(s). Police tactics are not complicated or involved, but simple, quick, workable maneuvers to place you in the best position to respond to the threat(s) throughout the situation.

These tactics are nothing more than trained-in skills and planning. Trained-in skills allow you to employ your weapon and tactics instantly. Planning allows you to stay one or two steps ahead during the unfolding encounter. With proper training and practice you have cultivated an aware and prepared attitude. As such, you are always aware of the people, places, and events around you, and are prepared to respond if anything begins to occur. You are ready if an encounter begins to unfold, and once it starts you move right along with it, planning each and every move every step of the way.

Tactics and planning must flow with the encounter as they are dictated by it. They should be envisioned as "move and countermove" until the situation is concluded (remember, the first move can be yours or the threat's). You must stay ahead by continually being one or two moves in advance and always tactically positioned to respond, thereby solving the problem facing you and anticipating what the threat(s) may do and how you will respond. You use tactics to increase your advantage, to stack the deck against the threat(s).

Premier police tactics.   Several police tactics have become standard to police work and are used continually during any search or encounter, if at all possible. These are especially important to the approach of any possibly dangerous scene.

1. *Hidden approach/positioning.* On the initial approach of any possibly dangerous scene or during the continuing search, officers must approach and/or search in such a manner as to keep the threat(s) from seeing or hearing them. Often this is not possible, but it should always be strived for. Even though it may appear impossible, the threat(s) may be momentarily occupied with something else and the officer(s) will slip into the area unnoticed. Also, even if one officer is seen, other officers may not be seen. If the second tactic, surprise, is to be used effectively, hidden approach/positioning must be used.

Even if hidden approach/positioning has not worked initially, it can work throughout the continuing encounter or search by the officers becoming hidden again. Continually use hidden movement. Even if your hidden movement is blown initially, keep using it and become hidden again. Sure, the threat(s) knows the officers are there, but now the threat(s) do not know exactly where the officers are and what they are doing.

2. *Surprise.* This is used throughout the search or encounter. If the threat(s) can be initially surprised and controlled, the encounter can often be quickly concluded. Surprise is used throughout the search or encounter to keep the threat(s) guessing as to what you are going to do next or where you are going to appear next. Even in the use of cover, an officer will pop out at different locations to fire and/or observe. Once threats know what you are going to do or where you are going to appear next, they have got you if they know what they are doing (luckily, most do not). Surprise can give you an excellent advantage and must be used whenever possible.

3. *Use of cover and concealment.* Even though listed third, the use of cover and concealment is your most important tactic. It places you in a concealed and/or safe position while helping you remain hidden. To gain a hidden approach/positioning and surprise, you must use cover and concealment as you move into the area and search it. The use of cover and concealment is discussed in Chapter 8.

4. *Time advantage.* Always use time to your advantage. Once the perimeter is secured, take the time necessary to conduct the search safely and effectively. There may be situations where you do not have the necessary time, but these will be few. The tactic of time allows you the advantage of gathering information slowly—be it actual information from sources, or information gathered from the search that is proceeding, or mistakes by the threat(s). Time allows the communication of this information to all units involved on the scene and the correct tactical decisions to be made. If used, the advantage of time will lessen or stop many of the mistakes that otherwise would have been made.

5. *Locate and control first, arrest second.* The search is conducted to locate and control the threat(s) first, then with sufficient backup arrest it. Obviously, both can occur simultaneously, but one need not instantly follow the other. Many officers have rushed in to make a quick arrest, only to be attacked by a secondary threat hidden at another location. Take the time and have sufficient backup to make a safe arrest.

Use these premier police tactics whenever approaching and searching possible dangerous locations. On the scene, use a hidden approach/positioning by taking advantage of all cover and concealment options, so that you can possibly surprise the threat(s), while using time to your advantage when locating and controlling the threat(s) before the arrest is made.

WHEN SEARCHING

The search of an area involves many tactical considerations and skills on the part of the officers conducting it. Always use the basic search rules as the basis of your search. These will keep you cued up to what is occurring. Also, use the premier police tactics throughout the search. This section covers further thoughts and tactical considerations when searching.

Preparing for the Search

Before starting the search make sure that you are prepared for it. The first search mistakes are often made by officers not being properly prepared to conduct the search.

Check Your Equipment First.   You must make sure that everything is in working order and properly placed for the search. This usually takes only 5 or 6 seconds, but can catch problems that may occur during the search. One large problem is noise that your equipment may make. Walk back and forth a few times and listen for anything making noise. If anything is making noise, correct the problem. Make sure that you do not have any key rings hanging from your belt.

Your flashlight must be in good working order and you must have a spare flashlight if engaging in an extensive search. Carrying a small spare flashlight, such as a "minilight," is a good idea anyway, as secondary illumination may be needed when least expected. But when engaging in an extended search, the spare flashlight should be full-sized and full-powered. During any low-light conditions, the flashlight will be critical to your search. Make sure that it is in good working order.

Make sure that you have communicated properly with the dispatcher and other officers on the scene. You must make sure that the proper communications have taken place: that the dispatcher knows exactly what is going on, and that other officers on the scene are fully informed. Take the time to communicate so that everybody knows what is happening. Use communications to your advantage. A haphazard, uninformed start will cause problems during a search.

Find Out All Information before Searching.   Do not just instantly begin a search; find out every piece of information available on what is occurring. Take an extra couple of minutes to talk to any witnesses, property owners, and other suspects already apprehended. What you learn may make the difference. It usually does not take long to get this information, but may save a lot of time, provide help in apprehending other threat(s), but most important, it may save an officer from injury or death. At times the information will be worthless, but at other times it can mean life or death. Once you and the other officers are prepared, begin the search.

Approach and Entry

When you begin, use a hidden approach/positioning to try and remain unobserved. This may or may not work, depending on the positioning of the threat(s), but it will definitely not work if you do not try it. Use C&C to accomplish your approach.

If a hidden approach cannot be made during low-light conditions, use your flashlight to light up all dark areas around you as you approach. When approaching a building be watchful of any windows from which you could be viewed. It is almost always darker inside a building than outside it, especially at night, when windows appear as solid black openings in the wall of a building. A threat can be standing just inside a window and you will not notice it, but the threat can observe every move you make if you let it. Try to be covered and hide your movements as much as possible. Also, the windows can be illuminated to spot the threat and/or keep it back.

Where you enter the building will be decided by the design of the building in almost every case. Many officers like to enter as high as possible, to search the building from the top down, as they think the high-ground advantage is preferable on stairways between floors. Actually, the high-ground advantage is not important in the types of encounters you will find when searching.

When entering a building, you will have to enter where you can and proceed with the search. The actual entry will be a critical time; maintain your total tactics and keep sharp. Once inside, continually gather information while searching. Often the best place to start is where the threat(s) entered the building, if you can locate that spot. This does not necessarily mean entering where the threat(s) entered; you can enter at another location and then proceed to the place where the threat(s) entered.

Search Systematically Using Total Tactics

From your entry point into an area, to searching and finally clearing all involved area, search systematically. When searching, usually moving from one area to another on the continuing search, always use total tactics. Do not become relaxed and proceed by half-searching and using half-tactics. Search systematically and use total tactics at all times.

If you proceed with a half-search, many areas will not be covered and the threat(s) may be missed or may be behind you and attack from where you least expect it. Check everything if at all possible. Searching systematically is nothing more than thoroughly clearing all areas as you search through them. When you start skipping, you start missing.

Total tactics must be used to keep you prepared when you find the threat(s) and/or if the threat(s) attacks. Maintain your total tactics throughout the search. Do not decide that any search is probably a false one, even though it may seem to be. Make it real each time. Always expect the threat(s) to be around every piece of cover you check and always be positioned to deal with an attack. Police officers will often slack off during a search they have decided is false or when they believe the threat(s) is gone. Do not go tactically soft; maintain total tactics until the search is completed.

Distance and Time Margins

You must use proper tactics to provide you with these margins and increase your ability to control the situation safely. Stay back from any corners when turning cover to find out what is in a hidden area. You must increase the distance between yourself and any possible threat cover you are going to turn. Use the maximum distance allowable and reasonable for the situation. In reality, this is most often determined by the structure of the area you are searching through. In many locations you will have to be right on top of possible threat cover when turning it. Increase the distance as much as possible, as even several feet of intervening distance can make a difference, especially against a threat with a knife or club.

Distance and time margins function virtually the same, with an increase in either providing an increase in your response and safety margins. Basically, if either a distance or time margin is increased, you will have an increased response margin. Giving you more time to respond usually provides an improved safety margin. With an increased response margin, your ability to counter attack, increase the distance, or move to cover is improved.

Often one of the best defenses is distance. Distance, coupled with the use of cover and the handgun held in a firing position, will greatly improve your ability to respond to an attack safely and effectively. This increased distance can also provide you with a buffer that can possibly stop an unintentional shooting of an innocent who may suddenly appear around the corner instead of a threat. With increased distance, a good position, and handgun ready, your chances of controlling the situation without the use of deadly force also improve.

Other Thoughts When Searching

When searching, your main objective is locating and controlling the threat(s) in the safest and most effective manner possible. You must not forget this objective. Keep it in mind and do not take unnecessary chances. Do not be in a hurry. Take the time necessary and use backup officers as the situation merits.

You must be balanced and flexible while searching. These two terms always function together. You must be flexible and ready to move instantly in any direction if the threat(s) attacks, which can be done only if you are balanced. Stay out of awkward, unbalanced, or restricted positions that will reduce your flexibility and render you vulnerable to attack. Your movement must be smooth and sure when searching. Avoid sudden movements, running, or jumping unless necessary (at times they will be necessary). This will mean paying more attention to where you place your feet and picking them up a little higher so that they do not scrape on the floor or ground, causing you to possibly trip and/or make sounds. Walking forward or backward usually presents no problems when moving, but if you must move sideways, do not cross one leg over the other, but shuffle to the side (first one foot and then the other). Stay balanced to be flexible.

Beware of Telegraphing Your Presence. Everything from sound, to movement, to light, to reflections can give away your presence, telegraphing your location and possibly your intentions. Sometimes referred to as your signature, it can give the threat(s) the advantage of knowing when and where you are coming from. In buildings the threat(s) may know this already, but try not to give it any extra information.

Use glancing and controlling techniques before entering any area and/or turning possible threat cover. It takes only a couple of seconds to use the glancing and controlling technique to visually clear the hidden area before entering it. These techniques are not 100 percent effective, but their use will reveal almost all threat(s), especially those that are close and preparing to attack you. While you are turning cover to reveal hidden areas, always keep up your 360-degree scan. Use all your senses when scanning—look, listen, and feel your way through the area as you are clearing it. Even though you keep your back to an area that has already been cleared, you still maintain your 360-degree scan.

Be careful not to totally concentrate on certain areas, but constantly keep checking your entire surroundings. Keep expanding your vision to include everything around you. No matter how systematically you search, a threat(s) can keep moving and get behind you. Many officers tend to think of physical structures as the entire search area, but this is often a fallacy. The walls of a building (its envelope) provide a prime example. When most officers are inside a building, they forget about the outside area; similarly, if outside, they concentrate on that area exclusively, forgetting that a threat inside the building can see out. Fences, hedges, and other physical barriers all tend to create the same illusion. Just keep in mind that a threat(s) can be anywhere around you. Remember, what you do not see can kill you; keep up your 360-degree scan into all areas around you.

Search fatigue. A quick note on search fatigue is appropriate. Any position kept for too long will begin to feel uncomfortable, and if allowed to continue will degrade your ability to function. If an action should start, your response will not be as quick or precise as it should be. Some searches or barricades can last for several hours. Watch officers handling weapons for a long period of time and see how quickly their weapons start to drop down or how they inappropriately hold them. One particular area that fatigues during a search is the strong hand's grip on the handgun. Take brief moments during the search (especially if it is prolonged) to ease the grip on the handgun and reduce the strong hand's fatigue. When doing this, make sure that you have completely secured your immediate area and that you are behind cover. This relaxing technique will only take 5 to 10 seconds, but make sure that you are positioned safely before you start.

Easing the strong hand's fatigue is accomplished by holding the handgun directly in front of the body with the insides of both forearms touching the sides of the body. The support hand then grips the handgun around the barrel (slide for an auto) and front part of the frame, keeping well back from the muzzle, and supports it (make sure that a S-A auto's safety is "on"). The strong hand's master grip is relaxed and the hand is removed from the handgun's grip. The strong hand opens up and leaves the grip, going only about 4 inches back from it, and stays at that position. Now the strong hand is gently flexed and the fingers moved back and forth to restimulate the strong hand and reduce fatigue. The support hand holds the handgun in the exact same position as the strong hand left it. Held in such a position, the strong hand can instantly regrip the handgun if something should occur.

TEAMWORK

Whenever engaging in a search, two or three officers should be used as the search team. Unless otherwise indicated, no more than three officers should be used as a search team. Most of the time, officers conducting a search will not have worked together extensively enough to have become a team, or maybe will not have worked together at all. This section covers the basics of teamwork, which each officer must understand when performing a search with another officer(s). With this understanding, and very few decisions, the officers can form a very effective team to perform the police task at hand.

Individual Skills and the Team Function

The team function is built from each officer's individual skills. Each officer will bring his or her own trained-in reflexive sets of individual skills and combine with one or two other officers for the team function. Most of the time, officers will not have worked together enough as a team to function smoothly together (many times they will never have worked together as a team). As a rule in police work, individual officers will come together for a team function to solve the problem at hand. When the problem is solved, they will return to their individual assignments. Each must bring his or her individually trained-in skills to the team function, and work together with the other officer(s) to perform a search effectively.

As long as each officer has an understanding of basic teamwork and the officers decide who will perform what task, the team function will work well. One of the secrets of the team function is to "KIS-U": keep it simple and uncomplicated. In the team function, keep the tactics and planning simple and uncomplicated or problems will occur. There is no need for intricate or complicated planning: all that is needed are simple, quick, and flexible plans that can be changed instantly to meet the situation. Any complicated planning can cause serious problems for the team.

The two-officer team concept is best unless the situation calls for more officers on the search team. With the two-officer team there is less chance of plans and communications going wrong and the team's flexibility is increased. The two-officer team is not only the best, but also the minimum number that will perform a search. No officer ever searches alone. Two or more officers are always used to search. One of the realities of police work is the lack of officers available at certain times to respond and secure a scene and perform the search. Often a two-officer search team is required if an area is to be secured. Make no mistake, though, if the situation warrants it, call in as many officers as necessary to perform the search safely and effectively. A three-officer team also works very well, but any more than three officers would have to be justified by the situation.

The officers of a search team must not fall into the "safety in numbers" syndrome. Whenever a search team is clearing an area, at times there is a pervasive feeling of safety in numbers, with a reduction in proper tactics. If searching alone, each officer would be aware and use total tactics, but place individual officers together and their collective awareness and use of tactics will usually be reduced. Also, each officer may assume that the other officers are keeping aware and tactically ready, and that he or she can ease up a little. Interdependency can breed poor awareness and tactics if you let it. There is also the feeling that no one will attack all of us (especially a three-officer search team). Of course, at the first indication of the threat(s), every officer will snap back into total tactics and proper search procedures. But if the first indication is an attack by the threat(s), the search team may be caught unaware and unprepared. Guard against this when searching by making sure that every officer on the search team takes the search seriously and keeps ready.

Communications and Support

Communication is extremely important and each officer must communicate with the other(s) throughout the search. Whether you communicate with words, gestures, or signals, make sure that you are understood. Being understood is the most important factor; make sure that you understand each other. If every officer of the search team is searching properly, communications are greatly improved, as every officer is concentrating on the search, with awareness high and ready to receive all informational input, including communications from the other member(s) of the team. Make yourself understood; if necessary, yell out the information in a loud voice. You must make sure that you are understood; no one else will do it for you. Also, do not assume that the other team member(s) knows that something is occurring; communicate the information.

Part of keeping the communications flowing throughout a search is constantly staying together and supporting each other. The team members must be close enough to support each other and close enough to be able to communicate effectively. The team always works in close support of one another when searching and clearing areas. Do not loose visual contact with any member of the team and know exactly where each member is. It is every team member's job to know exactly where the other member(s) is and be ready to communicate any information found.

When communicating, it does not have to be in loud, verbal form. It can be anything from whispers, to hand signals (using precise signals with prearranged meanings), to gestures, to signaling with a flashlight. But in the final analysis, if another team member does not see some danger, you may have to resort to a loud shout. Remember, being understood is the most important factor.

Team Movement and Cover

Each member of the search team must be in close support of the other member(s), but separated enough not to be a tempting target. Stay close enough to support and communicate with each other effectively, but do not bunch up to make an easy target. As a rule the maximum spread for a two-officer team should be 25 feet and the maximum spread for a three-officer team should be 45 feet (between the team members on either end, either side to side or front to back, depending on how the team is spread out). Obviously, situations may exist where the distances would have to be increased. Usually, team members will be working closer together, as the area searched will funnel them together. When this occurs, do not bunch up either side to side or front to rear, but keep spread apart as much as the area allows (but within the maximum spread). Remember, the area will usually dictate the amount of spread the team can take, but separate as much as the area and effective support and communications allow.

On the majority of searches, though, officers are searching right next to one another, walking side by side, talking back and forth as they search, making very tempting targets. This can cause both officers to be taken easily. With a determined threat(s), an ambush situation becomes a much greater possibility if both officers are searching together (shoulder to shoulder). Avoid being taken easily by separating as much as the area, support, and communications allow, and use one of the two movement methods.

There is no question that officers will ease up at times and search right next to each other, as the search will seem to be false; even the best will do it at times. Many times you may be searching with other officers who will not take the search seriously. When searching in these circumstances, you must be doubly aware throughout the search. Remember, you are the one ultimately responsible for your own survival. Keep aware and stay prepared.

Two Movement Methods.   One of two movement methods can be used by the team: pointman/backup and leapfrogging. In the pointman/backup method, one officer of the team (often the most experienced) takes the pointman position in front and the other officer(s) maintains a covering backup position. The pointman is the leader and makes the decisions, communicating these to the backup officer(s). These positions can be held throughout the search or changed at some point during the search. In the leapfrogging method, one officer covers while the other moves up to the next covered position, continually switching positions throughout the search (exactly the same movement that the children's game describes). With a three-officer team, only the first two officers need to perform the leapfrogging movement, with the third officer remaining as a backup for the first two. Both are excellent ways for a search team to advance through an area safely.

Team Firing Areas

Generally, team firing areas for each member breaks down to what threat(s) is presenting a lethal problem at that particular moment. As a rule, the officer in the forward position will take care of any problem occurring to the immediate front and sides. The backup officer(s) will take care of any other threat(s) and if no other threat is present, will concentrate his or her fire on the initial threat the forward officer is engaging. While doing this, the backup officer must continually expand his or her tunnel vision for additional threats. The forward officer must be free to engage the forward threat(s). This is not complicated at all and will flow with the situation, which can quickly change. The main idea is to support each other throughout the engagement.

If a threat appears, beware of converging and continuing tunnel vision, where all team member's attention is locked on that one threat. When the initial exchange occurs, it will be extremely overwhelming and all team members will no doubt concentrate on the threat(s) presenting itself. Once the initial engagement is over with and fire has been placed on the threat(s), the backup officer(s) must instantly break out of the tunnel vision and expand his or her vision to cover the larger surroundings. This must be done to be aware of any additional threat(s) appearing at the same or different location from the original threat. The initial threat may only be a decoy to draw the team's attention as another threat(s) prepares to attack from a different location. After the initial exchange, the officers must instantly expand their vision, especially the officer(s) in the backup position, who must constantly be watching all around his or her location. With a to-the-rear position, the backup officer(s) has a better view of the entire area and is in a better position to catch any additional threat(s).

When engaged in the team function, every officer will bring his or her own trained-in individual skills, which is the basis of the team function. Each search team member already knows how to perform all the tactics and weapon use skills necessary; but now they are combining to form a team that must function together. These basic team tactics must be understood by every officer to coordinate the team's movement and efforts successfully when searching. With this understanding, the officers can form a very effective team to perform the police task at hand.

Handling a Threat(s) from Control to Arrest

When a threat(s) is found, you must maintain your advantage and handle the control and arrest situation correctly. Your main purpose when handling any threat(s) is to begin with the advantage and maintain it throughout the situation, while keeping the threat(s) at a disadvantage. In this way you can stop the threat occurrence, by making it very difficult for the threat to attack you successfully. You must begin with the advantage and maintain it by your actions, as the advantage can be lost very easily if you let up.

Control and Arrest.   Once a threat(s) is found, your first priority is to control it, which means controlling its movements and actions. Control can extend from verbal commands to placing "hits" to stop the threat(s). The choice is the threat(s), as it can give up, try to escape, or attack. Once control has been established, the threat's options are very limited, and if the officers are obviously in control of the situation and have the advantage, the threat(s) will usually give up. This by no means guarantees what the threat(s) will do, but when controlled properly, the majority will give up.

[*Note:* The vast majority of armed threats that officers will be facing are one or two threats possessing mainly handguns—sometimes shotguns or rifles, cut down or full length—with limited expertise in shooting. But a new crop of threats are emerging that have practiced and become more skilled in the use of their weapons: not experts, but practiced and determined not to be taken. Add this to biker gangs and the growth of terrorist (both domestic and foreign) and other trained paramilitary groups, and there is an increased likelihood of finding practiced and trained threats possessing above-average skills and/or superior weapons. Controlling first is becoming more and more appropriate, as the lethality level of any situation may be high.]

Once properly controlled, the arrest is far safer and easier. Control first, then arrest. Avoid the temptation to rush in and arrest the threat as soon as you locate it. The situation may be far different than it appears on the surface. When you initially locate the threat(s), instantly *stop* in a covered position and control it. Keep your distance and cover the threat(s) until the situation is completely controlled. Use time, distance, and teamwork to your advantage. Once the entire situation is controlled, proceed with the arrest of the threat(s). Handcuff first, then search.

Control the threat(s) by having it assume a restricted position, where both hands can be seen. You must be able to see both hands. If a threat will not initially show one or both hands, there is a good chance that the hidden hand(s) is wrapped around a weapon. If a gun is seen, command the threat to drop it now. The longer the threat has possession of the gun, the longer it has to decide to attack you. Maintain total tactics and be prepared. The speed of an attack can be incredibly fast at times, and your response must be equally fast. If you are prepared, it will be.

Do not converse with the threat(s), but tell it what to do. By conversing with the threat(s), you are increasing your reaction time if the threat(s) should attack. You must maintain control, both physical and verbal. The threat may be talking, but do not answer it. Only give very short, to-the-point commands. The threat may also try to move closer as it is talking; do not let it. Maintain your distance advantage and keep cover between you and the threat(s) (an object between you and the threat will interrupt and slow down its movements if it attacks).

Assume nothing initially, while you maintain your advantage. No officer on the search team is to "assume" anything until it is fully checked out. As one team member might say to another: "If you ASSUME anything, it may make an ASS out of U and ME." The truth will rise to the surface in time, which will always be against the threat.

Cover Is King.   Think cover and use it whenever possible. Stay covered and in a ready position when controlling the threat(s). When you initially find a threat(s), you may not really know what is going on or there may be additional threats close-by. Stay covered and concentrate on the threat(s), while maintaining your 360-degree scan [teamwork is used, with your backup checking the entire area as you control the threat(s) you can see].

Again, you must get out of the habit of approaching and arresting instantly (unless other circumstances require it). Maintain your covered position, distance, and time advantages. You become an extremely hard target to hit when behind cover, in a firing position, with at least 7 yards (21 feet) between you and the threat(s). If the threat has a gun and decides to fire, it will have to bring the gun up and try to aim before firing—usually taking a second—while you are prepared instantly and can easily "hit" the threat in well under a second, even with your reaction time.

Reaction Time.   Few officers ever think of how reaction time can influence a situation. The most prominent demonstrations of this are confrontations with armed threats. Officers, with their handguns held in an aimed firing position, will stand in the open and/or approach an armed threat holding a lowered handgun. These officers think they can fire and "hit" the threat before the threat raises its handgun and fires. They are wrong and may possibly be dead wrong if the threat decides to fire. If the threat acts, bringing the handgun up and firing, it is initiating the action and the officer is reacting to the threat. As such, the officer will not even begin to move until some degree of reaction time has passed. When you preceive the need to react, reaction time will occur between the instant you perceived the need and when you first started to move. On the average, reaction time is three-tenths of a second (0.3 second), but if you are slightly distracted or your reaction time is slightly slower, it can be as high as eight-tenths of a second (0.8 second). Balance this against the fact that a person can fire a revolver three to five times in a second. As is readily apparent, the threat can get off one to three shots before you can fire.

You must have as many advantages as you can in a confrontation such as this. Do not throw away any advantages. As a rule, officers want to get close to the threat(s), as ultimately the threat(s) will be arrested and transported and the situation will be over with. Resist the urge to move in during the initial stages of a confrontation. Understand that your reaction time can work against you.

SUMMARY

In this chapter we covered the searching tactics and techniques used when negotiating the search area. The search is filled with many unknowns, as officers enter unfamiliar surroundings to locate, control, and apprehend any threat(s) safely and effectively. Many obstacles and problems will increase the danger of this undertaking. Usually, officers get only one chance to search an area: right or wrong, safe and effective or not.

When searching, officers must flow with the search and be flexible for any changes that can occur. In this chapter we discussed the search tactics that are used for the twofold purpose of safely negotiating the search environment where a possible threat(s) may be located, and applying the weapon use techniques to the search. These must be used to keep officers aware and prepared and one step ahead when searching.

11

Searching and Shooting in Low-Light Conditions

As a time of diminished visual perception, darkness creates its own unique set of problems that officers must solve to function safely/effectively within low-light conditions. For police officers responding to and clearing potentially lethal calls, low-light situations can increase the level of danger to all parties involved: officers, innocents, and threats. Officers must be able to locate/identify the threat(s) and effectively stop or contain it, with minimal risk of injury to themselves or other innocents on the scene. With proper low-light searching and firing techniques, officers can function and fire in darkness almost as well as in daylight.

For police officers who respond to dangerous situations (B&Es, robberies, assaults, etc.) where the threat(s) may still be on the scene, low-light conditions can increase the potential lethality of a situation many times over. All too often criminals use the blanket of night to cover their activities. Most of the officers killed in the line of duty are killed during hours of darkness. Officers must be trained to function and fire during low-light situations, and it must be a large part of any police firearms training program.

A new direction in low-light firearms training. In recent years, many firearms instructors have come to the realization that a redirection in training methods for low-light conditions has been long overdue. The days of the FBI flashlight technique being taught as the only night firing method are over. The use of handgun and flashlight must be dynamic and fluid during the search, flowing with it.

From this realization many new methods have been developed—some good, some not so good. The main techniques will be explained and examined. Major emphasis is also placed on the realistic flashlight search rule for using your flashlight when searching and firing. You must have the correct flashlight techniques to increase your quick/effective use during low-light conditions.

FOUR SCHOOLS OF THOUGHT ON HANDGUN AND FLASHLIGHT USE

When searching and/or firing in low-light conditions, there are four schools of thought on how to use the flashlight and handgun most effectively. Over the years, these schools have resulted from the development of various techniques that offered solutions to the searching and firing problems surrounding low-light conditions. Good and bad points came with each school, but with each new technique or development, the knowledge of how to deal with low-light conditions expanded. From this collective knowledge, the fourth school was developed, selecting and modifying the best techniques of the other three and also developing its own, fitting these low-light techniques to the varied low-light situations that can occur.

The Four Schools of Thought

The Separate-Use School. In the oldest of the schools, the flashlight and handgun are held separately throughout searching and/or firing. The old FBI flashlight technique was the predominate technique used, the flashlight being held at arm's length out to the side and head high during any searching and/or firing. Its good point was that the flashlight was held away from the officer during the search. The bad point was the lack of coordination, handgun support, and ability to hit when firing.

The Combined-Use School. A newer school resulted from practical handgun testing and developed techniques to quickly get on target and fire during low light conditions; the flashlight and handgun being held together during all searching and/or firing. The Harries technique is a prime example of this school—flashlight and handgun locked together throughout the search and/or firing. The good point was that it held the handgun and flashlight directly together and made firing fast and sure (with beam and barrel aligned). The bad point was that many of the techniques were far too locked in and rigid for the realities of the search: opening doors, climbing, moving objects, shining the light into awkward places, and so on. Some combined techniques, though, are nonrigid and work very well when searching. Another bad point is that the beam is locked into the body and could be used as an aiming point by a threat.

The Nonuse School. This is the newest of the schools and developed in response to the ability of officers to use stance-directed fire and other techniques to hit the threat in low-light conditions without using a flashlight. The flashlight is used only when searching, not when firing. The flashlight is either held but not turned on, dropped, or placed down to form a curtain of light that the officer moves away from and/or fires from behind. The good point is that these techniques will work without using the flashlight; some are excellent. The bad point is that the officer is giving up the flashlight and/or its ability to illuminate the threat(s), the area around it, and any other information its beam may reveal.

The Separate- and Combined-Use School. Appearing at the same time as the combined-use school, this school selected and refined the best techniques originally from the first two schools and later from the third school, and developed its own. These low-light techniques were combined to form a group capable of handling the many different low-light situations encountered. Thus, when a particular low-light situation occurs, the most appropriate techniques for that particular situation are used.

The low-light techniques described in this book subscribe to this school of thought, which takes the best techniques available and applies them to the varied low-light situations that can occur.

THE REALISTIC FLASHLIGHT SEARCH RULE

Any understanding of low-light search techniques begins with the realistic flashlight search rule, which dictates your basic use of the flashlight during any search. It is amazing how many officers do not understand the basic rule that answers the question; When do you turn the flashlight beam on and off?

Officers must face the dangerous problem of searching for a threat(s) which is invariably hiding, waiting for the officers to get close before the threat(s) attacks. The threat(s) has the advantage if it knows how to use it, but most do not. During low-light situations, the use of this simple flashlight rule helps you reduce the threat's advantage and increase your own.

The realistic flashlight search rule: If you are in the dark, keep it dark; if you are in the light, light it up. With this rule, the use of the flashlight's beam when searching is determined by the lighting condition surrounding the officer. By lighting condition surrounding the officer, we mean: Is the officer *in the light* [enough ambient or direct light for the threat(s) to see the officer easily] or *in the dark* [too dark for the threat(s) to see the officer easily].

How the Rule Works

While you are searching during low-light conditions, you will move in and out of light and dark areas, whether in a warehouse, home, or wooded area. You will have to judge the lighting condition you are *now in* while moving through the search, every step of the way. You will be judging whether or not you can easily be seen. The use of the flashlight's beam is dictated by the lighting condition you are in.

Moving within a light area. When you are searching and move within a light area [enough light to be seen easily by a threat(s)], you must use the flashlight's beam to improve your advantage. The problem with moving through a light area is that it is usually surrounded by dark areas in which a threat(s) could be hiding.

While you are moving through a light area, you can be seen easily. A threat hiding in a surrounding dark area, can stand fully out in the open and will not be visible unless you light up the area. In the dark, the threat can take its time aiming on you, preparing to fire. You must use your flashlight's beam to light up all surrounding dark areas. When in the light, keep your flashlight on at all times, directing the beam into any dark areas around you. You can react to the threat(s) only if you can see it.

As you use the flashlight, be sure you take full advantage of cover. Use cover in your movement by moving from covered position to covered position at all times, if possible. Whenever scanning an area with the flashlight (stopping for a brief moment while checking out an area around you), be behind cover if possible. Cover is the most important tactic you can use during an armed encounter. Whenever using the flashlight in low-light conditions, the use of cover is critical. Always be behind cover when using the flashlight. When you think flashlight, think cover; do not separate them. (*Note:* Concealment is included in the overall usage of the term "cover" as used here. Commonly known as C&C, it reflects the fact that, if cover is not available, concealment will have to be used.)

Some advise moving quickly through light areas: Move through them fast and get back into the dark again. This is unrealistic much of the time, especially in buildings, where most of the search will be channelized by the way the building is constructed. Sure everybody likes to stay out of the light, but do not run through it into a dark area where the threat(s) could be hiding; take whatever time you need to scan with your flashlight.

Moving within a dark area. When you are searching and moving within a dark area [not enough light to be seen easily by a threat(s)], you must limit your use of the flashlight's beam. The problem now switches from one of being easily seen by the threat(s) to one of giving your location away, as you are much harder to locate/pinpoint. You and the threat(s) are both in a dark area, each attempting to locate the other, and you must locate the threat(s) without increasing your danger by pinpointing your location.

When your in a dark area, even though the threat(s) knows that you are there (because it has heard you, seen your light, or seen you moving into the area), the threat(s) cannot easily see you and you are hard to locate/pinpoint. Keep the flashlight off and use it only for three reasons:

1. To see where you are going
2. To locate/identify the threat(s)
3. To shoot by, if needed

The two-second/move flashlight technique.   When the flashlight's beam is used, you must incorporate a technique that limits your exposure. The two-second/move flashlight technique accomplishes this rather well. The technique involves two parts: the brief use of the flashlight and then moving instantly immediately after the flashlight is turned off.

The technique consists of two parts: (1) turn the flashlight's beam on for less than 2 seconds (to accomplish whatever you are using it for; note the aforementioned three reasons) and turn it off, and (2) then move instantly at least two steps away from where you were standing. Turn on the flashlight briefly; turn it off and move. If the threat(s) tries to aim at the light, it will go out before the threat(s) can fire, and if it attempts to fire where the light was, you have moved.

You must be completely ready before the flashlight is turned on. In the dark, you decide to use the flashlight in your attempt to locate the threat(s). Before it is turned on, you must be prepared from three standpoints: be in a covered position with the flashlight directed at the point you want to illuminate first, know what area will be searched with the flashlight, and be in a position to fire if necessary.

First, you must be in a covered, ready position and have the flashlight prepared so that you can begin the search instantly. As stated earlier, whenever using the flashlight, be in a covered position. This must be your first consideration before the flashlight is turned on. Once you are behind cover, assume a ready position from which to turn on and direct the beam. The flashlight's beam, before it is turned on, must be directed at the point you want to illuminate first. When the beam is turned on, the area search is started instantly, with no time lost. Make sure that you use a flashlight with both a button and a switch, not one with a switch only. This eliminates the need for a precise finger movement to turn off the flashlight, as just the release of pressure turns it off. In the ready position, make sure that the hand placement on the flashlight and button is right. This will vary depending on the flashlight technique you are using (these will be covered in detail further on in this chapter).

Second, you must know what area the flashlight beam will cover during the brief time it is on. Even in the dark, the general dimensions of the area will be apparent most of the time. You must decide which part of the area you will search each time, before the flashlight is turned on. Make sure that you clear the areas closest to you first, as you must first secure the areas around you, only then expanding into the larger area. This is easily done as you clear successive dark areas around your location. The flashlight's beam will be on only for very short 2-second bursts, and you must be able to take in as much as possible during these periods of illumination. If the area to be searched runs laterally from point A to point B, the flashlight should be on one of these points. Thus when it is turned on, you can make your 2-second sweep from one point to the other, with no lost time or motion. You will be surprised just how much you can see in 2 seconds. [*Note:* Most vertical searching can be accomplished during a lateral sweep, but if large vertical areas (trees are a good example) are encountered, use the two points to enclose the entire vertical area that you wish to search.]

Third, you must be in a position to fire if necessary. The service handgun must be in a position to fire if the threat(s) suddenly presents itself. You must be prepared at all times for this eventuality. While clearing areas with the flashlight by using these short 2-second bursts, you may suddenly locate/identify the threat(s), which is now attacking. If this occurs, you must be able to respond to the threat(s) and it can be done only if you are already in a position to fire. If you suddenly light up the threat(s), fire several quick shots, turn the flashlight off, and move instantly. As soon as you move, take up a new position and be ready to fire. Firing the service handgun using the two-second/move technique works like this: Turn the beam on, shoot, turn it off, and move.

[*Note:* If you can use the flashlight to shoot by without unnecessarily placing yourself in danger, use it. The flashlight gives you the decided advantage of totally viewing the threat(s) and area and blinding the threat(s) momentarily. At close range, though, the flashlight is not necessary to place effective "hits" on the threat(s). Remember, though, you still must locate/identify the threat(s) before you can shoot. Use these techniques to locate/identify the threat(s) first and be ready to fire.]

As shown, using the flashlight's beam while searching follows the realistic flashlight search rule: When you are in the dark, keep it dark; when you are in the light, light it up. This rule is simple and is dictated by the light condition the officer is in now, at any time during the search. When moving through dark areas you are not easily seen or located; turn the flashlight on for only 2 seconds at a time, turn it off, and move at least two steps away. Repeat this process in any dark areas. When moving through light areas (and you will have to move through a lot of them) you are easily seen; use the flashlight's beam to penetrate the dark areas surrounding you where a threat(s) may be hiding. Avoid rushing through light areas; take the time needed to scan an area.

As you are searching, take full advantage of cover. Whenever the flashlight is used, be behind cover. Think flashlight/think cover. Understand that the proper use of cover is one of the most important tactics you will use during a lethal encounter. During low-light situations, cover is a must. Move from covered position to covered position at all times, if possible. If no cover is available, use concealment. Obviously, you should attempt to hide your movement in the dark areas as much as possible and as much as the surroundings will allow. Your search must be fluid and flexible, responding to the changes that occur, and your use of the flashlight must flow with these changes during the search.

You must understand and use the realistic flashlight search rule whenever searching in low-light conditions. It is a simple but extremely important rule.

SEPARATE AND COMBINED USE OF THE HANDGUN AND FLASHLIGHT WHEN SEARCHING

General searching is a combination of two modes, searching and approaching, that are used throughout the search depending on the possible threat location and/or area to be searched. Searching is concerned with the larger, total area you are moving through, with no precise location to focus on. Approaching is concerned with moving toward a precise location where a threat(s) could be hiding. They flow one into the other throughout the search as you clear all areas involved.

For example, you are searching through an area, watching all locations as you move through and clear that area, with no precise location on which to concentrate. While you are searching, you are also picking areas where a threat(s) may be hiding and watching those areas more carefully. If one merits your attention more than the others [a good place the threat(s) could be hiding, noise, movement, it does not feel right], you approach that location very carefully. Obviously, you do not disregard other areas, but this one location is where a major part of your attention is focused. Once your approach has cleared that location, you go back to searching until another possible threat location needs to be approached.

Using the handgun and flashlight separately and combined follows the concept of searching and approaching. Generally, when searching, the handgun and flashlight are held and used *separately,* and when approaching, they are held and used together as a *combined* unit.

Searching and Separate Use

When searching, watching all areas with no precise location where the threat is possibly hiding, the handgun is held in the belt-level position and the flashlight is held to the side and slightly in front of the body (with the arm bent, not straight). The handgun, in the controlled belt-level location, is positioned to react instantly by firing one-handed if attacked at very close quarters (0 to 4 yards) or snapping up into a locked-in two-handed firing stance and firing (a two-handed stance should be used whenever possible). The flashlight is held naturally in the support hand out to the side of the body during the search. From this position its beam can be directed quickly and surely into any dark area around you to clear the area. Whenever using the flashlight's beam, you must use cover and concealment if possible. With handgun and flashlight held separately while searching, you are flexible, ready to move and/or snap into a firing position if the threat(s) appears, no matter where it is located around you.

If a threat attacks at very close-quarters (0 to 4 yards), the handgun is moved instantly into a point-shooting firing position, as the flashlight's beam is centered on the threat, and is fired almost instantly. It does not matter where the handgun is in relation to the flashlight. Just instantly place the flashlight's beam on the threat while aligning the handgun, and fire. Especially at very close quarters, you do not need to thrust the flashlight out as the handgun is pointed at the threat. The only consideration is placing the beam on the threat as quickly as possible. At this very close distance, there is no time or need to try to assume a two-handed firing stance to fire on the threat. If the threat is moving toward you, it will be on top of you before the two-handed stance can be assumed. Remember, 4 yards is only 12 feet, a very close distance, requiring fast firing. (*Note:* Point shooting is discussed in Chapter 14.)

If the threat attacks beyond very close distances (over 4 yards), or if you suddenly know/feel a threat(s) is close while you are searching, snap into a locked-in two-handed firing stance with the flashlight and handgun held together. When holding the handgun and flashlight separate as you are searching, a good two-handed firing stance can be achieved in less than a second. If the threat(s) is not right on top of you, snap into a locked-in two-handed firing stance, to fire or be prepared to fire if necessary. Several combined handgun and flashlight techniques are described later. Remember, the flashlight does not have to be turned on just because it is part of the locked-in two-handed firing stance. In partial-light conditions, the flashlight may not be needed to fire effectively (discussed in detail later).

When searching you must be flexible enough to respond to the realities of the search, yet ready to respond instantly if the threat(s) attacks. Holding and using the handgun and flashlight separately will allow you the flexibility needed during the search: mainly being able to use the flashlight's beam efficiently when illuminating areas around you, while not having the flashlight locked into your body. Remember, you are using the realistic flashlight search rule and cover and concealment throughout the search.

Approaching and Combined Use

When approaching, moving toward a precise location where a threat(s) could be hiding, the handgun and flashlight are held and used as a unit. This combines two functions into one: directing both the flashlight's beam and the handgun's barrel at the threat. As such, with both the beam and barrel up and in line, you are ready to fire instantly if the threat(s) attacks.

In preparation to close-approach possible threat cover, you snap into a locked-in two-handed firing stance with the flashlight being held in the support hand. Now, both beam and barrel are aligned and functioning as a unit. The closer together the beam and barrel are, as long as they are parallel, the better the flashlight's beam and path of the bullet will align. This will help the beam, barrel, and sights point at the same spot, which will help aligning and improve "hitting." (*Note:* The beam is not used to aim the barrel. The handgun is aimed by being able to see the sights within the beam, or using stance-directed fire on a completely illuminated threat.) When close-approaching possible threat cover, the chances are greatest of having to respond instantly to a threat's attack. You must be as prepared as possible when close-approaching. To survive, your response may have to be instantaneous. Having the handgun and flashlight aligned and functioning together as a locked-in unit will position you to be as close as you can get to responding instantly. The combined handgun and flashlight techniques are described later in this chapter.

The flow of the total search.   As can readily be seen, searching and approaching flow into one another throughout the total search, just as separate and combined use of the handgun and flashlight flow back and forth. As you are searching, holding the handgun and flashlight separate, you notice a piece of possible threat cover. You now snap into a locked-in two-handed firing stance with the flashlight in the support hand (combined use), then approach and clear the possible threat cover [being ready to fire instantly if the threat(s) is there and attacks]. Once cleared, you return to the searching mode, with the handgun and flashlight held separately (handgun returning to the belt-level position and flashlight held naturally to the side and slightly in front of you). As you continue searching, a noise is heard, and you instantly snap into the two-handed firing stance and begin approaching the area to check it out. Once cleared, you return to the searching mode again, with handgun and flashlight functioning separately. Back and forth, moving from one into the other and back again, your separate and combined use flow with the total search.

The total search must be flexible, following no hard-and-fast method. Your understanding and use of the searching and approaching modes will give you the flexibility and instant readiness necessary to accomplish any search effectively and realistically. Searching and approaching flow into one another and become almost inseparable at times; with a small amount of practice, each flows effortlessly and smoothly into the other. In a short amount of time, each will function almost by itself as you move through the search.

Never forget, the search must be flexible. If you try to use one method of searching, you will find it cannot be done that one way all the time, and at times cannot be done that way at all. The problem is that people build buildings that throw all the pet methods out the window. You must have a good set of flexible basics to use when searching.

LOW-LIGHT CONDITIONS

Two distinct low-light conditions exist: partial-light and dark conditions. Each must be defined and understood to give direction for the searching and firing techniques that will be used. As such, whenever officers are moving through either of these low-light conditions, they will know what techniques will work, and why. The low-light searching and firing techniques use the flashlight and handgun separately and in conjunction to perform the primary function of the search: to locate/identify the threat(s) and effectively control or stop it, with minimal risk of injury to officers and innocents. To accomplish this, each officer must clearly understand these two low-light conditions and the techniques for each.

Low-light conditions are divided into two distinct illumination levels:

1. Partial-light conditions: Enough light present for an officer to locate/identify the threat(s), but not enough to use the handgun's sights
2. Dark conditions: not enough light present for an officer to either locate/identify the threat(s) or use the handgun's sights

Locating/Identifying the Threat(s) Is Critical before Firing

In any low-light situations, you must be able to locate/identify the threat(s) before you can fire. "Locate" and "identify" are the key words, as you must be able to locate the threat(s) to place "hits" on it, and you must positively identify it as a threat. During low-light conditions mistakes are easier to make, due to reduced visual acuity. Make sure that the threat is real before you fire.

The techniques shown here will increase your ability to use the handgun and flashlight safely and effectively to locate/identify the threat(s) during the search and/or fire on it if needed. You must be ready at all times during approaching/searching, especially during low-light conditions, to place rounds instantly on a threat(s) that presents itself. This does not mean suddenly having to switch the handgun and flashlight from one position to another to fire, but to be able to fire instantly from the position you are then in. The closer the threat(s) is to you, the more instantaneous your firing must usually be. The secret to this is being able to use the handgun and flashlight separately and combined to locate/identify the threat(s) and fire on it quickly/effectively.

Remember, in any low-light situation; you must be able to locate/identify the threat(s) to control or stop it, with minimal risk of injury to yourself or innocents. Always make sure you positively identify the threat before firing. The low-light techniques will help you do just that, in a safe and effective manner.

PARTIAL-LIGHT CONDITIONS

Partial-light conditions are locations and/or times of day when there is enough light present to locate/identify the threat(s), but not enough to use the handgun's sights to aim. In other words, you can locate/identify the threat(s) but cannot see the handgun's sights to aim with. Generally, during partial-light conditions, you do not need to use the flashlight when firing on a threat(s) at close range. One main technique and a secondary one are used to fire on a threat(s) without using your flashlight. By firing without using the flashlight, the only indication of your exact location is the muzzle flash.

Remember, you must be extremely careful and know exactly what you are firing at when firing without using the flashlight. When firing in partial-light conditions, you must know exactly where the threat is, that it is a threat, and direct every bullet at it—which is no easy undertaking at times.

Stance-Directed Fire

The main firing technique used during partial-light conditions, without using the flashlight to aid sight alignment, is stance-directed fire. At close-quarter handgun fighting distances this firing technique is very effective.

The technique centers on your practiced two-handed firing stance, that is, locked out at the end of the holster-to-stance reflex. This two-handed firing stance is the bread and butter of defensive pistolcraft and your most practiced firing stance. You have practiced locking into and/or firing from this two-handed firing stance hundreds of times, and your body has developed a kinesthetic feedback mechanism to tell you when the stance is right. Your muscles have specialized receptors (kinesthetic) built in which are triggered by muscular contractions. As such, the kinesthetic return from muscular movement produces a stimulus that can call forth, by previous learning, another set position or movement. You have repeated it, locked into it, and fired from it hundreds of times. Your body, in short, has a feel for it. Now, whenever you lock into the stance, your body tells you when it is right: Lock into your stance directed at the threat and fire without using the sights. Your locked-in stance will do the rest. Just by snapping up into your stance, you should be able to place shots effectively on a threat up to 10 yards. In low-light situations, with enough light to locate/identify the threat(s), your firing stance alone will work very well when firing on the threat.

(*Note:* Stance-directed firing techiques are discussed in detail in Chapter 14. Refer to the information there when working to developing your stance-directed firing technique.)

Training with Flashlight in Hand. When training and practicing stance-directed fire, you must train with the flashlight and handgun held together (combined use). During much of your searching, the flashlight will be used and held together with the handgun. Even though you will not need the flashlight to fire in partial-light conditions (the flashlight will not be turned on), it will often be held together with the handgun in a locked-in two-handed combined firing grip. You must become use to applying stance-directed fire with the flashlight held in the two-handed grip. In short, you must practice your stance-directed fire both with and without a flashlight being held.

In the partial-light condition you have located/identified the threat. Snap into your locked-in two-handed firing stance directed at the threat and fire. Also remember your tactics; do not forget to move immediately after firing. As soon as you fire the rounds at the threat, move to a new covered location and assume a ready position. There may be more than one threat; keep up your 360-degree scan of the surrounding area.

Typical handgun fight distances do not require the use of a flashlight to place rounds effectively on the threat in partial-light conditions. If there is enough light to locate/identify the threat(s), your firing stance alone will work very well to place rounds on the threat(s). This is one area where dry practice will definitely improve your skill level.

The Sighting by Back-Light Technique

A much more restricted partial-light-condition firing technique, sighting by back-light, can be applied effectively when the situation allows it. At some point during the encounter, if the threat is positioned close to or behind any source of direct or ambient light, you have the ability to verify a sight picture, place it on the threat, and fire.

The technique is fairly easy to use and works rather well. But it will work only if the technique is precisely followed. Two situational prerequisites must be present for the technique to be used: Both the threat and officer are not moving, and any light source is close to or behind the threat. With these two prerequisites occurring, you can use the technique.

The sighting by backlight technique follows these steps:

1. Lock into a two-handed firing stance directed at the threat (which has a light source close to or behind it).
2. Move the sights to the light source by moving the entire locked-in upper body from the waist up, and align them correctly.
3. Move the whole stance (upper body from the waist up) back until the handgun appears aligned on the threat.
4. Squeeze the trigger, making sure that you achieve a surprise break of the trigger.

Each one of these four steps must be done correctly for the technique to work.

Begin working on the technique by practicing it in daylight. In daylight you can see how the sights stay aligned, and that it works. With an unloaded handgun (check it twice), pick out a target that is about 10 yards away; this is the threat. Lock into a two-handed firing stance directed at the target and make no attempt to align the sights on it. Now slightly shift the entire locked-in stance (from the waist up) to one side of the target and align the sights (pretending you are aligning the sights on a light source). Then shift the entire locked-in stance back onto the target and check your sights. The sights will still be perfectly aligned if you did not change the stance while slightly shifting it back onto the target. Once you have seen that the sights are still aligned, squeeze the trigger for the surprise break. The technique is accomplished easily and fairly quickly following these steps.

During low-light conditions, the threat will appear as a black silhouette in front of or close to a light source. When you lock into the firing stance directed at the threat, the handgun will be slightly discernible as a black mass in front of the threat. When the entire locked-in stance is shifted slightly to one side (or up, if that is where the light source is located), the sights suddenly appear as the handgun is pointed at the light source. The sights are then aligned. When the handgun is directed back onto the target, by the entire locked-in stance shifting slightly, the sights again disappear as the handgun is once again that discernible black mass in front of the threat. Center that black mass on the threat and begin squeezing the trigger by smoothly increasing the pressure until the handgun fires—the surprise break. Do not jerk the trigger. In low-light situations, officers tend to get in a rush. Take your time and squeeze the trigger.

11.1.   **11.2.**

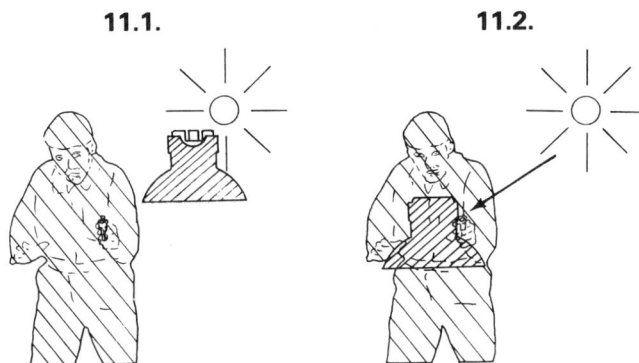

Figures 11.1 and 11.2 Lock into a two-handed firing stance directed at the threat, then move the sights to a close light source and align them by moving the whole locked-in stance from the waist (Fig. 11.1). Now move the locked-in stance until the dark handgun is directly centered on the threat and squeeze the trigger (Fig. 11.2).

This is a "must have the time" technique that requires a lull in the action. Everyone must be in stable positions for a few seconds while the technique is being used. All that is required is 2 or 3 seconds in which to follow the four steps of the technique. Sighting by backlight is an extremely effective partial-light firing technique that will greatly increase your round placement.

Flashlight Use

The last techniques for partial-light conditions are those using the flashlight. They are the same as discussed for dark conditions. When using these flashlight techniques, you must fully use the advantage given by the partial light, allowing you to be fully prepared before switching on the flashlight. In partial light you move into position and locate/identify the threat(s); now prepare by aiming the handgun and flashlight together right on the threat; then surprise the threat as you light it up and are ready to fire instantly. Use this advantage fully to become as prepared as possible before making your move.

Partial-light opening.   All of the techniques for separate and combined use, covered under dark conditions are used when searching, no matter what the low-light condition. If a partial-light opening presents itself—where you have enough light to fire on a threat(s)—use either of the two firing methods described here to place "hits" on a threat(s). When a partial light opening occurs, take advantage of it and do not turn the flashlight on when firing.

Partial-light conditions deal only with two methods of firing without using the flashlight. The remainder of low-light searching and firing will be done using the techniques described for dark conditions.

DARK CONDITIONS

Dark conditions are locations and/or times of day when there is not enough light present to either locate/identify the threat(s) or use the sights. There is not enough light for either of the two tasks to be accomplished without the aid of a flashlight. Techniques for using the flashlight are now employed and used in conjunction with the realistic flashlight search rule when searching.

The main problem will be locating/identifying the threat(s) in the close-quarters search situation, and being able to respond instantly if attacked. In dark conditions the flashlight will greatly increase your ability to locate/identify the threat(s) and reduce the mistakes you make along the way. Remember, you must know exactly where the threat is, that it is a threat, and direct every bullet at it. At times this is no easy undertaking in the dark. Once located and identified, the flashlight and handgun combine to place the shots on the threat(s).

Use of Stance-Directed Fire in Dark Conditions

We begin the techniques with stance-directed fire as it was described under partial light conditions. Flashlight techniques should be used if at all possible, but stance-directed fire may be appropriate in certain situations.

In dark conditions there is usually still some degree of ambient light, possibly enough to roughly define gross forms. At very close quarters to the threat(s), it is possible to use stance-directed fire to place the rounds if three conditions exist: You know it is the threat, you know the threat's exact loation, and you know that your fire will not endanger anyone else. All three conditions would be readily apparent if you used the flashlight to illuminate the area. But if you are positive of all three conditions, you can use stance-directed fire on the threat(s) without using the flashlight's beam to verify and/or fire by.

Why would you use stance-directed fire when flashlight techniques are available? For two reasons: if the use of the flashlight, before or during firing, would place you in danger, or if you do not have a working flashlight available. Under certain situations it may be imperative to use stance-directed fire in dark conditions;

otherwise, the combined use of handgun and flashlight to place your "hits" is preferred.

One very valid reason for not using the flashlight if at all possible is the presence of more than one threat (as a rule you always expect other threats to be present—always one more threat than you have found). By using the flashlight, your position will be completely defined, with the expectation of drawing fire from the other threats. Firing without the flashlight will produce, along with the destabilizing effects of instant shock and noise, small jets of fire and light from the handgun that will end almost as quickly as they began. When using the flashlight, there is the overwhelming tendency to take more time than necessary (this will occur even with flashlight techniques such as the Harries, where handgun and flashlight are mated as one). The tendency occurs before and after firing: before to completely verify the sight picture (using much more verification than is necessary) and after to verify the "hits" on the threat, and its condition. Extra time before firing allows the threat(s) you are firing on to react; extra time after firing allows any additional threats an extended time frame during which to direct fire to you.

Stance-directed fire, if used effectively, reduces your exposure to a minimum. Your presence is exposed only by the sudden noise, shock and light of close fire, which ends almost as instantly as it begins—and you are gone, having moved to another position. By the time the threat(s) has realized what is occurring, it is over with and you have moved, taking up another covered, ready position.

The main truth is: Stance-directed fire can be used during dark conditions to place "hits" on the threat(s), but its use must be undertaken with the utmost care, being completely sure that the three conditions are met before using the technique. It is a very effective technique, but you will ultimately have to answer if a mistake is made because one of the three conditions was not met.

Separate Use of the Handgun and Flashlight

When searching you use the handgun and flashlight separately. Separate use is a must to keep you as flexible as possible. Just keep the handgun in the belt-level position and the flashlight held out to the side and slightly in front of the body when using the beam. The separately held flashlight provides more freedom, coverage, and speed of movement when directing a beam into any dark area around your location (by the arm and hand's ability to angle and direct the beam instantly). If the handgun and flashlight were always held together, the beam movement would be much more restricted. You must have the coverage and ease of beam movement for the larger search area.

Fanning the Beam. With the flashlight held separate from the handgun, it can be fanned to increase the area instantly covered by the flashlight's beam. When fanning, you rock the flashlight back and forth very quickly by wrist action, which throws light instantly into a much larger area. This increases the chances of catching an instant glimpse of a threat(s) hiding there. The eyes pick up images very quickly and a quick fanning of an area can reveal quite a bit. Generally, you should fan an area quickly, then slow the beam down and cover the area completely.

Separate Use and Firing the Handgun. If suddenly attacked by a threat while holding the handgun and flashlight separate, several methods of firing can be used. If the threat attacks at extremely close quarters (0 to 4 feet), the handgun uses the speed rock for extremely close firing. If very close quarters (4 to 12 feet), the handgun moves into a point-shooting firing position. In any of these close-quarter situations, the flashlight's beam is centered on the threat or its eyes, as the firing is done instantly. The relationship between the handgun and flashlight does not matter; just get both instantly on the threat, and fire. They do not come together at this very close range (0 to 12 feet), as there is no time or need to try to assume a two-handed firing stance. The threat may be on top of you or its attack complete before a two-handed stance with the flashlight can be assumed. Also remember that at very close quarters, the flashlight is not thrust out; the flashlight's beam is merely placed on the threat to illuminate it. The only consideration for the flashlight is to illuminate the threat as quickly as possible.

If the threat attacks beyond very close-quarter distances (over 4 yards), or if you suddenly know/feel a threat(s) is close while you are searching, always snap into a two-handed firing stance. A good two-handed firing stance can be achieved in less than a second. If the threat is not right on top of you, snap into a locked-in two-handed firing stance, to fire or be prepared to fire if necessary. Combined use (discussed later in this chapter) will show you the necessary techniques.

Separate Use When Close Approaching. Separate use may be required when close approaching possible threat cover if the corner to be turned is a very restricted space. When close approaching you always try to use a locked-in two-handed firing stance with the flashlight ready, but the corner to be turned may make this impossible. If a restricted corner makes separate use mandatory, you use the flashlight-high technique: Hold the flashlight above your head level, with the handgun held in a point-shooting position at or a little above waist level. Close-approach the corner and prepare before turning the edge, and then turn the edge with only the flashlight, head, and handgun showing (flashlight on top, head in the middle, and handgun on the bottom). Make sure that the flashlight is around the corner before it is turned on. If it is on before the corner is turned, it is a dead giveaway. Also, when coming back out again, use a different level, either higher or lower.

Bodily Mass and C&C. By holding the flashlight out from your body (halfway or fully) and slightly in front of it, you will be less of a target if the threat(s) decides to shoot at the flashlight. Usually, though, the threat(s) can see you or your dark form well enough as you are searching. A human form is easily recognized in the dark, but if you break up your form or hide a large part of it, you will become much harder to locate and the threat(s) may be much less inclined to shoot. This is accomplished by breaking up or hiding your mass behind some intervening cover or concealment. When searching, always move from one C&C position to another and whenever using the flashlight, be behind C&C (if available). This will provide you with the excellent advantage of blending in with another object by exposing only a part of your head and flashlight.

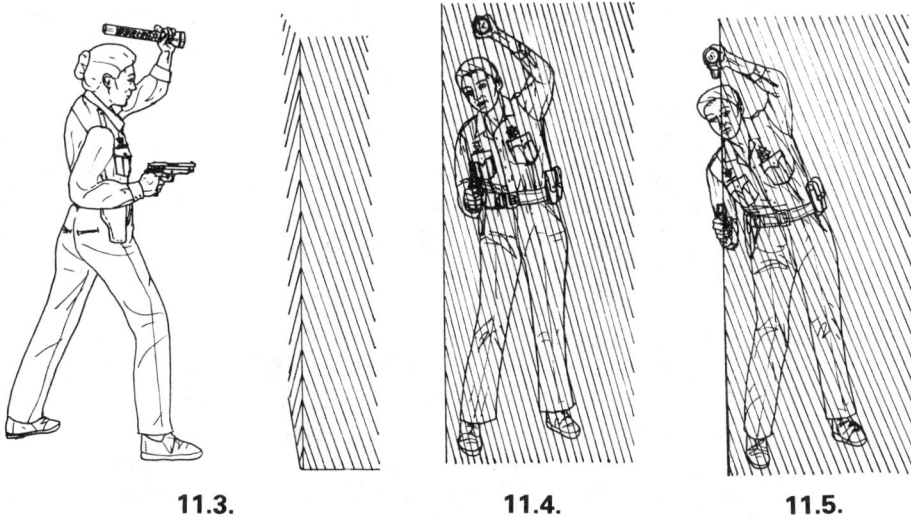

11.3.   **11.4.**   **11.5.**

Figures 11.3–11.5   Become prepared behind the edge, with flashlight held high and beam off; use a reverse grip: side and front views (Figs. 11.3 and 11.4). When the edge is cleared, the beam is turned on (Fig. 11.5).

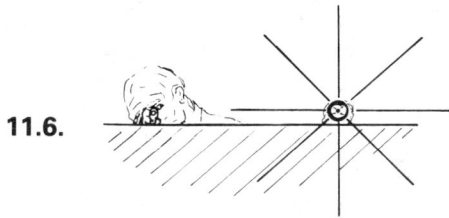

11.6.

Figure 11.6   With the officer behind cover and flashlight held to the side, the bodily form is greatly reduced or broken up. Also, with the beam forward of the body, it can further hide the form.

Combined Use

In combined use the handgun and flashlight are held together and manipulated as a unit, combining two functions into one. When this is done, the officer will have the advantage of the greater control of a locked-in two-handed firing grip, while having the ability to direct the flashlight's beam and the handgun's barrel together.

The main function of combined use is to coordinate the handgun and flashlight as a unit to produce a locked-in two-handed firing stance, with the flashlight ready instantly to help locate/identify the threat(s) and/or firing on it. When searching, you hold the handgun and flashlight separately. When you must become prepared instantly for a possible threat(s) and/or fire on it (if farther away than 4 yards), the two hands lock together. By locking them together, combining their use, you are taking advantage of the superior two-handed firing grip, which will improve your ability to "hit" quickly. Much of the time the flashlight will not even be used, but it is there, locked in with the handgun and ready for instant tactical use and/or to help aim when firing. Some recommend that you throw down the flashlight, assume a normal two-handed firing grip, and fire on the threat(s). This is unrealistic, as you should not dump the flashlight, which may be vital during the continuing encounter. In the combined-use firing grip, you can "hit" better and the flashlight is ready for instant tactical use and/or to help aim when firing.

If the threat(s) is under 7 yards away and you can locate/identify the continuing threat, use stance-directed fire to "hit" it. There is no need to turn on the flashlight. Simply lock out in the two-handed firing stance (with the flashlight held next to the handgun), fire, and move. The flashlight remains off when you fire. Remember, in the dark, there can be no doubt that it is a continuing threat and definitely not an innocent.

If the threat(s) is more than 7 yards away and/or its location has not been pinpointed, you will have to use your flashlight to locate/identify and/or fire on the threat(s), depending on whether or not the threat attacks or gives up. Locking the hands together in combined use produces good beam-to-barrel alignment (coaxiality—aligning along the same axis) and you will be able to backlight your sights and align them on the threat. Follow these steps: Lock out the handgun and flashlight together in your line of sight, pointed at the threat; turn the beam on for the shortest possible time to fire the shot(s); turn it off; and move instantly. As soon as the beam comes on, the handgun's sights (which were already in your line of sight) will appear; instantly verify your sight picture and/or make the minor corrections and fire. You must be completely prepared before the flashlight is turned on. Remember, move as soon as the beam goes off. Now, in the darkness you suddenly surprise the threat(s) with light and fire; then you are gone—the beam is off and you have moved: very quick and very effective.

Using the flashlight makes it quick to "HIT" but pinpoints your location. Many view using the flashlight's beam during combined use in a positive/negative light: on the positive side, providing a dramatically improved ability to view the scene totally and quickly "hit" (especially a hiding threat), but on the negative side, the flashlight's beam instantly locating you as a target. With the flashlight and handgun held together, the beam is centered on your body. If the threat(s) has no other point of reference to aim at, it will probably shoot at the flashlight—either directly at it or around it. In fact, prisoners have been shown training to shoot at officers holding flashlights, training to fire low and to the left of the flashlight (assuming that an officer is right-handed and using the old FBI flashlight technique).

Your improved ability to "hit" quickly in dark conditions must take precedence for several reasons. First, many officers are under the mistaken impression that the threat(s) cannot see you most of the time. In reality, the threat(s) can see you much of the time; do not fool yourself into thinking that the threat(s) cannot see you. Many officers, thinking they are hidden in the darkness, stay in the open and take far too long to prepare (aim). As such, they become easy targets. If the threat cannot see you, well and good, but always assume that the threat(s) can see you and always use cover. Also, where is the threat(s) located around you, and how is it positioned in relationship to the flashlight you are holding? It may not always be in front of you, with the flashlight's beam directly between you and the threat(s). It is not always as cut-and-dried as many make it out to be.

Light splash is also rarely considered by most officers when searching. Your flashlight's beam can reflect off of walls or other reflective surfaces enough to easily light you up. During the search you will inadvertently light yourself up a number of times, while trying to cover the dark areas around you. The search is fluid and you must also be fluid and flexible in your search, including the use of the flashlight's beam. At times lighting yourself up accidentally cannot be avoided, but work to keep it to a minimum. Even thin light splashes from other light sources can give your position away. You must make sure that you are not backlighted, as this will make you stand out and be an easy target.

Another interesting factor is the ability of a high-intensity flashlight's beam to slow down or stop a threat. Studies have shown that a strong flashlight beam, shown directly into the threat's face, can slow down its attack, at times stopping it completely. The instantaneous blinding effect of a high-intensity beam can often stop a threat cold. This cannot be counted upon, but it has worked many times and will no doubt continue to work.

Whenever you are in the dark, use the two-second/move flashlight technique: Always use the cover or concealment before the beam is turned on, only use the beam for 2 seconds or less, and move when it is shut off. Always (if possible) be behind C&C, as that can change your bodily form dramatically, making it hard for the threat(s) to decide what to fire at. When the beam is turned on, it is never for more than 2 seconds. As soon as the beam is turned off, move laterally to either side, at least a full step away. From the threat's point of view, a sudden curtain of light will appear, blocking out virtually all behind it (assuming that a high-intensity flashlight is used), while causing the threat's eyes to hurt and partially close. Almost as instantly as the light appears, rounds are fired striking the threat. Suddenly it is over with (time lapse was 2 seconds or less); the light is out and nothing is there. If the threat does return fire, it will just have to throw the gun up and fire, as aiming into the high-intensity light curtain will be hard.

When done correctly, the following is what the threat will view. Just like a light switch being turned on: Suddenly, light and gun fire were turned on, and just as suddenly they were turned off. If secondary threats try to fire on you, they will have to get their guns up, aim, and fire in 2 seconds or less. If not, the light is out and you have moved. Also, the sudden shock of the instantaneously turned-on light and gun fire will almost certainly delay their responses by a second or more.

The biggest problem involves not pinpointing the threat with your beam or possible other threats that may not be affected by your curtain of light—being at an angle to it or at its side. You can stop this only by checking out all areas around you while moving through the search area. Keep your head up and your 360-degree scan going.

You must remember that no technique will work 100 percent of the time. Your flashlight can become the target very easily or its use can be directly responsible for giving you the ability to stop the threat(s). The flashlight is more likely to be the target while you are generally searching (which is why it is held away from your body when searching) than when you are close approaching with your handgun and flashlight completely ready to respond to an attack.

Combined use occurs when you know/feel that the threat(s) may be close, especially when close approaching possible threat cover. You are very close to the initial exchange of gunfire if a determined threat(s) is hiding there—either hiding directly at the corner or back from it. As such, you must be prepared to fire instantly if attacked and use the techniques that will get you the quickest and best "hits" possible for whatever situation you find. The flashlight may, in fact, not be needed if the threat(s) is close, located, and identified. If not, the flashlight's beam must be used. The point is: You may not know what you will need until you need it. You must be prepared for both flashlight and nonflashlight use. An instantly occurring threat(s) must be fired upon just as instantly, and you must be properly positioned to do just that. This is accomplished by being tactically ready to use the flashlight if necessary to identify and/or fire with. Quickly "hitting" is the secret, stopping the threat(s) before it can fire on you.

Also consider how searching is accomplished. When searching generally, the flashlight is held separately to your side and flexible when used to illuminate all dark areas around you, while using the realistic flashlight search rule and C&C. When close approaching a possible threat location, combined use prepares you for whatever may occur. If the threat(s) attacks at close range (under 7 yards), the flashlight's beam may not be needed to "hit" the threat(s), provided that you know it is a threat and not an innocent. If you need to illuminate the threat(s) to locate/identify it, the flashlight is positioned for instant use and properly directed with the handgun's barrel. You are ready for any eventuality.

COMBINED-USE TECHNIQUES

Four combined-use techniques are used when coordinating the flashlight and handgun: Harries, modified Harries, Chapman, and Ayoob. Two of these can be assumed and used almost instantly (modified Harries and Ayoob), while the other two take slightly longer to assume and use properly (Harries and Chapman). Also, two favor the Weaver stance (modified Harries and Harries) and two favor the Isosceles stance (Ayoob and Chapman). All four should be learned and used, though, as the situation and structure will mainly determine which is used.

The Harries technique.   The Harries technique was designed to be used for general nightshooting and speciality searching during low light conditions. It was developed by Michael Harries of California, a former member of the Southwest Pistol League, and a founding member of IPSC (International Practical Shooting Confederation) and the Tactical Combat Program of Southern California, American Pistol Institute instructor, and excellent defensive trainer. Mike has been involved with defensive handgun use for years and has developed a number of other techniques for the defensive handgun.

This technique effectively locks the handgun and flashlight together—directing them as a unit when searching in low light situations. When you know the threat(s) is close in the dark, this is a very effective technique to switch to and use. The position was directly adapted for the Weaver stance, which is readily seen when the Harries technique is assumed. It is the best locked-in combined-use technique.

To use this technique the support hand must reverse grip the flashlight so that the little finger is on the flashlight's head and the middle finger is used to press the flashlight's button. Bring the handgun up into a Weaver stance as you normally would. Now the support hand (holding the flashlight head forward) goes under the strong hand (never in front of the muzzle) and the back of the support hand is placed against the back of the strong hand. Not just the backs of the hands, but

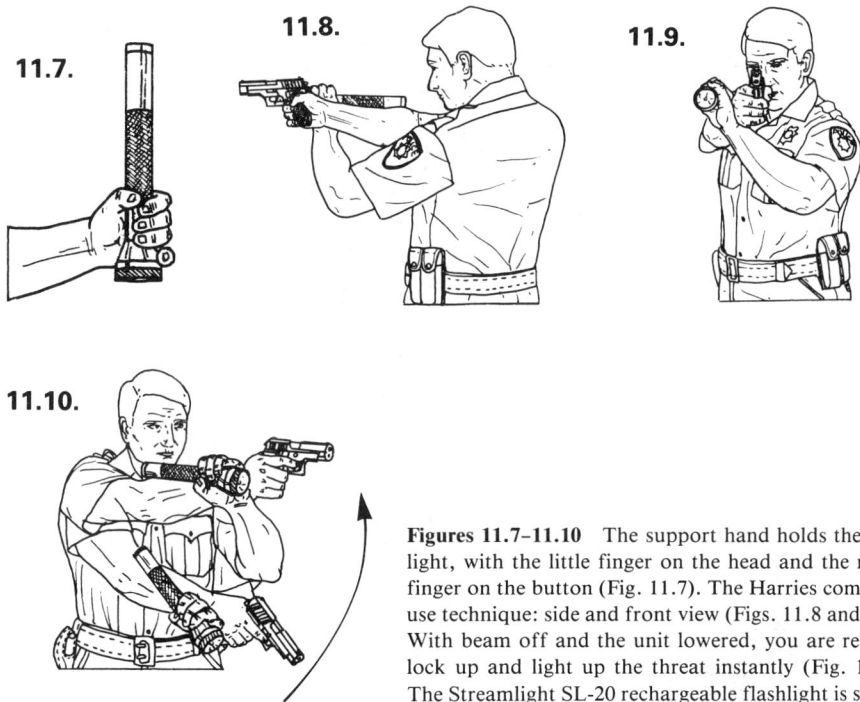

Figures 11.7–11.10   The support hand holds the flashlight, with the little finger on the head and the middle finger on the button (Fig. 11.7). The Harries combined-use technique: side and front view (Figs. 11.8 and 11.9). With beam off and the unit lowered, you are ready to lock up and light up the threat instantly (Fig. 11.10). The Streamlight SL-20 rechargeable flashlight is shown.

also the wrist areas lock in and press together to create the isometric press. While the strong hand's wrist is straight, the support hand's wrist is slightly curled upward (toward the back of the wrist) to make the two-handed lock fit a little stronger. The end of the flashlight is held along the arm. It may touch past the elbow, on the bicep, depending on the length of the flashlight. To align the beam and barrel together, while locking the position in, keep the flashlight arm's elbow down, making sure the flashlight and its supporting hand are solid against the strongarm and hand.

The Harries technique is assumed if you think a possible threat(s) is close and/or approaching possible threat cover with the flashlight off, usually with the handgun and flashlight held slightly down in a ready position. When you have located the threat(s), the stance is locked up, the flashlight turned on, the shot(s) fired, the flashlight turned off, and you move. Always be behind C&C. There are only two small drawbacks: It takes time to assume and if continually used throughout a long search it can be very fatiguing.

The modified Harries technique.   This technique is excellent for very close-range encounters, where the handgun and flashlight are held separately, then come together as they are instantly snapped up. We developed this modified version of the Harries technique to produce one that can be assumed almost instantly from a natural search position, even though producing a slightly less locked-in grip. What was needed for officers using the Weaver stance was a quick "hitting" technique that would quickly lock the handgun and flashlight together (with the flashlight held naturally) and work with the Weaver stance. Do not misunderstand; The Harries is

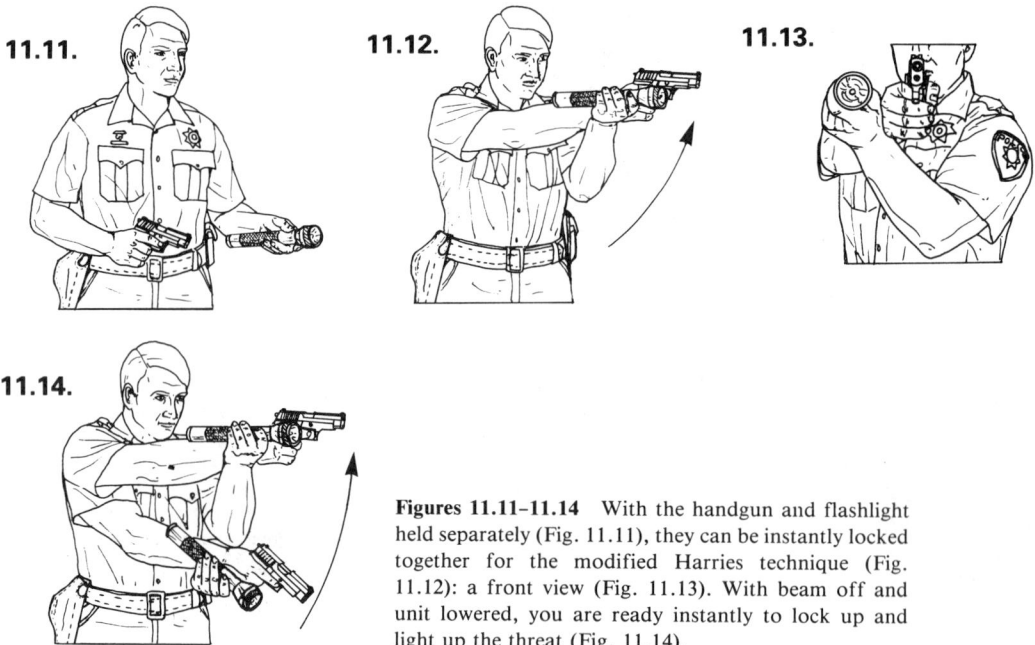

11.11.

11.12.

11.13.

11.14.

Figures 11.11–11.14   With the handgun and flashlight held separately (Fig. 11.11), they can be instantly locked together for the modified Harries technique (Fig. 11.12): a front view (Fig. 11.13). With beam off and unit lowered, you are ready instantly to lock up and light up the threat (Fig. 11.14).

used if you have the time to assume it. But if a need arises quickly, the modified Harries can be instantly assumed and used almost instantly to stop an instantly occurring threat(s). With the flashlight held naturally when searching, the modified Harries can be instantly assumed, without having to reverse the flashlight.

To use this technique the support hand holds the flashlight naturally, with the thumb used to press the flashlight's button. Bring the handgun up into a Weaver stance as you normally would. Now the support hand (holding the flashlight naturally forward) goes under the strong hand and places the base of the thumb and top of the wrist against the back of the strong hand. Both are pressed together to form the isometric pressure. The end of the flashlight cannot be placed on the elbow or forearm, due to the way it is being held.

The modified Harries technique can be assumed instantly to meet an instantly occurring attack. Just instantly lock up and fire. It can also be used when close approaching possible threat cover to quickly lock the handgun and flashlight together. Also, the ready position can be used with the modified Harries.

The Chapman technique. The Chapman technique is a good locked-in position for officers using the isosceles stance. This technique was developed by Ray Chapman, who has been part of the defensive handgun movement from the 1950s and was involved in the first leatherslaps held at Big Bear Lake, California, where the foundations of practical handgun use began. He was the first World Champion of Practical Pistol Shooting in 1975 and is a renowned police and civilian survival instructor and defensive tactician. Ray is the founder and director of the Chapman Academy at Columbia, Missouri, which provides excellent defensive training in pistol, shotgun, and rifle and their associated tactics.

This technique cannot be assumed as quickly, but is a good locked-in combined-use position. It works very well for an officer using the Isosceles stance.

To use this technique, the support hand's thumb and index finger are used to hold the flashlight naturally, with the thumb working the flashlight's button. When the hands come together, the other three fingers of the support hand wrap around the three strong-hand fingers. The flashlight's tube is placed against the side of the strong hand's thumb (the hand gripping the handgun), with the support hand's three fingers wrapping around the strong hand's three fingers holding the grip. This will hold the flashlight's beam parallel with the barrel.

The hands must be locked together and nothing must come in contact with the trigger finger when firing the handgun. Many officers find that the support hand's index finger (around the flashlight) should fit between the bottom of the strong hand's thumb and the top of its second finger. This allows much more comfort, a stronger lock between the hands, and keeps the support hand's index finger out of contact with the trigger finger (which could possibly interfere with its movement).

The Chapman technique is assumed if you think a possible threat is close and/or approaching possible threat cover with the flashlight off, usually with the hands held in a ready position. When you have located the threat(s), the stance is locked up, the flashlight turned on, the shot(s) fired, the flashlight is then turned off and you move. Always be behind C&C.

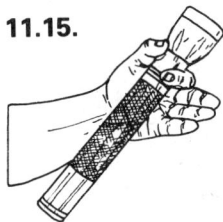

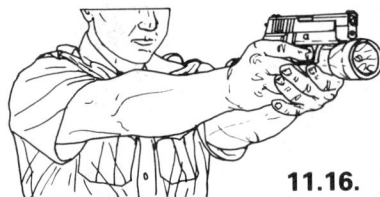

Figures 11.15–11.17 The index finger and thumb hold the flashlight, with the thumb working the button (Fig. 11.15). When the hands come together the other three fingers wrap around the strong-hand fingers (Fig. 11.16). The unit can be held close to the body and instantly snapped up into a locked-out firing stance (Fig. 11.17). The Mag-Lite MagCharger is shown.

The Ayoob technique. This technique is excellent for very close-range encounters, where the handgun and flashlight are held separately, then come together as they are instantly snapped up, effectively placing light and fire to stop a very close instant attack. The Ayoob technique was named after Massad Ayoob, a very well known defensive tactician and firearms instructor, and well-read writer on these subjects. He is the founder and director of the Lethal Force Institute, in Concord, New Hampshire, which provides one of the best defensive training programs to both police officers and civilians alike. His ongoing training programs have been especially effective in improving officer survivability.

This is one of the many defensive firearms techniques that he has developed. The main feature of this technique is optimally directing the flashlight's beam into the threat's face, which throws blinding light into the threat's eyes. The threat's reaction to the sudden blinding light would be to jerk its head away (back and/or to the side), which will also throw its weapon use off, at the moment of attack. This is not a locked-in two-handed technique, but two separate hands coming together for combined use. This technique is extremely fast to use when stopping a very close attack.

To use this technique, the handgun and flashlight are held separately while engaged in general searching. Suddenly the threat attacks. Instantly both the handgun and flashlight come together as they are snapped up and thrust out in front of your body. As the two hands come together, the bases of the two thumbs align, with the handgun pointing straight out at the threat's chest area and the flashlight slightly pointed upward into its eyes. At this close range, there is no need to use the sights—as long as the beam is in the threat's face, firing will place the bullets in its chest. Slight wrist action will help align the beam exactly. If time exists to use the sights, the light's beam will illuminate them. Also note that the position is perfectly suited for those using the Isosceles stance.

Out to about 7 yards the beam will be directly in the threat's face and the barrel pointed at its chest. With the beam going in the threat's face, the bullets will

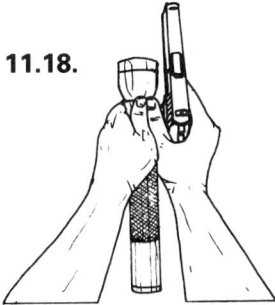

Figures 11.18–11.20 The bases of the thumbs align (Fig. 11.18). The hands do not interlock, but one holds the flashlight and one holds the handgun (Fig. 11.19). While searching with the hands held separately, the threat appears and the hands are snapped together, with the bases of the thumbs aligning, which places the beam in the face and bullets in the chest (Fig. 11.20).

go in its chest. After 7 yards, the beam will go over the threat's head and be of little effect. This technique is used for instantly occurring attacks at very close range. Both hands instantly come together and snap up into position and the shot(s) is fired.

These are the four combined use techniques to hold the flashlight and handgun together and manipulate them as a unit. When combining two functions into one, you have the advantage of a locked-in two-handed firing grip, with the flashlight tactically ready to help locate/identify the threat(s) and/or to help aim when firing. Being tactically ready is the key, and combined use places you, the handgun, and the flashlight in a tactically ready position.

One-Handed Use and Quick Fixes

A point that seems generally lost to many instructors is that low-light searching cannot be performed with both hands continually wrapped around the service handgun and flashlight. A number of times during the search, an officer will need an empty hand to perform some task: open a door, move something, carry something, to climb with, and so on. This is commonly referred to as the needed-third-hand syndrome. Lacking a third hand, the question then arises: What do you do with the flashlight when one hand is needed for a task? Three options are used to secure the flashlight while the hand is needed: (1) place it in the belt or flashlight holder on the belt, (2) put it under your armpit, or (3) use the double-up technique to hold the flashlight on the revolver (for revolvers only).

Option 1 provides the best way to hold the flashlight when it is not needed and it can be quickly retrieved. Options 2 and 3 are quick fixes for situations where you need one hand and sometimes light to perform a task that will usually take only 1 to 3 seconds. Once the task is completed (remember, a short-duration task of only 1 to 3 seconds), the support hand retrieves the flashlight and you are quickly back in your search position continuing the search.

11.21.    **11.22.**

Figures 11.21 and 11.22   In option 1 the flashlight is turned off and placed under the belt in the front on the support side (Fig. 11.21). If instantly needed, the support hand draws the flashlight and meets the strong hand for a combined-use technique (Fig. 11.22).

Option 1.   When one hand is needed, the flashlight is turned off and placed under your Sam Browne belt, in the front on the support-hand side. Thus positioned, you can instantly find it for a quick grab with virtually no arm movement. Many officers prefer to place the flashlight in the small of the back to secure it. The main problem is that the arm has to bend around to grab it instead of instantly coming up for the flashlight when it is placed under the belt in the front.

A secondary method for option 1 is to place the flashlight in a flashlight ring on the belt. A specialized leather belt loop for the flashlight is also available. Make sure that these are positioned on the support-hand side of the body, so that they can be quickly grabbed. The only problem associated with rings or loops is that they sometimes do not instantly release the flashlight, but bind on it as you are trying to remove it quickly. If you are going to use one of these, work with your equipment to make sure that it functions correctly.

Option 2.   When one hand is needed, the flashlight can also be placed under the strong-hand armpit, with the flashlight either on or off. This is the first of the quick fixes, used to solve a need quickly. When one hand is needed, the flashlight is placed under the armpit, the hand performs the task (turning a door knob to open a door, for instance), and the flashlight is retrieved again, all taking no more than 3 seconds. The reason the flashlight is placed under the strong-hand armpit is to allow the support hand and arm a full range of movement to perform the task.

If light is needed, leave the flashlight on and use the movement of the shoulder (while the flashlight is held in the armpit) to control where it points. No one likes the fact that the light is locked into the body for a possible threat(s) to fire at, but there are times when you must have the light to perform the task. You must judge the situation and where you think the threat(s) may be located. If the threat(s) does attack, you can fire instantly at close quarters by pointing the handgun out. You can also turn off the flashlight before placing it under the armpit when light is not needed.

Figures 11.23 and 11.24 In option 2 the support hand places the flashlight under the armpit (Fig. 11.23). The support hand is free to turn a door knob (Fig. 11.24).

Option 3.   When one hand is needed, the flashlight can be put on the revolver's grip (it must be a revolver) and held in place by the fingers of the strong hand. The flashlight is placed directly on the revolver's grip and the strong hand's fingers hold it in place on the grip (the thumb and middle finger open to accept the flashlight and then close to hold it in place). As such, the beam and barrel are aligned and held in one hand. In this position you can fire instantly if need be while holding the flashlight, but you cannot switch it on or off. The flashlight is placed on the gun hand either on or off and can be changed only when the support hand takes the flashlight back. It's amazing that very small to very large flashlights can be held this way with no problem.

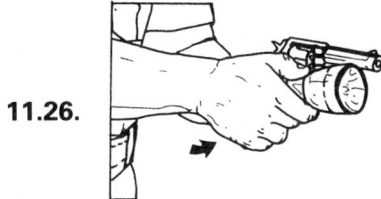

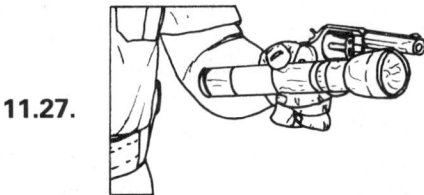

Figures 11.25–11.28 The support hand is holding the flashlight away from the revolver (Fig. 11.25). The support hand places the flashlight on the revolver, as the strong hand's thumb and middle finger open up to accept it (Fig. 11.26). The flashlight is now held on the revolver (Fig. 11.27). Top and front views show the relationship of revolver and flashlight (Fig. 11.28).

When searching and one hand is needed for a task, the flashlight must be secured by using one of these three options. The flashlight is never laid down. You must have control of your equipment at all times.

FLASHLIGHT TRUTHS

Several flashlight truths are particularly important and must be discussed. These truths are straightforward and more a matter of common sense than anything else. For some reason, though, many officers do not follow these simple flashlight truths when engaging in searches. They are thus placing themselves in danger by failing to use the proper equipment and techniques to maximize their survival advantage.

1. You never enter or search any building or dark area without a flashlight, no matter what time of day it is.   Obviously, you never search at night without a flashlight. But just because it is daytime, you never go into a building without a flashlight. Many dark areas will exist where a flashlight is a must. Without a flashlight, you will increase your response time [the longer it takes for you to see the threat(s), the longer it will take you to respond to it].

Being able to locate/identify the threat(s) early is critical to your survival. You are a sitting duck if you do not have the capability to penetrate the darkness around you to locate the threat(s). In the dark area, a threat can stand fully in the open and take careful aim at you and you will not be able to see it unless you can illuminate it.

2. You must purchase and use a flashlight that will effectively increase your survival advantage.   Using an inexpensive, low-intensity flashlight will greatly decrease your ability to locate/identify the threat(s), which is critical when responding to control or stop the threat(s). It is false survival economy to save a few dollars on a piece of equipment that may mean the difference in your survival.

The flashlight must be a high-intensity flashlight with enough candlepower to penetrate dark areas effectively. Two excellent examples of high-intensity, rechargeable flashlights are Streamlight and Mag-Lite. The Mag-Lite MagCharger and the Streamlight Excalibre series are state-of-the-art flashlights for police work. Both offer basically the same packages: extremely durable and rugged rechargeable flashlights, with three-position switches (on, off, and blink), and recharging units for cruiser or home. These flashlights have brightness ranges from 20,000 to 40,000 candlepower, averaging 10 times brighter than ordinary flashlights, and can easily provide the advantage necessary on searches. Your ability to locate the threat(s) is critical, especially during low-light conditions, which can hide them further. High-intensity flashlights such as these are vastly superior to ordinary flashlights and dramatically penetrate the darkness with a flood of illumination to reveal what is hidden. The primary function of the flashlight is to provide an increased ability to locate and identify threat(s) in low-light conditions. Your primary flashlight must be a high-intensity flashlight such as these. Using anything less reduces your ability during low-light conditions.

Both of these flashlights have a three-position switch: on, off, and blink. This type of switch is a must for a police flashlight. The on and off function is used for normal police duties, and the blink function is used when searching with a flashlight. The blink function, produced by slight finger pressure on the switch, provides you with the instant on/off capabilities needed when using the two-second/move technique. Also, if the flashlight is dropped inadvertently, it will go off instantly when in the blink mode and not light you up.

3. Every officer must have his or her own flashlight to use when searching.   If any officer does not bring and use a flashlight when searching, he or she is cutting down the efficiency of the search team. This can only cause problems, as the other officers will, throughout the search, have to help the officer who does not have a flashlight. Try to use someone else's flashlight to guide your path or meet a possible quick need, and you will see what we mean.

Five other points show the need for every officer to use a flashlight when searching: (a) increased illumination (more light) can definitely be very useful at times; (b) if there is only one light between two officers and it breaks, they are both in trouble; (c) if the officers separate for some reason (even for a short period of time), they will each have to function as a single unit, but one will not have a flashlight; (d) if the officer with the flashlight gets shot, the other one now does not have a flashlight; and (e) if two officers are attacked from two directions by separate threats, the one that does not have a flashlight is out of luck. These five points drive the reality home, but they need not be a concern if every officer searching would merely bring and use a flashlight.

4. You must have a backup flashlight before starting any prolonged search.   This is a must, as your primary flashlight can go out for a number of reasons, and without a backup flashlight you will be in the dark and reduce the search team's efficiency. On large buildings, opt for carrying a two- or three-cell flashlight (C- or D-cell) as your backup flashlight. Excellent examples are also produced by Streamlight and Mag-Lite, with each producing a full range of C- and D-cell flashlights. These contain reasonable candlepower and a three-function switch, so you can continue with the search.

Even during a short search, you should have some type of secondary light source. The minilights, such as the Streamlight Jr and Mini Mag-Lite, are perfectly suited for this. They are small and light and will slip readily into your pocket or fit on your Sam Browne belt with the slip-on minilight belt holsters. They have almost no bulk and are surprisingly bright for a very small flashlight. As secondary light sources to have on hand always, they are excellent, but do not use them as your primary light source or backup flashlight on prolonged searches.

These four flashlight truths are very important. Make sure you follow them to help maximize your ability to search the darkness.

OTHER LOW-LIGHT CONSIDERATIONS

Muzzle Flash and Firing Shock

Both muzzle flash and firing shock from the threat's weapon can cause unstabilizing effects that officers must understand and prepare for. Most nighttime searches will be conducted in a quiet, dark environment. When the initial exchange occurs, the environment suddenly explodes with shock and light. It can be an extremely violent shock to an unprepared officer as the threat(s) opens up. If not prepared for, this sudden shock can be bad enough to make an officer freeze momentarily. New officers in academy classes have quit police work when exposed to the shock of muzzle flash and firing shock during realistic nighttime encounter simulations. The best way to prepare for this is to train for it in realistic nighttime simulations, but many departments do not provide this training. The next best way is to know that these violent shocks can occur. If they do, you have expected that it could happen and are now instantly getting down to the work of stopping the threat(s). Remember, the muzzle flash and firing shock will not hurt you, but the bullets will if you freeze and do not begin working to stop the threat(s).

The muzzle flash from your handgun creates two main problems: giving your position away and interfering with your night vision. Muzzle flash will give your position away and there is no way to avoid it. What you must do constantly is to move after firing; either move laterally one or two steps to the side, or move to another location. If you were out in the open when you fired, get behind cover fast. As soon as you have fired, move.

Muzzle flash can also interfere with your night vision, which is explained further in the next section. The major cause of this is excessive muzzle flash in the ammunition. A number of different cartridges of the same caliber will produce varying degrees of muzzle flash, some quite excessive. This problem can be lessened by careful selection of ammunition for departmental issue. The various ammunition brands and loads should be tested at night. Any with excessive muzzle flash should not be considered.

Muzzle Flash Can Help. First, muzzle flash can reveal a threat's location when it fires on you. The small tongues of flame will pinpoint the threat(s) and if it does not move instantly, you know where to fire. As soon as a threat fires and is pinpointed, you must quickly return fire by laying down a pattern of three or four rounds on and around the threat's muzzle flash. There is no need to use your flashlight (unless unsure of the situation for some reason, or too far away, where the sights must be used). This must be done quickly, as the threat may move after firing. Remember, once you have fired, move!

Second, muzzle flash can verify your sight alignment when you follow through after firing. As the handgun fires, the muzzle flash will for an instant light up the handgun's sights and their alignment. If held in place, you can see where the sights were aligned. The sights will be illuminated for the briefest instant, but enough for you to see where they were.

You must be aware of all the advantages and disadvantages associated with muzzle flash and be prepared for the instant light, noise, and shock when a threat fires on you.

Understanding and Using Night Vision

Night vision is nothing more than allowing the eyes to become adapted to the dark conditions you are in. It takes about half an hour for the eye's rod cells to produce enough visual purple to activate them. As a police officer on a search, night vision can very seldom be achieved and usually cannot work. This is due to the use of flashlights by officers engaged in the search and any other light sources present, which will effectively block any night vision adaptation. Some advocate closing one eye whenever any light source is used or encountered on the search, then opening that eye again when in a dark area. This technique is hard to accomplish success-fully, as light splash can occur instantly, even in dark areas, effectively ending night vision. It will also reduce your field of vision from 180 degrees to 120 degrees and your depth perception will be off. Keep both eyes open when searching, closing the nonaiming eye only when firing.

The only time that night vision can be used is when you are stationed in a dark area waiting for a possible threat(s) to appear. The rolls are reversed; you are waiting in the dark for the threat(s). If you have the time to adapt your eyes to the dark and can remain in a dark area, it will work. When waiting in the dark and scanning for the threat(s), use off-centered vision by looking slightly to the left, right, above, or below the area or suspect object being scanned. This is done so that fresh rod cells are continually being used. If you stare at a suspect object, the visual purple being used bleaches out in 6 to 10 seconds and the object disappears. Use off-center vision to keep using fresh rod cells. Also, glancing back and forth quickly can bring an object out from its background. This scanning technique is accomplished by glancing back and forth quickly over an area several times (not moving the head, just moving the eyes back and forth over an area several times). Any predominate object that was hidden by the darkness will begin to stand out from the background. It will not remain apparent for long, but it will stand out for a few seconds so that you can see its form.

Another night vision problem occurs with excessive muzzle flash. When your ammunition produces a very bright muzzle flash, the effect on you can be temporary blindness, the same as that which occurs when a very bright light is shined in your eyes. Once this occurs, the eyes will take several seconds to readjust—for the irises to open back up. Usually, this problem occurs for several moments until the eyes readjust, but in some persons it can take longer. The way to offset this effect is to close the nonaiming eye when firing. Many officers do this naturally anyway, but all officers must be trained to close the nonaiming eye when firing. (*Note:* All the reasoning behind this is presented in Chapter 5.) Once the shot(s) is fired and the flashlight is turned off, the nonaiming eye is opened instantly and the officer moves. It is easy to use this technique, and it works.

The eyes will adapt much more quickly for less dramatic changes in lighting conditions. A good example is that of going inside a dark bar from the daylight. As you walk through the door into the bar, your eyes take 10 to 15 seconds to adjust— a short amount of time usually, but plenty of time for a threat(s) to aim and fire at you while your eyes are adjusting to the sudden darkness. Whenever going from a light area into a dark area, close your aiming eye for 10 to 15 seconds to allow it to adjust to the dark. Although this is a short amount of time, it will effectively prepare your aiming eye for the dark inside. Then enter the dark area and open the closed eye, which has been adjusting itself for the dark area. A simple technique, but very effective in bridging a critical few seconds while your eye would otherwise be adjusting. Also, take your sunglasses off before entering any structure, whether on a call or just getting a cup of coffee.

Thoughts on the Flashlight Roll Technique and Leaving Your Flashlight

The flashlight roll technique has appeared within the past few years and is used mainly as a room-entry technique. Two officers crouch down on either side of a doorway; one officer sticks a flashlight just inside the doorway and turns it on, with the beam shining into the room. The officer then rolls it across the floor to the other officer, who will roll it back. The purpose is to illuminate the inside of the room from the doorway, while both officers view the interior. It is also supposed to create a curtain of light that the officers can stay behind. There are a number of problems with this technique: The curtain of light produced is faulty as the flashlight rolls from one side to the other; one officer loses control of his or her flashlight; and it locates both officers at the edges of either side of the doorway and has them remain positioned there rolling the flashlight back and forth. This technique should not be used; instead, use the beam fanning technique to quickly cover the interior of a room. This is done by sticking the flashlight just inside the doorway and rocking it back and forth very quickly by wrist action, which throws light instantly into the whole room. This increases the chances of catching an instant glimpse of a threat(s) hiding there, as the eyes can pick up images very quickly. The flashlight is out and fans for about a second, with every part of the room being viewed by the officer. If two officers fan at the same time (one high and one low from opposite sides of the doorway), they will not only confuse the threat(s) but throw twice as much light into the room.

Some instructors are now teaching officers to place their flashlight down and leave it as a curtain of light to hide behind and fire from behind. This should not be done except in very rare situations. Every officer must maintain and use his or her own flashlight! An exception to this would be to place your backup flashlight down to blind and misdirect the threat(s). The curtain-of-light idea is a good one, but has one big disadvantage: The threat(s) must be directly centered in the beam and stay there. If the threat(s) has any brains, it will get out of the beam very quickly. When the threat(s) moves to one side, even several steps, the curtain of light does not work. When you direct the beam right on the threat(s) for 2 seconds or less, the curtain of light is working while you surprise and fire on the threat(s); then turn the beam off and move.

A more critical problem with any technique where the flashlight is placed down and left is that you may not be able to retrieve it, and thus you lose the tactical advantage a flashlight can give you. In effect you will be in the dark and not able to take tactical advantage of illuminating an area and the threat(s) if needed. Do not reduce your advantage by leaving your flashlight.

Blend with the Night

A last thought, which possibly should have been first: Blending with the night becomes very important during low-light searches. Most officers view low-light conditions as a completely negative environment, but it also has many positive aspects that officers can use to their advantage. Officers must know how to blend with the night, which is nothing more than using the camouflage that the darkness provides. Become one with the night by blending with it. Keep to the dark areas when moving (if possible) and scan from them. Just as the night may be hiding the threat(s), it can also hide you. The darkness can work to your advantage if you let it. Do not be afraid of it, blend with it.

SUMMARY

In this chapter we have covered techniques used to solve problems associated with low-light conditions and increase your survival advantage. Remember, you must be able to locate/identify the threat(s) and effectively control or stop it, with minimal risk of injury to yourself or other innocents on the scene. This task is complicated by low-light conditions, which can increase the potential lethality of a situation many times over. Use the techniques and methods covered here to function safely/effectively within low-light conditions and conclude the situation successfully.

12

Tactical Reloading and Clearing Stoppages

Once a lethal encounter is under way, at one or more points during it, reloading may be necessary. Reloading occurs at two times during an encounter: (1) when you decide to and can usually find the few seconds needed during a lull in the action, or (2) when you've run dry during the action, with the slide locked-back or when the hammer falls on an empty case (a bad situation). Your ability to maintain the action throughout the encounter may depend on your trained-in reloading skills. Too many officers have died while in the process of reloading. Reloading, and the tactics involved, must be trained-in skills that keep the service handgun well fed throughout an encounter.

All reloading is tactical in use. Most of the defensive reloading techniques used today are called either speed or tactical reloading. "Speed reloading" commonly refers to the speed reloading techniques developed in IPSC competition. "Tactical reloading" commonly refers to reloading a partially depleted handgun (reloading one, two, or three rounds in the revolver, or replacing a partially depleted magazine with a fresh one and not dumping any extra live rounds). These two separate references are in fact both tactical in use; both are used as a reloading tactic for the particular reloading situation at hand. We use the terms complete and partial reloading to describe more correctly the two tactical reloading techniques, each having its own particular tactical application. Reloading techniques are part of your trained-in reflexive sets of weapon use skills and always used tactically during a situation.

COMPLETE AND PARTIAL RELOADING: THE TWO TYPES OF TACTICAL RELOADING

For each of the service handguns, tactical reloading involves techniques to resupply the handgun with ammunition quickly. Tactical reloading is comprised of two types of reloading: complete (completely reloading all ammo) and partial (reloading a partially depleted handgun). All reloading is tactical and dependent on the continuing encounter. You must have the trained-in skills and tactical knowledge to reload your handgun, completely or partially and be ready to use either instantly during an unfolding encounter.

Complete Reloading.   This type of reloading completely reloads the handgun by instantly dumping out any ammo, empty cases, and/or magazines in the handgun, then completely reloading it using either a speed loader or a fresh magazine. It is usually done with the utmost speed, as the situation is pressing. Complete reloading usually occurs when you must instantly reload as the handgun has run dry, a bad situation to let occur unless it was a tactical necessity. Whatever the reason, you must now use complete reloading techniques to resupply the handgun with ammunition quickly, while behind cover. Remember, all reloading is done from behind cover or concealment and/or on the move. If the beginning encounter has caught you in the open with no chance to move, when the initial exchange of rounds has been fired, instantly move to a covered or concealed position to continue the encounter and as a place to reload.

Partial Reloading.   This type of reloading reloads a partially depleted handgun by removing and replacing only the empty cases in a revolver's cylinder (reloading one, two, or three rounds) or exchanging a fresh magazine for a partially depleted one in an auto, while saving any live rounds for the continuing encounter. Whenever a lull occurs in the action after the handgun has been fired, it can then be partially reloaded to make it fully loaded again. By using this technique, you can continually keep your handgun fully loaded throughout the encounter, while not dumping any live rounds that may be needed as the encounter continues.

To be tactically ready for any reloading situation, you must know how to reload your service handgun both completely and partially. During the encounter, partial reloading is the way to go, by always keeping your handgun fully loaded while saving any live rounds that would otherwise be dumped. Complete reloading may be needed to quickly replenish a run dry handgun during the action when reloading speed is the utmost consideration. Quickly dump everything and reload completely, to get back into the action as fast as possible. There will also be times when no reloading needs to be done, depending on the situation.

Reloading speed versus ammo considerations.   Thrown into the reloading mix is the trade-off between reloading speed (how fast you have to reload at that moment) and ammo considerations for the continuing encounter (as yet unknown, but whether you need the extra ammo in the next few moments). These are related directly to reloading the handgun completely and partially. Reloading speed becomes the all-important consideration when the handgun is run dry during the action or the threat(s) is charging you while you are reloading. Reloading must be done as fast as possible to stop the attacking threat(s). Most of the time, though, you can take the few extra seconds during a lull in the action to reload partially, and conserve ammo that may be important during the continuing encounter. Of the two, reloading speed is obviously more critical, as the handgun must be kept ready for action. But if you can find the few extra seconds during a lull, use partial reloading techniques to conserve ammo.

You must use the tactics at your disposal to keep your handgun from running dry; thus reducing or eliminating the need to reload instantly during the action. By tactically using partial reloading, you keep the handgun fully loaded throughout the encounter, while saving live rounds that will be very valuable if the encounter continues—and many have.

Complete and partial reloading techniques are discussed fully for each of the service handguns and for right- and left-handed officers. There are only two reloading techniques, complete and partial, that an officer must learn (provided the officer is using only one type of service handgun and/or backup/off-duty handgun). There are just two techniques for each of the service handgun types; that is all you have to learn.

The when and the how of reloading.   Tactical reloading is more concerned with the *when* of reloading than with the *how* of reloading. The when of reloading refers to the tactical use of reloading techniques during an encounter: When do you reload? The how of reloading refers to the reloading techniques that you will use.

The How of Reloading.   The first step is training-in the tactical reloading reflexive sets until they will occur automatically when it is time to reload. When it is tactically time to reload, you must know how to perform the reload—the skills being trained-in to function automatically.

We say that "tactical reloading is more concerned with the when of reloading than with the how of reloading" with the understanding that you have trained-in and maintained your reloading skills. As one thing is very true: Once you know when to reload, you must already know how to reload. This can occur only when the reloading skills are trained-in reflexive sets.

The When of Reloading.   When to reload is the part that is the most difficult to work with, as it is a variable every time, whereas how to reload is a constant. When to reload follows the general rule: Reload at the first available lull after you fire; don't wait and run dry. The how of reloading consists of the trained-in reflexive sets that function automatically when the time comes to reload.

Reloading occurs at some point after the initial exchange. The action has started, you have fired an unknown number of shots, and you are in a covered position ready to fire instantly if the action starts again.

The question is: "When should I reload?" The rule is: Reload at the first available lull after you fire. Reload during the lulls so that you will not have to reload during the action. Obviously, you must not be forced to reload during the action, because at that point you are out of ammo with a run dry handgun (a bad situation). You want to reload when it is tactically advantageous to do so, to keep a constant flow of ammunition going into the handgun. Replenish the handgun during the lulls when you think it is necessary to keep it fully loaded. You must choose the time to reload and not let yourself be so caught up in the situation that you forget and run out of bullets. Similarly, do not holster or move with a handgun that is depleted. Reload the handgun before doing either of these. Especially make sure that you do not leave your covered position for another one with a partially loaded handgun (unless absolutely necessary).

You must think reloading after you fire and not forget to accomplish this task during a highly charged situation. Do not attempt to count the rounds as you fire them and use that as the gauge of when to reload. Invariably your count will be wrong and you will be out of ammo at the wrong time. Reload in the lulls, when they occur, and think of it as part of your lull tasks (as outlined in Chapter 9, under the post-exchange rules).

INITIAL UNDERSTANDING REGARDING RELOADING TECHNIQUES

The functions of the strong hand and support hand during reloading.   Of your two hands, one is the strong hand (if you are right-handed, your right hand), which possesses the greatest amount of dexterity, and the other is the support hand, which is not as well coordinated (much of the time the support hand is referred to as the weak hand). When reloading, there are only two tasks performed by the hands: One hand holds the handgun and the other picks up and reloads the fresh ammo. The question is: Which hand do you use for each task when reloading the revolver or the auto? The answer is: The strong hand is used for whichever task requires the most dexterity.

Most shooters do not understand that the function of the strong hand during reloading is different for the revolver and the auto. The strong hand is used to perform the most difficult task during the reloading process (as it is the more dextrous and can perform better), and this task is different for the revolver and the auto.

For the Auto.   The task requiring the most dexterity when reloading is handling the auto, as grabbing and inserting the fresh magazine is accomplished very easily by the support hand. Little dexterity is needed to place the top of the fresh magazine into the magazine well opening and lock it home. Even a partial reload, inserting the fresh magazine while catching the partially depleted magazine falling from the auto, does not require much dexterity and is easily accomplished with the support hand. During reloading, the auto stays in the strong hand, while the support hand reloads it. The auto does not switch from one hand to the other.

For the Revolver.   On the other hand, the task requiring the most dexterity when reloading the revolver is manipulating the speed loader or reloading single cartridges. During reloading, the revolver switches from the strong hand to the support hand, while the strong hand performs the reload, and then it is switched back into the strong hand. With the revolver you must switch hands to accomplish the reload efficiently. This must be done for the strong hand to manipulate the fresh ammo in the most dextrous manner to reduce the problems that can occur when reloading a revolver.

A number of problems can occur. With the speed loader, there are six bullets to line up and insert into their corresponding cylinder holes; then the cartridges are released into the cylinder. If the sharp edges on the cylinder holes (at the star) have not been knocked off, the case openings can catch on them, thus adding to the problem. Additionally, reloading single cartridges one at a time requires a great amount of dexterity to position the cartridges in the hand and then insert them into the cylinder—repeating the process six times. Also, if the need arises to partially reload one, two, or three cartridges during a lull in the action, dexterity will be called upon to accomplish this task.

Any reloading of a revolver or auto will follow this rule: Reloading revolver, strong hand on rounds; reloading auto, strong hand on gun.

There is only one method for reloading a revolver that goes against this rule (not including one-handed reloading methods). This is a speed reloading method used in competition, where the revolver is continually held in the right hand throughout reloading (the technique works only for right-handed shooters). This is done to decrease the time used in switching the revolver between the hands. The cylinder is opened by the right hand, while the left hand goes for the fresh rounds, reloads them, and closes the cylinder as it reassumes the two-handed firing grip. This is very fast but takes extensive practice and does not hold up during defensive encounters. The main problem is that finite movements are needed to perform the reload and the cylinder is not held tightly but rotates freely. As we know, finite movements break down during a lethal encounter; gross reloading movements must be used. Also, standing still during a match, this is fine, but on the move during an encounter you will have problems, and this technique breaks down quickly.

All other reloading techniques follow this rule, as you must understand the functions of the strong hand and the support hand during the reloading process.

Reloading Must Work When Moving.   Any reloading technique that is used must be able to be done while moving. If it will not hold up while you are moving, it should not be used. The handgun must be controlled when reloading. For the automatic this is not a problem and is accomplished easily, as the magazine fits into the auto. For the revolver, the reloading techniques must control the cylinder and hold it locked open while the reload is accomplished. Reloading may have to occur while quickly moving to cover, and the techniques must work. Try them out for yourself and see how they function on the move.

Reloading Is Done by Feel. Reloading techniques must not only become trained-in, but must be done by feel, while you keep your eyes on the action/threat(s) during the encounter. [*Note:* A slight glance to aid in reloading can save seconds and get the handgun back into action quicker, but the vast majority of time, attention is on the action/threat(s).]

Train-in your reloading skills by practicing eyes off. While practicing, keep your attention at any spot designated as the action/threat(s) and perform the reload, training-it-in completely by feel.

Using the touch index when reloading. As in many of the techniques that build your defensive weapon use skills, reloading is aided by a touch index that helps control the technique to reduce fumbling and increase speed. To accomplish this, the handgun is brought out of the firing position by the arms bending at the elbows until the elbows touch the sides of your body, creating a touch index as soon as the elbows touch the body. As the handgun is reloaded, the forearms slide (in reality, skim lightly) along the sides of the body during the process. At times, the forearms will not touch the body at all (while picking up extra ammo), but will return to touch the body lightly, creating a touch index that helps control the technique.

The main function of the touch index is to help train-in the reflexive sets of reloading skills and produce an increased eyes-off reloading ability. During a lethal situation you should be watching the action/threat(s) at all times and the ability to reload by feel must be trained-in to accomplish this. A slight glance to aid in reloading can save seconds in getting the handgun quickly back into action, but the vast majority of your attention is on the action/threat(s).

METHODS OF CARRYING AND LOADING AMMUNITION

For each of the two distinct mechanical designs—revolver and auto—there are preferred methods for carrying extra ammunition. For the auto, there is only one choice: All extra ammunition is carried in extra magazines. For the revolver, the preferred method of carrying extra ammunition is a combination of speed loaders and extra cartridges in belt loops, due to tactical reloading considerations. Every officer must understand that reloading must be approached from a tactical reloading standpoint, and the methods of carrying extra ammo and its placement is the first step. The following outlines the ammo carrying methods and placement for both the revolver and the auto.

Ammo Carrying and Reloading Methods for the Auto

The ammo carrying methods for the auto are addressed very quickly and easily. First and foremost, all extra ammunition is carried in extra magazines. It is just that simple: Extra ammunition is carried only in extra magazines. Without a magazine, the auto can hold only the chambered round (unlike the revolver, which can hold one to six cartridges). As such, the magazine functions in conjunction with the auto as a unit when firing. The magazine is loaded beforehand and is ready instantly to be inserted and locked into the auto, to replenish the ammunition supply completely in one, quick stroke.

The belt pouches holding the extra magazines are located on the support side of the body (on the side of the body opposite the holster). They must be located there, as the support hand will pick up and insert the extra magazine when reloading, while the strong hand manipulates the auto.

A police officer must carry at least two extra magazines for the auto. A magazine can be rendered nonfunctional and an officer must have at least two extras. The chances of this occurring are minimal, but we train and plan for the worst breakdown in situation and equipment. Damage can occur to the magazine's lips, the floorplate can come off, or foreign matter within the magazine can cause the rounds to jam in the magazine itself. Even though the chances of these occurring are minimal, you must have at least two extra magazines—one for the auto and one for a reload—if your initial magazine fails.

How to grip the spare magazine when reloading. The proper method of gripping the spare magazine begins with the correct placement of the spare magazine in the pouch on your Sam Browne belt. The magazine pouch is located on the opposite side of the belt from the holster for the support hand to easily grasp and pull the magazine free from the pouch. The spare magazines are inserted into the pouch with their floorplates up and fronts facing forward. This positioning allows the index finger to lay along the front of the magazine when it is pulled from the pouch, thus properly aligned when the hand turns the magazine's end up and inserts it into the auto.

The proper grip on the magazine places the index finger along the magazine's front, with the floorplate resting in the palm and the other fingers wrapped around and holding the magazine in place. The tip of the index finger extends just forward of the first round in the magazine, forming a touch index to improve alignment of the magazine and magazine well.

When the support hand goes for the magazine in the pouch, the proper grip is begun as the magazine is started out of the pouch and fully achieved as it clears the pouch. As the spare magazine is pulled from the pouch, the hand turns its top toward the magazine well to align it. Once the depleted magazine falls free, the spare magazine is aligned (with the help of the index finger tip feeling the front of the magazine well). As the top of the magazine is started in, the fingers release it and the palm pushes it home until a click indicates that the magazine catch is engaged.

A proper grip on the spare magazine is very important to a smooth, quick reload. After a while the magazine will feel right in your hand.

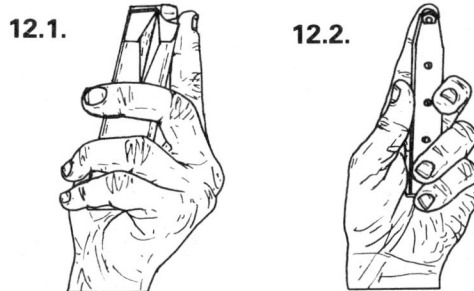

12.1.   **12.2.**

Figures 12.1 and 12.2   Both views showing the index finger held straight along the front of the magazine, floorplate in palm, and fingers securely holding the magazine.

Ammo Carrying and Reloading Methods for the REVOLVER

There are three methods of carrying extra ammunition for the revolver: in speed loaders, speed strips, and belt loops. Each of these methods of carrying extra ammunition has its own method of loading it into the revolver.

Speed loaders.   (Par time for reloading, 6 seconds.) There are two types of speed loaders in general use: (1) the HKS speed loader, with a knob on top that has to be turned to release the cartridges, and (2) the Safariland speed loader, which releases the cartridges by the tip of the cylinder's star pushing in a central pin on the speed loader, which occurs automatically as the speed loader is pushed in. Once you have decided which you will use, use that type exclusively. Do not switch back and forth, or worse, carry both types, as there is little room for mistake when reloading during a real encounter.

The speed loaders have two areas that are held and/or manipulated when reloading the revolver: the barrel (the black cylinder holding the cartridges) and the knob (the smaller top; on the HKS this top is turned to release the cartridges). When inserting the cartridges into the revolver's cylinder holes, the speed loader is held by the barrel no matter which type you use. Under no circumstances do you hold the knob when initially aligning and inserting the cartridges into the cylinder. When it is time to release the cartridges: (1) the Safariland speed loader is pushed in firmly (a slight push forward), causing the internal mechanism to release the cartridges automatically, or (2) the HKS speed loader knob is gripped and turned (by the thumb and index finger sliding off the speed loader's barrel) which releases the cartridges. Once the speed loader has released the cartridges, it is instantly dropped out of the hand, which is now involved with closing the cylinder and reassuming a two-handed grip.

Right- and left-handed use of the speed loader and their touch index. There are two methods of gripping the speed loader, for right- and left-handed officers. The reason two methods exist is because of the relationship between the open cylinder, the side of the revolver, and the thumb and fingers holding and inserting the speed loader. It is nothing more than a gripping method which takes human engineering into consideration. The main idea is to keep the thumb and fingers holding the speed loader properly positioned so that two things are accomplished: (1) the fingers must not interfere with aligning the speed loader and inserting the bullets into the cylinder (which will occur if they come in contact with the left side of the revolver or the grips), and (2) the fingers must be positioned to allow for the touch index to aid when aligning speed loader and cylinder. This positioning is accomplished by keeping the thumb and fingers on only one side (one half) of the speed loader, the side that is away from the frame and grip.

The Touch Index When Using the Speed Loader. A touch index is used when gripping the speed loader and inserting the bullets into the cylinder. Either the index or second finger (depending on whether the right- or left-handed method is used) will ride along the cartridge cases with its tip extended just forward of the bullet tips. In this position the fingertip can *feel* the edge of the cylinder. When initially lining up the speed loader with the cylinder, the touch index greatly improves the coordination between these two. It becomes much easier for the hand and speed loader to find the cylinder and align with it. Remember, reloading must be trained-in to be an eyes-off process. You should be able to reload with your eyes closed. The touch index, the fingertip touching the cylinder wall, will greatly improve your ability to perform eyes-off reloading. Methods are shown for both right- and left-handed officers. Use the method shown for whichever is your strong hand.

The Right-Handed Method and the Touch Index. Once unloaded, the left hand holds the revolver almost laying on its right side, with the cylinder held open. To use the speed loader, the right hand will have to bring it *overtop of and across* the left side of the revolver to align it with the cylinder. The thumb and second finger (middle finger) are thus positioned directly across from each other, holding the barrel of the speed loader (the tip of the thumb is on the barrel, as is the second pad of the second finger, its tip held along the cartridge cases). The index finger is held along the cartridge cases with its tip extended just forward of the bullet tips— positioned as the touch index.

The Left-Handed Method and the Touch Index. Once unloaded, the right hand holds the revolver almost straight up and down but at a slight angle to the right, with the cylinder held open. To use the speed loader, the left hand will bring it "next to" the left side of the revolver, to align it with the cylinder. The thumb and index finger are thus positioned directly across from each other, holding the barrel of the speed loader (the tip of both holding the barrel). The second finger (middle finger) rides next to the index finger, with the second finger's tip extended just forward of the bullet tips—positioned as the touch index.

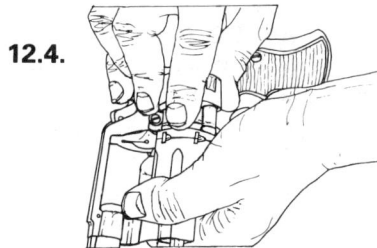

Figures 12.3 and 12.4 When the right-handed officer holds the speed loader, the thumb and middle finger are positioned directly across from each other on the barrel, with the index finger's tip held forward for the touch index (Fig. 12.3). When inserting the cartridges into the cylinder nothing gets in the way and the touch index is working (Fig. 12.4).

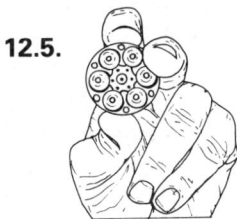

Figures 12.5 and 12.6 When the left-handed officer holds the speed loader, the thumb and index finger are positioned directly across from each other on the barrel, with the middle finger tip held forward for the touch index (Fig. 12.5). When inserting the cartridges into the cylinder nothing gets in the way and the touch index is working (Fig. 12.6).

In both of these methods, when the speed loader is brought into position and aligned initially, the thumb and fingers are not in the way (not in contact with the frame or grip) and the touch index improves eyes-off alignment. Also, in either the right- or the left-handed method, the third and fourth fingers are extended out and away from the speed loader during the reloading process. Keep them out of the way.

Aligning the Speed Loader with the Cylinder. There are two methods of aligning the speed loader with the cylinder. The straight method inserts the tips of all the bullets directly into the holes of the cylinder (speed loader and cylinder aligned straight on), "jiggling" the speed loader slightly to aid the bullet tips and case rims as they start into the cylinder holes. The cartridges are then inserted all the way and released. The angled method brings the speed loader in at an angle to the cylinder and starts the two outer bullet tips into the two outer holes of the cylinder. As soon as these two bullet tips are placed into the holes (at a slight angle), the speed loader is then aligned straight on with the cylinder, with the remaining bullet tips going into their corresponding holes. The cartridges are then inserted all the way and released.

Either of the methods will work well. Both methods require some degree of "jiggling" when aligning and inserting the bullet tips in the cylinder holes. The straight method pushes the speed loader straight on to the cylinder, "jiggling" the speed loader (using a slight back-and-forth motion) to start the bullet tips into the holes. The angled method brings the speed loader in at an angle, placing the two outer bullet tips into two outer holes of the cylinder to align the bullets and holes initially, then instantly rotating the speed loader straight on with the cylinder, with the remaining bullet tips going right into their holes. For the angled method, the touch index can be improved by placing the tip of the second finger between two cartridges. When initially aligning the two bullet tips, they are placed into the two cylinder holes that are farthest away from the revolver. The tip of the second finger touches the cylinder wall at this point to help alignment. Both methods are greatly improved by using the touch index.

Whichever method you use is trained-in as an eyes-off procedure to make them as automatic as they can possibly be. One point on eyes-off reloading: When initially aligning the bullet tips in the cylinder holes, a slight glance may be required. If everything is going fine and you feel the bullet tips go into the cylinder holes, no glance is needed. But if you feel that the alignment is not going right (in all probability due to stress), an instant glance can straighten out the problem quickly, saving precious seconds. Using a quick glance to verify the alignment usually takes a second or less. As soon as the bullet tips enter the cylinder holes you look back up, the remainder of the reload being done by feel. The only time you glance at the reloading process, if at all, is during the initial alignment of the bullet tips in the cylinder holes (unless a malfunction occurs).

Again, as with any dual techniques, you must pick one and use it exclusively, no switching back and forth. You must pick one style of speed loader and one method of using it.

Check for Worn or Damaged Speed Loaders.   Through excessive use and/ or being damaged, speed loaders can become defective and not hold the cartridges securely. This is simple to test for merely by loading a speed loader and shaking it back and forth. Obviously, no cartridges should become loose or fall out. If a problem is found, replace the speed loader.

Speed strips.   (Par time for reloading, 10 seconds.) The speed strip, by Bianchi International, is a straight piece of hard rubber holding six cartridges in a straight line. The cartridges are held in place by rubber lips gripping the rims of the cartridges. To release a cartridge, simply turn it sideways to the speed strip, which will pull the rim out of the rubber lips holding it. A small rubber tab is attached to one end of the speed strip, to facilitate removing it from a carrying pouch. Thus positioned, all the cartridges are aligned next to each other in a straight line, one right after the other.

Next in order of speed from a speed loader, the speed strip improves the reloading process over loose rounds by having all the cartridges already positioned to reload. When using the speed strip you can reload two cartridges at a time. Two cartridges are placed halfway into two cylinder holes and the speed strip is turned sideways, releasing the two cartridges to fall completely into the holes. Rotate the cylinder to optimally position the next two holes and repeat the process. When this process is done three times, the revolver is reloaded and the speed strip is discarded.

The speed strip is usually carried in a dump pouch (a pouch that holds loose cartridges and when unsnapped, dumps the loose rounds into the hand), with the rubber tab on top (folded into the pouch with the leather cover snapped over it). When time to remove the speed strip, the pouch is unsnapped, the rubber tab pops up and is grasped by the fingers, and then the speed strip is pulled from the pouch. The cartridges are reloaded two at a time until the revolver is reloaded.

The speed strip is also easily carried in the pocket. Instead of the bulge of loose cartridges rattling around in the pocket, a straight line of cartridges lays flat and makes no noise by hitting together.

When partial reloading is required and your Sam Browne belt does not have loops, the speed strip is the next best alternative. Cartridges can be loaded into the cylinder holes one or two at a time, easily reloading the one, two, or three fired cases which have been removed from the cylinder during partial reloading.

Loose rounds. (Par time for all six, 10 to 12 seconds.) Loose rounds (not held in any device) can either be carried in cartridge loops or dump pouches on the belt. Most Sam Browne gun belts have 12 cartridge loops sewn onto them. These hold the cartridges one right after the other in a straight line. Dump pouches (either single or double) are separate from the belt and slide onto it, being positioned most effectively for the reload. For these two methods of carrying extra ammunition, there are two different ways of handling the loose cartridges, as discussed next.

Cartridge loops. (Par time for all six, 10 seconds.) When extra rounds are reloaded from cartridge loops, they are removed two at a time and placed into adjoining cylinder holes. The beauty of this method is that only two cartridges have to be handled at one time, which greatly reduces fumbling and dropped cartridges. The hand only has to manipulate two cartridges into position. This method works extremely well.

Reloading from the Cartridge Loops. When reloading from the cartridge loops, the rounds are taken two at a time. The rounds in the cartridge loops will invariably be pushed all the way into the loops until their rims are resting on the top of the loops. When time to remove the two cartridges, the index, second, and third fingers go to the bullet tips and push them up as far as they will go in the loops. The fingers then switch from the bullet tips to the case rims (primer end of the cartridge), grasping and pulling free two cartridges, which are held by the three fingers and the thumb. At the cylinder, insert the two cartridges together instead of one at a time.

[*Note:* When pulling two cartridges out, if fumbling begins to occur (some binding of the cartridges in the loops, clothing gets in the way, the cartridges are not pushed up enough), stop trying to remove two cartridges at once. Quickly remove the first cartridge and then the second one. The three fingers and thumb will position the cartridges to be together.]

At the cylinder, insert the two cartridges together instead of one at a time. As soon as they drop into the cylinder holes, the strong hand returns for two more cartridges. The support hand, holding the opened cylinder, rotates it slightly to optimally position the next two empty holes. The strong hand brings two more cartridges to reload them simultaneously. As the bullet tips are initially started into the holes, a quick glance may be needed to verify the alignment.

Dump pouch.   (Par time for all six, 12 seconds.) When extra cartridges are taken from a dump pouch, they all fall into the hand at once and the hand moves to the revolver to reload. The problem with this method is that the hand has to handle all six cartridges at once, while trying to manipulate them one after the other into the cylinder holes. This greatly increases fumbling and dropped cartridges. If any cartridges are dropped, do not try to pick them up. It is better to have a partially loaded cylinder than to increase the time needed to reload by trying to pick up, clean up, and insert dropped cartridges. Reload the revolver first and become ready if the situation should start instantly. If the opportunity presents itself, retrieve the dropped cartridges only after you have reloaded (even partially) and are ready if the action starts.

Reloading from the Dump Pouch.   When reloading from the dump pouch, all the cartridges are dumped into the hand at once. The trick is to juggle the cartridges in the hand while manipulating them into position one after the other into the cylinder holes. The thumb, index, and second fingers are used to accomplish the task.

As soon as the pouch dumps all the cartridges, the thumb and two fingers go to work. The hand is held in a cupped position with the cartridges resting in the cup. The thumb and index finger will pick one cartridge at a time out of the cup, manipulating it so that the bullet tip points straight forward (using the second finger as needed) and inserting it into the cylinder hole. About half of the time, the thumb and index fingers will need no help in picking up and pointing the cartridge straight forward. The other half of the time, the second finger will be used to flip the cartridge 180 degrees (being held at the rim by the thumb and index finger) to point forward. These three must be used to manipulate the cartridges one at a time into a straight-on, bullet-tip-first position to be inserted into the cylinder hole. At times, the hand will have to be "juggled" slightly to move the cartridges forward in the hand to help the thumb and index finger pick them up.

Only through practice can this manipulation be perfected. Again, as the bullet tips enter the cylinder holes, a quick glance may be needed to verify the alignment. In reality, almost all can be inserted without having to verify the alignment by a quick glance. Usually, the last one or two empty holes require a quick glance to find them. The cylinder should be rotated to present the empty holes in their optimum position, away from the side of the revolver and thus easier to reach.

Realistic ammunition carrying methods. As have been shown, there are three methods of carrying extra ammunition, with their associated methods of loading it into the revolver. The question arises: Which method or methods are realistic, and why? The answer has several parts and is always part of your tactical considerations.

First, you must be able to perform both types of tactical reloading: complete and partial. Both can be done with either the speed strip or loose rounds, but both cannot be done just with speed loaders. With only speed loaders, a partial reload cannot be accomplished. This dictates that if carrying speed loaders, you must also carry a speed strip or loose rounds. You must have the ability to reload partially if the situation arises.

Second, you should be able to perform a complete reload as fast as possible. This dictates the carrying of speed loaders as the fastest method of completely reloading the revolver. A situation may arise where speed of reloading can mean survival. Too many dead or wounded officers have been caught trying to reload their revolvers. Many other officers have survived by the sheer luck of the situation, where they could easily have died due to lack of reloading speed. Speed loaders must be used to give you the ability to reload quickly during a situation. This means not only reloading while you are stationary, but being able to reload on the move, if forced to, while moving instantly to a covered position from which to respond. Speed loaders give you increased ability to perform a reload on the move.

Third (a combination of the first and second), you must carry speed loaders and either a speed strip or loose rounds, to respond quickly/effectively to any tactical reloading situation that may occur. To cover all the bases and all the reloading possibilities that could occur, two methods of carrying and reloading extra ammo for the revolver must be used, one of which is the speed loader. The best way for uniformed officers to carry extra ammo is in the cartridge loops on their Sam Browne belt, with the addition of a double speed loader pouch. As such, officers have 24 extra rounds equally divided between the tactical reloading situations that can occur.

A note on locking the cylinder and cylinder rotation. When locking the cylinder closed, the hand closing it will invariably turn the cylinder that last little bit so that the cylinder stop (on the bottom of the frame) locks up into one of its recesses in the cylinder wall. This is not necessary for the revolver to function properly (the cylinder stop does not have to lock the cylinder in place when you close it), as the next pull of the trigger will rotate and lock the cylinder in place. The hand (which rotates the cylinder each time the trigger is pulled or hammer cocked) will rotate the next cylinder hole into alignment with the firing pin and barrel, even if the cylinder stop is not initially locked in place. As a rule, though, the cylinder is eased closed (never swung closed as sometimes occurs on TV) and the cylinder slightly rotated until the lock is felt.

Another question often asked is: Which way does the cylinder rotate? There are all sorts of ways of remembering which way a Smith & Wesson, Colt, Ruger, and so on, rotates. Which way a cylinder rotates is answered very simply by looking at the recesses on the rear part of the cylinder, which the cylinder stop fits into. These recesses appear as arrowheads on the cylinder. Now look at the cylinder, and whichever way the arrowheads are pointing is the way the cylinder turns: a very simple way of instantly telling which way any cylinder rotates. This information can be important with a partially loaded cylinder, as knowing which way the cylinder rotates will tell you where to place the first round so that it aligns with the firing pin and barrel on the next pull of the trigger.

TACTICAL RELOADING TECHNIQUES

Tactical reloading techniques are covered for the three service handguns, giving the complete and partial reloading technique for each—only two reloading techniques for each handgun. The two techniques for each service handgun will be shown for both right- and left-handed officers. All too often, left-handed officers are taught to use reloading techniques that are for right-handed shooters, which reduces a left-handed officer's performance level. Left-handed officers must use left-handed reloading techniques.

When learning these reloading techniques, you need only concentrate on the two reloading techniques for your particular type of service handgun and whatever handed you are. Only instructors or students of total pistolcraft need understand all of these. Also, for continuity, all reloading techniques are shown returning to the locked-out two-handed firing stance. In reality, the reloading techniques can start from any position and return to any position.

Remember, all reloading is tactical in nature and used in conjunction with proper tactics at all times. Complete and partial reloading techniques will completely cover the reloading procedures needed during an encounter.

The Double-Action Revolver

Completely reloading.   (Par time, 6 to 12 seconds, depending on how the ammo is carried and reloaded.) Usually, if the revolver has been run dry in the middle of the encounter, or during a slight lull in the action, the officer completely reloads the revolver as fast as possible to get it back in the action.

Right-handed officers follow these steps:

The time has come to completely reload the revolver.

1. As the revolver is started down, out of the firing stance, the trigger finger is out of the trigger guard (throughout all reloading). The right-hand thumb is placed on the cylinder release (if necessary, the master grip is eased and slightly shifted for better thumb contact on the cylinder release), as the left hand slides up to grasp the cylinder lightly (thumb on the left side and index and second fingers on the right side).

2. As the revolver is brought down further, the right-hand thumb pushes the cylinder release and the index and second fingers push the cylinder out to the left, both fingers following it through the frame. The two fingers (placed through the frame) and the thumb now securely hold the opened cylinder, as the right hand leaves the revolver (becoming positioned to strike the ejector rod).

3. The revolver is tilted muzzle up as the large muscle area on the side of the right hand sharply strikes the ejector rod, forcefully ejecting the empty cases from the cylinder. Note that the muzzle is slightly angled rearward as the ejector rod is struck, but is still not pointing at the body.

4. The right hand now goes for the fresh ammo as the revolver is turned muzzle down in preparation to be reloaded.

5. The fresh ammo is inserted into the cylinder holes. A speed loader should be used when completely reloading the revolver, as it is the fastest means of replenishing the revolver.

6. Just as soon as the cartridges have left the speed loader, the right hand releases it and moves to regrip the revolver (note the trigger finger held straight along the frame) as the left hand closes the cylinder.

7. The two-handed grip is resumed.

Left-handed officers follow these steps:

The time has come to completely reload the revolver.

1. As the revolver is started down, out of the firing stance, the trigger finger is out of the trigger guard (throughout all reloading). The left hand shifts back on the grip (the three fingers still holding onto the front of the grip) with the trigger finger resting on the cylinder release, as the right hand positions itself (by merely raising up from its support position) to open and catch the cylinder (the right-hand thumb is touching the right side of the cylinder to push it open and the index and second fingers are on the other side to catch it).

2. As the trigger finger pushes on the cylinder release, the right-hand thumb pushes the cylinder out to the left and goes through the frame following the

12.7.

12.8.

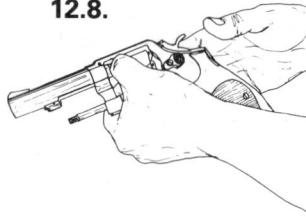

12.9.

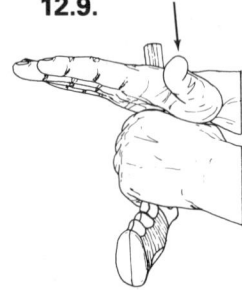

12.10.

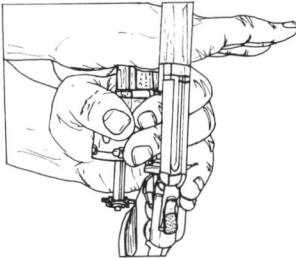

12.11.

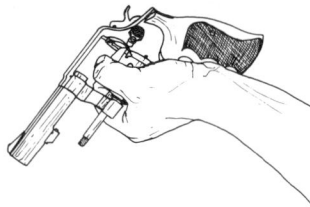

12.12.

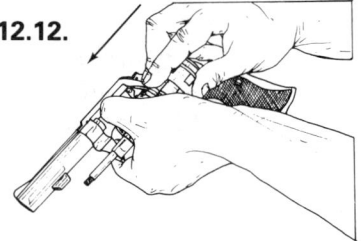

12.13.

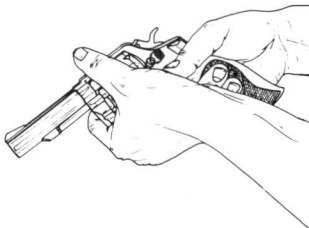

12.14.

Right-Handed Technique

Figure 12.7   Step 1.   **Figure 12.8**   Step 2.
Figure 12.9   Step 3.   **Figure 12.10**   Inside view of step 3.
Figure 12.11   Step 4.   **Figure 12.12**   Step 5.
Figure 12.13   Step 6.   **Figure 12.14**   Step 7.
(Smith & Wesson Model 10 shown.)

cylinder (the underside of the top strap may rest on top of the thumb). The right-hand thumb, index, and second fingers instantly close on the cylinder to control it as the left hand leaves the revolver (becoming positioned to strike the ejector rod).

3. The revolver is tilted up as the large muscle area below the thumb of the left hand sharply strikes the ejector rod, ejecting the empty cases. Note that the muzzle is angled rearward as the ejector rod is struck, but is still not pointing at the body.

4. The left hand now goes for the fresh ammo as the revolver is turned muzzle-down to receive it.

5. The fresh ammo is inserted into the cylinder holes.

6. Just as soon as the cartridges have left the speed loader, the left hand releases the loader and moves to regrip the revolver (note the trigger finger held straight), as the right-hand fingers close the cylinder.

7. The two-handed grip is resumed.

12.15. 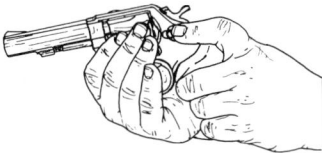 **12.16.** 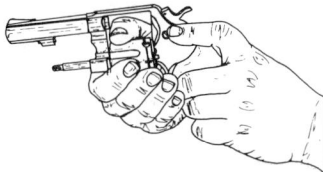 **12.17.**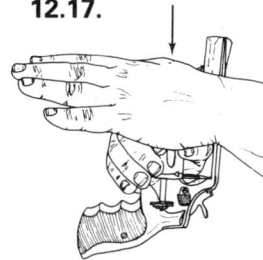

12.18. 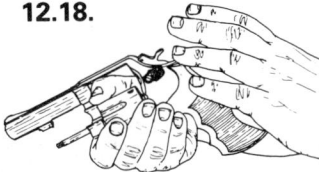 **12.19.**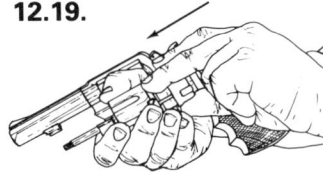

12.20.

12.21.

Left-Handed Technique

Figure 12.15	Step 1.	**Figure 12.16**	Step 2.
Figure 12.17	Step 3.	**Figure 12.18**	Step 4.
Figure 12.19	Step 5.	**Figure 12.20**	Step 6.
Figure 12.21	Step 7.		

(Smith & Wesson Model 10 shown.)

Completely reloading the revolver has been shown in its expanded version, covering all aspects of the technique. In reality it consists of just four movements: (1) opening the cylinder (steps 1 and 2 performed as a set), (2) ejecting the empty cases (step 3), (3) reloading fresh ammo (steps 4 and 5 as a set), and (4) closing the cylinder and reassuming the two-handed grip (steps 6 and 7 as a set).

In each of the four movements, the actions indicated (in parentheses) are performed as one set. The entire technique flows from one movement to the next. With a little practice it is easily accomplished and begins to become a completely fluid reloading technique, with a commensurate increase in reloading speed.

When using the speed loader make sure that you use proper finger placement to facilitate aligning it with the cylinder. The speed loader is held by the thumb, index, and second fingers, with either the index or second finger (or both) touching the cases becoming the touch index to aid aligning. This was explained previously for both right- and left-handed officers.

A Note on Design Features That May Interfere with Ejection. Two design features that can interfere with ejection are short ejector rods and oversized grips. Many short-barreled revolvers are equipped with equally short ejector rods. Problems can occur if these are not struck forcefully enough to extract the empty cases completely. This problem can also occur with oversized (or improperly cut) grips that block the empty cases when they are trying to be ejected.

The real problem that can occur is an empty case being forced under the extractor star, with the star now resting on top of it. If this should occur, time will be needed to remove the empty case and the revolver will be inoperative until it is done. Doing it does not take long, but under the stress of a lethal encounter, the time will no doubt increase as your fumble factor goes up. With the cylinder open and the ejector rod held up so that the star is raised, the empty case must be picked out with the fingernails and angled outward to let its rim get out from under the star. Once clear, the revolver is quickly reloaded.

Partial reloading.   (Par time, 4 to 6 seconds, depending on how many rounds need to be loaded.) During a lull in the action, an officer may decide to replace the one, two, or three fired rounds without completely reloading the revolver. By opening the cylinder and pushing the ejector rod halfway up and then releasing it, the empty cases will remain standing (due to their being expanded when fired) as the unfired cartridges will fall back into the cylinder. As such, the empty cases are easily removed from the cylinder.

Right-handed officers follow these steps:
The time has come to partially reload the revolver.

1. As the revolver is started down, out of the firing stance, the trigger finger is out of the trigger guard (throughout all reloading). The right-hand thumb is placed on the cylinder release (if necessary, the master grip is eased and shifted slightly for better thumb contact with the cylinder release) as the left hand slides up to grasp the cylinder lightly (thumb on the left side and second and third fingers on the right side). The index finger is resting on the right side of the barrel and will be used to push up the ejector rod.

2. As the revolver is brought to waist level, with the muzzle pointing down, several things occur: The right-hand thumb pushed the cylinder release as the second and third fingers of the left hand push the cylinder out to the left (they do not follow it through but stay on the right side of the frame), the left-hand thumb hooks overtop the opened cylinder, locking it in place; the left-hand index finger places its tip or middle on the end of the ejector rod and pushes it up halfway, pushing all the cases halfway up in the cylinder. The revolver is still controlled by the right hand with a loose hold on the grip.

3. When the left-hand index finger releases the ejector rod, the empty cases remain standing while the live cartridges fall back into the cylinder holes. As this occurs, the left-hand index finger releases the ejector rod and locks down on top of the crane (the piece that attaches the cylinder to the frame) as the right hand releases the grip and begins extracting the empty cases left standing in the cylinder.

4. When all the empty cases are removed, the right hand picks up the extra, loose rounds and replenishes the one, two, or three fired rounds.

5. When the cylinder is again reloaded, the right hand reassumes its grip (note the straight trigger finger) and the left hand closes the cylinder.

6. The two-handed firing grip is reassumed.

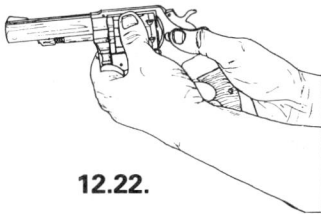

12.22.

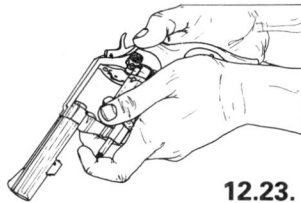

12.23.

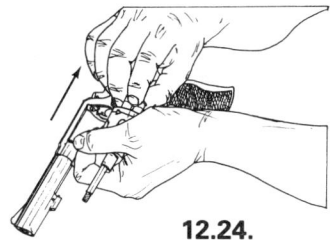

12.24.

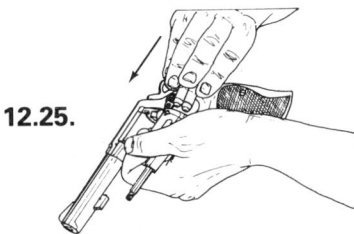

12.25.

12.26.

Figure 12.22 Step 1.   **Figure 12.23** Step 2.
Figure 12.24 Step 3.   **Figure 12.25** Step 4.
Figure 12.26 Step 5.
(Smith & Wesson Model 10 shown.)

Left-handed officers follow these steps:
The time has come to partially reload the revolver.

1. As the revolver is started down, out of the firing stance, the trigger finger is out of the trigger guard (throughout all reloading). The left hand shifts back on the grip (the three fingers still holding onto the front of the grip) with the trigger finger resting on the cylinder release as the right hand positions itself (merely by raising up from its support position) to open and catch the cylinder (the right-hand thumb is touching the right side of the cylinder to push it open and the second and third fingers are on the left side of the cylinder). The index

finger is resting on the left side of the barrel and will be used to push up on the ejector rod.

2. As the revolver is brought to waist level, with the muzzle pointing down, several things occur: The trigger finger pushes the cylinder release, as the right-hand thumb pushes the cylinder out to the left and follows it through, the second and third fingers and thumb locking the cylinder in place as the index finger places its tip or middle on the end of the ejector rod and pushes it up halfway, pushing all the cases halfway up in the cylinder. The revolver is still controlled by the left hand loosely holding the grip.

3. When the right-hand index finger releases the ejector rod, the empty cases remain standing while the live cartridges fall back into the cylinder holes. As this occurs, the right-hand index finger releases the ejector rod and locks down on the crane (the piece that attaches the cylinder to the frame) as the left hand releases the grip and begins extracting the empty cases left standing in the cylinder.

4. When all the empty cases are removed, the left hand picks up the extra, loose rounds and replenishes the one, two, or three fired rounds.

5. When the cylinder is again reloaded, the left hand reassumes its grip (note the straight trigger finger along the frame) and the right hand closes the cylinder.

6. The two-handed firing grip is reassumed.

12.27.
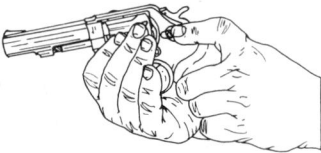

12.28.

12.29.
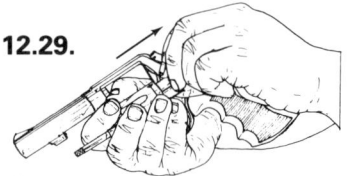

12.30.
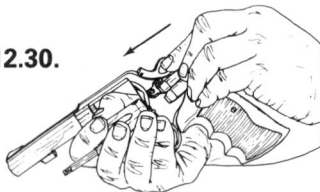

12.31.
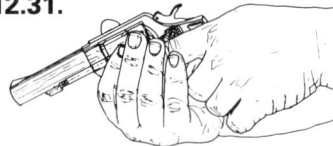

Figure 12.27   Step 1.   Figure 12.28   Step 2.
Figure 12.29   Step 3.   Figure 12.30   Step 4.
Figure 12.31   Step 5.
(Smith & Wesson Model 10 shown.)

Partially reloading the revolver has been shown in its expanded version, covering all aspects of the technique. In reality it consists of just four movements: (1) opening the cylinder and raising the cases (steps 1 and 2 performed as a set), (2) removing the empty cases left standing (step 3), (3) reloading fresh loose rounds (step 4), and (4) closing the cylinder and resuming the two-handed grip (steps 5 and 6 as a set).

In each of the four movements, the actions indicated (in parentheses) are performed as one set. The whole technique flows from one movement to the next. With a little practice it is easily accomplished and begins to become a completely fluid reloading technique, with a commensurate increase in reloading speed.

The Double-Action and Single-Action Automatics

Completely reloading the D-A or S-A auto. (Par time for reloading, 3 seconds.) Usually, if the auto has been run dry in the middle of the encounter or during a slight lull in the action, the officer completely reloads the auto as fast as possible to get it back in the action.

Right-handed officers follow these steps:
The time has come to completely reload the auto. Keep your trigger finger out of the trigger guard (throughout all reloading).

1. As the auto is started down out of the firing stance, take an instant glance at the top of the slide (to catch any problem) as the left hand releases its two-handed grip and goes for the fresh magazine. The downward motion of the auto stops as the elbow touches the side of the body (the auto is not brought as far down and into the body as the revolver), the auto is canted slightly in the hand so that the thumb can easily reach the magazine release, and the wrist slightly turns the auto to the right to aid magazine insertion and/or extraction).

2. The left hand grasps and removes the fresh magazine from the pouch and holds it in a ready position close to the auto. Remember, the magazine is gripped with the index finger held along the front of the magazine and extending slightly past the first round, creating the touch index.

3. As one motion, the thumb pushes the magazine release, the depleted (or empty) magazine falls free, and the fresh magazine is inserted into the magazine well and locked home. These actions occur one right after the other.
(For the remainder of the complete reloading process, step 4a is used if the auto still has a round chambered, or step 4b is used if the auto has been run dry with the slide locked back.)

4a. With a round still chambered—The master grip has already been fully assumed (the auto was canted in the hand), the left hand assumes a two-handed grip, and the auto is locked out in a two-handed firing stance.

4b. Run dry with the slide locked back—The right-hand thumb depresses the slide release (causing the slide to go forward, chambering the first round from the magazine), the master grip is fully assumed instantly (the auto was still slightly canted to help the thumb easily reach the slide release), the left hand assumes a two-handed grip, and the auto is locked out in a two-handed firing stance.

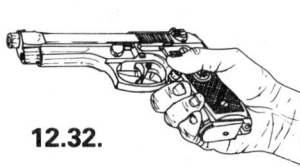

12.32.

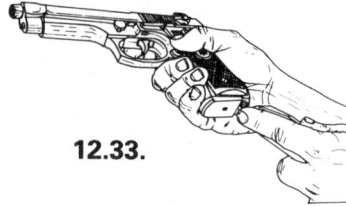

12.33.

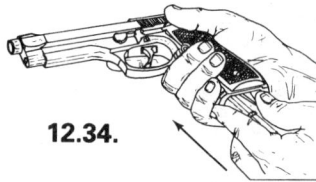

12.34.

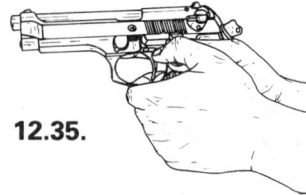

12.35.

Figure 12.32 Step 1.   Figure 12.33 Step 2.
Figure 12.34 Step 3.   Figure 12.35 Step 4a.
(Beretta 92-F shown.)

Left-handed officers follow these steps:

The time has come to completely reload the auto. Keep your trigger finger out of the trigger guard (throughout all reloading).

1. As the auto is started down, out of the firing stance, take an instant glance at the top of the slide (to catch any problem) as the right hand releases its two-handed grip and goes for the fresh magazine. The downward motion of the auto stops as the elbow touches the side of the body (the auto is not brought as far down and into the body as the revolver), the left hand's grip is slightly eased so that the trigger finger can easily reach the magazine release, and the wrist turns the auto slightly to the left to aid magazine insertion and/or extraction.

2. The right hand grasps and removes the fresh magazine from the pouch and holds it in a ready position close to the auto. Remember, the magazine is gripped with the index finger held along the front of the magazine and extending slightly past the first round, creating a touch index.

3. As one motion, the trigger finger pushes the magazine release, the depleted (or empty) magazine falls free, and the fresh magazine is inserted into the magazine well and locked home. These actions occur one right after the other. (For the remainder of the complete reloading process, step 4a is used if the auto still has a round in the chamber, or step 4b is used if the auto has been run dry with the slide locked back.)

4a. With a round still chambered—The master grip is already fully assumed (as the grip was slightly eased), the right hand assumed a two-handed grip, and the auto is locked-out in a two-handed firing stance.

4b. Run dry with the slide locked back—The trigger finger depresses the slide release (causing the slide to go forward chambering the first round from the magazine), the master grip is fully assumed instantly (the grip was eased slightly to help the trigger finger reach the slide release), the right hand assumes a two-handed grip, and the auto is locked out in a two-handed firing stance.

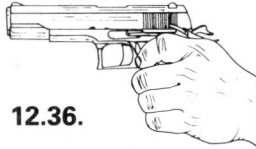

12.36.

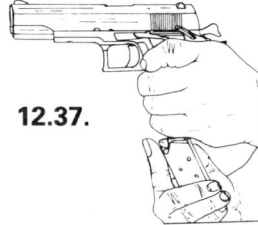

12.37.

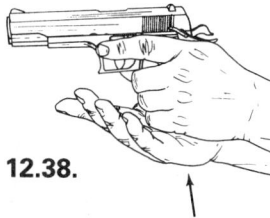

12.38.

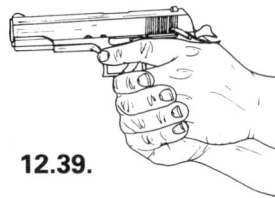

12.39.

Figure 12.36 Step 1.   **Figure 12.37** Step 2.
Figure 12.38 Step 3.   **Figure 12.39** Step 4a.
(Colt .45 auto shown.)

Completely reloading the auto has been shown in its expanded version, covering all aspects of the technique. In reality it consists of just three movements: (1) picking up the fresh magazine and holding it in a ready position next to the auto (steps 1 and 2 performed as a set), (2) the magazine exchange (step 3), and (3) reassuming the two-handed grip (step 4).

In each of the three movements, the actions indicated (in parentheses) are performed as one set. The whole technique flows from one movement to the next. With a little practice it becomes a fluid reloading technique and is very fast.

Glancing at the Top of the Slide.   As the auto was started down to reload completely, the top of the slide was given an instant glance. This is done to catch a run dry or malfunctioning auto. If the auto is run dry, the slide will almost always be locked back. If a malfunction, the slide will not be all the way forward (in battery). A quick glance will catch these. As the auto is started down, it is directly in the line of sight and the glance is easily done. If no problem is seen, fine. But if a problem is noted, you will save precious seconds and/or fumbling as you have spotted the problem. This will generally work in partial-light conditions but will not work in dark conditions.

An Alternative Method of Releasing the Locked-Open Slide.   With the slide locked back on a run dry auto and a fresh magazine locked in, there is an alternative method of releasing the slide. This is done by the support hand grasping and pulling the slide to the rear—which will disengage the slide release—and then releasing it fully. The support hand grasps the slide by wrapping overtop it, with the tips of the fingers and base of the thumb holding either side. Once grasped, pull it slightly to the rear and fully release it. When releasing, you must let it fly forward, by fully releasing it. If not, it may malfunction by not completely chambering the first round from the magazine. Even though this method does employ larger and grosser movements, there is a greater chance that a problem can occur if not done correctly.

The Auto was Unknowingly Designed for Left-Handed Shooters.   Being a left-handed automatic shooter is easy, as few understand that the automatic was designed for the left-handed shooter (although not the intention when it was designed). The classic Browning automatic design, which has influenced virtually all succeeding automatic designs, places all the reloading controls—the magazine release and slide release—on the left side of the auto. This was done so that predominately right-handed shooters would not press them inadvertently. For a right-handed officer to use the reloading controls effectively, he or she has to cant the auto in the right hand to reach them. For a left-handed officer, the reloading controls are easily reached with a very slight easing of the grip; the trigger finger is used to depress both the magazine release and the slide release. All automatic reloading functions for right- and left-handed officers are the same, except which finger depresses the reloading controls.

Magazine Info.   The "QAQ" (*Q*uickly, *A*ccurately, *Q*uickly) drill is a varying speed drill to train in the different speeds for the three movements involved in exchanging magazines. The QAQ drill: Quickly pick up and position the fresh magazine next to the auto, accurately align and insert the magazine's top into the magazine well, and quickly lock it home by pressing it up with the palm. You must go fast by quickly picking up and positioning the magazine, then slow down a little to insert the top accurately, and then go fast by quickly locking it home. Three speeds—fast, medium, fast—are used for the three movements of the magazine.

Inserting the Magazine.   When initially inserting the magazine top, place the magazine in the magazine well back to back—the back of the magazine against the back of the magazine well. The magazine is held at a slight rear angle to the well during this initial alignment. As soon as the back-to-back meeting occurs, the butt of the magazine is rocked forward—so that it is straight up and down—and locked home.

Some officers prefer to push the magazine straight in, as one move. If you practice enough, this certainly works and is very fast, especially if the auto has a beveled-out magazine well opening. Double-stack magazines (9-mm high-capacity autos) work especially well, as their tops are tapered, which helps initial insertion. Whereas single-stack magazines (.45 ACP and some 9-mm autos) have to be aligned more precisely when inserted initially. During a stress-filled lethal encounter aligning and pushing the magazine in as one move may not function as well.

If the Magazine Does Not Fall Free. A service handgun's magazine should fall free of its own weight, but during the course of events the magazine may not fully fall free. This can occur if the magazine's sides become damaged or if dirty. If this occurs, the remedy is simple; just use the support hand's little finger to pull it free. Before the magazine release was pushed, the support hand is positioned next to the auto with a fresh magazine. When the release is pushed and the magazine does not fall free, the strong hand lays the auto on its side (magazine's floorplate pointing directly at the support hand) and the support hand's little finger and area where it attaches to the hand lay over the front part of the magazine's floorplate (the front lip) and pulls it free. Once the well is clear, the fresh magazine is locked home. If you notice this problem, take care of it now.

Make two tests of the magazine's ability to fall free. First, place an empty magazine into the auto and see if it will fall free. If it falls free easily, continue; if it does not, find out what the problem is. Second, place a partially full magazine (half of its capacity) into the auto and test it. If that also works, fine. Then test all your magazines.

[*Note:* The H&K P-7's slide release mechanism is part of the squeeze-cocking mechanism. If the slide is locked open (having been run dry), release the squeeze-cocker and exchange magazines. Once that is done, reapply your grip to press in the squeeze-cocker and the slide will go forward automatically, chambering the first round from the magazine.]

Partially reloading. (Par time for reloading, 4 seconds.) During a lull in the action, an officer may decide to replace the partially depleted magazine with a full one. When the partially depleted magazine is removed from the auto, it is not discarded but retained, thus retaining any extra rounds it holds, which could come in handy later if the encounter continues. The difference between complete and partial reloading is that the partially depleted magazine is caught by the hand and saved.

Right-handed officers follow these steps:
The time has come to partially reload the auto. Keep your trigger finger out of the trigger guard (throughout all reloading).

1. As the auto is started down, out of the firing stance, take an instant glance at the top of the slide (to catch any problems) as the left hand releases its two-handed grip and goes for the fresh magazine. The downward motion of the auto stops as the elbow touches the side of the body, the auto is canted slightly in the hand so that the thumb can easily reach the magazine release, and the wrist turns the auto slightly to the right to aid magazine insertion and/or extraction.

2. The left hand grasps and removes the fresh magazine from the pouch and holds it in a ready position close to the auto. When partially reloading, the

magazine is gripped differently, to enable the left hand to receive and hold the depleted magazine as it comes from the auto. The thumb and index finger now wrap around the lower part of the magazine as it is pulled from the pouch. The other three fingers are held away from the magazine.

3. The exchange of magazines now takes place. The left hand, with the last three fingers held opened and slightly cupped, is held directly below the magazine well. The magazine release is depressed, releasing the depleted magazine, which is caught, held, and pulled the remaining way from the auto (the floor-plate of the magazine usually rests on the little finger, with the other two fingers wrapping around the magazine). Once pulled free, the left hand turns slightly and the fresh magazine is inserted and locked home (by the thumb and index finger releasing it and the palm pushing it home).

4. The left hand places the depleted magazine in a pocket to secure it. A partially depleted magazine is never replaced in the magazine pouch; it is secured in a pocket. You do not want to mistake it for a fully charged magazine later in the encounter, instantly reloading from the pouch and finding out that the magazine contains only several rounds.

5. The left hand reassumes a two-handed grip as the auto is locked out in a two-handed firing stance.

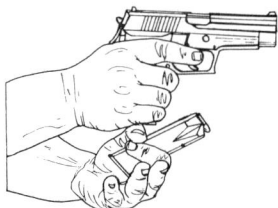  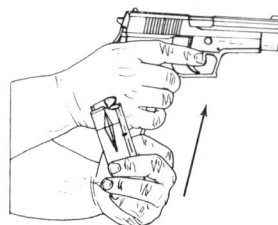

12.40.   **12.41.**   **12.42.**

Figure 12.40   Step 2.
Figure 12.41   Step 3 (first part).
Figure 12.42   Step 3 (second part).
Only the central two steps are shown, which visually depicts the method for gripping
and holding the magazines.
(Sig P-226 shown.)

Left-handed officers follow these steps:
The time has come to partially reload the auto. Keep your trigger finger out of the trigger guard (throughout all reloading).

1. As the auto is started down out of the firing stance, take an instant glance at the top of the slide (to catch any problem) as the right hand releases its two-handed grip and goes for the fresh magazine. The downward motion of the auto stops as the elbow touches the side of the body, the grip is eased so that

the trigger finger can easily reach the magazine release, and the wrist turns the auto slightly to the left to aid magazine insertion and/or extraction.

2. The right hand grasps and removes the fresh magazine from the pouch and holds it in a ready position close to the auto. When partially reloading, the magazine is gripped differently, to enable the right hand to receive and hold the depleted magazine as it comes from the auto. The thumb and index finger now wrap around the lower part of the magazine as it is pulled from the pouch. The other three fingers are held away from the magazine.

3. The exchange of magazines now takes place. The right hand, with the last three fingers held opened and slightly cupped, is held directly below the magazine well. The magazine release is depressed, releasing the depleted magazine, which is caught, held, and pulled the remaining way from the auto (the floorplate of the magazine usually rests on the little finger, with the other two wrapping around the magazine). Once pulled free, the right hand turns slightly and the fresh magazine is inserted and locked home (by the thumb and index finger releasing it and the palm pushing it home).

4. The right hand places the depleted magazine in a pocket to secure it. A partially depleted magazine is never replaced in the magazine pouch; it is secured in a pocket. You do not want to mistake it for a fully charged magazine later in the encounter, instantly reloading from the pouch and finding out that the magazine contains only several rounds.

5. The right hand reassumes a two-handed grip as the auto is locked out in a two-handed firing stance.

  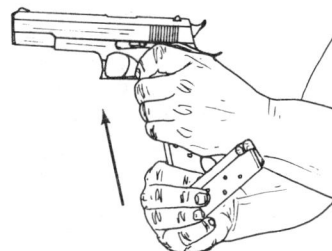

12.43.   **12.44.**   **12.45.**

Figure 12.43 Step 2.
Figure 12.44 Step 3 (first part).
Figure 12.45 Step 3 (second part).
Only the central two steps are shown, which visually depicts the method for gripping and holding the magazines.
(Colt .45 auto shown.)

Partially reloading the auto has been shown in its expanded version, covering all aspects of the technique. In reality it consists of just four movements: (1) picking up the fresh magazine and holding it in a ready position next to the auto (steps 1 and 2 performed as a set), (2) the magazine exchange (step 3), (3) securing the partially depleted magazine (step 4), and (4) reassuming the two-handed grip (step 5).

In each of the four movements, the actions indicated (in parentheses) are performed as one set. The whole technique flows from one movement to the next. With a little practice it becomes a fluid reloading technique.

A Safety Note. Whenever any S-A auto is partially reloaded, push the safety "on" to keep the auto cocked and locked. Also, the H&K P-7's squeeze-cocking mechanism is allowed to come fully forward, by the master grip being eased, during any reloading.

The butt magazine release.   Magazine releases are located at one of two places on autos: at the rear of the trigger guard and at the bottom of the magazine well. The release at the rear of the trigger guard frees the support hand to go instantly for the fresh magazine, as the strong hand can depress the button. The release at the bottom of the magazine well, requires the support hand—holding the fresh magazine—to depress the release lever and pull the magazine from the auto (some will fall free). All previous reloading techniques have been described for the release at the rear of the trigger guard, as this constitutes the vast majority of service autos in use today. The following method is used for butt magazine releases.

Using the butt magazine release:

1. The support hand first picks up a fresh magazine and becomes positioned to extract the depleted magazine in the auto. The support hand's grasp on the fresh magazine changes, with the magazine being held between the index and second (middle) fingers, the floorplate on the palm.
2. The support hand now prepares to extract the magazine. The thumb is resting on the floorplate and pressed against the magazine release lever at the rear of the magazine well. The index finger is bent to form a hook that is hooked over the front lip of the magazine's floorplate.
3. As one push-pull movement, push the magazine release lever to the rear with the thumb as you pull the magazine out of the auto by the index finger pulling down on the magazine's front lip.
4. Depending on whether you are reloading completely or partially, either drop the magazine or secure it between the second (middle) and third fingers (pull it halfway out and then grasp it between the fingers). Then insert the fresh magazine and lock it home. (*Note:* When inserting the magazine, stick it into the magazine well at an angle to the front, then rock it back—depressing the magazine release lever as the magazine is straightened up into the well—and lock it home.)

(*Note:* On the older H&K P-7's, the magazine release lever, at the rear of the magazine well, is pushed into the rear of the gun's butt—opposite from other butt-release levers. Once the lever is pushed in, the magazine will fall freely from the auto. On the new P-7's, the magazine release is to the rear of the trigger guard.)

Positioning of the auto during reloading.   There are two points of view with reference to the positioning of the auto when reloading. One point of view is that the auto is brought about halfway toward the body, where the reloading can proceed with the greatest control. The other point of view is that the auto is held in position (the locked-out two-handed firing stance) when reloading to be ready to fire instantly when reloading is completed. Those who adhere to the held-in-position point of view maintain that it will allow a quicker alignment on target when reloading is completed—thus quicker firing. They argue that speed is the ultimate consideration toward your survival, especially when completely reloading the auto during the action.

There is no doubt that speed is critical at this time, but three other considerations must also be involved: your reloading ability, your unobstructed view of the encounter zone, and moving to cover. In reality, the difference in firing speed (if just standing there and reloading), when held in position or brought down slightly to reload, is so small that it can barely be measured; often it is the same. But you must also consider the tactical moves necessary.

First is your trained-in and improved ability to reload. When the auto is held in position, it takes more practice and finer attunement, which may disappear completely under the stress of the encounter. Bringing the auto slightly down toward the body (until the elbow touches the side) creates the touch index so important to eyes-off reloading. You must have one way of reloading that will hold up in all situations, being a trained-in reflexive set. Also, you must be able to reload on the move.

Second is your unobstructed view of the encounter zone during the brief reloading pause. By lowering the auto just out of your line of sight, you have "unobstructed" your view of the encounter zone. With the greater viewing ability, you may catch something important which you might otherwise have missed. This will help you expand your vision for the brief reloading pause and help reduce the tunnel vision that will occur.

Third is your need to move to cover instantly. Whenever reloading you should be behind cover or concealment if at all possible. If not initially behind cover, you move to it instantly. With the handgun brought down toward the body, you can move and reload at the same time. With an auto there is a good chance that you will be completely reloaded as you go behind cover. Even if not completely finished before you are behind cover, at least the reloading process has been started and the auto is closer to being reloaded.

As you can see, reloading also has a number of tactical considerations thrown into the mix. Whenever reloading, the auto is brought down toward the body and done the same way everytime.

MALFUNCTIONS

As we in law enforcement know: Anything that can happen will happen. During a lethal encounter anything can occur. Malfunctions, although rare, can occur at the worst time and officers must be trained to handle them quickly and get back in the action. In defensive handgun use, we train and prepare to handle the worst situational breakdowns that can occur, which invariably will come at the worst time. A malfunction occurs as one of these breakdowns and must be cleared instantly to continue the encounter.

During a lethal encounter a malfunction occurs when your handgun suddenly fails to fire as you pull the trigger—whether first shot, last shot, or any time in between. You must instantly engage in the immediate action drill to clear the malfunction and get back in the action. Making the handgun function again is critical to your survival; you must perform the drills reflexively, with no time lost trying to figure out what is wrong. Knowing exactly why the handgun is malfunctioning is not important; getting it functioning is.

The immediate action drill is a reflexive set of trained-in skills that occur automatically to get the handgun functioning again. The two drills—one for the revolver and the other for both autos—contain four options to clear the malfunction and get back in the action. We call these the immediate action "ABCD" drills, as there are four options that are used one right after the other. The drill you will use must be a trained-in reflexive set of skills, done one right after the other involving no decision making, done by feel and employing only gross movements. (*Note:* Option B is not an option if you do not carry a backup gun.)

You train for the breakdowns that can occur, but with a properly cared for service handgun and proper ammunition, malfunctions will be a rare occurrence. Rare or not, you must be prepared to handle a malfunction instantly.

Double-Action Revolver

IMMEDIATE ACTION ABCD DRILL FOR THE D-A REVOLVER

A. Always keep the revolver in the firing position, fully release the trigger, and pull it again. If the revolver does not fire, go to either B or C.

B. The backup gun option is available to you if you carry one. Instantly stick the service handgun back in the holster and draw your second gun. If no second gun, go from A to C.

C. Completely reload as you move instantly to cover. Completely reload the revolver from a covered position; dump everything, reload fresh cartridges, and attempt to fire. If the revolver does not fire, go to D.

D. Disengagement may now be your best survival option if the service handgun is out of commission and you do not have a backup gun.

Option A. When the trigger is pulled the revolver may not fire due to an officer error, defective primer or light primer strike, or being out of ammo (the most common reason for a failure to fire). After firing a round, officer error can occur if the trigger is not allowed to go forward fully before the trigger is again pulled, which may rotate the cylinder but not fire the revolver although the trigger was pulled. Also, a defective primer may not have worked or the revolver is out of ammo. In any case the immediate action is to release the trigger fully and then pull it again. If the cylinder is frozen—due to everything from high primers to bullets moving forward in the cylinder—pulling the trigger will do no good until the problem is corrected, during option C.

Option B. This is the best reasoning for carrying a backup gun and makes good sense, as even the best service handgun can malfunction at the worst possible time. A backup gun is just insurance against this occurrence. Make sure that you do not just throw down the service handgun, but quickly stick it back in the holster. You may be able to get it functioning if the encounter continues. (*Note:* This is the only exception to not placing an unloaded handgun back in the holster. It is done as the handgun can be holstered very quickly, while sticking it under the Sam Browne belt can easily become a fumble situation, and at times an unsafe situation. Place it in the holster quickly.)

Option C. At this point the revolver must be unloaded and then reloaded completely while moving to and taking up a covered position. This process begins immediately as you are moving to cover; do not wait until you are behind cover to start it. Immediately, both hands work to open the cylinder and eject the cartridges/ empty cases. This should be done instantly while moving to cover. If the cylinder is frozen, usually the only way to free it is with a blow by the right hand while the left hand holds the revolver on the leg and presses the cylinder release. Make the right hand into a fist and with the side of the hand, firmly strike the right side of the cylinder, which should free it. This procedure will have to be done behind cover. Once the cylinder is open and empty, reload fresh cartridges into it, close the cylinder, and attempt to fire. Unloading and reloading completely the revolver will usually take care of the problem.

Option D. If the revolver cannot be made to function, disengagement may be your best survival option. Move away from the threat(s) by moving between C&C positions and exit the encounter zone. You are exiting the encounter zone now, but you will be back with a functioning weapon and troops.

D-A and S-A Automatics

IMMEDIATE ACTION ABCD DRILL FOR THE D-A and S-A AUTOS

A. Always keep the auto in the firing position. With the support hand tap the floorplate of the magazine to make sure that it is locked in place. Then grasp the rear of the slide, pull it forcefully to the rear, and release it fully. The support hand reassumes the two-handed grip and you attempt to fire. This is commonly referred to as tap, rack, bang. If the auto does not fire, go to either B or C.

B. The backup gun option is available to you if you carry one. Instantly stick the service handgun back in the holster and draw your backup gun. If no backup gun, go from A to C.

C. Completely reload as you instantly move to cover. Completely reload the auto from a covered position. Lock the slide open and eject the magazine to dump everything. Work the slide back and forth several times, lock home a fresh magazine, forcefully pull the slide to the rear and release it fully and attempt to fire. If the auto does not fire, go to D.

D. Disengagement may now be your best survival option if the service handgun is out of commission and you do not have a backup gun.

Option A.   In all probability, if the round does not fire when the trigger is pulled the first time, no round has been chambered or it may possibly be a defective primer. By performing option A, tapping the magazine to make sure that it is locked in and racking the slide, these problems and a lot of others can be taken care of. The support hand is touching or almost touching the floorplate of the magazine in the two-handed grip. It instantly taps the magazine to make sure that is it locked in place. Now the support hand wraps overtop the rear of the slide (keeping back from the ejection port) and grabs it, forcefully pulling it to the rear and fully releasing it—chambering the next round from the magazine. A number of problems can be cleared this way.

Option B.   This is the best reasoning for carrying a backup gun and makes good sense, as even the best service handgun can malfunction at the worse possible time. A backup gun is just insurance against this occurrence. Make sure that you do not just throw down the service handgun, but quickly stick it back in the holster. You may be able to get it functioning again if the encounter continues. (*Note:* This is the only exception to not placing an unloaded handgun back in the holster. It is done as the handgun can be holstered very quickly, while sticking it under the Sam Browne belt can easily become a fumble situation, and at times an unsafe situation. Place it in the holster quickly.)

Option C.   At this point the automatic must be unloaded and then reloaded completely while moving to and taking up a covered position. This process begins immediately as you are moving to cover; do not wait until you are behind cover to start it. The support hand wraps overtop the slide (fingertips applying pressure on one side of the slide and the area below the thumb on the other) and forcefully pulls it to the rear as the slide release is pushed up, locking the slide open (this is done just in case the magazine has to be pulled out and the support hand is free to do it). The magazine is instantly released, which may have to be forcefully pulled from the auto. The slide is then worked back and forth to free up any problems, and then fully released. Instantly pick up a fresh magazine and lock it in place, pull the slide to the rear, fully release it to chamber the first round from the magazine, and attempt to fire again. (*Note:* When using an H&K P-7, make sure that you relax your master grip so that the squeeze-cocker mechanism returns to its fully out rest position while completely reloading the auto. This is done for safety.)

Option D.   If the automatic cannot be made to function, disengagement may be your best survival option. Move away from the threat(s) by moving between C&C

positions and exit the encounter zone. You are exiting the encounter zone now, but you will be back with a functioning weapon and troops.

Two automatic malfunction tricks.   For two particular types of malfunctions, two things can be done to help remedy the problem. These two malfunction tricks may be able to get you back in action quicker. The problem with any tricks is that you have to stop and find out what the problem is. With these two, it will take only a glance. These two malfunctions can be handled through the immediate action ABCD drill, but if spotted can be taken care of by using these tricks. All other malfunctions are handled through the drill.

Failure to Eject (Stovepipe).   An empty case is caught between the slide, breech face, and barrel. The support hand grips the slide as before, except that the hand is overtop the ejection port and the index finger is directly against the protruding empty case. In one quick motion the slide is racked to the rear, throwing the empty case completely clear. Keep the handgun in a firing position, with the strong arm held rigid when performing this.

Failure to Go Fully into Battery.   The slide does not go completely forward into battery. A glance, especially at the hammer area, will spot this. The immediate action is to hit the rear end of the slide with the palm of the support hand, which will push the slide fully into battery. This is usually caused by either dirt or residue between the slide and frame or an improperly sized case that the slide was not able to force into the chamber.

To handle a malfunction, go to the immediate action ABCD drill and work through the four options one right after the other (skipping option B if you do not carry a backup gun). Train in the drill; you never know when you may need it.

SUMMARY

Reloading and clearing malfunctions may be critical to your survival during a lethal encounter. In this chapter we have covered the tactical reloading techniques necessary for you to keep your service handgun fully loaded throughout the encounter and the techniques to clear malfunctions and get the handgun back into action if a problem occurs. The techniques for both reloading and clearing malfunctions must become reflexive sets of trained-in skills that occur automatically when needed.

13

Lowered Firing Positions and Pivoting

During lethal encounters many tactical options will appear quickly and disappear just as quickly. If officers can capitalize on these options, their survival advantage will increase. But to take advantage of these, the officer must know how to use them successfully. Some of the most overlooked tactical options are lowered firing positions that can enable an officer to become less of a target, assume a more stable position when returning fire, take better advantage of C&C, reduce the danger to anyone behind the threat(s) while still being able to fire, and be able to respond more quickly and be more flexible. Many advantages are offered by the ability to assume lower-to-the-ground firing positions.

Most officers are taught mainly to stand and fire, with little training given to lowered firing positions. Consequently, officers reflect this training and often stand and fire when a lowered position would have offered a better survival advantage. If not trained to assume these lowered firing positions, many tactical options will be lost. Along with lowered firing positions, pivoting and traversing must be used to quickly turn, lock on, and direct fire at threat(s) to either side or behind you. With minimal practice these techniques work very effectively when turning your firing stance to stop threat(s) around you.

Lowered Firing Positions: the Reasons

When firing the handgun, a number of positions are available to us, but the excessive majority of the time—virtually all the time—firing is done in the standing position. Lowered firing positions are virtually nontaught, and if taught, are very rarely practiced. Many firearms instructors and officers alike have disregarded these positions for two main reasons: being lazy and not wanting to get dirty. During a suddenly occurring encounter these positions can save their lives, but only if trained-in and practiced.

Shooting flexibility when conforming to the situation and structures is the key. There will be times when a shot cannot be taken from a standing position as the target cannot be seen, but dropping down into a lowered position it comes into view. Cover is always an important consideration, and lowered positions enable you successfully to use a greater variety of it, especially waist height to very low cover. It also allows you to drop instantly out of a threat's line of sight as you take a lowered position and return fire. This can be vital when returning fire if innocents are directly behind the threat. By dropping down to a lowered position your bullets will be angling up into the threat and not be a danger to those behind the threat. As will be shown, many other advantages make it imperative to train-in and practice these positions.

Remember, these low firing positions must be trained-in long before the encounter occurs. If you do not have these skills available, you will not to be able to take advantage of many tactical options that occur.

THE TWO KNEELING POSITIONS

The Unsupported Kneeling Position

This is the most versatile and quickest lowered firing position to assume, and lowers you instantly into a very stable and controlled firing position. Much of its versatility comes from the ability of the upper body to traverse back and forth just as in the standing position and to raise and lower to the varying levels of cover. Further versatility comes from the instant directional change that can occur by switching the knees or spinning on the down knee. This position is especially good if you have been running and are out of breath. By lowering your body into a more stable and controlled firing position, you will be better able to "hit." It can be assumed whether standing still, walking or from a dead run, or when instantly pivoting. Quick and effective, it is often quite a surprise to a threat(s).

The Unsupported Kneeling Position is assumed by

1. You are either facing the target with one leg forward or step out towards it, with your hand on the holstered handgun.

2. Now the position is assumed all in one move; draw/drop, as you lock out.

Drop the rear leg's knee to the ground while keeping the upper body erect, as the handgun is drawn and locked out into a two-handed firing grip.

Technique Points.   Whenever assuming a kneeling position, either foot can be forward and just drop the rear leg knee to the ground: very simple and very quick. Whatever position you are in, merely drop the rear leg knee to the ground. If both feet are parallel, simply step out on one. Step out in the direction you want to face and drop into the position. Whenever assuming a kneeling position, either foot can be forward and just drop the rear knee to the ground. This is stated as you must know that you can drop instantly into an unsupported kneeling position without doing anything else—to meet an instantly occurring threat(s). Assume the position as described by starting with the handgun holstered, but it will be in-hand most of the time when assuming the position instantly. Merely drop and lock out.

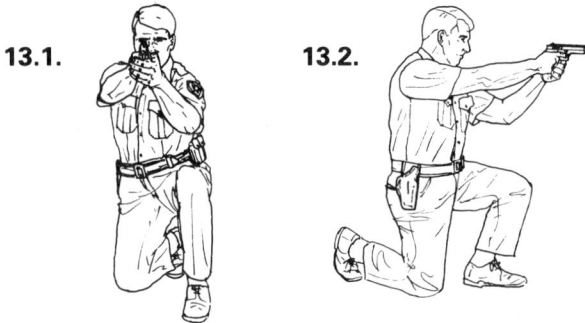

13.1.   **13.2.**

Figures 13.1 and 13.2   The unsupported kneeling position: front and side views.

Although either knee can be up or down, the knee preferred to be up is the support leg knee. This will give you the option of further locking in the position by dropping into a supported kneeling position. Most officers become used to standing in the interview stance with their holster side to the rear and support leg to the front; the support leg knee is thus usually the one that will be up when the kneeling position is taken. Remember, either knee can be up or down, but it is preferred to have the support leg knee up.

The kneeling position provides three-point stability (two feet and a knee), as opposed to a standing position, which provides two-point stability (the two feet). The position is balanced between the forward foot, rear knee, and rear-foot toes. For flexibility you must stay on the toes/ball of the rear foot. Balance is very good in this position and the stance is very stable.

Lowering and Raising the Upper Body.   Once in the kneeling position, you can raise or lower the upper body by about 2 feet. This is done by bending at the waist and raising or lowering the legs while still kneeling. This will help you fit the cover you are behind and make it possible to rock up and down overtop of cover when glancing and/or firing.

When in the highest position, the upper body is straight up and down and the legs hold the rear end up as high as it can go without coming out of the kneeling position. When in the lowest position, the upper body is bent forward at the waist and the legs are lowered so that the rear end rests on the heel of the rear foot.

Turning in the Kneeling Position.   Initially, you should turn the kneeling stance to face the threat(s) directly by simply stepping out towards the threat(s) with the support leg, and dropping into a kneeling position. The quickly assumed kneeling position forms a more stable, lowered firing position that can be turned in any direction. In the unsupported kneeling position, the upper body—being able to turn at the waist—can traverse the same firing arc as a standing position (the 270-degree firing arc, with the 90 degrees to your rear requiring you to turn in your stance).

If the need to pivot to the rear, either the knee switch or spin technique is used. The knee switch is accomplished simply by switching the knees as one movement (placing the one that was up on the ground, and raising the one that was on the ground), which will pivot the hips and position around. Just switch the knees—the one that was up is now down, and the one that was down is now up. This technique turns the position about 180 degrees, or directly to the rear. The spin is accomplished by spinning on the knee that is on the ground, with the feet rotating the position in the direction you want to turn. This technique can instantly turn the position to any angle, precisely where you want to be.

Both are very quick methods of pivoting the kneeling position and both must be learned. Depending on a number of factors—your positioning, which knee is up, objects next to you that would interfere with either of the turning methods, where the threat(s) is located—one pivoting method may be much more effective than the other. Learn both to be prepared for all situations and structures that can occur.

When training officers no guns can be used, as standard ranges have only one firing direction. Have the officers assume the kneeling position with only the hands locked out in a mock firing grip and perform the pivoting methods. They are learned quite quickly and easily, but you must work with them a little bit to get their feel.

The quickness of dropping and firing.   It is amazing to some that you can drop and fire, in an unsupported kneeling position, as quickly as you can stand and fire at standard encounter distances, 7 yards and under. The fact that you can draw and shoot just as fast kneeling as standing can open up quite a few options to you. In a direct confrontation, you can instantly drop out of a threat's line of sight and return fire. This is especially important if innocents are directly behind the threat. By dropping to a lowered position, your bullets will be angling up into the threat, and if any continue past the threat, they will be well over the innocent's heads. Also, if there is any intervening cover, you are behind it instantly.

To make this work, everything must be done at once: As the upper body draws the handgun and locks out into a firing stance, the lower body simply drops into an unsupported kneeling position as the eyes constantly watch the target. You continually watch the action/threat(s) as the body drops; do not look down at where you are kneeling. The body instantly drops, but the knee does not instantly slam into the ground. The body drops as fast as possible, but the knee is halted just short of the ground and then quickly sets in the last several inches (this is done without looking down; the body will tell you when). Many times firing will already be in progress as the knee is set on the ground, which is fine, as the position is still very stable. The main idea in making this work is to do everything at once. As you drop instantly into the kneeling position, the handgun is in your line of sight and you are firing.

The unsupported kneeling position has many advantages. The first advantage is that the kneeling position can be assumed almost instantly—just by dropping to one knee—to take advantage of a quickly appearing tactical option. Speed when using a tactical option is very important, and this kneeling position is fast. Tactical options—cover, better view of a threat, lowering your angle of fire if innocents are behind the threat, dropping out of the threat's line of sight—must be taken advantage of quickly, as the option may not remain open for long.

This position is a more stable, balanced, and flexible position, giving you the ability to assume it quickly and move in any direction from it. When used with cover, the position is nicely balanced when coming out from behind the cover.

When a more stable firing position is called for, the unsupported kneeling position can quickly become the supported kneeling position, merely by dropping the elbow to the support leg knee (assuming that the support leg knee was up).

The Supported Kneeling Position

This is not as versatile and quick as the unsupported kneeling position, but offers you greater stability for shots that are a longer distance and/or require greater precision. Assuming this position will help prepare you for this greater precision by slowing you down, even though the position takes only about 1.5 seconds to assume. This position is perfect for the Weaver stance, with the support arm's elbow resting on the support leg's knee. If you use an Isosceles stance, you should train-in this elbow-on-knee supported position by changing the position of your support arm.

The Supported Kneeling Position is assumed by following these steps:

1. Begin by stepping toward the target on the support leg. No matter where the target is located around you, simply step toward it with the support leg, with your hand on the holstered handgun.

2. Now the position is assumed all in one move: Draw/drop and support. Drop the rear leg knee to the ground as the handgun is drawn and locked out into a two-handed grip and the support arm's elbow rests on the support leg's knee.

Technique Points.   The support-side knee is pointing directly at the target, with the elbow resting on the knee and the elbow bone's point slightly forward of the knee, not bone on bone; the strong arm must be directly over the knee for a good locked-in position, with the cheek laying on it; the strong foot is on its toes/ball and you are setting on its heel; and the hands must be locked together in a good two-handed grip, maintaining power. Once the supported kneeling position is locked in, you can test your positioning by relaxing slightly while keeping a firm firing grip, and the front sight should stay on target. If it does not, adjust your position and two-handed firing grip. Assume the position is described by starting with the handgun holstered, but it will be in-hand most of the time when assuming the position instantly. Merely drop and lock up.

13.3.    **13.4.**

Figures 13.3 and 13.4 The supported kneeling position: front and side views.

Remember Your Trigger.   Once the position is locked in and you are sighting properly, the only problem left is poor trigger manipulation. As you have taken this position for a more precise shot, your trigger manipulation must be a smooth, continually increasing pressure until the surprise break occurs. Anything less and you will probably miss.

To Cock or Not to Cock.   The supported kneeling position is used when a more precise shot is needed. If you are using a D-A revolver or D-A auto and a particularly precise shot is needed, you may want to cock the hammer for the single-action firing mode. Remember, cocking the hammer on a D-A revolver is rarely used, and there is no slack to be taken out of the trigger once the hammer is cocked. If you decide to cock the hammer, use the support hand's thumb to cock it while keeping the trigger finger out of the trigger guard. The hammer is only cocked once the position is almost fully assumed, with the handgun out in front of the support-leg knee. (*A Safety Note:* Single-action firing of the D-A revolver is only used rarely. Before it is used, you must have trained-in single-action firing and the technique for safely lowering the cocked hammer. These are covered in Chapter 3.)

Using the single-action firing mode provides you with a shorter and lighter trigger pull that can help in placing precise shots. This is rarely necessary during lethal encounters, as the double-action mode is fine for virtually every situation for which you would use the supported position. But on rare occasions, with a particularly precise shot, the single-action mode can help.

The Supported Kneeling Position's Strengths Also Creates It's Weaknesses.
When a precise problem needs to be solved, the supported kneeling position can
give you the ability to solve the singular task quickly. As a speciality technique, it
is pulled from your bag of tricks to solve a precise problem. Its strength—a very
solid, locked-in firing position—also creates its weaknesses, as once the supported
position is locked in, it becomes non-flexible. When the time is right, it works excellently, but often cannot be used over some cover, to engage a threat(s) to the side,
to track a moving threat, and so on. As with any speciality technique, use it in its
proper context and it will give you the ability to solve precise problems that otherwise you might not be able to solve.

THE TWO PRONE FIRING POSITIONS

Prone positions are the least practiced of all firing positions but can give you the
ability of taking advantage of a tactical option during an encounter. The ability to
get very low can be critical and you must learn and practice both types of prone
positions. As a rule, prone positions are mainly taught as laying on your belly with
the handgun held in a locked-out grip, firing at a threat(s) farther away. This is
certainly a very valid application but by no means the only use that prone positions
have. They give you the ability to conform to the available cover and situation and
become a real surprise to a threat(s).

The main advantages of the prone positions are to assume the most stable
firing position for longer shots, conform to the available cover (usually very low or
firing under objects), acquire a target that could not otherwise be seen, direct fire
from a surprise location, and return fire if you go down (if hit or if you fall).

The main disadvantages are that it takes slightly longer to assume a prone
position, your flexibility is reduced if you need to move instantly, bullets can be
richoeted into your position, and your ability to view the entire encounter zone is
restricted.The first two—taking time to assume the position and to move from it—
are really not as much of a disadvantage as many officers think. You should be able
to drop into a locked-in rollover prone position in 2 seconds and place a controlled
"hit" at 50 yards by the third second. When moving from the position, you should
be on your feet and moving in under 1 second: really not much of a disadvantage
if used at the tactically proper time.

We begin with the most noted of all prone positions, the rollover prone position. Once you understand this excellent and most stable firing position, we will
continue into the other style of prone positions, the flexible prone positions.

Rollover Prone Position

Another one of Ray Chapman's excellent defensive handgun techniques, the rollover prone position has proved to be the most stable firing position available. It is
especially useful when firing at longer distances and under objects. The rollover

prone position also provides greater use of cover, as the body is angled to the target, being angled behind the cover.

Assuming the rollover prone position follows these steps:

1. The body is positioned at an angle to the target (the same as in the Weaver stance or the interview stance) before you drop to the knees. Drop to both knees as the handgun is drawn and held pointing downrange (about a 135-degree bend in the elbow, which is just touching the body or slightly in front of it, handgun pointing directly downrange) and the support hand (held down and ready to make contact with the ground) is positioned about a foot below the handgun. Make sure that the muzzle is in front of and above the support hand and that it did not cross the hand any time. The waist is not bent, the upper body being straight up and down. The trigger finger is out of the trigger guard.

2. Now, in one move, the body bends forward as the support hand makes contact with the ground to lower the upper body instantly and the strong arm and handgun go straight out toward the target as the body is laid on its strong side (the toe of the strong foot is turned in to help position the body on the strong side). The strong arm does not touch the ground until it is straight out and the support arm (which has been lowering the "forward-moving" body) drops the body the last several inches to the ground; the strong arm comes straight-out and the body hits the ground at almost the same instant. The cheek lays on the strong arm and shoulder.

3. The instant the upper body is positioned on the ground, the support hand snaps forward to assume the two-handed grip. The support leg is bent and its foot is placed overtop the knee of the strong leg. When the two-handed grip is assumed, the trigger finger is placed into the trigger guard and any safety pushed "off."

Technique Points. Before the drop is made, make sure that the strong side is angled back from the target; try not to drop while standing straight to the target. If you do, simply adjust your angle as you are continuing into the position. Make sure that the trigger finger is out of the trigger guard and the S-A auto's safety is "on" until the two-handed grip is assumed. Also, the H&K P-7's grip is not fully taken, to press in the squeeze-cocker, until the two-handed grip is assumed. Make sure that the muzzle is pointed downrange at the target and never crosses any part of your body, especially the support hand.

Once in position, make sure that the two-handed grip is correct. The support hand is wrapped around the strong hand as is normally done, but make sure that the support hand's index finger is underneath the trigger guard and that the edge of the hand is on the ground. Both of these are necessary for the handgun's support. Lock both hands together in a strong grip and lock the arms. Maintain a strong two-handed grip. The handgun should never come out of the support hand and the

13.5.

13.6.

13.7.

13.8.

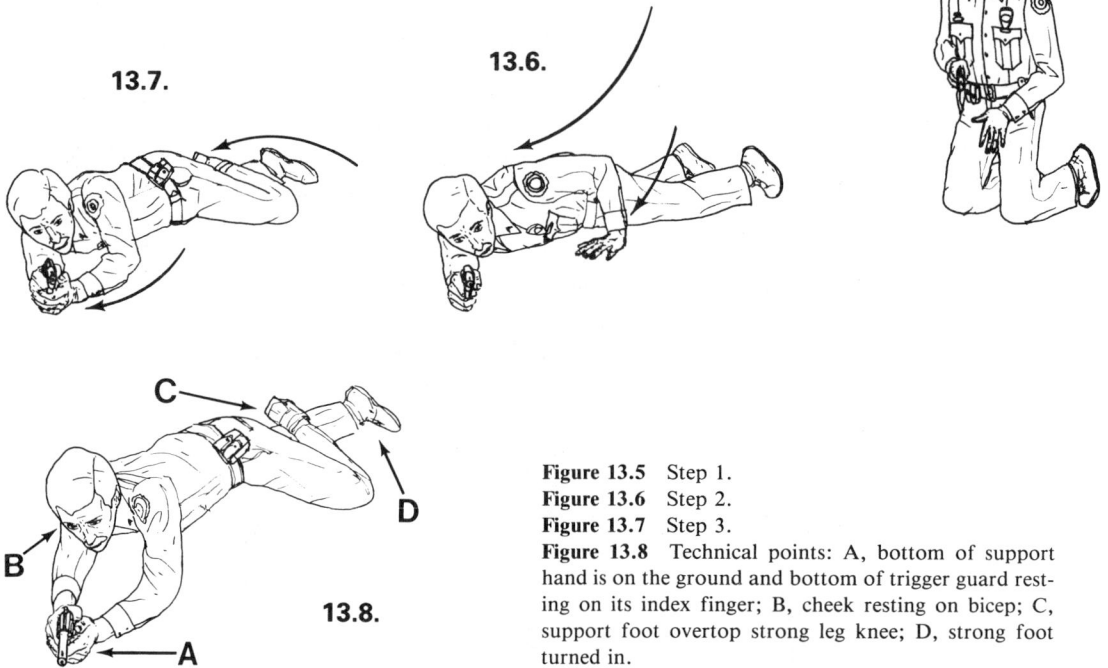

Figure 13.5 Step 1.
Figure 13.6 Step 2.
Figure 13.7 Step 3.
Figure 13.8 Technical points: A, bottom of support hand is on the ground and bottom of trigger guard resting on its index finger; B, cheek resting on bicep; C, support foot overtop strong leg knee; D, strong foot turned in.

muzzle should not come up very much. If either of these is occurring, increase the grip's strength (but not to the point where the handgun is shaking slightly; just use a good firm grip).

Once you are in the position, make it feel right for you by slightly adjusting and positioning your body. As every one is different, slight adjustments will increase your ability to use the position and its comfort. When laying your cheek on the strong arm and shoulder, adjust it until the feel is right. Make sure that the support leg is properly positioned at an angle and that its foot is placed overtop the strong leg at the knee. You must work with the position until you get a feel for it.

After you have gotten the idea of the position and practiced it a few times, you can test the position to see if it is correct. This is done by locking into the position and concentrating on the front sight. Now relax the body slightly, while keeping the strength in the hands, and if the position is correct, the sights should remain stationary. The handgun and sights must not move.

The rollover prone position is the most stable defensive handgun firing position there is, as the handgun and body are locked onto the ground. There is no more stable firing position. When placing longer and/or more precise shots and the situation is right, no firing position is better. Also, its use is excellent when firing under objects that require a very low position.

Angled Behind Cover and Switching the Handgun.   When using low cover, the angled positioning of the body allows virtually the whole body to be hidden behind cover, with only the handgun, hands, and part of the head sticking out. This works perfectly for the strong side of cover, but when using the support side of cover, the handgun must be switched to the support hand. (*Note:* The handgun switching techniques are described in Chapter 8.)

Behind the support side of cover, your body is angled with the support side to the rear. The handgun switching is done before you begin to drop into the position. Simply switch the handgun to the support hand and then drop into the position as you normally would except on the support side. There is nothing hard about this, but it must be practiced a few times.

Flexible Prone Positions

During many situations a completely locked-in rollover prone position will not work and consequently cannot be used, but a low prone, supine, or side position can instantly function to solve the problem. You must be able to use quick and flexible low prone (laying face down), supine (laying on the back), or side positions, in one- or two-handed firing grips, to take advantage or recover from certain situations. The key word in these low prone positions is flexible; they must be flexible to work.

Assuming these flexible prone positions is not as cut-and-dried as for the roll-over prone position. Basically, these low positions conform you to the structures and situations you are faced with, but assuming them follows some basic steps:

1. The positions begin with the body becoming ready to be lowered to the ground. The body is bent forward at the waist, both knees are deeply bent, either foot can be forward, the handgun is held out in front of your body, and the support hand is held down, close to the ground. The handgun's muzzle is pointing downrange, in front of and well above the support hand. The trigger finger is out of the trigger guard.

2. The body is facing the target but does not have to be precisely positioned to the target. The drop is done by the support hand coming in contact with the ground as one knee and then the strong arm touch the ground, and then the body is lowered quickly until it is on the ground with one leg straight back and the other leg out to the side with its knee bent (which leg is straight or bent will depend on the direction you are firing and the structures or objects around you).

3. Once the body is down, the firing position is assumed and conformed to the structures and objects surrounding you. Either a one- or a two-handed firing grip can be used.

(*Note:* The example shown is one of many that can be assumed.)

Technical Points.   Only after the firing position has been assumed, with a one- or two-handed firing grip, do you push the S-A auto's safety "off" and/or place your trigger finger into the trigger guard. Make sure that the muzzle is always pointed downrange and never crosses your body, especially your support hand. Also, on the H&K P-7's, the grip is not fully taken, to press in the squeeze-cocker, until the firing position is assumed.

The exact positioning cannot be precisely stated, as many different methods of using a flexible prone position exist. Start out slowly with the method shown and learn how to conform your flexible lowered position to the many structures and situations that can occur. Once you can smoothly drop into a flexible lowered position, practice assuming it (with an unloaded handgun—check it twice) while walking and instantly after slowing down from a run. By quickly dropping into position this way, you are not slamming into the ground but quickly lowering yourself into position. If you slam into the ground, you can be injured; control yourself as you drop into position. Always remember safety; keep the muzzle pointed downrange and away from your body and the trigger finger out of the trigger guard.

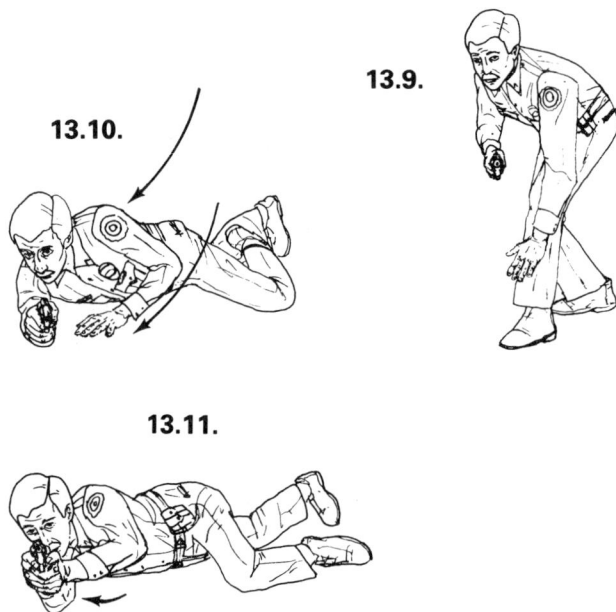

13.9.

13.10.

13.11.

Figures 13.9–13.11 When dropping into a flexible lowered position, there are really no precise steps to follow. Initially bend at the waist and knees with the support hand almost to the ground (Fig. 13.9). Then drop to the ground, with the support hand instantly lowering you, firing one-handed if needed (Fig. 13.10). Or assume a flexible two-handed firing grip (Fig. 13.11). Many flexible lowered positions can be assumed.

The body's positioning is important so that you can be flexible in position and move quickly from the position. One leg is bent at the knee and placed out to the side of the body for two reasons: first, this adds stability to the position while you are in it, and second, when moving from the position, as soon as the body is raised, the knee is instantly under the body (it is harder to bring a knee under the body from straight back). When it is time to move, the hands become positioned first: The support hand is drawn back to the body (if it is not already there) and the strong hand comes in slightly (not all the way) while holding the wrist angled backward so that the handgun is up and the heel of the hand is on the ground. (*Note:* If using an S-A auto, the safety lever is pushed "on" before you start to move. If using an H&K P-7, the grip is eased before you move, so the squeeze-cocker is not pressed in. Also, the trigger finger is out of the trigger guard. These are done for safety while you are moving.) As the hands are positioned, they push the body up instantly, with the bent knee automatically sliding under the body; both arms and legs now spring up. When moving around in position, both arms and legs are used for quick spiderlike movements to the side, forward, or back.

More Flexible Firing Angles.   This position allows the handgun to be directed at virtually any angle of fire. By raising the upper body on the elbows, or lying on your side, the handgun is very flexible and can cover virtually any firing angle, from low to high. The support arm can be used in a two-handed firing grip or used to rock the firing position either up and down or out and back from behind cover. Flexibility is the key: flexible firing angles, flexible positioning for the area you are in, and flexible movement from the position. When you understand the flexibility these positions afford you, dropping down fast and quickly assuming a firing position whenever a tactical option appears is a snap.

Do not forget to surprise the threat(s) by appearing where least expected. Low positions are rarely used or thought about, and always the last place to be checked along with high positions. A low firing position behind cover can give you a very good advantage in certain situations. In these positions, you can challenge the threat(s) while being less readily seen, especially if several pieces or areas of cover are between you and the threat(s). This does not always work, by any means, but it can work very well.

When Unintentionally Going Low.   This will occur at two times: when you are hit and when you fall down. Once down, there is a good possibility that you will have to fight from the ground instead of trying to get back up to continue the fight. If you have the time and ability to get back up instantly and/or move to a covered position, do it. Rarely, though, will an officer take advantage of a low position if suddenly there and fighting for his or her life. Tactically there may be no time to try and get up and/or move to cover and then fire. Simply go into a flexible lowered position and return fire.

Lying on your back and/or side may be the best position if the threat(s) is pressing its attack. Laying prone (laying face down), you have a limited area in which you can fire and you have to arch the back up to raise the position. Lying on your back and/or going from side to side, you have the ability to fire in a 360-degree circle around you and you can aim and fire the handgun much more easily. In part of the circle, the handgun will be fired upside down, but this is no problem if the threat(s) is close. Returning fire instantly to stop the threat(s) may be your only chance to survive. As you go down, assume a firing position instantly and return fire. Also, if you went down because you were hit, lying on your back can make returning fire much less painful then if you were prone.

At the first possible moment, move to a covered position. This does not necessarily mean that you must get back up; just get behind cover.

Prone positions can give you the advantage if you understand how they function and use them correctly. They provide you with the ability to use certain tactical options that appear, but are generally not recognized.

PIVOTING AND TRAVERSING

At some point in an engagement it may become necessary to instantly pivot your firing position, to engage a threat(s) that is to either side or behind you. Pivoting must be used for a threat(s) directly behind you, but its use is not limited to that area. The pivot is also used to align your firing stance more precisely on the threat when you fire. Its use is not complicated and functions easily with minimal practice.

Traversing and Pivoting: Where the First Ends and the Other Begins

The General View.   Traversing is the lateral movement of the handgun to engage threats to the front and sides of an officer. This movement is done by the upper body and locked-in firing stance rotating from the waist, while the feet do not move or move very slightly. In either locked-in two-handed firing stance, the handgun can easily cover 270 degrees (135 degrees to either side from facing directly forward), with a small area (90 degrees) directly behind an officer that cannot easily be covered, without moving the feet or contorting the body. Pivoting must begin where traversing ends, to cover the 90 degrees directly behind an officer. This is easily accomplished by moving one foot and pivoting on the other, which will turn the firing stance to direct its fire to the rear. That is the general view of the functions of traversing and pivoting; traverse to cover all areas around you whenever possible and pivot only when you have to, for the area directly behind you.

Somewhere along the line in defensive handgun use the general view that traversing and pivoting are wholly different functions came into being. Traversing was always used to direct the firing stance at targets around you and pivoting was used only when the firing stance had to be turned to the rear. This is by no means the total functioning of the two. In reality, the two interact together to keep your firing stance balanced, comfortable, and flexible. When these two functions work together, they make it as easy as possible for you to place "hits" on targets located around you.

The Interacting View.   In this view, traversing and pivoting interact together to center the firing stance on the threat(s), to keep it balanced, comfortable, and flexible. Whenever centering the firing stance on a threat anywhere around you, traversing (turning at the waist) and pivoting (turning on the feet) interact together, to place the firing stance instantly and precisely facing the threat(s). Even if the threat is only at a small angle to the side, do not just use traversing, but also slightly pivot the feet to be completely centered on the threat. This small pivot loses no time, but optimally centers the firing stance on the threat, allowing the stance to function at its best.

As everyone knows, you will function better when the firing stance is balanced, comfortable, and flexible, especially for techniques such as stance-directed fire. Intuitively, the human organism knows this and will naturally align its body on the target when firing. Watch officers running an assault course; they will naturally align their bodies for the best use of their firing stance. Given the situation, officers will always (without even thinking about it) move to align their firing stance on the target when firing. This is nothing more than optimumly positioning your firing stance on the target, wherever it is located.

Traversing and pivoting did not just suddenly begin when you used them to turn your firing stance to a target. They were used together throughout every search to position your firing stance and movements toward the danger (or where you thought the danger was). They did not just suddenly go into action when a threat appeared but were always working to place you in the best position to respond to danger (or where you thought the danger was). The human body can fight better when facing the danger, and traversing and pivoting point you toward it.

When Pivoting is Not Used. During certain circumstances and situations, only traversing is used, as pivoting cannot or will not be used. Traversing can work better by itself to place "hits" instantly on close, multiple threats in front of you (well within the front 180 degrees), and there is no need to pivot each time. In reality, having threats positioned 180 degrees apart is a very rare occurrence, as usually they are much closer together. Any further angle may require pivoting to turn the firing stance. Also, your position and objects around you may restrict your ability to pivot, with traversing still being able to cover a 270-degree firing arc. Positions such as setting, climbing over objects, and moving through tight areas will readily restrict your ability to pivot instantly. Unless engaging close, multiple threats in front of you or your positioning restricts it, pivoting should be used to optimally position your firing stance.

Pivoting

Pivoting is easily done and does not need extensive practice. It is learned quickly and will function naturally to center your firing stance on the danger. Functioning naturally is the key. In your general movements throughout a search, pivoting is always done to center you on the danger (or where you think it is) and flows with the search or situation.

As will be shown, pivoting is very fast and easily done. It is used throughout any search to position your stance and movements toward danger. When a sudden threat occurs, as the handgun is either drawn or brought up and the body is turning to meet the threat, the traverse and pivot are done and locked-in place as the handgun comes up into your line-of-sight: nothing slow about it. The threat appeared somewhere around you (except straight ahead, where no turn is required), and as the handgun was coming up, the traverse and pivot place the stance directly on the threat. Remember, pivoting must be done as the handgun is coming up, with the feet being planted and legs locked as the handgun comes into the line of sight.

Feet Movement and Lock.   Each foot has a function when pivoting, one being the pivoting foot and the other being the moving foot. When it is time to pivot, the feet instantly perform their functions and the stance is turned. As the turn begins, the moving foot's heel raises and the toes push it in the direction that the stance will turn, with the foot traveling only several inches off the ground. The instant this is occurring, the pivot foot's heel raises and the foot pivots on the toes. The instant the turn is completed, both feet lock into the ground to plant the stance. The moving foot and leg swing, which would draw a small or large arc on the ground if the foot were touching. At no time do the feet cross, and nothing telegraphs the move; it just starts instantly. Crossing the feet makes the stance unbalanced and telegraphs the move; neither are done when pivoting. The legs must be steady to catch the body instantly if a slip should suddenly occur.

The most important technical point is that only one foot moves when pivoting. Do not attempt to move both feet when pivoting; one foot moves while you pivot on the other. Your stance must be balanced and flexible, with the weight slightly forward and the knees slightly bent. When you normally are pivoting during the search, it is easily done, with the moving foot turning the stance and lightly touching down, without the leg muscles locking the instant the feet plant. But when turning to fire on a threat, the leg muscles lock as soon as the feet plant. The knees do not lock straight; only the leg muscles lock, while the knees are still slightly bent, instantly flexible for another move. When pivoting as you are searching, you pivot and move. When pivoting and firing, you pivot-and-lock.

Stance Movement.   Each of the stances (the Weaver and Isosceles) has a particular pivoting method and rule. This difference is due to the way the stances are facing: the Weaver is angled with one foot pointing toward the threat, while the Isosceles is straight with both feet the same distance from the threat.

Weaver stance pivoting follows this rule: Either step toward the threat with the support foot or step away from the threat with the strong foot. Pivoting with the Weaver stance is easy to understand; wherever the threat is located around you, either precise foot movement (either your strong foot or support foot has only one movement it makes) will properly position your feet and stance centered on the threat.

Isosceles stance pivoting follows this rule: The foot closest to the threat steps away from it, or the foot farthest from the threat steps toward it; either foot can be used when the threat is directly to the rear. Pivoting with the Isosceles stance is slightly more complicated. Wherever the threat is located around you, one foot is closest to the threat (if anywhere on the right side of your body, the right foot is

Figures 13.12–13.14 All the pivots are accomplished by pivoting on one foot, while the other swings toward or away from the threat: 180-degree pivot (Fig. 13.12) and two 45-degree pivots: one to the right (Fig. 13.13) and one to the left (Fig. 13.14). Remember to pivot and lock into the firing stance. The Weaver stance is shown.

closest to the threat) and the other foot is farthest from the threat. Either foot movement will position your feet properly, centering it on the threat.

Working with, Then Forgetting the Rules. Work with the rule for your firing stance. With an unloaded handgun (check it twice), pick out a target, stand at different angles to it, and use the rule to turn your firing stance toward it. After a while, it will become quite natural and you will begin easily pivoting at any angle around you. Now, begin practicing the pivot when walking, picking out targets around you as you move, then pivoting to them. Pivoting on the move is very important for the skills needed when moving throughout a search, and when you pivot to engage a threat you will probably be moving. Also, practice the pivot and move (when moving through a search) and the pivot and lock (when turning to fire on a threat).

Once you become proficient in pivoting, forget the rule, as you will not need it anymore. There is no need to clutter up your mental process with something that is not needed anymore. The rule starts you in the right direction, which your trained-in abilities will continue without having to reflect on the rule.

Stepping Away or Toward the Threat. Why are there two methods of pivoting for each stance? There are three reasons for this: the location of the threat, its closeness, and your position. First, where is the threat located around you? By being able to pivot instantly to either the left or right, you can make the quickest turn to the threat.

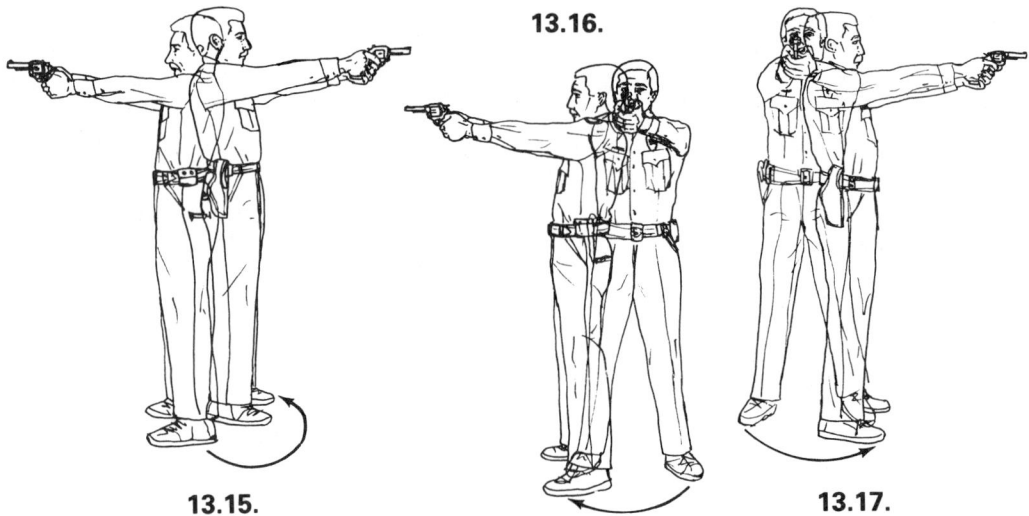

Figures 13.15–13.17   The Isosceles pivot rule is different from the Weaver, but again one foot is used to pivot on, while the other swings toward or away from the threat: 180-degree pivot (Fig. 13.15) and two 45-degree pivots: one to the right (Fig. 13.16) and one to the left (Fig. 13.17). Remember to pivot and lock into the firing stance.

Second, how close is the threat? By using either foot, you will usually be closer to or farther away from the threat (depending on which leg you pivot on). When pivoting, stepping away from the threat(s) is just as important as stepping toward the threat(s). Most officers are only taught to step toward a threat when turning, but if the threat(s) should suddenly appear at very close range (0 to 4 yards), it may be close enough to block or grab the handgun. By stepping away from the threat when pivoting, the extra distance you are giving yourself (even though only a few feet) could be all that is needed to keep the threat from blocking or grabbing your handgun. Look at either rule and you will see that one movement is toward and the other is away from the threat—away from the threat will increase your distance from it by several feet. You must know how to pivot away from a very close threat and fire. And you must also know how to backpeddle and sidestep to increase your distance farther and/or move to the side of the threat, as its body momentum may still carry it into you, even if well "hit."

Third, your position may restrict pivoting in a certain way. You will certainly not always be in the open with enough room to pivot any way you want to. There will be times when you can pivot only one way. You must have more than one pivoting option open to you.

Traversing and pivoting must be used together throughout the search and when engaging threats, to place your firing stance in the most balanced, comfortable, and flexible position. Only then can the stance perform optimumly.

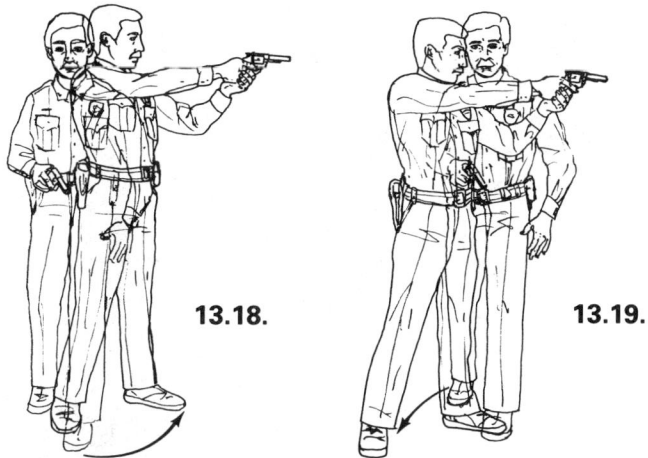

Figures 13.18 and 13.19 By stepping away from the threat when pivoting (if the threat is close), you may keep it from grabbing or blocking your handgun. Stepping toward the threat (Fig. 13.18) can place the handgun in easier reach, while stepping away from the threat (Fig. 13.19) can provide the extra distance needed to keep the handgun from being grabbed or blocked.

SUMMARY

In this chapter we described the lowered firing positions and traversing/pivoting techniques necessary to take advantage of tactical options that appear quickly. Without the trained-in ability to assume these positions, many options will go completely unnoticed. They are easy to learn and can save your life.

14

Point Shooting and Other Unaimed Firing Techniques

Point shooting and other unaimed firing techniques are vital to defensive handgun use. Whether used in close–quick–sudden encounters, during low-light conditions without using a flashlight, or where a restricted area does not allow eye-level aligning of the handgun, unaimed firing techniques can save your life. To a large number of officers, the thought of using unaimed fire is not even considered, as they just qualify each year and do not practice with their handgun. The thought of not using the sights to align the handgun seems like it cannot work without extensive practice. In fact, the techniques do work very well without that much practice. Remember, we are dealing with all the unaimed firing techniques that are used.

As you study this chapter, leave all preconceived or supposed realities to the side. This is very hard to do, as everyone's previous learning experiences bear heavily on how a particular subject is perceived. But there may exist new information, techniques, or previously un-thought-of realities that may change your perception. Drop preconceived notions and work through this chapter; it might just surprise you.

As stated in Chapter 1, there are three major thoughts on/followings of defensive handgun use: the left, middle, and right (borrowed from political usage to designate two extremes and a middle ground). The left believes that almost all defensive handgun use must be done with unaimed fire. The right, being at the opposite end of the spectrum, believes that almost all defensive handgun use must be done with a locked-in two-handed sighted firing stance. The middle, as a combination of the two, applies the best techniques of each to the total situations that can be encountered, by using both unaimed and aimed firing techniques to their most appropriate use and best advantage. This book is based on the middle philosophy—the most appropriate technique for the situation at hand. Work through these unaimed firing techniques and see how they fit into defensive handgun use; try them out and see how well they function.

Three unaimed firing techniques will be covered: point shooting, the speed rock, and stance-directed fire. (*Note:* The speed rock will be handled under point shooting, although they are, in fact, different techniques.)

POINT SHOOTING

Point shooting is the most misunderstood firing technique in defensive handgun use. When thought of, it usually invokes the image of a gunfighter, with revolver thrust neatly into a buscadero rig, stalking through a time of deadly encounters. To some degree that image has validity. But those who used point shooting in the past knew what it was good for, just as we do today—very close, sudden, deadly encounters: time frames squeezed until almost no time exists; instantaneous-appearing attackers; no time to think, only time to react instantly.

The ability to gain the fighting advantage instantaneously during extremely close and quick lethal encounters, which usually occur in less-than-favorable conditions, may depend on your use of point shooting. When the lethal encounter is very close and quick, you must get on target extremely fast: "Hit" and keep on "hitting" to survive. Point shooting can provide you with a very definite fighting advantage by giving you the ability to use the handgun functionally below eye level. Usually, the need for point shooting occurs when a threat(s) attacks at very close range—from touching to 4 yards. When an attack is this close, the action of merely pointing out the in-hand gun and firing is extremely fast. Also, point shooting can be used in a variety of situations that limit your ability to either assume or use a two-handed firing stance. There is also the fact that one hand may be needed for a task (using a flashlight, opening a door, carrying something, climbing). Suddenly the threat(s) attacks: no time to readjust what you are doing and attempt to acquire a two-handed grip to fire the handgun. In all of these, you must instantly react to save your life when a close and quick threat(s) attacks. Point shooting can be used to solve these unique shooting situations.

Let there be no mistake: The locked-in two-handed firing stance is the preferred firing technique of defensive handgun use. If realistically available with reference to situation and structure, use it at all times. But one- and two-handed unaimed firing techniques must be used in certain situations to provide you with the fighting advantage necessary to survive. There is no "one" supreme firing position for all situations. The closest is the locked-in two-handed sighted firing stance, but that cannot work for all situations. Unaimed firing techniques must be learned and practiced to deal effectively with situations where aimed firing techniques cannot be used.

At certain times, point shooting can be pulled from your bag of tricks (techniques) to save your life, by instantaneous gaining the fighting advantage with lightning-quick reactions. If the situation were to occur to you right now—precariously close, deadly, and quick (PDQ)—you would probably point that handgun out and start pulling the trigger. Do not kid yourself, in all probability you would do just that, no matter how much you have practiced your favorite two-handed firing stance. When it is that close, you know that you have got to be the fastest to survive. Given slightly more time and distance and you will instantly go into your locked-in two-handed firing stance. But exceedingly close work, with the threat(s) trying to press its advantage [the threat(s) usually being first to start, first to fire, and possibly having caught you completely unaware], requires the fastest answer. This has been shown time and time again during very close-quarters encounters. Police officers are only kidding themselves if they do not have a good point-shooting technique. Learn how to do it correctly before you are going to do it for real.

An example of this occurred to a police officer who is an extremely talented IPSC shooter. At that time the officer had been involved in IPSC competition and match direction for over three years and was rated the best practical shooter in a five-state area; when he arrived at a match, he usually won. He consistently used and trained in the Weaver stance, from which he was exceedingly fast, placing "hits" from touching distance on out. One afternoon he responded to a call for possible hold-up suspects that the manager of a local fast-food restaurant thought he recognized from a previous holdup. Two units responded to the scene. As the officer pulled onto the scene, he spotted two individuals matching the suspects' descriptions walking away from the restaurant, both having a drink in one hand and a burger in the other. He approached, with his hand on the holstered service revolver, and advised both to stop which they did and turned around. The distance was now 8 feet. As he began questioning them, the suspect on his right suddenly dropped the food and drink from his hands, with his right hand going under his jacket. The officer's revolver was out in a flash, with three bullets leaving it in a split second, fired by point shooting. The suspect's .44 Magnum revolver fell to the pavement with the suspect, who had tried to draw and kill the officer. The object is simple; a highly trained two-handed shooter used a point-shooting technique in an instantly occurring, close-quarters shoot-out when faced with the life-threatening need for speed. It must also be stated that he had previously learned and only casually practiced the point-shooting technique.

The methodology involved in point shooting follows the shooter's learned eye and hand coordination and is as simple as the common reflex of pointing your finger at an object. Most will say that is too simplistic, and they are right. The problem is to overcome faulty handgun-handling habits, which leads to poor performance and an oh-this-doesn't-work-attitude. Point shooting is not as difficult as you think and quickly becomes a natural function that you do not have to think about. If ever called upon to use it in a PDQ situation, just point and fire. If you are serious about your defensive shooting skills, point shooting must be in your bag of tricks. This chapter describes the technique to make it work.

The Handgun In Hand and the Belt-Level Position

The learning process to develop point-shooting skills begins by establishing a set of positions to begin training-in the bodily mechanics. These starting positions are used to consistently train-in the pointing movement—making it the same every time you do it. Within a short period of time, these positions become trained-in and second nature, and the pointing movement starts becoming a smooth, fluid movement.

Once trained-in, the pointing movement is used to "hit" very close targets merely by pointing out the handgun at the target and correctly manipulating the trigger. The pointing movement is trained-in consistently from the belt-level position first, as this is where the handgun will be a majority of the time, when point shooting is needed in a real situation. Once the pointing movement is trained-in, it can be used from any place the hand and gun are, no matter from where the handgun starts the movement.

The technique begins with proper placement of the handgun in relationship to the body. We use the belt-level position to hold the handgun at the belt line close to the body. This position is the one you trained-in previously as part of the holster-to-stance reflex, and its main points are:

1. The handgun is properly gripped—firmly but not tightly—with the web of the hand high on the back strap.
2. It is held in the belt-level position, with your thumb touching the belt and the barrel pointing safely out in front of you at the ground. In this position, even if you send an unintentional round out of the barrel, it will not put a hole through your foot but strike about 9 feet in front of you. Also, the handgun is not held directly at the side but about halfway between the belt buckle and pants seam; it should feel natural.
3. The trigger finger is out of the trigger guard for safety and kept there until the handgun is in front of your body and pointed-out at the target, just before firing. You are safe with your trigger finger out of the trigger guard, until you are ready to shoot. There is no need to worry; you will have plenty of time to insert the trigger finger as the handgun is pointed out. When point shooting is transfered to real situations, the trigger finger is always out of the trigger guard before the handgun is brought up.
4. The wrist must be straight, with the elbow, wrist, and handgun forming a straight line. Some officers have a tendency to bend the wrist inward, wrapping the arm, wrist, and handgun around the body. Do not let this happen; keep it straight.

When beginning, look down every now and then to check that everything is proper, especially that the wrist is straight. In training, you start in the belt-level position before you point shoot and return the handgun to this position after you shoot. Do not let the handgun hang down or stick out; do not be sloppy with your handgun. There is no excuse for poor gun handling anytime, anywhere.

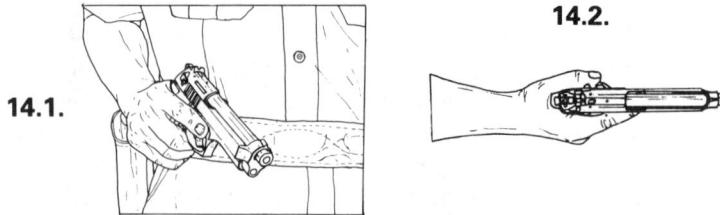

14.2.

14.1.

Figures 14.1 and 14.2   The belt-level position holds the handgun at the belt (Fig. 14.1). Remember to keep the handgun, wrist, and forearm straight (Fig. 14.2).

Why the belt-level position.   The belt-level position serves you several ways in training and definitely in real situations. Remember, we never train-in anything that will not serve us in a real situation. The belt-level position serves you in three ways:

1. This is an excellent position when close-quarters searching with a handgun. In the belt-level position, the handgun is ready for instantaneous use—for close point shooting or for snapping up into a locked-in two-handed firing stance. The handgun is close to the body and a very hard target for an attacker to try for. Also, the other hand is free to use a flashlight, open doors, move things, or to climb with.

2. You are safe with your trigger finger out of the trigger guard, so a startled reaction or slip does not instantly send a shot off—not only dangerous, but it would give your position away completely. In case you do send an unintentional round out of the barrel, you will not put a hole through your foot, as the barrel will be pointing at a spot on the floor about 9 feet in front of you.

3. The belt-level position is ideally located between the holstered handgun and a locked-out two-handed firing stance. During the holster-to-stance reflex, the handgun travels up through the belt-level position, with all firing positions beyond it. It is all one package—from holster or belt-level position, up to fire by point shooting or from a two-handed firing stance, and then back again. Each complements the other and the belt-level position is just the midpoint. When preparing for action, a quick draw and short movement of the arm places the handgun in the belt-level position ready for the upcoming action.

The belt-level position is the start. Attempt nothing until you read and understand the rest of this chapter, then dry practice with an unloaded handgun in front of a mirror until the technique begins to feel right and you can easily create the pointing movement.

Point-Shooting Techniques

Point shooting consists of the eye and hand taking over to place the shot(s), as opposed to sight alignment or any other method of locking the handgun to the body as a way of aligning to place the shots.

When you naturally point at something, your finger is more than likely right on whatever you are pointing at, and if it was the barrel of a handgun, you would "hit" what you were pointing at. This comes from years of practice you never knew you were engaging in—each time you pointed at something. From this natural pointing act, several truths surfaced:

1. As in pointing your finger, you do not look at your finger, but what you are pointing at. You look at the target, exactly where you want to hit. In natural pointing, you never find yourself looking at your finger while you point, but looking directly and precisely at what you are pointing at. The same must be done when point shooting.
2. The eye's peripheral vision is used when pointing. The handgun is extended and the eyes' peripheral vision picks up the barrel and aligns it (the same as naturally accomplished with the finger).
3. Once the handgun is pointed out, an imperceptible hesitation of about one-eighth to one-sixteenth of a second is needed for alignment before the shot is fired. The handgun is not pointed out fast and fired the moment it is extended: rather, it is pointed out fast, there is an imperceptible hesitation during the alignment, and the shot is fired. (*Note:* The hesitation is initially for the peripheral vision to align the barrel, but the kinesthetic mechanism takes over once point shooting has been practiced enough. Thus both work together and if there is not enough light for the peripheral vision to see the barrel, the kinesthetic mechanism still functions to align the handgun.)

Basically, you look at the target, the handgun is pointed straight out at the target, your eyes' peripheral vision picks up the barrel and aligns it during an almost imperceptible hesitation, and the shot is fired.

With practice, and not as much as you might think, the eye and hand begin functioning together to place the shot easily. As practice continues, the body will become used to the feel (kinesthetic feel) of point shooting.

Four Techniques That Must Be Followed

When point shooting there are four techniques that are used to create the smooth, fluid pointing movement to make point-shooting work. When initially learning point shooting, keep checking yourself to make sure that these four techniques are done correctly.

1. The Wrist Must Be Straight Throughout Point Shooting.   The wrist must be straight in the belt-level position before pointing and kept straight throughout the pointing movement (not up or down or canted to either side). You must not bend the wrist either up, down, left, or right. Start with the wrist straight and keep it straight. If not, the bullet will go high, low, left, or right. Start with an unloaded handgun (check it twice). Practice frontways and sideways to a mirror while making the pointing movement, to make sure that the wrist is straight.

The wrist may have to be bent slightly depending on your bodily construction. A very slight angling of the wrist may be necessary depending on your own physical build, as it must feel natural and comfortable to you. Also, a slight rearward bend to the wrist can occur when point shooting at a target in front of you, as the arm comes slightly in. Train with the wrist always straight at first, until you work into point shooting and the pointing movement, making sure that you are getting "hits" on the target. Work into point shooting by slightly modifying the techniques if necessary to fit you. Remember, these are very slight modifications only.

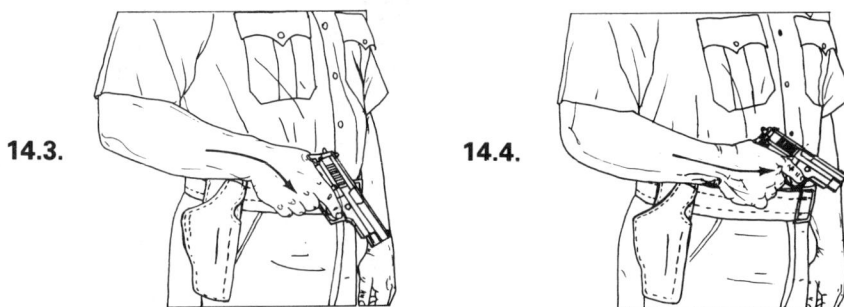

Figures 14.3 and 14.4   Two wrist bending problems sometimes occur when holding the handgun in the belt-level position: either bending the wrist downward (Fig. 14.3) or wrapping it around the stomach (Fig. 14.4). The wrist must be straight in the belt-level position.

2. The Target's Centerline is Used for the Initial Shot.   When the handgun is brought forward and up in the pointing movement for the first shot on the target, the barrel swings up the centerline of the target. This does not mean that the arm is stiff, bringing the handgun and barrel swinging up, but it bends in a natural pointing movement, just as you naturally bring the arm up to point at something. The handgun is brought forward in the pointing movement, which brings the muzzle from a low position to a higher one and stops at the firing point, all the time tracking up the centerline of the target. This is not an exaggerated sweep but is a natural pointing movement. The shots may be either high or low at first, but they should be on the centerline of the target. The main idea is to get the centerline down; then with a small amount of practice you can place the shots anywhere along that line.

This will often enable you to "hit" the threat somewhere if the firstshot is pulled off too soon. A "hit" in the lower legs or lower torso is better than no hit at all. Even if the first shot is pulled off too soon, usually due to the urgency of the

14.5.

14.6.

Figures 14.5 and 14.6 The barrel and muzzle swing up the centerline of the target: side and top views.

situation, the other shot(s) can be placed right on target, as the pointing movement continues.

3. No Erratic Movement of the Handgun.   With some shooters, two problems occur in pointing the handgun out: side movement of the handgun and bringing the barrel first up and then down.

The first problem is side movement of the handgun. From the belt-level position, the handgun is moved straight forward in a direct line toward the target. Some officers have a tendency to make it swing to the outside or inside of the body and then get back on track as the pointing finishes. If this occurs, it will throw the shot off. The handgun must be kept in a straight line. Remember, a straight line is the shortest distance between two points and naturally used when pointing; any extra movements can void the natural point. (*Note:* Any unnecessary movements must be greatly reduced or eliminated in all your weapon use skills.)

The second problem is bringing the barrel up and then down when pointing. This can also void the natural point. When bringing the handgun forward and up, the end of the barrel swings from a low position in an upward arc (not an exaggerated swing, but a very small, fast one). Any raising and then lowering of the handgun will not work.

Both of these can be overcome by starting out slowly and watching yourself in the first stages of learning how to point shoot.

4. The Bend in the Elbow Is Important.   The bend in the elbow and the distance that the handgun is extended from the body at the firing point (when you fire) are determined by how close an attacker is to you.

0 to 4 Feet. When the threat is right on top of you, this is the time for just turning the handgun straight with virtually no pointing movement and firing. The technique is generally known as the speed rock.

4 to 8 Feet. With a threat a little farther away, the arm moves farther forward in the pointing movement, with the bend in the elbow at 90 degrees, or slightly more, and the inside of the elbow just barely touching the side of the body. The handgun should be just above waist level.

14.7.

14.8.

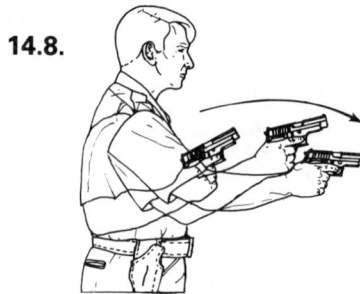

right   **wrong**

Figures 14.7–14.10 The barrel only sweeps forward and upward, coming up the centerline of the target (Fig. 14.7). The barrel is never brought up and then down (Fig. 14.8). Also, the barrel is pointed straight forward (Fig. 14.9) with no side movement (Fig. 14.10).

14.9.

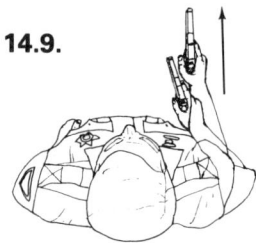

14.10.

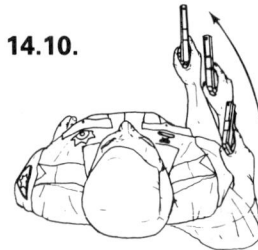

right   **wrong**

8 to 12 Feet. With the threat farther away, the arm is raised to about midway between the position next to your body (90 degrees) and straight out (as if you were aiming one-handed). The elbow is bent in about a 130-degree angle.

14.11.

14.12.

14.13.

Figures 14.11–14.13 The three general bends in the elbow and distance the handgun is extended from the body: the speed rock (Fig. 14.11), the 90-degree bend (Fig. 14.12), and the 130-degree bend (Fig. 14.13).

Through these three basic positions you can see that the farther the attacker is away, the farther the arm extends and the greater the elbow's angle. Also, the higher the handgun is, the greater the eye and barrel alignment. Practice these until they feel right. Remember, the pointing movement is a smooth, fluid movement that brings the handgun up into a natural pointing position.

After a distance of 12 feet, point shooting is stopped and either stance-directed or aimed firing techniques are used. This is not to say that point shooting ends abruptly at this arbitrary distance, but its application to lethal encounters ends. Point shooting can give you an instant fighting advantage during PDQ situations, but once the distance increases, its use ends in favor of superior firing techniques—stance-directed or aimed firing techniques.

The speed rock, not really point shooting. Although the speed rock is covered under point shooting, the technique is very different. As the name implies, the handgun is instantly rocked up into a close-to-the-body firing position. No pointing movement is made; the handgun is simply rocked up, with the wrist bending a little to bring the handgun's muzzle up.

When searching with the handgun held in the belt-level position, if a threat suddenly attacks at very close range (0 to 4 feet), the handgun is instantly rocked up into a firing position and fired from belt-level (never having left the waist). This will place the "hits" directly into the threat's center mass. If the handgun was holstered, it is drawn and rocked up into this position to fire.

The support hand is out of the way by being held up to fend off the threat. As such, it is well away from the handgun's muzzle. Also while shooting, one or two quick backward steps (back peddling) can be taken to help absorb the bodily momentum of the threat's attack (sidesteps can also be used to move out of the way of the threat's attack). This is the only time the trigger finger enters the trigger guard before the handgun is out in front of the body after position 3. When you begin practicing the speed rock, use an unloaded handgun (check it twice).

14.14.

Figure 14.14 The speed rock is used with the support hand being held up to fend off an attacker.

TRAINING

Once you have learned the techniques by engaging in dry-fire practice, live-fire training is begun. Safety is heavily stressed by doing three things: (1) starting the handgun from the belt-level position and returning to it to that position after firing (with the muzzle pointed well in front of you at the floor), (2) keeping your trigger finger out of the trigger guard until the pointing movement is started and the handgun's muzzle is well in front of your body, and (3) making sure that you keep the support hand out of the way and do not let it cross the centerline of the body or be placed in front of the muzzle.

Live-fire training starts with a target at a distance of about 12 feet. You can use a regular combat target to see where your shots are going, but the side of a dirt bank with a small target (cartridge box size) is preferable. (*Note:* Do not fire into a rocky area where ricochets may occur.) Bring the handgun up along the centerline of the target and shoot when you think it is right, allowing a brief pause at the end of the pointing movement before the first shot is fired. Do not just thrust it out fast and pull the trigger. Take your time, point it out slowly to get the feel and allow a second to go by, and when you think it is right, press the trigger.

The handgun must not move while you are manipulating the trigger. If it does, your shot will be off, just as it would if aiming with the sights. Many times your natural pointing technique is fine (producing the handgun right on target) but as you manipulate the trigger, the handgun moves and the shot goes wide. Take your time to watch for this when you start. Also, keep your wrist straight and fully locked while keeping full strength in the master grip.

Practice by starting with the handgun in the belt-level position, bringing it up, out, and firing, and returning it to the belt-level position. Do not allow the handgun to hang down, pointing at your feet; control it.

The pointing movement follows these steps:

1. The wrist, forearm, and handgun are held in a straight line in the belt-level position.
2. The pointing movement is started by the handgun being pointed at the target, the moment it moves from the belt-level position. The handgun, wrist, and forearm are held in a straight line as the handgun is brought out straight toward the target in a pointing movement (no inside or outside movement).
3. The barrel travels up the centerline of the target.
4. You look at the target and not at the handgun as you point it out (your eyes' peripheral vision will align the barrel on the target).
5. As the handgun arrives at the firing point an imperceptible hesitation elapses during alignment (one-eighth to one-sixteenth of a second).
6. The shot(s) is fired by using correct trigger manipulation. These six steps flow together instantly when point shooting.

Drawing

Only after you are thoroughly familiar with the technique should you integrate drawing from a holster into your practice. Remember, when drawing from a holster, keep your trigger finger out of the trigger guard, indexing it (placing it into the trigger guard on the trigger) only as the handgun begins pointing at the target and the muzzle is in front of your body. You must be safe; always be thinking safety. Also be aware that the trigger finger stays out of the trigger guard not only when drawing, but also when reholstering.

Point shooting will feel the same with the added draw as the handgun travels right through the belt-level position on its way into the pointing movement. Your wrist may be bent on the draw but is straightened out instantly as you begin the pointing movement. Forearm, wrist, and handgun must be in a straight line.

14.15.   **14.16.**

Figures 14.15 and 14.16 The pointing movement is shown from the belt-level position to the 90-degree bend in the elbow: front and side views.

APPLIED TECHNIQUES

Once the technique has been trained-in, its use follows the applied pointing of your finger. Wherever the target is located around you, simply point at it, turning the body for the rear 180-degree arc. It is thus highly versatile in coping with threats that present themselves at different angles around you.

Point shooting should be viewed as one technique in your bag of tricks (your trained-in reflexive sets of weapon use skills) and is used in conjunction with the other techniques. Always select the best technique for the situation at hand.

Traversing and Pivoting

Point shooting works easily for the 180-degree firing arc in front of the officer, with slight traversing (turning the upper body at the waist) for shots to either side. To cover the rear 180-degree firing arc, traversing and pivoting are used to turn the body when aligning the strong arm on the target. If pressed by the situation or structure, you can use point shooting with little turning to cover much of this rear 180-degree arc, but you will be in an unnatural position. Remember, you want the pointing movement to be as natural as possible. Turning at the waist and/or pivoting on the feet to cover any side or rear area, as the pointing movement points the handgun out, helps the strong arm to be aligned more naturally on the target. Remember to keep the handgun, wrist, and forearm held straight when pointing at any target around you.

Multiple Targets

In point shooting, as in all forms of defensive firing, placing "hits" on multiple targets must be practiced. When shooting multiple targets with a locked-in two-handed firing stance, the arms are kept straight and moved from one target to the next. In point shooting this is not done. Instead, you must point the handgun each time you move to another target. It is not an exaggerated pointing action. Just draw the arm and handgun back slightly as they are traveling to the next target and then point them back out just enough to get a pointing movement as you are coming on target.

As an example of the natural point, just stick your finger out and point at one object, then another. You will find yourself making a slight pointing movement between the two objects. That is all you have to do when pointing the handgun between two objects—just use a slight pointing motion. Just keep it natural. If the arm is kept straight, you have a tendency to swing past the second target and at times miss it. With the pointing movement you are pointing directly at the second target, with no time lost or overswing occurring.

When firing on multiple targets, if you can go into a locked-in two-handed firing stance for the second or third targets, do it (or if again placing "hits" on the first target). The support hand can catch the handgun as it is moving to the second target and lock into the two-handed grip just as it locks out to fire. Remember to keep the support hand well back from the muzzle.

14.17.   14.18.

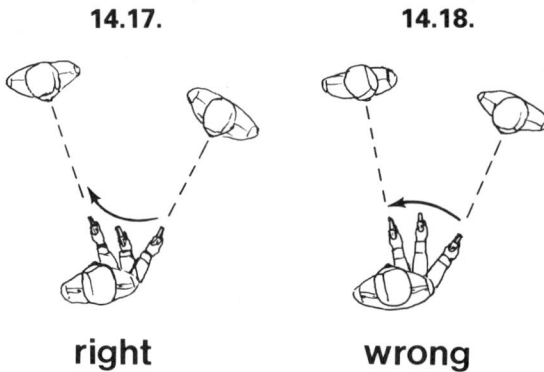

right   **wrong**

Figures 14.17 and 14.18   When firing on multiple targets, the arm is pulled back slightly, as it moves toward the other target and then pointed out at that target (Fig. 14.17), for a better pointing movement and to make sure that you do not "swing past." The arm is not just swung from one target to the next (Fig. 14.18).

From Point Shooting to a Two-Handed Firing Stance

In your practice you must integrate point shooting into your two-handed shooting. Begin with a quick shot using point shooting, then (once the point shooting shot has been fired) continue out and up into a two-handed firing stance (with the support hand assuming a two-handed grip). In many lethal encounters this is exactly what is called for. Your quick shots with point shooting have hopefully solved the close, urgent problem and you instantly go into the superior two-handed stance to continue firing or while moving to cover for the rest of the fight.

Practice switching into the two-handed firing stance after point shooting, as it forms one defensive weapon use package. Be careful not to place the support hand in front of the muzzle when assuming the two-handed grip. Keep the support hand ready, but back, until it is needed. Only when the muzzle is in front of the support hand will the hand come across the centerline of the body and begin the two-handed grip. Also, become accustomed to assuming the two-handed grip while the handgun is held in the support position (at position 3)—prepared to lock out instantly into a two-handed firing stance.

Point shooting and the speed rock have been discussed; we now move into the stance-directed fire technique, the last of the unaimed firing techniques.

STANCE-DIRECTED FIRE

This unaimed firing technique was described in Chapter 11, as a low-light firing technique for partial-light conditions: enough light present to locate/identify the threat(s), but not enough to use the handgun's sights to aim with. With stance-directed fire, the officer's locked-in two-handed firing stance alone, without the use of the sights, is enough to fire successfully on an identifiable threat.

The technique centers on your practiced, two-handed firing stance that is locked out at the end of the holster-to-stance reflex. This is your most practiced firing stance. You have practiced locking into and/or firing from this two-handed firing stance hundreds of times, and your body has developed a kinesthetic feedback mechanism to tell you when the stance is right. Your muscles have specialized receptors (kinesthetic) built in which are triggered by muscular contractions. The kinesthetic return from muscular movement thus produces a stimulus that can call forth, by previous learning, another set position or movement. You have repeated it, locked into it, and fired from it hundreds of times. Your body, in short, has a feel for it. Now, whenever you lock into the stance, your body tells you when it is right. When using stance-directed fire, just lock into your stance without using the sights and fire. Your locked-in stance will do the rest.

Just by snapping up into your stance, you should be able to place shots effectively on a threat up to 10 yards. This works well in all conditions: daylight, partial-light, and dark conditions. (*Note:* In dark conditions, you must know that it is a threat, know exactly where it is, and direct every shot at it.) Simply snap into your locked-in two-handed firing stance directed at the threat, and fire.

Techniques That Make It Work

There are several techniques that will make stance-directed fire work smoothly. Understand and follow these when practicing this unaimed firing technique.

   1. *Use one stance consistently.* You have no doubt selected either the Weaver

or Isosceles stance as your locked-in two-handed firing stance. Whichever stance you have selected, use it exclusively; no switching back and forth. Also, you must practice the firing stance the same way each time to program your body to the feel of the stance. Only by doing this will the body become programmed to the kinesthetic return that tells you the stance is locked in and right. Practice the locked-in two-handed firing stance the same way every time you do it, again and again and again. Only through repetition will the stance be trained-in for the kinesthetic return required. Pick one stance and use it exclusively.

2. *Look through the handgun.* When engaging in stance-directed fire, which is unaimed, make sure that you use the stance exactly the same as you do when engaging in aimed fire. Most of the problems occur when officers do not lock into the stance at eye level when using unaimed fire, but hold the handgun below eye level (below the line of sight), as they want to see more of the threat. You have already located/identified the threat; now you must fully lock into the stance to fire on it. Even when fully locked up in the two-handed stance, you can still see almost all of the threat. Make sure that you fully lock up into your line of sight, looking through the handgun at the target. Remember, it must be the same each time, whether live-fire practice, dry practice, or during a real encounter. You know it's right when you are looking through the handgun at the target.

3. *Smooth trigger manipulation.* Maintain a stable stance while smoothly manipulating the trigger. Make sure that you do not rush or "jerk" the trigger, but manipulate it smoothly when firing. Your two-handed firing stance can be perfect for a good "hit" on the threat, but a sloppy trigger will throw the round off, possibly missing the target completely.

The Kinesthetic Return Test

Anytime during your practice you can test yourself to see how the kinesthetic return is functioning. When engaging in dry-fire practice with an unloaded handgun (check it twice), you normally pick out a target (aiming point) on a wall, lock out in your two-handed firing stance while aligning the sights, and manipulate the trigger.

Now you reverse the sighting process to test the kinesthetic return. While looking at the target, you lock out into the stance first, then verify the sights to see if they are aligned on target. Look at the target, then lock out in your two-handed firing stance at eye level while still focused on the target (looking through the handgun, which is held between your eyes and the target). Now shift your focus to the sights and see if they are aligned on the target. Make sure that you hold the handgun completely still while you are verifying the sight alignment. If the sights are aligned, your kinesthetic return is working. At first, practice without manipulating the trigger to see if the kinesthetic return is working.

Dry firing must also be done to train-in and verify that the correct trigger manipulation is being used. With an unloaded handgun (check it twice), lock out into your two-handed firing stance at eye level (while focusing on the target) and manipulate the trigger. Now shift your focus to the sights and see if they are aligned on the target. You may have an excellent kinesthetic return, but your trigger manipulation may jerk the handgun off target. Proper trigger manipulation must also be trained-in whatever firing technique is used.

Live firing will complete the practice/testing needed for stance-directed fire, to make sure that everything is actually working when firing the handgun. On the range, with the handgun loaded, lock out into your two-handed firing stance at eye level (while looking through the handgun and focusing on the target) and manipulate the trigger. Fire one or two shots while keeping the stance locked on target. Once the firing is completed, shift your focus and check for sight alignment on the target. The sights should be aligned. Also, check the target for round placement.

The more you practice your two-handed firing stance, the better your kinesthetic return will be. Use all three testing mechanisms on a continual basis: basic alignment (with no trigger manipulation), dry firing (pulling the trigger to make sure your trigger manipulation is correct), and live firing (to make sure that everything is working when actually firing the handgun). These tests will help you practice your skills and build your confidence in stance-directed fire.

SUMMARY

In this chapter we covered the three unaimed firing techniques that can be used during lethal encounters. Training-in these one- and two-handed unaimed firing techniques will increase your survival advantage if aimed firing techniques cannot be used. We train for all situations that can occur, to be prepared for a breakdown in situation and/or structure. Unaimed firing techniques prepare you for some of the worst breakdowns.

15

Backup and Concealed Handguns and Concealment Drawing Techniques

In this chapter we discuss the three areas of hidden handguns: backup handguns, concealed handguns, and the concealment drawing techniques for both. Backup handguns are concealed second guns carried by uniformed and plain clothes officers as insurance policies against the possibility of their service handguns malfunctioning or if reloading cannot be accomplished instantly during a pressing attack. Concealed handguns are the issued service handguns carried by plain clothes officers or any handgun carried by off-duty officers under a jacket. There are a number of realities and concealment drawing techniques which will be covered with each concealment mode.

BACKUP HANDGUNS

Few firearms issues come under such departmental attack as carrying backup handguns. Nationwide estimates say that 50 to 60 percent of all police officers, whether or not sanctioned by their respective departments, carry backup handguns. Many departments, including the giant New York City Police Department, allow their officers to carry a backup handgun in case the situation goes bad.

Any lethal encounter that officers are involved in can instantly go bad for any number of reasons. The backup handgun is just a form of insurance against the breakdown or loss of your service handgun. Police officers, carrying a service handgun as their main piece of emergency equipment, should have a backup handgun in case the service handgun fails. During any encounter your service handgun can malfunction or become completely "jammed," greatly reducing your ability to survive. Also, your service handgun can become lost in a chase or struggle, or can be taken from you during a hostage situation. Remember, we train and prepare for the ultimate breakdown in situation. If it never occurs, all well and good, but if it occurs tomorrow, you are ready to meet the situation and survive.

To reload or use a backup handgun.   Many officers consider their backup handguns as their first reload. Instead of reloading their service revolver after the initial exchange, they instantly go for their backup handgun, feeling that the fastest reload is the second gun. In reality, officers must use their trained-in reloading techniques to keep their service handguns well fed during the encounter, resorting to the backup handgun only if a malfunction occurs or the situation instantly demands it. Usually, enough time exists to reload during lulls in the action. A situation may exist, such as multiple threats still continuing to attack your position after the initial exchange, where there is no time to reload. Obviously, the backup handgun would be used. But if time to reload, reload the service handgun and continue to use it.

Backup Handgun Type and Ammunition Compared to Service Handgun

An initial question about a backup handgun is whether it should be of the same design type and caliber as the officer's service handgun. Many say that it should—which has limited advantages. For example, if a .38 special D-A revolver is carried as the service handgun, a .38 special D-A revolver would be carried as the backup handgun. The sizes would be different, but both service handgun and backup handgun would function the same and use the same ammunition.

The first advantage of both being the same type and caliber relates to training and qualification. When officers are trained in the use of their service handgun, they are being automatically trained in the use of their backup handgun. Both function the same and will require the same reflexive sets. Thus the extra and possibly confusing training needed with two different handgun designs will not be needed. Also, this would preclude the need to carry extra ammo, as the service handgun ammo would fit the backup handgun.

In reality, it is not that easy. First, the same handgun design type can certainly aid in training (using only one design type), but the backup must still be trained-in thoroughly even though of the same design type. When allowed to make personal selections, officers are more likely to practice with the backup handgun. Often, the backup handgun will be a small off-duty handgun with which officers are very familiar and comfortable. As a rule they have already engaged in a good amount of practice, with only departmental qualification needed. Let there be no mistake; you must be qualified with a backup handgun.

Second, ammunition compatibility often becomes unrealistic. Considering the actual small handguns available, the .38 special is no problem to match with a small backup handgun, but for ammunition compatibility, the .357 Magnum, 9mm, and .45 ACP are not as easily matched in a small backup. Also, some hot .38 special service loads may not be suitable for the small handguns. If an auto, the backup handgun must also have its own magazine, even if the same caliber.

Officers should be allowed to select a small backup handgun, either revolver or automatic, within certain established parameters. This system of individual selection, with the controls necessary, will function best.

Types of Backup Handguns and Modifications

Types of backup handguns.   To be considered as a backup, a handgun must be small enough to be readily concealed, while the caliber can range from adequate to downright excellent in defensive ability. Generally, most backup handguns fall into two categories: small revolvers in .38 special caliber and small automatics in .380 caliber (Charter Arms Police Undercover .38 special and S&W Chief .38 special revolvers and Walter PPK/S .380 and Sig P230 .380 autos are excellent examples). The third category is the larger-caliber handguns that come in small packages (excellent examples are the Charter Arms Bulldog .44 special revolver, a lot of backup power in a little package, and the S&W 469 9mm auto, a lot of 9mm's in a small package).

15.1.

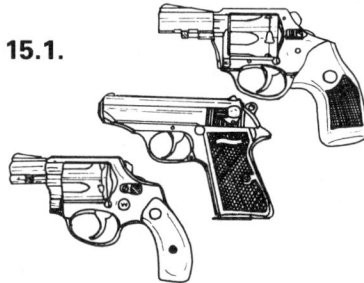

Figure 15.1   Three backup handguns, from top to bottom: Charter Arms .44 Special, Walther PPK/S .380, and S&W .38 Sl.

38/380 Floor.   No caliber below a .38 special for a revolver or a .380 for an automatic should be considered as a backup handgun. Many fine examples of true "hideout" handguns—mainly .22 long rifle and .25 ACP calibers—exist, but these should not be used as backup (secondary) handguns. Their use is relegated to the true hideout handgun variety (tertiary guns), which would be deeply concealed and are not covered here. (*Note:* There are generally three levels of handguns used: service/primary handguns—largest variety with longer barrels; backup/secondary handguns—medium to small variety, with shorter barrels; and hideout/tertiary handguns—small to very small variety. Here we are dealing only with backup handguns.)

Modifications.   Just as with the service handgun, the backup must be completely reliable and fully test fired by you (a minimum test of 100 rounds must be fired). Reliability is the primary factor, as the backup must work the first time and every time you use it. Only use and purchase a handgun of reliable manufacture and in good condition (if unsure, have a gunsmith check it out). Any modifications must not reduce the backup's mechanical and functional reliability.

Usually, a backup handgun is modified to improve its smooth and snag-free exterior. The backup must be as smooth and free of sharp corners as possible. If not, it can catch and bind on clothing when drawing. The sights must be simple and fixed, with the sharp corners taken off/rounded. A revolver's hammer spur should be removed so that it will not catch in clothing when drawing. The backup handgun should feel smooth to the touch. Do not use rubber grips or grips with sharp checkering, as they will only catch on clothing and wear holes in it. For backup handguns, the grips should be small and smooth. If a revolver, they should be of the round butt style and the left grip panel must easily accept a speed loader. Keep modifications to a minimum and do not compromise reliability.

Backup Concealment Locations

A number of backup concealment locations exist, but only some can be used, depending on the clothing worn. We will be talking about two levels of concealment (for both backup and concealed handguns): deep (under a garment that is not easily opened, although it can be opened quickly) and surface (under a garment that is easily opened). First several concealment carrying factors must be understood.

Concealment carrying factors.   First, any concealed carry must effectively conceal the backup handgun, the primary function of any concealment carry. This is your first consideration: Is the backup well concealed? Second, you must be consistent in your placement of the backup. Once you decide on a carrying location for the backup, it must be used consistently: no switching back and forth. You must know instantly where to go for the backup. Third, the backup must be securely carried in a holster so that the handgun will stay in place during any strenuous physical activity. You must be able to run after and struggle with a suspect without loosing your backup handgun. Avoid sticking it under the pants belt or in a loose pocket. Also, it should be hard to grab if a suspect sees it (if it should appear from concealment). Fourth, the draw must be able to be performed very quickly. The major loser in this area is the ankle holster, as the body has to bend down or the leg has to be raised when drawing. Fifth, the backup must be relatively comfortable for prolonged wear. On an 8-hour tour, the backup will be with you for 8 hours. Only you will be able to tell what is right for you; test the carrying modes.

Make sure that you have weighed and tested these factors thoroughly when selecting a concealment carrying location that will be suited to you. Everyone is different; work with the fit and feel of different concealment carrying locations, and find what is right for you.

Deep concealment.   This level of concealment is used to place the backup handgun under standard clothing: a shirt and pants, with no jacket needed to aid concealment. The garment is not easily opened (unbuttoning a shirt), but it can be opened quickly when needed (popping the shirt open, with the buttons flying). The backup is available only after pulling some clothing free, which usually requires two hands.

Any uniformed, plain clothes, or off-duty officer not wearing some type of jacket has three deep concealment options for concealing a backup handgun: belly-band holster, Horan-Hide-Out holster (for the bullet proof vest), and below-the-knee leg holster.

Bellyband and Horan-Hide-Out Holsters.   These holsters will be handled to-gether, as they are both worn under the shirt. The bellyband holster by Bianchi is an elastic band with a holster attached to it. It goes around your stomach, under your shirt, to hold the backup into your side. The elastic band supports the backup and pulls it in slightly. If the shirt is not skin tight, the backup is nicely hidden. The Horan-Hide-Out holster by Calibre Press attaches to the two side straps of a bullet proof vest and fits under your arm, the same as a shoulder holster. This is really a slick holster that conceals the backup very well.

The drawing method for both of these begins by popping the shirt open with one hand (sticking the fingers into the front of the shirt and pulling hard, which will pop the buttons off) while the other hand draws the backup. The draw is like a crossdraw or a shoulder holster and averages about 1.5 seconds. Practice with a tucked-in shirt and the front unbuttoned to get the hang of it. Tactically, as you are drawing, you stay upright on your feet, moving for cover if not already behind it.

Below-the-Knee Holster.   This leg holster is positioned on the inside of the leg, just below the knee. The problem with any leg holster is the slower drawing speed and having to either hop around on one foot or drop down when drawing. Also, since this holster is directly below the knee, the pants leg has to be pulled up to the knee to draw the weapon. Thus two hands must be used when drawing; both pull up the pants leg then the strong hand draws the backup. This is the least desir-able position for deep concealment but is an option.

Surface concealment.   This level of concealment is used to place the backup handgun under a jacket. As such, the garment is easily opened and the backup can be drawn quickly. Obviously, the concealed backup locations described under deep concealment will also work, but a speed advantage can be gained by using surface concealment locations.

Once a jacket is worn, three surface concealment options appear for conceal-ing the backup handgun: upside-down shoulder holster, inside-the-pants holster, and ankle holster.

Upside-Down Shoulder Holster.   A light and comfortable shoulder holster, with no tiedown straps for either side, is easily concealed under the jacket and holds

15.2.   **15.3.**   **15.4.**

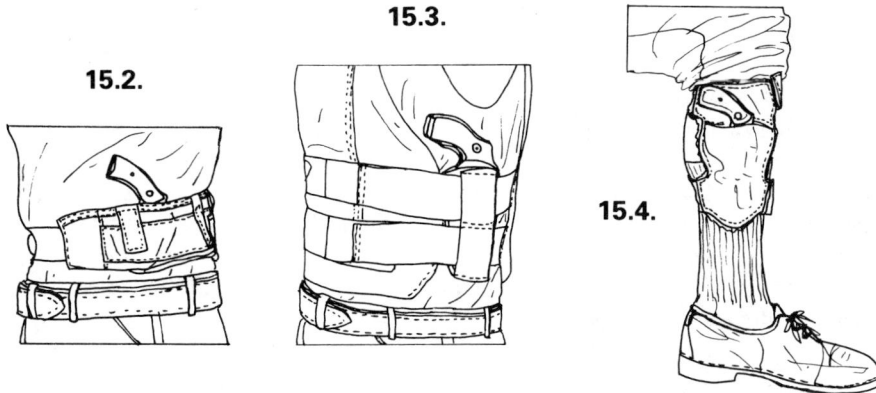

Figures 15.2–15.4   Three types of deep concealment holsters are shown: the belly-band holster by Bianchi (Fig. 15.2), the Horan-Hide-Out holster by Calibre Press (Fig. 15.3), and the leg holster by Bianchi (Fig. 15.4).

a small backup well. The upside-down positioning of the backup handgun conceals it better and makes it very easy for the strong hand to reach the grip. When drawing, the support hand pulls the jacket out of the way while the strong hand instantly goes to the backup and makes the draw. The support hand is used if available but does not have to be used if needed for another urgent task. Also note that the holster must be well secured against the handgun falling out.

Inside-the-Pants Holster.   These soft leather/clip holsters or thicker leather/belt snap holsters can fit anywhere around the belt and ride between the inside of the pants and the shirt, with only the grip showing above the pants. The best positioning is on the strong side below the kidney, with the backup handgun facing forward. Only the strong hand is ever used when drawing. This positioning will give you the fastest draw, especially when the grip is tilted slightly forward and the barrel slightly to the rear. The holster can also be positioned in the small of the back, but this can become very uncomfortable, especially if driving.

When drawing, the strong hand must sweep the side of the jacket out of the way as it goes for the backup. This is done by the strong-hand fingers being held slightly apart and naturally, as the hand starts rearward. The little finger hooks the edge of the jacket and pulls it quickly back and out of the way, actually throwing it well to the rear of the backup's position, at the end of the sweep. When doing this the fingertips will be in contact with the shirt during the first part of the sweep, until the jacket is thrown to the rear the instant before the grip is made. Once the hand is at the backup, it instantly forms the master grip and draws the gun. Before the draw, the hand can be positioned at the belt line, with the little finger already hooked under the edge of the jacket, ready instantly. Also note that extra ammo can be carried in the strong-side jacket pocket. This additional weight will help throw the jacket away from the backup, especially helpful on very light jackets.

Also, the extra ammo is on the right side for the strong hand to grab if using a revolver.

Ankle Holster.   This holster is located on the inside of the ankle and concealed below the lower pants leg. If right-handed, the holster is on your left leg; if left-handed, on your right leg. The main problem with the ankle holster is the slower drawing speed and having to either hop around on one foot or drop down when drawing. Also, two hands must be used when drawing; one pulls up the pants leg while the other draws the backup. This is the least desirable position for surface concealment but is a concealment option. Make sure that the holster has a good security device; if not, you will lose the gun quickly.

15.5.   **15.6.**

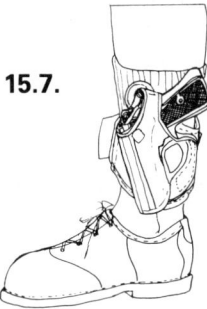

15.7.

Figures 15.5–15.7 Three types of surface concealment holsters are shown: two upside-down shoulder holsters (Fig. 15.5, the slant shoulder rig by DeSantis shown with a full-sized, auto and the Silent Partner by Bianchi shown with a small revolver), an inside-the-pants holster by Horseshoe Leather (Fig. 15.6), and the ankle rig by DeSantis (Fig. 15.7).

(*Note:* A reference on the pocket carry should be included here. Carrying a small .38 special revolver or .380 auto backup handgun in your pocket has some definite advantages, but it goes against everything most departments will allow. This is especially good with a small .38 special revolver with the hammer spur cut off. With your hand in your pocket, on the backup, you are ready to draw and fire instantly. The only problem is catching the backup on the pocket lip; with the hammer spur cut off, this is usually not a problem.)

Training with the Backup

Backup handguns are often not a part of departmental firearms training and qualification. This must not occur. Firearms instructors must make sure that officers have the necessary skills with their backup handguns, and departmental qualification with the backup must be done along with the service handgun. If qualification is not done, vicarious liability problems can emerge after a shooting, justifiable or not, where an officer used a backup handgun.

Individually, officers must practice with their backups quite a bit, engaging in both dry and live practice. If nothing else, officers must make sure that they are thoroughly knowledgeable in their backup handgun's functioning and firing, especially safe handling and carrying modes.

Officers must have trained-in skills for the backup handgun just as they do for the service handgun. Whenever engaging in dry- and live-fire practice with the service handgun, the backup handgun must also be part of the practice. At times the backup is easily neglected. Do not let this happen; make sure that the backup is part of your training regimen.

CONCEALED HANDGUNS

Concealed handguns are service/primary handguns used by plain clothes and off-duty officers wearing some type of jacket. This is nothing more than appropriately carrying the service/primary handgun while concealing its bulk.

For this purpose, two main concealed carrying locations are used: the strong side/kidney carry and the shoulder holster. Positions and holsters that are crossdraw (excluding shoulder holsters) and/or worn forward of the hip bone should not be used, as neither provide good concealment and the crossdraw is very inviting for a suspect to try to grab (if the gun is seen). Also, for a crossdraw to be concealed, it must ride behind the hip bone and positioned there, it is very hard to grip instantly when drawing. Position nothing forward of the hip bone and do not use a crossdraw holster.

Strong Side Kidney Holster. These holsters ride on the outside of the pants belt directly under the kidney, with the handgun facing forward. The holster should have a snap-and-strap arrangement as a primary securing device, cover the trigger guard and trigger, and the leather formed to the handgun as a secondary securing device. The holster should also fit tight on the belt, with the handgun fitting close to the body.

When drawing, the method is the same as described under surface concealment. As the draw is made, the strong hand sweeps the jacket out of the way as it goes for the handgun, by the little finger hooking the edge of the jacket and pulling it quickly back and out of the way, throwing it well to the rear at the end of the sweep. Once the hand is at the handgun, it instantly forms the master grip and draws the gun. Before the draw, the hand can be positioned at the beltline, with the little finger already hooked under the edge of the jacket, instantly ready. Again, the extra ammo can be carried in the strong-side jacket pocket for the additional weight to help throw the jacket away from the handgun.

Shoulder Holster.   These holsters can either be upside down or straight up and down, depending on the style of holster and handgun you are using. In reality it is a matter of choice, as both work very well.

When drawing, the method is the same as described under surface conceal-

15.8.

 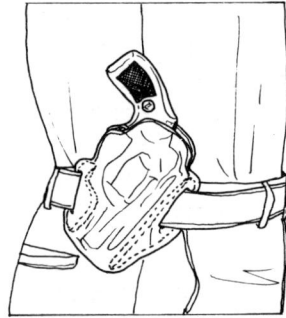

15.9.   **15.10.**

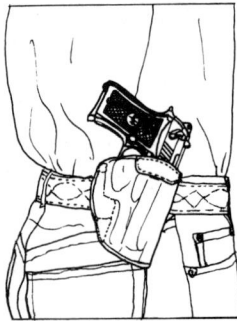 

Figures 15.8–15.10   Generally concealed handguns are carried in two main locations: strong side/kidney carry and shoulder holsters. The strong side/kidney carry holsters shown are the DeSantis thumb-break scabbard (with full-sized auto) and speed scabbard (with small revolver) (Fig. 15.8) and the concealed carry holster by Horseshoe Leather (Fig. 15.9). The shoulder holster shown is the Phantom by Bianchi (Fig. 15.10).

ment. As the draw is started, the support hand pulls the jacket out of the way while the strong hand instantly goes to the handgun and makes the draw. The support hand is used if available but does not have to be used if needed for another urgent task. Also note that the holster must be well secured against the handgun falling out.

SUMMARY

In this brief chapter we have discussed the best concealment locations for both backup and concealed handguns. These locations and the drawing techniques are the first step. Once one is decided on, you must practice with it to produce the skill to use it quickly and correctly; work for smoothness first, only then working on speed. Remember, you must know the safe handling procedures and carrying modes for your backup handgun.

Conceaiment holsters, as with any holsters, are a compromise between concealability, speed, security, and wearability. These four factors produce a mix that must be lived with throughout your working hours. Choose what is right for you and what works the best for you. Again, once chosen, the skills must be developed.

Bibliography

ARNOLD, DAVE. *Handguns for Home Defense.* Los Angeles: Peterson Publishing Co., 1982.

ASKINS, CHARLES. *Gun Fighters.* Washington, DC: National Rifle Association, 1981.

AYOOB, MASSAD. *In the Gravest Extreme.* Concord, NH, 1975.

AYOOB, MASSAD. *Stressfire.* Concord, NH, 1984.

AYOOB, MASSAD. *The Truth About Self-Protection.* New York: Bantam Books, 1983.

BIANCHI, JOHN E. *Bluesteel & Gunleather.* Temecula, CA, 1978.

BOOTHROYD, GEOFFREY. *The Handgun.* New York: Bonanza Books, 1970.

CHAPMAN, SAMUEL. *Police Murders and Effective Countermeasures.* Santa Cruz, CA: Davis Publishing Co., 1976.

CLEDE, BILL. *Police Handgun Manual.* Harrisburg, PA: Stackpole Books, 1985.

COOPER, JEFF. *Complete Book of Modern Handgunning.* Englewood Cliffs, NJ: Prentice-Hall, 1961.

COOPER, JEFF. *Jeff Cooper on Handguns.* Los Angeles: Peterson Publishing Co., 1979.

COOPER, JEFF. *Principles of Personal Defense.* Boulder, CO: Paladin Press, 1972.

FAIRBAIRN, W. E., and SYKES, E. A. *Shooting to Live.* Houston: Lancer Militaria, 1971.

FARNAM, JOHN. *Basic Combat Shooting—Volumes I and II.* Aspen, CO, 1984.

FARNAM, JOHN. *The Street Smart Gun Book.* Aspen, CO, 1987.

HOGG, IAN V. and WEEKS, JOHN. *Pistols of the World.* San Rafael, CA: Presidio Press, 1978.

JORDAN, W. H. *No Second Place Winner.* Shreveport, LA, 1965.

MASON, JAMES D. *Combat Handgun Shooting.* Springfield, IL: Charles C. Thomas, Publisher, 1976.

McGIVERN, ED. *Fast and Fancy Revolver Shooting.* Piscataway, NJ: New Century Publishers, 1984.

NONTE, GEORGE JR. *Combat Handguns.* Harrisburg, PA: Stackpole Books, 1980.

REMSBURG, CHARLES; ADAMS, RONALD J., and McTERNAN, THOMAS M. *Street Survival: Tactics for Armed Encounters.* Evanston, IL: Calibre Press, 1980.

REMSBURG, CHARLES. *The Tactical Edge: Surviving High-Risk Patrol.* Northbrook, IL: Calibre Press, 1986.

SHAW, JOHN. *Shoot to Win.* Memphis, TN, 1985.

SHAW, JOHN. *You Can't Miss.* Memphis, TN, 1982.

TAYLOR, CHUCK. *The Complete Book of Combat Handgunning.* Cornville, AZ: Desert Publications, 1982.

WINOKUR, JON. *Master Tips.* Pacific Palisades, CA: Potshot Press, 1985.

———. ".45 Auto Handbook," New York: Modern Day Periodicals, 1982.

Glossary

Action/Threat(s) The immediate danger during an encounter; what you always must be watching.

Approaching Moving toward a precise location where a threat could be hiding (possible threat cover). Used in conjunction with searching.

ASSETS System Acronym for Assessing the Situation and Structure for the most Effective Tactic Selection. A system to detect what is occurring and how to respond to it appropriately.

Awareness Progression From the first recognition of a danger sign until the threat(s) presents itself, you progress through stages of awareness by observing continuing danger signs that an encounter is at hand.

Belt-Level Position The handgun is held in close to the body, with the thumb touching the belt, and the muzzle pointing safely at the floor in front of you. A good controlled position when searching.

Canting Bending the firing stance toward the side of cover to be turned or fired around.

Coaxiality Good flashlight beam to handgun barrel alignment—aligning along the same axis.

Cocked-and-Locked The correct carrying mode of a single-action automatic: where the hammer is cocked and the safety is locked "on."

Color Code System Describes four or five levels of alertness or readiness that you progress through during an encounter.

Contingency Plans One or two moves you've decided on in advance. If the first plan does not work or if a change occurs, these plans are ready instantly.

Continuum Line A line stretching from the past into the future, with the possible occurrences of life-threatening encounters as points along it.

Controlling Technique Used to look into a hidden area when turning cover and then remaining there, controlling it with the handgun.

Critical Time Reference The time interval from threat recognition through threat occurrence, and finally to your defensive response, including any lag interval. Runs through the opening ceremony where the initial exchange of gunfire usually takes place.

Danger Signs Any indication that is viewed, heard, felt, or sensed that something is not right.

DA/SA Switch Trigger mode switch when using a double-action auto, between the first shot in the double-action mode and the second shot in the single-action mode.

Defensive Response Quick and effective actions taken to stop the threat(s). Can occur before the threat(s) makes its move. Part of the critical time reference.

Distance Margins Increasing your distance from the danger will give you more time to respond to it.

Double-Action (D-A) Firing Mode The trigger is smoothly pulled to the rear, which will mechanically cock and drop the hammer, firing the handgun.

Double-Joint-Pull Whenever using the double-action firing mode, use the finger's joint position, and pull the trigger for the longer/heavier manipulation.

Draw to Belt-Level The draw into the belt-level position. The second part of the holster-to-stance reflex.

Dry Practice With an unloaded handgun, an officer can practice every weapon use skill except actually firing.

DVC The three principles of IPSC—accuracy, power, and speed.

Edge An imaginary line extending away from any corner to be turned, where a small movement beyond it will show the hidden side.

Expanded Focus Used to break out of tunnel vision during an encounter.

Expect Always expect the threat(s) to be there and be prepared. Part of the basic search rules (the "E" in the acronym SPECTR).

Eyes-Off Techniques Must keep your eyes on the action/threat(s) by reducing the need to look at the handgun (eyes off the handgun).

Fanning the Beam Rocking the flashlight back and forth very quickly by wrist action that throws light into a much larger area.

Feeling Times when certain bodily mechanisms or senses can "feel" that something is wrong. Possibly subliminal or precognitive in nature.

Fight or Flight Reflex Physical changes to the body due to stress dump that create changes in your functional ability—some positive and some negative.

Finite Movements Small, precise movements that usually break down during high stress situations.

Firing Positions Three positions in which the barrel is pointed at the threat or a possible threat location. Used when approaching possibly dangerous areas and when firing.

Firing Reflex Made up of four parts: locked-in firing stance, combat sight picture, trigger manipulation, and follow-through.

Firing Shock Violent shock that can occur when suddenly fired upon from close quarters.

Firing Speed The total time it takes to bring the handgun up and fire. Firing Speed = Presentation Speed + Triggering Speed.

Follow-The-Movement (FTM) Used to "hit" moving targets. Concentrate on Front sight, Track the moving target, and smoothly Manipulate the trigger.

Follow-Through After firing, reestablish sight picture immediately, then if further firing is not immediately necessary, lower the handgun to a "ready position." Stay ready to fire.

Glancing Technique Take a very fast look into a hidden area when turning cover and then instantly go back behind cover.

Grip Initial movement of the hand when gripping the holstered handgun. The first part of the holster-to-stance reflex.

Gross Movements Larger, sweeping movements and physical strength that usually hold up during high stress situations.

Hidden Approach Approach and/or search in such a manner to keep the threat(s) from seeing or hearing you.

Holding Positions Three positions where the barrel is pointed down in a non-threatening position. Used when searching for safety and when maneuvering around obstacles.

Holster-to-Stance Reflex The reflexive set of movements for instantly drawing and locking into a firing position. Made up of four movements: the grip, draw to belt-level, support position, and locked-out position.

Indexing the Trigger Finger Placing the trigger finger into the trigger guard on the trigger. ·

Initial Exchange The first exchange of gunfire, often times deciding the outcome.

Isosceles Stance A locked-in, two-handed firing stance with the chest facing straight toward the target, and the arms and elbows locked straight out.

Kinesthetic Mechanism When a position is repeatedly trained-in, the body develops a feel for it and can tell when it is right. The mechanism that makes stance directed fire work.

"KIS-U" Keep It Simple and Uncomplicated.

Lag Interval Will occur when the officer did not know the encounter was about to happen and is caught flatfooted. The longer the interval, the longer the officer's defensive response.

Locked-Out Position The two-handed firing stance is locked-out.

Machine-Gunning Panic firing as fast as you can, causing almost all misses. Sometimes referred to as "spraying and praying."

Manipulating the Handgun Maneuvering the handgun in the holding and firing positions in response to changes that occur while searching.

Master Grip The strong hand's grip on the handgun which is initially assumed when the gun is in the holster. In a two-handed grip, the master grip is not altered but the support hand adds to it.

Mental-Set A pre-set state of mind that is produced when officers mentally condition and prepare themselves for the realities of lethal encounters.

Modern Technique Modern defensive pistolcraft techniques stemming from the Weaver stance and IPSC freestyle competition, developed by the civilian practical community.

Muzzle Flash Flame from the handgun's muzzle caused by unburned powder.

On-Hand Factors That which you have "in you" and "on you" when an encounter starts (mentally, physically, and equipmentally).

Opening Ceremony When the lethal action begins, usually when the bullets start flying.

Par Time An average time taken to accomplish certain weapon use skills, such as drawing, reloading, etc.

Partial Light Opening At certain locations when searching in dark conditions, you may have enough light to fire without using your flashlight.

"PDQ" Situations Precariously close, deadly, and quick situations. The majority of lethal encounters.

Pivoting Turning your firing stance by moving one foot and pivoting on the other. Used when turning the firing stance to engage threat(s) to either side or to the rear.

Plan Take advantage of lull to plan, rethink, and evaluate. Part of the post exchange rules.

Possible Threat Cover (PTC) A location where a threat(s) could possibly be hiding. These are constantly being selected and carefully approached as you are searching an area.

Post Exchange Rules Used after any exchange of gunfire to follow-through in case the encounter suddenly starts up again. There are four rules reference to: cover, scan, reload, and plan.

Preparatory Response Your preparation for the encounter once a danger sign has been read correctly. Part of the critical time reference.

Presentation Speed The time it takes to present the handgun in a position to fire. Firing Speed = Presentation Speed + Triggering Speed.

Pressure Wall Increased pressure that is reached when the trigger's slack is taken up.

"QAQ" Drill A varying speed (quickly, accurately, quickly) procedure for picking up, aligning/inserting, and locking the magazine into the pistol.

Quick Fixes A method for quickly placing the flashlight in a controlled position while the support hand is used for some other task.

Quick Switch A method for quickly changing the handgun from one hand to another.

Readiness Conditions Conditions appropriate for the handgun's intended use and situation, which dictate the sequence necessary to fire the handgun. There are only three: carrying mode, loaded storage, and unloaded storage.

Realistic Flashlight Search Rule A rule that dictates your basic use of the flashlight during low light situations.

Reflexive Sets Trained-in sets of firearm skills that are critical to the defensive operation of the service handgun. Repetitious training produces these sets that occur almost automatically, at a subconscious level.

Reliability The first and foremost requirement of a service handgun. It must function reliably the first time and every time.

Reloading Once an exchange of gunfire has occurred, the used rounds must/may be quickly replaced in the service handgun. Two methods are used: complete and partial reloading.

Respond Always be in a position to respond and be ready to make a shoot/no-shoot decision. (The "R" in SPECTR.)

Reversal Condition During high stress situations, emotions begin to take control and reasoning ability is lowered—a reversal of the usual mental condition.

Run Dry Firing the handgun until it is completely empty.

Safety Reflex The four basic safety rules are trained-in until they are a reflex that is in place and working at all times.

Scanning Keeping a 360 degree visual check around you at all times while searching. Also used to cover the whole encounter zone as one of the post exchange rules.

Scenario Imaging Forming a mental image of a possibly pending encounter and quickly selecting a course of action. This method trains-in your ability to quickly decide what to do.

Search Fatigue Any position kept for too long will begin to feel uncomfortable and can degrade your ability to function.

Searching Checking the larger, total area you are moving through, with no precise location to focus on. Used in conjunction with approaching.

Short Trigger (You are on a) Due to a high stress situation you are instantly ready to fire. You must be extremely careful during these times as an unintentional shooting can easily occur.

Sighting Shift The eye's focus shifts from the target to the front sight the instant the sights are snapped up into your line of sight.

Single-Action (S-A) Firing Mode The trigger is pressed which will drop an "already cocked" hammer firing the handgun. The trigger does not mechanically cock the hammer.

Single-Pad-Press Whenever using the single-action firing mode, use the finger's pad position, and press the trigger for the shorter/lighter manipulation.

Slack The initial, extremely small rearward movement of the trigger from its rest position, until a pressure wall is met.

Smoke Over Initially viewing an area or situation for danger, usually from cover.

"SPECTR" A learning key for the six basic search rules that keep you alert, prepared, and ready if the action starts. The six parts of the acronym are: scan, plan, expect, cover, trouble-spot(s), and respond.

Speed Rock The handgun is held very close to the body while firing at an extremely close threat.

Speed Stroke A very fast draw to locked-out firing stance.

Stance Directed Fire A firing technique that utilizes and relies on the kinesthetic feed-back mechanism from your trained-in firing stance to place the "hits."

Strong Hand Your favored hand—if right handed, your right hand.

Subconscious Level The level your trained-in reflexive sets of weapon use skills should occur on. Constant, repetitive practice will produce these trained-in skills that require little or no conscious thought during a lethal encounter.

Subsequent Exchange Any exchange of gunfire that occurs after the initial exchange or opening ceremony.

Support Hand Your non-favored hand—if right handed, your left hand.

Support Position As the handgun moves forward from the belt-level position, the support hand forms a two-handed grip on the handgun. The third position in the holster-to-stance reflex.

Surprise Break Smooth, increasing pressure on the trigger building to a surprise break—you are not precisely sure when the handgun will fire during the pressure build-up.

Survival Reinforcement Mentally creating simulations of varied lethal encounters and working through every aspect of them, while always reinforcing that you will survive.

Survival Response When a lethal encounter occurs, you'll revert to a response based on what you've practiced and prepared for. Survival Response = Conditioned Response + Mental Preparation.

Tactical Safety An understanding of the basic safety rules as they apply to tactical encounters or searches. Covers two areas: search safety and weapon etiquette.

Tap, Rack, Bang An immediate action procedure for clearing an automatic's malfunction.

Telegraphing Any movement or preparation that will signal your intention to make a move.

Threat Occurrence When the threat presents itself—announced and/or takes physical action to start the physical threat. Part of the critical time reference.

Threat Preparation Begins with the first danger sign and ends with threat occurrence. Part of the critical time reference.

Threat Recognition When an officer first spots and correctly interprets a danger sign that a possible threat could exist. Part of the critical time reference.

Time Advantage Take the time necessary to safely and effectively conduct a search or respond to a situation. Use time to your advantage.

Time Margins The time you have to respond in. When increasing it, you can improve your response and safety.

Time Pressure The feeling that you are running out of time. Can cause you to work and fire too fast during stress situations.

Total Tactics (Using) Not becoming lax and proceeding with half-searches and half-tactics.

Touch Indexing Touching one part of the body to another bodily part or handgun part, to help the body better align itself when performing a task—drawing, reloading, ready position, preparing, etc.

Traversing The lateral movement of the handgun to engage a threat(s) to either side of the body. Usually a locked-in firing stance turning at the waist.

Trigger Creep Any motion or irregular feel in the trigger as it is pulled to the rear (after slack is taken out) just before or when the sear breaks.

Trigger Finger Placement Two parts of the finger tip are used (the first joint and pad) and each of these goes with a firing mode: the first joint with D-A and the pad with S-A.

Trigger Manipulation Increasing pressure is applied to the trigger in a smooth and timely manner until the handgun fires. The main shooting problem.

Trigger Overtravel Any excessive rearward movement of the trigger after the sear breaks and the hammer (striker) falls to fire the handgun.

Trigger Timing How fast you have to manipulate the trigger for the situation at hand. Mainly dependent on the size and distance of the target, with the trigger manipulation being either a "slap" or a "squeeze."

Triggering Speed The time it takes to align the sights and manipulate the trigger. Firing Speed = Presentation Speed + Triggering Speed.

Trouble-Spot(s) Location where a threat(s) could possibly be hiding. These are continuously selected while searching. (The "T" in SPECTR.)

Tunnel Vision Totally focusing on the threat, while excluding just about everything else.

Two Second/Move Technique A technique that limits your exposure when using the flashlight. Consists of two parts: use beam for 2 seconds or less and turn it off, then move at least two steps away.

Unintentional Discharge Accidental discharge of the handgun.

Weaver Stance A locked-in, two-handed firing stance, where the strong side is angled slightly rearward, and the strong arm is locked (or almost locked) straight out, while the support arm's elbow is bent and pointing down.

Index

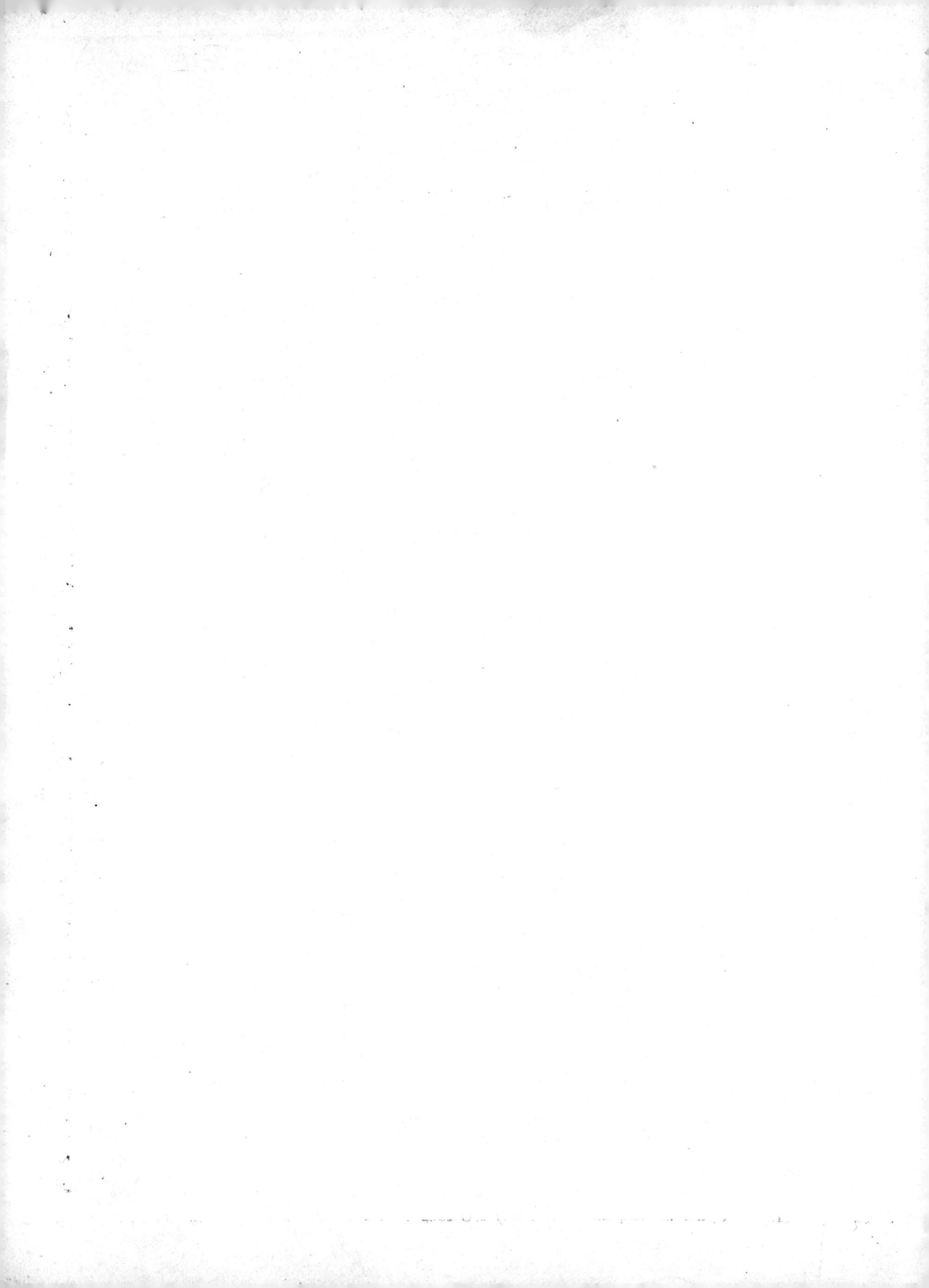